AGING AND ITS DISCONTENTS

AGING AND ITS DISCONTENTS
FREUD AND OTHER FICTIONS

Theories of Contemporary Culture
Center for Twentieth Century Studies
University of Wisconsin-Milwaukee

General Editor, KATHLEEN WOODWARD

AGING AND ITS DISCONTENTS

FREUD AND OTHER FICTIONS

KATHLEEN WOODWARD

INDIANA UNIVERSITY PRESS

BLOOMINGTON AND INDIANAPOLIS

The paper used in this publication meets the minimum requirements of American
National Standard for Information Sciences—Permanence of Paper for Printed
Library Materials, ANSI Z39.48-1984.

 ™

Manufactured in the United States of America

Library of Congress Cataloging-in-Publication Data

Woodward, Kathleen M.
    Aging and its discontents : Freud and other fictions / Kathleen
Woodward.
        p.   cm. — (Theories of contemporary culture)
    Includes bibliographical references.
    ISBN 0-253-36640-2 (alk. paper). — ISBN 0-253-20620-0 (pbk. :
alk. paper)
        1. French literature—20th century—History and criticism.
2. Aging in literature.   3. English literature—20th century—
History and criticism.   4. Freud, Sigmund, 1856–1939—Influence.
I. Title.   II. Series.
PQ307.A47W66   1991
840.9′354′0904—dc20   90-4535
                                                                                              CIP

1 2 3 4 5   95 94 93 92 91

FOR JESSAMYN

CONTENTS

ACKNOWLEDGMENTS

I want first to thank in this public and personal space the people at the Center for Twentieth Century Studies who have helped me in so many ways with this book. The Center has been my intellectual home; at times it seems to me to be my home, period. My heartfelt thanks, then, to Jean Lile and Carol Tennessen, to Barbara Obremski and Kate Kramer, to Mark Pizzato and Thomas Piontek. And to William Halloran, a friend and the creative Dean of The College of Letters and Science at the University of Wisconsin-Milwaukee, who found a way to provide me with the time I needed to finish this book.

I want also to acknowledge the generous support of a fellowship from the Camargo Foundation in the fall of 1984. Many of my ideas for this book took shape as I sat in the Camargo Library overlooking the glittering Mediterranean in Cassis. I am grateful for the comments of my colleagues and friends, some of them old, some new: Murray Schwartz and Patricia Mellencamp, Norman Holland and Susan Miller, Stephen Heath and David Wilbern, Tom Cole and Rick Moody, Gabriele Schwab and Susan Stewart, Ann Wyatt-Brown and Marolina Salvatori, and Margaret Gullette.

Some portions of this book have appeared in *SubStance*, *Discourse*, *Melanie Klein and Object Relations*, *Contemporary Literature*, and *Kenyan Review*. I'm grateful also for the opportunities I've had to present sections of the manuscript at the University of California at Irvine, the Center for Contemporary Cultural Studies at the University of Massachusetts at Amherst, the University of Southern Maine, the State University of New York at Buffalo, the Institute for Psychoanalysis in Chicago, the Center for Twentieth Century Studies at the University of Wisconsin-Milwaukee, and at various meetings of the Modern Language Association, the Northeast Modern Language Association, the American Studies Association, and the Gerontological Society of America. My deepest gratitude extends to my intellectual companion and confidant, my husband, Herbert Blau.

1. Introduction . . .
Aging, Difference, and Subjectivity

AGING AND ITS DISCONTENTS: *Freud and Other Fictions* is a study of representations of old age from the entwined perspectives of twentieth-century western fiction and psychoanalysis. I want to begin, however, with an anecdote about a photograph, not a literary text. In 1989 the theme of the annual meeting of the American Studies Association of France was the body in American culture. In conjunction with the conference, a gallery in Strasbourg organized an exhibit of photographs on the subject of the body. One photograph in particular solicited strong reactions. It was a portrait of a thin old man (actually he could have been in his early sixties) sitting on the side of his bed, his knees wide apart, his body naked except for the shuffling slippers on his feet. The black-and-white photograph told us that his old age—or his premature old age—was compounded by poverty and alcoholism. His body, positioned in the center of the photograph, was framed by his near-squalid room which was lined with a long overhead shelf full of liquor bottles, rather neatly arranged. Like his knees, his arms were spread apart on the bed. They supported the negligible weight of his upper body and his alcoholic stomach, which was as slack as his penis. His entire body seemed to be hanging down, depressed. He looked straight ahead at the photographer, and at us, expressing no particular affect, perhaps only listlessness.

We were all academics—with positions, families, futures, presumably accomplished pasts. I was finishing up this book on aging and hovered around the photograph, listening to reactions and talking with people. Many expressed disgust and outrage. They interrogated the absent photographer, Gundula Schultz, an East German. Why, several demanded to know, had the photographer *exploited* this man? (In her "defense," the story was circulated that she had lived with him for several weeks before taking this picture, a story which was met with predictably tasteless jokes.) I wondered aloud if this anger at the unknown photographer and this moral judgment of her intentions did not represent a displacement of their own fears. Most of them quickly turned their eyes away from the portrait, although the photograph remained in their minds' eye, generating conversation. If they were angry at the photographer, they also seemed angry at this old man whose body expressed no particular pride. For rather than soliciting our sympathetic gaze, this portrait avoided the consoling patina of pathos. It had something neutral about it. Although the man was clearly placed in the context of his environment, paradoxically his surroundings seemed to disappear. We were left with his naked body, all the more naked for the slippers. To this nakedness people responded neither with curiosity nor with voyeurism, nor with the generalized affection with which the body of a child is greeted. In turning away from this particular portrait, it was as if people were turning away from old age itself.

I talked about the photograph with a professor from Tours, a tall, finely featured man with a deeply lined face. His sensitivity and intelligence were striking. He was thoughtful, not abruptly dismissive, either of the photograph or of my reflections. But no, he did not want to look at this picture. No, he did not want to contemplate the body of old age. He would, he said, live that time when it came to him. As he spoke I thought of Virginia Woolf's pensive seventy-some-year-old Eleanor in *The Years* who murmurs, "old age they say is like this; but it isn't. It's different."[1] I thought, no doubt when old age came to this man, it would not be like that. But this professor, who refused to tell me his age (I would guess he was in his early fifties, but I am not very good at guessing ages), was a scholar of John Hawkes, not Virginia Woolf. I thought of the disturbing phantasy world of *The Passion Artist* which is charged with virulent representations of the aging female body. I seriously doubted that this middle-aged man from Tours would be persuaded by Woolf's gentler, yet scarcely benign world. For him the photograph of the old man, which so eloquently but matter-of-factly spoke of the circumscribed everyday life of this particular person, represented old age *in general*. We may conclude that his response to the photograph reflected his expectations about old age, the fears of a middle-aged man.

I want to complement this anecdote from academic life with one from the history of psychoanalysis. It presents the denial of old age in a different form.

About Freud's mother, this little story ostensibly has to do with vanity in old age. In his biography of Freud, Ernest Jones writes about Freud's mother, Amalia: "When she was ninety she declined the gift of a beautiful shawl, saying it would 'make her look too old.' When she was ninety-five, six weeks before she died, her photograph appeared in the newspaper; her comment was: 'A bad reproduction; it makes me look a hundred.' "[2] In her book on Freud, Lydia Flem tells the story this way: "in her youth Amalia had been a very beautiful woman. She remained feminine up until her last days, always interested in clothes and jewelry. For her eightieth birthday her two sons gave her a brooch and for her ninetieth birthday they gave her a huge sapphire ring surrounded by diamonds. Trying on a new hat at this age, she announced: 'I won't take it. It makes me look too old!' "[3]

In every version I have read, this story is told as a kind of joke about Freud's mother. We are asked to react to this old woman's interest in her appearance with a smiling and hence condescending indulgence (and in fact every time I have repeated this story to people, they have either smiled or laughed outright). We are asked to understand her continuing investment in the insignia of a gendered body (her "femininity," as Flem puts it) as foolish, but because harmless, charming. We are asked to conclude that she does not know how to act her age. The anecdote, of course, tells more about our culture's attitudes toward aging than it does about Freud's mother who is presented as a stock character. We are not meant to identify in any way with this woman or to entertain any complicated notions of her subjectivity, of her feelings, her desires, her fears. On the contrary, we are meant to laugh at her and her futile pretensions. But there is a complication here. Just as the teller of the tale wants to distance himself or herself from old age, so does Freud's mother want to keep old age at arm's length for as long as possible. At ninety-five she does not want to be mistaken for one hundred. If at ninety-five Amalia Freud found a way to affirm herself, it was at the expense of those years older than she.

It is my experience that when people do speak personally about their own experience of old age or their own fears of aging and death, especially when they are old, the common response of others is to reject what they say. Nervous anxiety is masked by a denial of another's subjectivity in a way that appears to be reassuring but is in reality silencing and repressive. You're not old, people will say to others whom they do in fact think old. I want to add to this collection of introductory anecdotes a third anecdote which illustrates this point in a complex and economic way. Simone de Beauvoir, whose omnibus book *The Coming of Age* was one of the first important indictments of the treatment of the elderly in western culture, nevertheless found herself often responding, for complex reasons, in such a way to Sartre during the last ten years of his life. I will return in my last chapter to her book *Adieux: A Farewell to Sartre*. Here I want only to note a passage, representative of the book as a whole, that combines the unflinching gaze of the photographer Gundula Schultz with Beauvoir's denial of Sartre's subjectivity. Here is Simone de Beauvoir on Sartre at sixty-seven: "One morning, as he lit his first cigarette, he said to me, 'I can't work anymore . . . I'm gaga, as they said. . . . ' Yet he retained his pleasure in life. When I was talking about Picasso, who died at the age of ninety-one, I observed, 'That's a fine age. It would give you another twenty-four years.' 'Twenty-four years is not much,' he replied."[4]

Beauvoir recorded Sartre's words but she could not accept what he said. She hated the prospect of losing the Sartre she knew to infirmity, senility, and death. I do not mean to reproach her with this. Who would feel differently? Still, Beauvoir could not absorb what Sartre said about his experience. To Sartre's fears of no longer being capable of work, which he equates with being senile, she adds a "yet," in effect accepting his dubious equation and thus reinscribing his fear in her own voice. And while she confronts the matter of old age and death directly by bringing up the "fine" age of Picasso when he died, she does so in the manner of bestowing cheery consolation. Ninety-one seems to her so reassuringly far away from sixty-seven. But Sartre is not Picasso. He is not comforted by being given an imaginary death age. What is truly interesting is Sartre's answer, which gives the lie to platitudes about a long life: "Twenty-four years," he asserts, "is not much." From the other side of the divide between youth and old age, which is where Beauvoir imagines herself, twenty-four years seems a long stretch of time. Not so to Sartre. Beauvoir lets his revealing comment dangle in her repressive silence, reducing his speech to just another sign of a general depression.

Anxiety, fear, denial, repression: I have evoked in the above paragraphs some of the concerns of psychoanalysis in opening the subject of aging and old age. As I will insist throughout this book, old age is a time in our lives about which many of us feel anxiety and fear. The symptoms of these feelings of apprehension are denial and repression of the very subject of aging and old age. But a fear of aging is not a strictly "personal" problem. Our culture's representations of aging are predominantly negative and thus are inextricably linked to our personal anxieties—for ourselves and for others. And denial, as I suggested above, can take many forms. In the West it often takes the form of a screen obsession with chronological age, of a concern with precise numbering which in the end collapses into the polar divide of youth and age.

From the moment of birth on (in fact even before), age is a fundamental and endlessly interesting category. New parents will tell you the age of their infants with a fantastic precision—a new father will tell you his baby is twenty-seven days old, for example, or six and a half weeks. Two-year-olds will insist on their proper place in the hierarchy of birthdays (I will have occasion to refer to this obliquely in the chapter on generational identity). Four-year-olds will rewrite the order of the birthdays of their friends and siblings with imaginative impunity. Adults will speculate on how many years separate a husband and wife. Women will ask how old other women were when they had their children. Colleagues will wonder about the ages of their other colleagues, posing the question silently to themselves or asking others or referring to the card catalogue. Adults will measure age by a subtle calculus of difference between their own bodies and the bodies of others through the medium of yet other bodies. All these bodies are themselves reflected through the prisms of personal phantasms and cultural representations. The aging body as imagined and experienced and the aging body as represented structure each other in endless and reciprocal reverberation. As Jacques Lacan has written, "language is not immaterial. It is a subtle body, but body it is. Words are trapped in all the corporeal images that captivate the subject."[5] Many of these corporeal images are concerned with age.

For an adult it is considered impolite to ask someone how old he or she is. But if chronological age is not an open subject of conversation in private life (often even best friends will keep how old they are a secret from each other, or will shave off a year or two or more), age is reported everywhere in the media. News stories typically begin with the name of the person followed by his or her age. We know the precise ages of our politicians and of politicians around the world, of celebrities, of the people who are getting married in our home towns, of the people who are arrested, and of the people who have died. As my colleague Patricia Mellencamp has pointed out, in a news story or a gossip item the age of the person in question is often the very piece of information for which the story exists.[6] The deep structure of the story is: name and age.

But our arithmetical precision about chronological age conceals the fact that our culture attaches remarkably few meanings to different ages across the life course. We can point of course to terms which are age-related—infancy, adolescence, maturity, adulthood, and old age, among them. Psychoanalysis has contributed much to theorizing these "stages" (I will come back to the question of "stages" later), and the histories of these stages are now being written. (Philippe Ariès's great book on childhood has become a model for this kind of research, and in the United States several historians have recently turned their attention to old age.)[7] But interestingly enough, we have not periodized the life course by proliferating a large number of categories. This can be seen in the fact that we use the various categories we have to modify each other and to produce new subcategories. We speak, for example, of a "mature" adolescence, or of old age as a "second childhood." Or we speak of "preadolescence" and "postadolescence." In suggesting that we have not been culturally inventive in producing age gradations (and I can imagine someone arguing the opposite), I am not insisting that we should be. Rather I am arguing that in our culture, these distinctions ultimately and precipitously devolve into a single binary—into youth and age.[8] Age is a subtle continuum, but we organize this continuum into "polar opposites."

In every culture, age, like any other important category, is organized hierarchically. In the West youth is the valued term, the point of reference for defining who is old. But if our cultural representations about aging and old age remain locked in primarily negative stereotypes, youth is, subjectively speaking, a remarkably fluid and seemingly almost infinitely expandable category. Youth is a point which in our psychic economy is not fixed. Youth—"being young"— is a moveable marker. Young and old may frame the continuum of the life course. But as people grow older, most of them—of *us*—take youth with them, as if it were a precious possession not to be left behind. Concomitantly, age— meaning "old age"—is pushed ahead. People often will label "old" only those who are older than they are. To a child, everyone is old. As Toni Morrison's preadolescent Claudia puts it in *The Bluest Eye*, "I had no interest in babies or the concept of motherhood. I was interested only in humans my own age and size, and could not generate any enthusiasm at the prospect of being a mother. Motherhood was old age."[9] Claudia was nine or ten at the time. To the ninety-five-year-old Amalia Freud, one hundred was old. In terms of value, then, as we grow older, youth comes to occupy the vast proportion of the continuum of the life course. Old age is relegated to the very end. I might add here that as I write, more and more people in the United States are reaching the age of one hundred. Centenarians constitute the fastest-growing segment of our population. The number has apparently tripled since the 1980 census, and it is projected that by the late 1990s there will be about 100,000 of us who are at least one hundred years old.

Within a few days of his seventy-second birthday, Freud wrote to Ernest Jones, " 'Young' and 'old' now appear to me to be the greatest opposites of which human life is capable." Freud added that "an understanding between the representatives of each is impossible."[10] While I would want to challenge this statement (I will return to this in a later chapter), I think it does approach a truth. Freud was referring to the impossibility of understanding old age without *experience* of it. But we may think about "the greatest opposites" in another way. Psychoanalysis itself has given us the concept of *splitting* which can help explain this psychic division of representations of age into polar opposites—

into youth and crabbèd age.[11] Splitting, as Melanie Klein has argued, is a primary mechanism of defense. Unable to tolerate feelings of ambivalence, the infant separates or *splits* what is most important into two representations—into the good and the bad. The infant phantasizes, for example, two mothers instead of one—a good mother who is loved and a bad mother who is hated. Only as the infant matures are these two images of a single object brought into focus, into a single but complex representation which is a synthesis of the primary feelings of love and hate. Such a synthesis is a sign of *tolerance*. In the world of Kleinian theory, tolerance for ambivalent feelings represents a psychic advance of immense proportions.

Analogously, we can understand our culture's representations of aging in terms of splitting. Youth, represented by the youthful body, is good; old age, represented by the aging body, is bad; in addition we find *subsplitting*: idealized images of old age constitute a polar opposite to those which express fear. But in the West our representations of old age reflect a dominant gerontophobia. Almost any text can confirm this. Here I select two almost at random. We can turn to a passage from Thomas Mann's relatively little known novel *The Black Swan*, which is a bizarre companion piece to *Death in Venice* in terms of gender. The plot (such as it is) revolves around a fifty-year-old widow who falls passionately in love with a twenty-four-year-old man. The appearance of Frau von Tümmler is described in terms of the presence of signs of youth and age: "Small in stature, but with a well preserved figure, with hair which, though now decidedly grey, was abundant and wavy, with delicate if somewhat aging hands, the backs of which the passage of years had discoloured with freckle-like spots that were far too many and far too large (a symptom to counteract which no medication has yet been discovered), she produced an impression of youth by virtue of a pair of fine, animated brown eyes, precisely the colour of husked chestnuts, which shone out of a womanly and winning face composed of the most pleasant features."[12] The tell-tale conjunctions "but," "though" and "if" signal the shift in value from youth, which is good, to age, which is bad.

Or we can turn to a more extreme instance of gerontophobia in a text to which I have already referred—Hawkes's *The Passion Artist*. In it we see aggression directed at the female body through the medium of age. The parts of the face of a very old woman—her teeth, ears, skin, facial hair, eyes—are figured as characteristics of the crone. She is presented as a type, not an individual. The fragments of her face do not belong to a person (we do not read about "her skin" but "the skin") but rather to a composite, that is, to an inhuman figure. Hawkes describes the parts of her "torn mask" this way: the "open mouth with its three amber-colored teeth and the breath of a great age, small twisted ears that appeared to have been sewn to the sides of the skull with coarse thread, the skin that was shriveled tightly to the bone beneath and cured in sun and salt until the wrinkles were deep and permanent, the soft facial hair that flowered around the cheeks like a parody of a bristling beard, and above all the yellow eyes, which alone reflected the ageless crafty spirit in a face that otherwise was only a small torn mask of leather."[13] With its many openings, the face is the most expressive part of the human body. Here the face of this old woman has been pulverized into a collection of disjunct parts which nonetheless expresses power ("the ageless crafty spirit") and thus incites fear in the spectator. Old age, tellingly gendered as woman in Hawkes's text, is the figure of horror and catastrophe.

I submit that the relative lack of ambiguity in our representations of aging, the relative paucity of their elaboration or differentiation, is a symptom that our culture as a whole has not succeeded in producing persuasive representations of aging—in particular of the aging body—which are characterized by *tolerance* in the Kleinian sense. Splitting is a defense against ambivalence. In our culture we are profoundly ambivalent, and primarily negative, about old age.

In the chapters that follow I turn to a select number of representations of aging in twentieth-century western literature. My intent is not to present a typology of literary figures of old age. Aging characters can serve as metaphors, for example, of the sterility of an age, just as aging can be used as a figure of speech for the exhaustion of energy or of the spirit.[14] I want instead to focus on old age itself rather than on old age as a metaphor for something else. Nor do I examine the question of late style, that is, how a writer's work (and his or her representations of old age) changes over time.[15] Nor do I survey twentieth-century literature and its representations of old age. My study is not meant to be exhaustive. Rather, I have chosen only a few of the many works of fiction and autobiographical writing (I have not drawn from poetry or from drama) that seem to me to resonate fruitfully with central concerns of psychoanalysis. My purpose is to present psychoanalytic interpretations of aging, with the emphasis on old age, through readings of literary and psychoanalytic texts.

In this book the relationship of literature and psychoanalysis is primarily one of imbrication, sometimes one of mutual interrogation. I read the literary texts and the psychoanalytic texts in a reciprocal fashion, asking what the two together can suggest to us about aging. Most of the chapters pair a single and basic category in psychoanalysis (narcissism, introjection, or mourning, for example) with a fictional scene or scenes drawn from literature. My aim is to take these scenes as paradigmatic of certain aspects of aging. It is not to provide full interpretations of the literary texts themselves.

How have I selected the texts which I have included? Psychoanalysis, with its emphasis on interiority and subjectivity, has influenced my choice of literary texts about aging. Thus, for example, I have written about scenes from Proust's *Remembrance of Things Past* and Woolf's *The Years*, whose subtle and highly serious evocations of interior consciousness correspond to the concerns (we might even say the very temperament) of psychoanalysis in ways that Muriel Spark's *Memento Mori* with its satiric impulse to black comedy and Leonora Carrington's caustic *The Hearing Trumpet* do not.

Reciprocally, the literary texts on aging which attracted my attention have themselves guided my decisions about which issues in psychoanalysis to consider in terms of aging. In fact as I think back over the way in which these chapters have taken shape, I realize to what a great extent it was the literary texts which themselves suggested their own particular approaches to aging through psychoanalysis. Thus it is the peculiar emphasis in Samuel Beckett's *Malone Dies* on tangible objects, which seem to disappear one by one, that led me to wonder if it might not be useful to think about transitional objects of old age in addition to transitional objects of infancy, as theorized by D. W. Winnicott. It was the closing party scene in *The Past Recaptured* which, with Lacan's mirror stage of infancy in mind, suggested to me the idea of a mirror stage of old age. And it was the final and moving paragraph of Eva Figes's lyrical novel *Waking*, whose narrator, dying, calls for her long-dead mother, which compelled me to think about the representation of gender and the role of the mother over the life course.

The arrangement of the chapters presents a kind of narrative in itself, although it is by no means continuous. I begin with a chapter on Freud, the founding father of psychoanalysis. The chapter is meant to be polemical. For Freud of course the autobiographical and the theoretical are interlaced and inseparable. For Freud old age is associated with castration, and the process of aging with an encroaching inertia that is felt in both the body and the psyche. We could not begin to imagine Freud ending his long life with the remark which concludes *Quartet in Autumn*, Barbara Pym's tragi-comic novel of manners in the everyday life of four elderly people: "life still held infinite possibilities for change."[16] Nor would it have been possible for Freud to substitute the word "ripening" for "aging," as Meridel Le Sueur has so forcefully done, or to speak of his eighties as puzzlingly "passionate," as Florida Scott-Maxwell has asserted.[17] For Freud aging presents a threat more serious than that of death itself, which he insisted is not contained in the unconscious. What then of old age? Where is it located? I argue that Freud repressed the subject of aging in his construction of a powerful discourse of subjectivity and generational relations so firmly anchored in infancy and early childhood.

The effect of this founding ethos of psychoanalysis is that in thinking through aging from its perspective, we will tend to reproduce dark if not tragic portraits of aging. With Freud we see aging through a glass darkly. Thus Freudian psychoanalysis, as well as many literary fictions of aging, is embedded in the fundamentally ageist ideology of western culture.[18] Hence the title of this book: *Aging and Its Discontents*. It is meant to recall Freud's *Civilization and Its Discontents* (1930) with its deeply grained pessimism. My point is that old age is one of the discontents of our civilization.

The depth of the implicit pessimism about aging contained in (or reproduced by) Freudian psychoanalysis could be clearly seen if we were to compare it with the positive teleology of Jungian psychoanalysis, which I do not take up in this book. It will suffice here, I hope, to recall that Jungian psychoanalysis (including its descendant in the work of James Hillman) envisions the reconciliation of opposites in old age (interesting enough, the reconciliation of opposites is largely figured in gendered terms). If opposites are reconciled in old age, the notion of polar opposites itself gives way to the notion of the complementarity of youth and age. Jungian psychoanalysis also gives us the figures of the wise old man and the wise old woman (the emphasis is on a certain balance in the *psyche*), unthinkable in Freudian psychoanalysis where we find instead the figure of heroic stoicism, always male, produced in response to the vicissitudes of the *body* in old age. The figure of the infirm body of the aged father is linked to this figure of stoicism.

In Freudian psychoanalysis the body is paramount. As we recall, in Freud's celebrated formulation in *The Ego and the Id* (1923), the ego is "first and foremost a bodily ego."[19] If, as Freud theorized, the ego "may thus be regarded as a mental projection of the surface of the body" (SE 19: 26), what kind of surface did he have in mind? The ego takes shape in infancy; the surface of the body is imagined as smooth, that is, as unwrinkled—in short, as *young*. Thus in Freudian discourse the aging body would be a sign of *deformation*. The aging body would represent a narcissistic wound to the ego. In Freudian psychoanalysis, then, the preoccupation with the body, which in old age is figured in terms of incontinence and decline, is complicit with the general emphasis—if not obsession—in western culture on the appearance of the body as the dominant signifier of old age. Neither in Freudian analysis nor in other major discourses of western culture do we find old age represented, for example, in terms of new forms of creativity in late life. But if Freudian psychoanalysis is dominant in *Aging and Its Discontents*, the work of other psychoanalysts, some of whom represent quite different traditions, is also present. There is Lacan, but there is also Winnicott, J. -B. Pontalis, Joan Riviere, and Heinz Kohut, among others.

After the chapter on Freud and with the exception of the chapter on Roland Barthes's *Camera Lucida*, all the other chapters leave authors behind—their intentions, their experience, their feelings, their other work. For the most part the chapters focus on isolated scenes taken from fiction and autobiographical writing. Roughly, *very* roughly, these scenes follow one another in the fictional time of a life and in the historical time of literary history. Thus the next two chapters concentrate on middle age and early old age. The scenes from Proust's *The Past Recaptured* (1927) dramatize the uncertain boundary between late middle age and old age. The scenes from Woolf's *The Years* (1937), while concerned with the distorted projections of the middle-aged upon the elderly, more importantly focus on early old age, or what the psychoanalyst Charlotte Herfray has called the latency period of old age, an expanse of time delimited not so much by chronological age as by relative health.[20]

The next two chapters are also paired. My discussion of both Figes's *Waking* (1981) and Barthes's *Camera Lucida* (1980) is predominantly concerned with a child's relation to his mother, and in particular to her death. But both chapters also deal more broadly with moments across the life course—with the introjection of the figure of the mother in *Waking* and with mourning and melancholia in *Camera Lucida*. The next chapter turns to an entirely different question—to our relation in advanced old age to objects, by which I mean literal objects. With Winnicott's notion of the transitional objects of infancy in mind, I read Beckett's *Malone Dies* (1951) where we see the transition from life to death accompanied by the progressive subtraction of objects from the environment.

Although all the chapters in *Aging and Its Discontents* deal with the body, the last two chapters focus explicitly on representations of the aging body from two distinct points of view. I consider first Joan Riviere's notion of masquerade in terms of the specular body of old age, drawing on scenes from Mann's *Death in Venice* (1913), from Patrick White's *Eye of the Storm* (1975), and finally, from mass culture. The last chapter is meant to serve as a kind of answer to, or expansion of, the previous chapter. The specular body of old age may dominate our representations of the aging body, but the image-repertoire of literature is by no means limited to it. I conclude, then, with a chapter on representations of the aging body which refer us to aspects of the body in old age other than the visual. These literary texts invite us to think about the aging body in terms of movement and stasis, in terms of the body as a container and its contents, and in terms of the body as a collection of articulated parts. I write about what I call the immobile body of old age in Marguerite Duras's *The Afternoon of Monsieur Andesmas* (1962), the empty body of old age in Beauvoir's *Adieux: A Farewell to Sartre* (1981), and the fragmenting body in *Waking* (1981). Taken together, the last three chapters in *Aging and Its Discontents* bring us closer to death, with which advanced old age or a frail old age must inevitably be associated.[21]

The question may be raised: why a psychoanalytic reading of aging? Psychoanalysis gives us both a theory and a method for an archeology of the past. Freudian psychoanalysis continually refers us back in time, to our infancy and childhood. As Lacan stresses, "the subject is there to rediscover *where it was.*" But Lacan immediately adds, "I anticipate—the real."[22] Where, I ask, will the subject be? In his *Journal* Kierkegaard wrote, "It is perfectly true, as philosophers say"—and I would add, as psychoanalysts say—that "life must be understood backwards. But they forget the other proposition, that it must be lived forwards."[23] In this book the impulse is prospective. The backward movement of the classical or canonical traditions of psychoanalysis is supplemented by a forward motion. For we are here to discover where we will be as well as to discover where we were. In psychic time we move backward and forward between the future and the past. We project ourselves into the future (although often not very far into the future consciously), and we bring our identifications from the past with us into those imagined futures. Psychoanalysis itself, then, invites us to think through the implications of some of the key concepts of psychoanalytic theory—castration, mourning, narcissism, introjection and projection—in a prospective as well as a retrospective mode.

Our experience in everyday life confirms this. Children play into the future as well as work through and out of the past. I remember my own daughter vividly enacting this some time ago. While I was talking with my friend Susan Suleiman one afternoon, my six-year-old played by herself—with her *selves.* She talked to herself, occasionally to me, pretending that she was eight, then eleven, then three, then one, all in the course of an hour. She threw herself into the future, reeled herself back in, and then turned to the past. She was of course always present. She was gone and yet here at the same time. She was enacting a kind of control over age in her life in a way similar to which Freud speculated his eighteen-month-old grandson, in throwing out a wooden spool that represented his mother and then reeling it back in, exercised control over his emotions in response to the absence of his mother.[24] But if for Freud's little grandson the scene represented his *renunciation* of certain satisfactions through the dramatization of symbolic compensations, my daughter's play represented the *assumption* of identifications with other ages, the working through of what she so manifestly remembered or anticipated with pleasure.

If children cannot project themselves very far into the future, I wonder how far ahead our psychic sense of time can take us when we are adults (I will refer to this obliquely in the last chapter). I cannot answer this question, although many works of literature confirm that some of us have a great psychic range in terms of age. Freud and much western literature also suggest that as we move into and out of middle age, identification with aging parents becomes problematic, if not fatal. A scene from the anthropologist Loren Eiseley's *All the Strange Hours* dramatizes this. Seeing his mother, nearly eighty, for the last time before her death, he also sees, written on their bodies conjoined by genetic as well as psychic history, the worm that will inhabit their graves after their deaths in old age:

> "Why," she said, surprised, running a finger down the blue vein of her forearm. "I believe I'm getting old." Again the bright sparrow's eye looked up at me, escaping as always. "Do you think that's it?" she repeated doubtfully. "Old age?"
>
> I shook my head wordlessly and turned away, raising my hand in a combined gesture of despair and farewell. The last I saw was the blue vein creeping down her arm as she repeated in a voice that seemed to emanate from another dimension, "I'm old. I think I'm old."
>
> The thought was contagious. I extended my own arm later on the airfield, while waiting in the blistering sun. By the powers of heredity a blue worm was beginning to inch its way . . . down my arm. . . . The same blue worm crawled faintly along my forearm. . . . The blue worm took everything in the end.[25]

Here the signifier of old age—again it is taken from the realm of the body—is associated with death. However much we may find a certain peculiar morbid fascination with death as signified by old age in this passage, I consider it important that Eiseley presents his final words with his mother as a scene of *conscious* identification. This is a necessary first step in understanding the many negative associations we have to old age in the West. It also represents an act of imaginative identification which may lead to understanding of the experience of old age. Beauvoir's project in *The Coming of Age* is to uncover the roots of the oppression of the elderly in our culture. But she also urges us to consciously exercise our faculties for prospective identification. She writes, "If we do not know what we are going to be, we cannot know what we are: let us recognize ourselves in this old man or that old woman. It must be done if we are to take upon ourselves the entirety of our human state." For Beauvoir such prospective identification has not just personal consequences but important political consequences as well. As she continues, "we will no longer acquiesce in the misery of the last age; we will no longer be indifferent, because we shall feel concerned, as indeed we are."[26] What happens, however, if the identification is *unconscious*? I take this up in the chapter on Freud.

I believe that the act of reading can help us exercise our psychic imagination of prospective time. Hence this highly conscious book about certain literary texts. But I also believe that much of our reading, and perhaps literature about old age in particular, may work subliminally, surfacing when we have need of it. I want to suggest there may be a *reading unconscious* into which these texts may recede. This reading unconscious would be one which functions not on the principle of repression but on the principle of *protection* and *preservation*. Almost all of the texts which I consider at length in *Aging and Its Discontents* I read many years ago. They are for me striking fictions which I am convinced have served to preform or preorient my experience. I cannot say for certain why they have surfaced in my writing now. But it may be that my own "horizon of expectations," to use Hans Robert Jauss's term, has expanded over time, that my own field of experience has broadened, allowing these texts to reenter my consciousness in a new way.[27] Jauss insists that literature can manifest "its genuine possibility only where the literary experience of the reader enters into the horizon of expectations of his lived praxis."[28] The experience of our own aging, or of the aging of our parents or of our neighbors, may call up the texts which we read in the past about old age. Memories about the past and phantasies about the future would coexist in a relationship of reciprocal interpretation in the present. It is in this way that I understand the reading of literature as having a potentially salutary social effect. Our reading can help shape the unacknowledged possibilities of our future experience in that largely unexplored realm of our cultural imagination—old age. But I do not want to sound too utopian here. What is the practical effect of my reading on my social behavior? Perhaps for the moment, my rereading and my teaching—and this book.

I want to mention briefly two other points in connection with the problematic relation between psychoanalysis and aging before turning to the question of gender. First, if the discourse of Freudian psychoanalysis itself tends to produce dark portraits of old age, a corollary is that the emphasis on infancy in psychoanalysis can tend to produce the stereotype of old age as a second childhood. In transposing or inverting some of the concepts of psychoanalysis, I may reproduce that very stereotype which I find so inimical. But neither can I consciously deny (although I might wish to) the disturbing similarities that can exist between infancy and old age. Secondly, if what I have been calling classical psychoanalysis did not admit the subject of aging, in recent years quite a few psychoanalysts and others who work within the domain of psychoanalysis have turned their attention to the subject of aging, including David Gutmann, George Pollock, and Bertram Cohler in the United States, and Charlotte Herfray, Michèle Dacher and Micheline Weinstein, and Michèle Grosclaude in France, whose work has all been useful to me in different ways.[29]

I want now to return to the Strasbourg exhibit of photographs on the body in order to open up the question of aging and gender, and more broadly, difference. In addition to the photograph of the old man with which I began *Aging and Its Discontents*, there was a photograph of an old woman which had also been made by Gundula Schultz. Unlike the old man, the woman, perhaps in her late sixties, had been photographed against a neutral background and thus was situated in no particular social context. She too was naked, at least from the waist up. We saw only her face and the upper half of her body—her shoulders, breasts, and upper arms. To me the most striking aspect of her nakedness was the skin on her arms. Down them ran finely striated wrinkles which were strongly vertical yet somehow subtle and distinctive, unlike her breasts. They also had a downward motion to them but seemed just the sagging—that is the common and unflattering word—breasts of any old woman.

This woman seemed to have prepared herself for this photograph in a way that the old man seemed to have not. I do not mean that she had made herself up in any elaborate way. Quite the opposite. Her hair was short, the shock of it somewhat punk. But she seemed to welcome the camera work in a way that the old man, while acquiescent, did not. Her steady gaze spoke to me of a pride in her acceptance of the vicissitudes of the body in old age. Predictably, in comparison with the portrait of the old man, people found the photograph of this woman easier to contemplate precisely because of her pride, but also because we saw only half of her. We did not see her pubis. Still, just as the eyes of the spectators avoided the old man's penis, they avoided her breasts, not knowing how in public to look at the sexual parts of the body in old age, or the sexual body of old age. But my point here is not so much that these two photographs challenged the western tradition of the nude as young and beautiful, although they surely did. Rather it is to introduce the question of gender and aging through the issue of spectatorship.

Much work in feminist film theory and criticism over the past ten years or so has been concerned with the gendering of the spectator and the fragmentation of the female body. Comparing these photographs, we cannot help but see that the old man's body is photographed in its entirety, while the old woman's body is, we might be tempted to say, fragmented. What is the effect of this? Is the effect of the photographer's framing of the woman's body in half aggressive in some way? Or is it cowardly? We see the man's body whole, but the woman's body cut in half. Is the photographer just repeating the gesture of fragmenting the female body?

A strange story circulated about this photograph as we circulated looking at the other photographs. It began in a conventional way. This woman had been very beautiful in her youth and middle age. This we could see for ourselves. She had the proud bearing of someone who is used to being looked at admiringly. She was "still handsome," as it is commonly—and I think bizarrely—said; the implication, of course, is that old age and beauty are antithetical. But what we could not see for ourselves was that in her old age her legs had had to be amputated, or at least that was what I was told. To see her naked body whole would have meant to see the parts that were not there, to see her body in parts, literally fragmented. It would have been unbearable. And thus the framing of the photograph was protective, tactfully allowing us to imagine for her an intact body.

My intention is not to rehearse the strong and subtle debates about the fragmented female body and the gendering of the gaze, in particular the fetishizing of the parts of a woman's body by the male gaze.[30] It is instead to suggest that the gaze solicited by these two photographs at the exhibition in France in 1989—one of an old man, one of an old woman—was not *primarily* a gendered gaze, neither a masculine gaze nor a female gaze. First and foremost at stake in these two representations of the aging body in the spectator's eye was *age*, not *gender*. (In the chapter on narcissism, I make a distinction between the "look," which is disfiguring, and the "gaze," which may be benevolent.) My point is that in western culture age takes precedence over and may swallow up gender.

Over fifteen years ago Susan Sontag referred to the double marginality of sexism and ageism to which women are subject in our society. She stressed that old age is "a genuine ordeal, one that men and women undergo in a similar way." But she emphasized that growing older, which in our society is considered a "social pathology," "afflicts women much more than it does men."[31] No one can dispute the incontrovertible fact that in our society women are more disadvantaged in old age in terms of social opportunities and resources than are men. In our culture, the sexual allure of a woman, still taken to be one of a woman's most important "economic" possessions, is understood to diminish much more rapidly with age than does that of a man. All this is self-evident, and I do not need to repeat the obvious here. But in this book I want to insist on the obvious—that aging and old age intersects all of our lives. I subordinate the question of gender to that of age. Aging is a woman's issue. It is also a man's issue. More polemically still, I want to suggest that in advanced old age, age may assume more importance than any of the other differences which distinguish our bodies from others, including gender, as my story about the two photographs suggests. I do not mean to imply that this is good—certainly not—only that this may well be the case: that in old age, and in our culture where aging is perceived negatively, old age becomes the dominant category to which we are consigned. If difference produces anxiety, what is the future of difference? For all of us, if we live long enough, that difference is constructed as old age.[32] Still, throughout this book I do deal implicitly, and sometimes explicitly, with concerns of gender.

But what of other differences? I believe that the literary texts I have chosen have paradigmatic value in several ways, ways which are at times contradictory. All of these texts, from the well-known novels by Proust and Beckett to the little-known novels by Figes and Duras, belong to the central tradition in twentieth-century western fiction, even if the latter two novels, for example, have not received the attention which constitutes formal admission into that canon. All of these texts are by white men and women and, notwithstanding their date of composition, are part of the modern literary tradition. As I will be insisting throughout this book, in western culture aging is represented primarily in negative terms. Freudian psychoanalysis, with its emphasis on castration, narcissism, mourning, and anxiety, reinforces a negative reading of aging. For the most part these texts do not resist this reading. On the contrary, they produce it— and they are symptomatic of it. But even as they represent our culture's dominant images of aging (images which are themselves often contradictory) and thus shape our experience, they also *speak* eloquently to the experiences of many of us—or to what we imagine will be our experiences. They are texts which in their subtlety and richness invite us to consider and confront growing old, and older, from a multitude of perspectives, if the perspectives are nonetheless limited. In other words, even as my reading of aging through the double lens of psychoanalysis and literature insists on the fundamentally ageist ideology of twentieth-century western culture and is a *critique* of it, I have wanted also to preserve the possibility that these literary texts, together with psychoanalysis, speak complexly and not reductively to our *experiences* and anticipatory phantasies of aging. In this book I am interested in producing more than a critique of representations of aging.

But whose experience? In suggesting that these texts are "paradigmatic," I do not mean that any of the literary or psychoanalytic scenes which I invoke in the following chapters can speak to or for all of us. Indeed many of them, as I have already mentioned, contradict one another. But in the interaction of these texts with psychoanalysis, I have been led to pose speculative questions that have, I think, paradigmatic value of a heuristic nature. Can we speak in the late twentieth century of a mirror stage of old age, for example? Or, what kinds of experience would the notion of a mirror stage of old age usefully describe? Is the work of mourning different in old age? Or, might mourning not be different for some of us in old age? Does the figure of the mother surface insistently in literary fictions and in our representations of our own experience as we near death? Can we speak of changing relations to parental figures as we grow older in terms of an inverse Oedipus complex?

In the literary texts that I have chosen to discuss, then, I have a certain confidence. But I do not want them to be understood as representing, either singly or together, old age in all of its complexity. That would be wrong. First, as I have already suggested, the propositions generated by one reading may be challenged by another. Thus, for example, the emphasis on the specular body of old age which is so strong in Proust, Woolf, Mann, and others is countered in the chapter on phantasms of the aging body where senses other than sight assume more importance. And secondly, what of other differences? What, for instance, of the differences of race or of color, class, and ethnicity in populations so heterogeneous as in the United States and western Europe? Or what of more radical cross-cultural difference, if that is any longer possible? What of the differences between the West and the Orient, differences which as I write are blurring, as in the United States where Oriental influence is growing much more dominant and where it increasingly makes less sense to speak of a "western" tradition?

I have wanted in at least some small way to suggest other texts about old age. Thus I have added after each chapter, simply and without commentary, an excerpt from another text as a brief counter-scene. I intend these excerpts to serve as visible reminders of other representations, other traditions, other work to be done. I should add that I have made no effort in choosing these counter-scenes to represent a wide spectrum of differences. Instead my choices have been guided primarily by my relatively recent reading.

In theorizing various forms of difference, we are inevitably led to the question of the difference biology makes. The debate in feminism on the relation of gender and sexuality to biological differences in the body has helped me think through—or at least ponder—the complicated issue of the relation of biology to the meanings attached to old age. In feminism the question often has been posed this way: to what degree, if any, is anatomy destiny? Positions on this issue range from biological essentialism, which often asserts various virtues of female bodies in relation to male bodies, to social constructivism, which maintains that all meanings attached to differences in gender are produced socially. In terms of aging, I basically subscribe to the latter position—or at least I want to (although in the chapter on generational identity and Figes's *Waking*, I have drawn on arguments from feminist psychoanalysis which verge on biological essentialism). But our language about the aging body is so heavily charged with negative connotations that it is difficult to even express the matter in a neutral register. If we speak of the aging body in terms of the *weakening* of various functions of the body (hearing diminishes, eyesight dims, etc.), we are necessarily invoking the corresponding notion of strength, which is associated with youth and gathers all positive value to itself.

With regard to the aging body, we are unable to adopt a position of pure social constructivism. We cannot detach the body in decline from the meanings we attach to old age. The inevitable and literal association of advanced old age with increasing frailty and ultimately death itself presents a limit beyond which we cannot go. The body in advanced old age not only represents death; it is close to death and will in due time be inhabited by death. The facticity of the mortal vulnerability of the body in old age, and the meanings we attach to it, cannot be explained away by insisting that an ideology of youth, with its corresponding semiotics, is responsible for negative representations of old age. Advanced old age is a trial, as many have told us in their diaries, essays, and memoirs, including Malcolm Cowley in *The View from Eighty*.[33] Apart from the social stigma attached to aging, the vicissitudes of the body may become all too palpable. In her journal *After the Stroke* May Sarton, speaking from her own experience (she had a stroke when she was seventy-three), succinctly links her subjective experience of old age with bodily adversity. "Youth, it occurs to me, has to do with not being aware of one's body," she writes, "whereas old age is often a matter of consciously *overcoming* some misery or other inside the body. One is acutely aware of it." As her body heals, her experience and construction of herself as *old* change: "now that I am well again I am not any longer the very old woman with a very old dog I was all spring and summer."[34]

Aging and old age are intimately related to biological phenomena. With the experience of the body being so central to the construction and experience of old age, I cannot agree with Bernice Neugarten that old age is an "empty variable," although I think her polemical assertion has done much to dispel stereotypes from the field of gerontology.[35] Nor, by analogy with feminist theory which quite correctly understands *woman* as an empty signifier,[36] would I accept the notion that *old age* is an empty signifier. At best, we may speak in the West of the compensations that may accompany the ordeals of old age, as did Bernard Berenson, for example, in his diaries, published under the title *Sunset and Twilight*. At the age of eighty-two, Berenson asked this rhetorical question in his diary: "How is one to understand without experience, and how is one to procure the experience before body and mind have matured for it?"[37] In great part his experience is of a failing body, of a body "too uncomfortable to live in" (239). But his experience also includes what he considered to be gifts of insight and gifts from others in old age. A certain kind of psychological work is implied. But to completely rewrite the ideology of the aging body in the West, we would have to rewrite the meaning of death. And this we are not likely to do so easily. The self-reflexivity that language gives to the human organism has allowed us to understand our mortality, which in the West has often been taken as the quintessential mark of what it is to be human. The body at the limit of its life is the bedrock of the *real*, in Lacanian terms. Here again Freudian psychoanalysis is in resonance with the subject of old age because it was Freud who so firmly yoked together biology and psychology, soma and psyche. I want to argue, then, as I will put it in the chapter on masquerade, that there cannot be a postmodern poetics of the aging body. But the problem here is in part precisely that of *representing aging primarily in terms of the body*. What of the psyche? I will return to this question in the chapter on phantasms of the aging body.

In thinking about old age, we must think about the increasing biological vulnerability of the body. But to what extent must we think about old age as a "stage"? In her novel *A Far Cry from Kensington* Muriel Spark introduces the owner of a 1950s London rooming-house with this two-sentence paragraph: "Milly was sixty years of age, a widow. She is now well over ninety, and still very much Milly."[38] What does the narrator, a Mrs. Hawkins, mean by describing Milly as "still very much Milly"? I take it as a gesture of affection toward someone she did not know intimately but did know well, affection colored perhaps by nostalgia and sustained by the reassuring stability of Milly's social persona over a period of thirty years of old age. Interestingly, at the same time that age is crucial to the description of Milly (she is sixty, then ninety), Hawkins (and through her, Spark perhaps) is in effect denying that age is a distinct period in our lives. The point is that Milly is defined in terms of her character, which is understood as the continuity of the personality (already fully formed) over the years, not in terms of her age.[39] Indeed the implication is that Milly has somehow succeeded in resisting change that might be brought about by time, and thus we are never given a sense of her body either at sixty or at ninety. That *A Far Cry from Kensington* was written by the author of *The Prime of Miss Jean Brody*, a novel about female adolescence,[40] sets the issue in relief. In the hands of Spark, adolescence is a period of intertwined bodily and psychological development, old age is not.

Freudian psychoanalysis periodizes our lives in terms of stages of libidinal development in infancy and in terms of the Oedipal stage of early childhood. Anna Freud and, more recently, Peter Blos have theorized adolescence in psychoanalytic terms as a period or stage in which gender identity is solidified and parental ties are loosened. David Gutmann has written provocatively of parenthood as a developmental time in the lives of adults.[41] As for old age, Erik Erikson is of course widely known for his schema of interlocking psychosocial stages across the life span, with the last stage dramatized in terms of an individual's psychological conflict between integrity and despair in the face of death. I have found much in developmental psychoanalysis that is useful, particularly its descriptive value. What is less persuasive if not sometimes outright offensive is its proscriptive or prescriptive stance. By and large the rhetoric of a developmental psychoanalysis revolves around the notion of *tasks* appropriate to that "stage" in life, tasks which must be completed properly. This rhetoric I want to avoid in my discussion of the representations of old age. At the same time, however, the perspective of literature and psychoanalysis, as well as the dictates of common sense, invite thinking about old age as a time in our lives when bodily vulnerability and changed generational relations present new problems—and challenges.[42]

In gerontological circles the term "life cycle" was not so long ago succeeded by the term "life span." More recently, "life span" (which has typically been the preferred term of developmental psychologists) has been replaced by "life course" (which has been used all along by sociologists). This shift in vocabulary represents, among other things, a conscious effort to move toward language which is less metaphorical and more neutral in its associations. "Life cycle" carries the damaging connotations of the return in old age to childhood, while "life span" suggests a smoothly continuous movement through the years structured like an arc which rises in the first half of life and descends in the second half. In both cases old age is necessarily and negatively associated with decline *generally*, not just in bodily terms.

Similarly, I have recently heard gerontologists correct themselves when they say "old age," substituting in its stead the term "late life," or "later life." They too want to avoid the notion of a proscriptive stage ("growing older," with its emphasis on a process rather than a fixed period, is also common now). More emphatically, they want to expunge the negative connotations associated with the term "old age" itself. While I understand this gesture, I will continue to use the phrase "old age" in this book without embarrassment. The guiding impulse of *Aging and Its Discontents: Freud and Other Fictions* is that we have repressed the subject of aging and old age and that we should look long and hard at it, for others and for ourselves. I do not in the process want to repress the term "old age" as well.

Over the past years I often found myself met by silence when I told people that I was working on a book on aging. In part, I think, this telling response is largely a sign of puzzlement stemming from the fact that in literary studies there is no established tradition of scholarship or well-known body of research on aging.[43] The relatively little research that has been done remains scattered and has not yet coalesced into a field marked by self-conscious debates over matters of method, canon, and position such as we find in feminist literary studies, for example. Scholars have no intellectual guideposts which would enable them to enter easily and effortlessly into an exchange. Hence an awkward silence. But I am also convinced that this silence all too often speaks of a suspicion that the subject of aging is, simply, morbid.

Two little stories will help, I think, to illustrate this point. One was told to me by Mary Russo who, along with Diana Hume George, Gabriele Schwab, and me, was on a panel on "Feminist Approaches to Aging" at the Modern Language Association in 1988. When Mary mentioned to one of her colleagues that she was going off to a session on aging, her friend remarked, "How depressing," and squeezed Mary's arm in a gesture of wordless and sympathetic consolation. As feminists most of us have politicized virtually everything— everything but aging.

The second story is mine. Recently I was explaining the project of this book to an accomplished scholar of American literature. I was speaking in animated tones. She was interested in what I had to say, but she paused to observe that I was "obsessed" with the subject of aging. I took her reaction as an index of *her* uneasiness with the subject. We would not describe feminist literary critics as "obsessed." Why then literary critics writing on aging?

But to these two stories I should add a third which complicates the analysis. It echoes the story I told earlier about Freud's mother. I well remember giving a lecture on literature and aging some five years ago to a group of people, all elderly, who were taking a course in my university's extension program. During the discussion afterwards, one woman asked me in a quite motherly way, "What's a nice young woman like you doing in old age?" She was not protecting her intellectual turf. She was protective of me, that is to say, of youth. She too found the subject of aging "depressing" and preferred to avoid it. I was reminded of Rebecca West's words. "I do not myself find it agreeable to be 90," she wrote some time before she died, "and I cannot imagine why it would seem so to other people." Amplifying tartly, she added, "It is not that you have your fears about your own death, it is that your upholstery is already dead around you."[44] Or as Herbert Blau has sardonically put it, alluding to the famous line in *King Lear* about ripeness being all, "we all know about what follows ripeness."[45] Yes, the subject of aging may be depressing—from many points of view. All the more reason to study it.

In the eyes of the woman in the class, I was young. In terms of chronological age I am in my mid-forties, middle-aged. In the recent practice of literary and cultural criticism of difference—gender, race, ethnicity, and postcolonial discourse—it has become almost axiomatic that one's body should resemble the subject of one's research. If it does not, one is vulnerable to the charge of speaking for others. Basically one's motivations are called into question. In the case of the study of old age by someone who is not yet old, one's motivations may be called into question in a particularly insidious way, devaluing the research. The accusation may be that one is *afraid* of aging, the implication being that one is psychologically unsound. I prefer to understand such a charge as a projection of the other person's fear and thus as a symptom of the denial of aging. But however much we may wish to construct alternative representations of aging for our culture and for ourselves, it remains true that in the West, if not in other societies, and perhaps particularly in the United States, as Robert Butler shows in his passionate book *Why Survive?: Being Old in America*, it is preeminently reasonable to have fears about growing old.[46] Aging is a subject in which we all have interests of our own. The difference of age is the one difference which we will ultimately all have in common, if we live long enough. The subject of aging is one that belongs to all of us.

I am often asked how I became interested in aging. There are many answers to this question—some professional, some more strictly personal. My first book, which was based on my dissertation, was on late style in American poetry. It grew out of my tonal preference for the late poems of several of our most accomplished twentieth-century American poets at a time when most of the literary criticism was concerned with their early work. Essentially I was asking myself why I found the later work of Eliot, Pound, Stevens, and Williams so much more satisfying than their early work. My answer revolved around the construction of a persuasive figure of the poet as an old man, a kind of calm, equilibrated, and quietly courageous antibody to the figure of youth which was and still is so dominant in America. At the same time that I was working on that book, I went to my first meeting of the Gerontological Society of America. I was struck at the time—it was 1976—by the number of impressive older women actively involved (this was not then a characteristic of the Modern Language Association). I made a kind of vow to remain associated with them (as it turns out, the role of the humanities in the Gerontological Society did not develop appreciably in the next ten years, and my participation in it diminished as my theoretical interests took a different direction). I should also add that I see *Aging and Its Discontents*, with its darker tone and with more of an emphasis on the body (or the bodies) of old age, as redressing an imbalance in the earlier book.

But it may be that most strongly in the background of this book and much of my other work on aging stand the figures of my four grandparents. They were very much a part of my weekend life when I was growing up. They were and still are very much a part of my psychic imagination. I appreciated one grandfather for the gentleness of his character which seemed to emanate from the quiescent corpulence of his body. His passivity, which projected stability, allowed those around him to be briskly involved in all kinds of projects. I imagine him sitting in a large armchair, reading. I imagine him a little bit like Duras's Mr. Andesmas, or Mr. Andesmas like him. I admired my other grandfather for his authoritativeness and his energy. He always seemed to be moving into another future, leaving achievements and projects behind (I remember one day in a library coming across a mathematics book he had written, just like that; I had never known he had been involved in that field too). He took on one organizational project after another in education, working in Africa for the Kennedy Administration after he "retired." He always knew what was going on in the news. He was handsome and, although still married to my grandmother until he died, a ladies' man (which I found out quite by accident one day when one of his companions called me with his greetings).

Of the four, I had the least sense of my mother's mother. She was a good-looking and aloof woman who had worked as a librarian. Although her household was managed efficiently and with apparent aplomb, she was irascible. There seemed to be something unpredictably eccentric about her which emerged more and more in her behavior as she grew older. I remember finding her setting the table for herself with newspapers. My other grandmother, my father's mother, I simply loved. We were companions. We traveled together, we went to museums together, we shopped together, we dieted together. She was the only one of my four grandparents to confide in me about some of the events and vulnerabilities and mistakes in her life. She had been a practicing member of the Theosophical Society of America and wore two wedding rings on her ring finger. She was in excellent health, and I imagined that after my grandfather died, she, somewhat like Eleanor in *The Years*, would travel to India to see her spiritual husband. Instead she was killed in a car accident when she was seventy-one.

I have wondered how she would have lived out her life. In my imaginings I hope that she would have lived into a "great" age, healthy and active in whatever way she chose to be, thus giving the lie to the experience of my other grandparents in old age. The other three all died relatively young and vastly diminished. My father's father had one stroke after another and spent the last years of his life in a nursing home and then in a hospital. My mother's parents both had Parkinson's disease and grew rapidly and increasingly frail. They died in the hospital wing of a retirement residence, where my grandmother lived on for many years after my grandfather had died. She was also incapacitated by a series of strokes. I remember her lying in that single bed in a room which she now shared with another old woman. My grandmother had been there for years. She was all bones, curled up into herself. She muttered and murmured—to herself. I could not make out what she was saying. I wanted to know what she was thinking, what she was feeling. She had never cultivated a language of intimacy, or at least not to my knowledge. Now she was physically incapable of communicating her experience. And I did not have the resources to imagine her experience. It seemed to me at that infinitely expandable moment that youth and age were indeed the greatest opposites of which life is capable, as Freud had remarked. I wanted a sense of her subjectivity, which so definitively escaped me. Hence, perhaps, this book. I wish too that the endings of the lives of my other grandparents, so painfully stretched out in incapacity, had been different and their experience more accessible to me. And hence, perhaps, my emphasis on the discontents of aging.

2. **Reading Freud . . .**
Aging, Castration, and Inertia

FREUDIAN PSYCHOANALYSIS, with its discoveries of infantile sexuality and the Oedipus complex, is preeminently a theory of childhood. With his theoretical eye turned toward our beginnings and with his clinical ear inclined toward young and middle-aged patients, Freud does not offer us an investigation of aging.[1] Still, Freudian psychoanalysis—in spite of and in great part because of its emphasis on infancy and youth—has colored our associations to aging and has subtly reinforced our culture's devaluation of age. In this chapter I want to focus on two aspects of aging which are part of Freud's strong and troubling legacy to our culture: identification with an aging or elderly parent as castration, and aging as a condition to be accepted as our fate. My approach will be indirect as I consider two points in Freud's life and work. As much as possible I intend to condense the particulars into two far-flung scenes—one from middle age, one from old age. They are separated from each other by almost forty years in writing, ranging from *The Interpretation of Dreams* (1900), which was published when Freud was forty-four, to "A Disturbance of Memory on the Acropolis" (1936), which was published when Freud was eighty.

Freud did not address himself in any systematic way to aging or old age theoretically, nor did he leave us in his writing any extensive meditations on his own old age. In his letters from the 1880s and 1890s we do find scattered references to age. As isolated asides they are by and large unremarkable. Yet taken together they fall into two distinct categories which reflect two of Freud's major preoccupations throughout his life in psychoanalysis—intergenerational family structures and his relation to his own work. As an example of the latter preoccupation, I want simply to note that in the four years preceding the publication of *The Interpretation of Dreams* Freud often described himself as old in his letters to Wilhelm Fliess, who was his intimate friend during those years. Freud also continued this theme after the publication of *The Interpretation of Dreams*. "I really am forty-four now," he wrote to Fliess in 1900, "an old, somewhat shabby Jew."[2] In his biography of Freud, Peter Gay reports that Freud's age—that is, his melancholic sense of being old—haunted Freud from then on and became an "obsession."[3] I submit that Freud's expressions of feeling old can be understood as condensing his anxieties about his father's infirmity in old age with his own anxieties about the progress of his writing. Feeling old, which was associated with *being* old (the two need not be connected), was linked with a lack of productivity which is typically, and negatively, ascribed to old age in the West. During these two decades Freud, who was in his late twenties, thirties, and early forties, was worried about growing old. Interestingly enough, he also described himself as having "never felt young."[4]

As a specific example of the particular inflection he gave to old age in terms of intergenerational family structures, I want to cite the peculiar way in which Freud, when he was engaged to Martha Bernays, figured their relation to her mother. It was as a struggle for possession and power that took a distinctly Freudian triangular form. But at stake was not so much sexual identity for the younger generation as *generational* identity, although the two were related. Reinscribing the scene of the Oedipus complex, Freud wrote of his dilemma to Martha's sister Minna who, as we know, came to live with them after he and Martha married (and thus was the triangle further complicated). Freud urged Minna to persuade Martha to reject her mother and to commit herself to him. But at times it seems as if he were urging Minna to do the same. The passage deserves to be quoted at length:

> Now, I don't want you to think that I feel hostile to her or that I have altered my high opinion of her or that I am on less affectionate terms with her. I do not think I am being unfair to her; I see her as a person of great mental and moral power standing in our midst, capable of high accomplishments, without a trace of the absurd weaknesses of old women, but there is no denying that she is taking a line against us all, like an old man. Because her charm and vitality have lasted so long, she still demands in return her full share of life—not the share of old age—and expects to be the center, the ruler, an end in herself. Every *man* who has grown old honorably wants the same, only in a woman one is not used to it. As a mother she ought to be content to know that her three children are fairly happy, and she ought to sacrifice her wishes to their needs. This she doesn't do,

she complains that she is superfluous and neglected, which we certainly give her no reason to feel; she wants to move to Hamburg at the behest of some extraordinary whim, oblivious of the fact that by so doing she would be separating you . . . and myself for years to come. This certainly isn't very noble-minded, nor is it downright wicked; it is simply the claim of age, the lack of consideration of energetic old age, an expression of the eternal conflict between age and youth which exists in every family, in which no member wants to make any sacrifice and each one wants a free rein to go his own way.[5]

Freud found it strategic to his argument to portray the mother as an "old woman." She was fifty-three at the time, and Freud, twenty-seven. Of course at the turn of the century old age was understood as arriving earlier than it does today.[6] But this does not account for the negative cast with which Freud branded their mother. By calling her "old," Freud hoped to strip his future mother-in-law of legitimate authority. But he could not overlook her apparently considerable strength. Nor for tactical reasons could he completely vilify her in a letter to her own daughter, although he comes perilously close to doing so. Bizarrely, Freud concludes that the energy and vigor of his future mother-in-law—those very qualities which set her off from the "absurd weaknesses of old women" in general—are *unnatural* for an old woman, a woman of her age. Unnatural, and thus threatening. So unnatural, in fact, that Freud can describe her only in terms of her gendered opposite; that is, she is like "an old *man*." This charge is intended as a crippling insult. The mother is condemned for not knowing her place as an *old woman*, which is a place of powerlessness. She is indicted for stubbornly refusing to understand that it is now her time in life to give up her children. In a passage I find astonishing in its crude casting of men and women in old age, Freud reserves to men of "honor" what he would refuse to old women: *power* (although he does assert that the mother has "moral power," but that is also part of the problem). At the same time Freud suggests that the old deserve less than the young, simply because they are old. It is right, he insists, that "the share of old age," as he coldly puts it in economic terms, be less than "the full share of life," which properly belongs to the young.

There is much that is blatantly prejudicial about old age in this passage, much that expresses our conventional stereotypes of old age. Gender and age: Freud bluntly confirms our cultural tenet that old age is tolerated less in women than in men. Old age and desire: when the elderly (particularly elderly women) express desire, it is to be promptly dismissed on the grounds that it is querulous if not frivolous, certainly selfish and irrational.[7] Old age and youth: the two are engaged in a power struggle. Freud unabashedly represents the relation between the generations—here divided simply into the young and old—as a conflict that is in the "èternal" order of things. Yet more insidiously, his implication is that in the *natural* order of the succession of generations there should be no struggle for power because the old should simply relinquish their claims on those younger. Thus Freud concludes that what is particularly threatening from the point of view of the young is "energetic old age," an old person who in Freud's capsule definition here displays the strength which marks youth. The semiotics of youth and age should be unambiguous. Youth is to be associated with energy, old age with passivity. Furthermore, the generations should keep to themselves. Freud warns that a daughter should on no account *identify* with her mother, nor should her mother insist that she do so: the future mother-in-law should have no interests of her own (I am alluding here to an essay by Alice Balint on mother love, to which I will refer in the chapter on gender and generational identity). Nor apparently should a daughter even try to sympathize with her mother's wishes. The implication is that identification of the young with the old is dangerous. As we will see, such identification can amount to castration.

In a section on the symbolic interpretation of dreams in *The Interpretation of Dreams*, Freud associates castration in general but not exclusively with typical physical signs of aging. A not-uncommon passage reads: "To represent castration symbolically, the dream-work makes use of baldness, hair-cutting, falling out of teeth and decapitation" (SE 5: 357). The equation is reversible. Aging is associated with castration. As I have already suggested, the period during which Freud was working on *The Interpretation of Dreams* was marked by his anxiety about his career, which in turn was linked in his mind to aging. One of the autobiographical themes of *The Interpretation of Dreams* is precisely this anxiety about aging, an anxiety which went largely unanalyzed.

Freud assumed, for example, that men who are older (that is to say, *his* age at the time) will desire to be younger. This is not necessarily so. I would even hazard a generalization here. It is my guess that while our cultural representations of aging emphasize the desire for youth, most individuals do not, consciously at least, literally wish themselves younger. Rather, they may wish to stay young while growing older. This is another way of understanding one of Freud's remarks—it borders on the pontifical—in *The Interpretation of Dreams*. The "deeply-rooted wish for youth," he asserts, is "one of the constantly gnawing wishes of a man who is growing older" (SE 5: 476). We might be tempted to dismiss this as a commonplace. But we should linger here for a moment. Freud was here referring to himself. He was speaking of one of his own dreams—it is one of his laboratory dreams—which reminded him, he says, of an altogether grim period in his career when he was working at the Chemical Institute and during which he suffered a "barren and indeed humiliating episode in my apprenticeship" (SE 5: 475):

In an indistinct part of the background of one of my laboratory dreams I was of an age which placed me precisely in the gloomiest and most unsuccessful year of my medical career. I was still without a post and had no idea how I could earn my living; but at the same time I suddenly discovered that I had a choice open to me between several women whom I might marry! So I was once more young, and, more than everything, *she* was once more young—the woman who had shared all these difficult years with me. The unconscious instigator of the dream was thus revealed as one of the constantly gnawing wishes of a man who is growing older. The conflict raging in other levels of the mind between vanity and self-criticism had, it is true, determined the content of the dream; but it was only the more deeply-rooted wish for youth that had made it possible for that conflict to appear as a dream. Even when we are awake we sometimes say to ourselves: "Things are going very well to-day and times were hard in the old days; all the same, it was lovely then—I was still young." (SE 5: 476)

We may read this dream as anxiety about the present, an anxiety that is displaced in the dream onto the past and is neutralized by the association of the past with what Freud assumed was unequivocal value—youth. Freud's analysis of the dream is, at the level of age, unexamined and banal. He offers us a cliché about the good old days *when we were young*. This is all obvious. But what is striking is that Freud displaces anxiety about performance in the sphere of work onto the sphere of sexual relations. Freud, fulfilling the theoretical desire that dreams represent the fulfillment of a wish, phantasizes himself as wildly successful with women—there was not only one woman but several who wanted to marry him! More significant still, I think, is that he imagines as young again the woman whom he had married and who thus by his particular accounting was now old—in part because he thought of himself as old, or at least as "growing older."[8] He underscores her transformation from an old woman to a young woman as the triumphant aspect of the dream: "So I was once more young, and, more than everything, *she* was once more young—the woman who had shared all these difficult years with me." The dreamer is, we cannot help but remember, a middle-aged man. Youth is valued by men even more in women than it is desired for themselves.

Thus Freud did not turn his analytic attention to aging even when it looked him in the face. A clear case is his dream "My Uncle with the Yellow Beard." Freud first reports this dream in a chapter on "Distortion in Dreams" (actually he tells us only the first half of the dream—the rest we never learn):

I. *My friend R. was my Uncle—I had a great feeling of affection for him.*
II. *I saw before me his face, somewhat changed. It was as though it had been drawn out lengthways. A yellow beard that surrounded it stood out especially clearly.* (SE 4: 137)

Freud returns to this dream some ten times in *The Interpretation of Dreams*, among other things using it consciously to illustrate the laws of displacement and condensation. In terms of his theory of dreams as the fulfillment of our unspeakable wishes, Freud interprets "My Uncle with the Yellow Beard" as a dream of professional ambition, as a dream which offered him the not insignificant pleasure of slandering a colleague whom he disliked profoundly and whom he thought stupid. As with many of his dreams, Freud read "My Uncle with the Yellow Beard" as a dream of revenge and of reassurance.

I do not want to reject Freud's interpretation, which is altogether persuasive. But we may also read the dream as expressing anxiety about aging—anxiety in terms of his career but more particularly, as we will see, in terms of his ambivalent identification with his invalid father. From this perspective we can understand Freud's own interpretation as a denial or coverup of his anxiety about aging—both in terms of the present and in terms of what he feared, perhaps unconsciously, was to come.

Leafing through the thoughts associated with the dream, Freud insists that the wavering identification at stake is that of his abhorred colleague with his Uncle Josef, whom in reality he did not like at all. In fact, this conclusion was already present in his text of the dream ("*My friend R. was my Uncle*"). But my point is that the more important identification is that of himself with his father, which is covered up by his association of R. with his Uncle. Freud repeatedly compares the face in the dream, the visual image, the "picture," with that of a composite photograph. The dream-image reminds him of the technique of superimposing photographs of various members of a family onto one other. This technique was used by the contemporary photographer Galton to "bring out family likenesses," as Freud puts it (SE 4: 139). In his commentary Freud repeatedly mentions himself and his father in connection with aging. But he dismisses these associations as "incidental." How can we not read this as an instance of negation?

Just what is the color of his Uncle's beard? Or more pertinently, what does the color "yellow" signify? I would argue that the yellow of the beard represents both youth and age. Freud's uncle, who is by Freud's measure "old," had a "fair" beard. And by identifying his colleague with his uncle, Freud ages his colleague. He defaces him, in effect castrating him. But unwittingly he also performs the same operation on himself. Freud notes in such precise detail the changing colors of R.'s beard (originally it had been dark) that we cannot but conclude that his interest is more than coincidental. Freud has his revenge. His colleague is getting old.[9] Freud describes the change in color as "unpleasing," and he refers to this aspect of aging as *punishment* for a good-looking youth: "My friend R. had originally been extremely dark; but when black-haired people begin to turn grey they pay for the splendour of their youth. Hair by hair, their black beards go through an unpleasing change of color: first they turn to a reddish brown, then to a yellowish brown, and only then to a definite grey. My

friend R.'s beard was at that time passing through this stage'' (SE 4: 138–39).
I imagine Freud looking into this mirror of a dream and, catching a glimpse of
himself, turning away.

In the associations to the dream was also the face of his father whose hair,
Freud tells us in the same paragraph, "turned grey from grief in a few days"
(SE 4: 138). Later in *The Interpretation of Dreams* Freud, commenting again
on "My Uncle with the Yellow Beard," notes in passing that "incidentally, the
beard further involved the allusion to my father and myself through the intermediate idea of growing grey" (SE 4: 293). Again, incidentally. Again, denial.
For the years of his father's infirmity in old age coincided with Freud's own
going gray. Just six months before his father died in October 1896, Freud wrote
to Fliess describing the state of his own health. "My state of health does not
deserve to be the subject of inquiry. Last week there was a recrudescence of
the suppuration on the left side, migraines rather frequently; the necessary ab-
stinence is hardly doing much good." He summed up the litany of medical
complaints with a reference to aging. "I have," he wrote, "rapidly turned
gray."[10] Two months later Freud reported to Fliess that he was suffering from
fears of dying.

Surely the identification of himself with his father through the idea of aging,
symbolized by the color of the beard, was not a matter of minor importance to
Freud. The beard is the most important visual aspect of the dream, as the very
title of the dream itself testifies. And the title of the dream also simultaneously
conceals what it reveals—that the color of the beard in question is not yellow
but *gray*.

Why should the matter of hair turning gray be of such obsessional importance
to some of us? Many look anxiously for their first gray hairs. Many women,
and now more men, color (as we say) their hair when it begins to go gray. I
will return to this in the chapter on masquerade. But for now I want to remark
that if gray hair is associated in general with *old* age, usually our hair tends to
start turning gray in *middle* age. What is in fact a marker of middle age is
relegated, culturally and psychologically, to old age, dismissed as a sign of *age*
itself as if it were a fearsome ontological category, pushed out of middle age
and into *old* age. For some, particularly ambitious people like Freud, gray hair
might serve as a disagreeable "reminder" in middle age of the coming of old
age, more specifically that life at the midpoint may be seen as half over, that
we should hurry up, that we should get ourselves together.

Freud is explicit on this point elsewhere in *The Interpretation of Dreams*.
In several places he comments on a dream in which one of his teachers gives
him the horrific task of dissecting his own body (his pelvis, to be exact). Freud
interprets this dream as expressing his anxieties about how his book, so revealing

of his own "private character," will be received when it is published (SE 5: 453). He fears, he says, discomfort, a "gruesome feeling" (*grauen*). Miraculously, in his dream this feeling does not materialize. His wish is fulfilled—or at least his fear is allayed. But *grauen* also means growing gray. Freud himself notes this: "I should also have been very glad to miss growing grey—'*Grauen*' in the other sense of the word. I was already growing quite grey, and the grey of my hair was another reminder that I must not delay any longer" (SE 5: 478).

One of Freud's cultural associations to this dream is H. Rider Haggard's strange novel *She*. The novel represents one of our culture's dominant utopian phantasies about aging—that we might live a very long time as adults with our youthful bodies displaying no traces of aging (we see this phantasy in *Brave New World*, and in *The Portrait of Dorian Gray* as well).[11] In *She*, as Freud puts it, "a person's identity is retained through a series of generations for over two thousand years" (SE 5: 455). Thus the novel embodies Freud's wish that he not grow old, which is signified by "growing grey." At this point we might also re-read *grauen* in the other sense of the word—as a "gruesome feeling" that Freud associated with the body of his father in advanced old age, the body which he unflinchingly dissected in his mind's eye, the body which might be *his* body in the future.

As we know, Freud wrote in his preface to the second edition of *The Interpretation of Dreams* that he realized in retrospect the writing of the book was itself in great part the working through of his reaction to his father's death (his father had died in 1896 at the age of eighty-one and one-half). His father's death was, Freud wrote (was he pontificating? was he postulating a psychic truth within the sphere of the intergenerational yet nuclear family?), "the most important event, the most poignant loss, of a man's life" (SE 4: xxvi). *The Interpretation of Dreams* may be read as a son's book of mourning for his father, albeit a strange one. But I also want to insist that to the extent the figure of the dead father dominates the book in the abstract, the figure of the infirm and aged father haunts it. It is aging, not death, which castrates the father. The dead father persists in the psyche as strong. The infirm father is all too literally present as painfully weak.

Here we should turn to Freud's dream of "Count Thun." Freud interprets this dream as fulfilling the wish of the rebellious son against the father—as indeed of his own revolt against his own father. Freud recalls that when he was only two, his father had reproached him for wetting his bed. He also recalls that when he was seven or so, he urinated in his parents' bedroom in front of his parents, and that his father, dealing a not-forgotten blow to Freud's ambitions, announced that "the boy will come to nothing" (250). (A reader of almost any age might well sympathize with the two-year-old Freud but wonder just what the seven-year-old Freud was doing. In *Freud* Gay wonders if indeed this incident ever happened at all but speculates that the young Freud may have wandered into his parents' bedroom and, in a state of sexual excitement, urinated [23].) In "Count Thun," revenge (it seems truly infantile revenge) is obtained through the medium of age. One need only wait. Revenge comes so easily, so "naturally." What we commonly refer to as the second childhood is a punishment. It is in Freud's words "a tragic requital" (SE 4: 217n).

In the dream it is the old and infirm "father," not the son, who now cannot take care of his bodily functions. The roles are reversed. The son is in charge of the father. As Freud transcribes the dream-images into words, "I was a sick-nurse and had to give him the urinal because he was blind" (SE 4: 210). (In fact it was Freud's sister who nursed Jacob Freud, not Freud himself.) This is an association to the final days of his father's life during which, as Freud puts it, his father "soil[ed] his bed like a child" (SE 4: 217n). Or as Freud tells us elsewhere in *The Interpretation of Dreams* (he is referring to the dream "His Father on His Death-Bed Like Garibaldi"), his father's last weeks were marked by "a complete paralysis (*obstruction*) of the intestines" (SE 5: 429). From this Freud reports tactfully yet unsparingly that "disrespectful thoughts of all kinds followed." Yet guilt—in the form of filial piety—demanded that these thoughts be silenced. Freud, speaking of the resentment that he assumed a child continued to feel toward his father into middle age, uses the charged word "censorship": "The authority wielded by a father provokes criticism from his children at an early age . . . but the filial piety called up in our minds by the figure of the father, particularly after his death, tightens the censorship which prohibits any such criticism from being consciously expressed" (SE 5: 435). Freud also mitigated the harshness of his "disrespectful thoughts" by highly respectful ones, writing to Fliess two months before his father died that he was living out his last days "with decency and dignity."[12]

In "Count Thun" we find the figure of the incontinent father. In "His Father on His Death-Bed Like Garibaldi" we find the figure of the constipated father. Both fathers are incapacitated and require assistance. Freud suggests indirectly but definitely that he took a kind of sadistic pleasure in his father's suffering, in witnessing the breaking up of the father's authority over his body. Freud concludes that his response was not unusual. To support his conclusion he could draw on his developing theory of the Oedipus complex. But he also called on the reactions of other people—his patients—to corroborate his own. To Fliess he wrote that several of his own patients had experienced similar feelings of pleasure and guilt when taking care of their aged parents. This is from a letter Freud wrote to Fliess in 1899: "Two of my patients have almost simultaneously come up with [self-]reproaches following the nursing and death of their parents and have shown me that my dreams about this were typical. The reproach is in every instance bound to attach itself to revenge, to spiteful glee, taking satisfaction in the ill person's excretory difficulties (urine and stools)."[13]

As Melanie Klein has shown us, our phantasied attacks on others produce guilt, which she theorizes gives rise to our impulse of reparation, the basis for love. Our attacks also give rise to the fear that we will be attacked in turn. For Freud himself, then, what would be *his* "tragic requital"? What would be his punishment for his "disrespectful thoughts of all kinds"? Would it not be a similar old age? An old age that was one of wasting away, of being neither really dead nor really alive in Freud's sense, which meant being able to work? This is what, according to Freud, the last part of his father's life was like. As Freud wrote to Fliess soon after the death of his father, "His life had been over a long time before he died."[14] Just what did Freud mean by "long"? I take it that he was referring to the period of about three and one-half years between the attack his father suffered on his seventy-eighth birthday—"now he is a shadow of his former self," Freud wrote to Fliess[15]—and his death. In Freud's words, and in our culture as a whole, an infirm old age is regarded as being something *other* than life, and it is implicitly understood as being worse than death.[16]

How old our parents were when they died (and of course how they died) works strongly in our psychic imagination, casting shadows on our foreboding of our own deaths. For we now assume that barring an abrupt medical catastrophe or an accident (they are referred to as "untimely") we will live into old age. We may wonder vaguely how long we will live. We may refer ourselves to the statistical averages of the life spans for men and women that are quoted to us almost daily in the media as if there were a promissory stock exchange for the duration of our lives. We may take a certain arithmetical comfort in the idea that surely we will live at least as long as our parents did. And given the fact that people are living longer, we may imagine that by all rights we should live longer than did those who preceded us. In our culture today a longer life span is assumed to be our technological birthright, another version—the prolongevity version—of generational "progress." The age at which our parents died (especially mothers for daughters, fathers for sons) is simultaneously a goal and a barrier. Will we break the death barrier? We invariably measure our hypothetical life span in reference to the age of our parents at their deaths. We take out a mental ruler and move from left to right.

As is well known, Freud was obsessed with the date of his own death. He did not wonder vaguely about the age at which he would die. He had forebodings that took concrete numerical shape. He focused first on the age of forty, then on the age of forty-one; having passed forty-one, he singled out the age fifty-one, which he associated with the climacteric.[17] Freud's obsession with the age at which he would die was unquestionably peculiar and had something of the superstitious about it. But there was a certain logic about it as well. Take the ages forty and forty-one, for instance. As it turns out, these two numbers represented the midpoint of his father's life. They pinpointed Freud to a certain fixed term. I suspect that no matter how long our parents have lived, when we apply the measure of their days to our own lives it seems an inadequate span of years. To us the age at which Freud's father died (or as we commonly say, the age to which he lived)—eighty-one and one-half—may seem sufficiently long. Certainly it was well beyond the statistical average of the time. But to Freud eighty-one and one-half seemed too short a life span. When he was only in his late fifties, we find Freud worrying that he might have only another twenty-some years to live. He was precise about the dismal mathematics: "My father reached the age of 81½ and my eldest brother the same age, so there's a gloomy prospect."[18] If living beyond the father is an overtaking of him, is there not also a sibling rivalry in the matter of longevity as well?

Just how our parents and our grandparents (Freud's father was old enough to be his grandfather) live out their old age has a strong influence on our own associations to it—on our particular fears or on our relative equanimity, as I suggested in the previous chapter. Freud feared that his old age might resemble his father's. "Hence, in spite of all the acceptance of fate which is appropriate to an honest man, I have one quite secret prayer: that I be spared any wasting away and crippling of my ability to work because of physical deterioration."[19] An infirm old age represented to Freud a threat worse than death.

Lacan has insisted that the "fear of castration is like a thread that perforates all the stages of development."[20] The paradigmatic model of identification and castration is the Freudian Oedipus complex which is located in childhood. How is the threat of castration escaped? Freud theorized that the little boy, desiring the mother and wishing to take the place of the father, chooses instead to identify with the father and the power he represents. In this way the little boy escapes punishment but must postpone pleasure and the assumption of power. More recently adolescence has been theorized as a reactivation of the Oedipus complex, as a time when what has been postponed can now be enjoyed. The adolescent (and then the young adult) does so not by threatening the parental marriage bed (for within the discourse of psychoanalysis the parents have after all now grown old) but by forming a family of his own within his own generation. We see here again how important it is in psychoanalysis to keep the generations separate and apart—and never equal.[21]

But in our long lives of shifting identifications with parental figures, we may imagine other paradigmatic moments in our lives when our psychic relations with them change. Freud's experience as he approached what forcibly struck him as the midpoint of his life—it coincided uncannily with his father's death—invites us to speculate that in middle age there is another replaying of identification with parental figures, who have now aged. Does not identification in middle age with a parent in an infirm old age represent precisely the future castration which the young son had hoped to escape? Presumably safe in the middle years[22] and in a position of power, the child, in a moment of ambivalent identification with an aging parent, may realize that he has in fact succeeded only too well in taking the place of the father. In an infirm old age the body of the father embodies the very fact of castration. And the father's features uncannily resemble his own, prefiguring the future, which is the decline of the guilty child.

Thus from a Freudian perspective, one way of understanding anxieties about aging in middle age is as a symptom of a reactivation of the Oedipus complex. But the "resolution" of the complex must necessarily be different. The aggressivity of the Oedipus complex of childhood is transcended by identifying with the father. Perhaps the aggressivity of what we might call the inverse Oedipus complex of middle age is transcended *positively* by identifying with one's own child (or with the younger generation in general)[23] and *negatively* by displacing that aggressivity onto the category of old age in general. In middle age, identification with the father is disagreeable. It is *grauen*, it is repressed, it is censored. I will return to this question in the next chapter on the mirror stage of old age.

I do not want to be understood as arguing that an inverse Oedipus complex in middle age is the only representation of and model for our experience. It does, however, help explain our culture's simultaneous obsession with and repression of old age. Moreover, it is important that we recognize to just what extent this model, itself a kind of knowledge, is produced by the discourse of Freudian psychoanalysis which is largely inimical to aging and old age. I could offer many counter-scenes,[24] and will take up later in some detail a scene in Figes's *Waking* of a middle-aged woman with her dying mother. But here it is appropriate to insist that the discourse of Freudian psychoanalysis, made as it is out of the stuff of Freud's life and writing, has worked to avoid if not repress the *theorization* or *analysis* of old age. Freudian psychoanalysis, as I am presenting it here, is quite in consonance with our culture's general attitudes toward aging—aging is something we would rather forget. Although Freud could not forget it. He reinforced our dominant cultural attitudes about aging.

The occlusion of old age in Freud's work—old age is a kind of scotoma or blind spot—is covered up by Freud's emphasis on death and by the dramatistic rhetoric of psychoanalysis itself. As we have so clearly come to see, psychoanalysis is haunted by death or, to borrow a term from J.-B. Pontalis, "deathwork."[25] Its obsession with death has been amply theorized and documented in many different kinds of texts, ranging from Freud's own theorization of the death instincts in *Beyond the Pleasure Principle* and Max Schur's *Freud: Living and Dying* to Jean Laplanche's *Life and Death in Psychoanalysis*, Samuel Weber's *The Legend of Freud*, Nicholas Abraham and Maria Torok's work on mourning (to which I will refer in a later chapter), and Stuart Schneiderman's *Jacques Lacan: The Death of an Intellectual Hero*, which returns us to Freud and the centrality of death to psychoanalysis.[26] There is no need to rehearse this well-traveled terrain here. I accept the argument that death is as central to psychoanalysis as is sexuality. I also entertain Pontalis's suggestive hypothesis that Freud *covered up* his obsession with death with his emphasis on sexuality.[27] I would go one step further: *if sexuality is a cover for death, death is a cover for aging. We may read Freud, in other words, as displacing his fear of old age onto death.*

Freud found aging more threatening than death itself. The emphasis on death, which we commonly find represented as an *event*, conceals a denial of aging, a *process* that usually stretches out over many years. The dramatistic rhetoric of psychoanalysis encourages this coverup. Freudian psychoanalysis is theatrical. I am not referring only to the fact that Freud formulated his theories of the Oedipus complex and of narcissism with Greek drama and mythology in his mind's eye. I mean more generally that psychoanalysis is predominantly a vivid discourse of sharply defined events, which are themselves characterized in terms of conflict and which are understood to "punctuate" our lives. Our lives are figured in terms of visually perceptible infantile stages (such as Lacan's mirror stage), in terms of scenes (such as the primal scene), and in terms of traumatic events (such as seduction scenes or scenes to which we are captive witnesses). In Freudian psychoanalysis these scenes are located in childhood. In old age, in contrast, *nothing dramatic happens* for a long period of time, although of course we will commonly speak of a person as having aged suddenly or overnight. Old age is more like a postmodern drama of interminable postponement, as we find it in *Waiting for Godot* and other Beckettian fictions, than it is like a Greek tragedy (with the exception of *Oedipus at Colonus*, which Freud never took as his text). Aging in old age is for the most part an infinitesimally incremental process of the addition of time. It is figured as the infinitesimally decremental process of the subtraction of strengths, of a cumulative series of losses. Thus the rhetorical figures of psychoanalysis, and not just the substance of the theory, colluded with Freud's own attitudes toward old age to block an analysis of aging.

But at the same time my method in this book is precisely to render aging and old age visible by reflecting on old age as it is given to us in psychoanalytic and literary terms. This means that I have necessarily *dramatized* aging and old age. I myself write in terms of scenes and struggle, of Oedipal conflicts and the mirror stage of old age, of castration and narcissistic wounds, of masquerade and phantasms which shadow the *mise-en-scène* of the psyche. Working with the dramatistic categories of psychoanalysis, I will necessarily produce a discourse that takes on a certain theatrical form.

I want to turn here from Freud's middle age to another time in Freud's life—that of his old age. We will see again how Freud's theoretical categories, his attitudes, and his experience worked together to give us a model of behavior in old age which is much admired if not vaunted in the West. For Freud old age was a largely bitter burden which was to be shouldered. He withstood old age, and he did so heroically, not querulously. His stoicism and resignation in the face of disabling disease and increasing infirmity were virtually unyielding. His discipline in continuing to work was prodigious, as was his tenacity in maintaining his position of power in psychoanalysis as an institution. He valued independence over dependence, silent resistance over complaint. Freud was no King Lear.

I do not want here to dispute overmuch this model of stoic behavior. From what we know of Freud's old age through his letters and the various testimonies and biographies about him, his behavior was as exemplary as his experience of suffering was acute. But I do want to observe that confronting old age stoically with one's own resources, however extensive they may be, means that one does not *impose* one's old age on others in particular, or on society in general.[28] If our culture values a model of an *undemanding* old age, how much more easily those in old age can be forgotten or ignored by others, and by society at large.

For Freud personally, the terms ''old'' and ''sick'' were inextricably correlated. During the last sixteen years of his life he underwent a series of painful operations for cancer of the jaw. He grew increasingly frail. For long periods at a time he was a semi-invalid. At the end of his life the disease was so advanced and its odors so strident that even his dog would not venture near him, as we read in Ernest Jones's biography of Freud. How would Freud meet old age which was defined in great part as illness? He would continue as much as possible the pattern of his previous years. He would see patients, consult with colleagues, and write and see his work through to publication. He would remain at home with his family, first in Vienna and then in London. He would continue to correspond with his friends and associates. Old age was not visibly conferred on him by those social rituals of retirement that divide for many the work years from the so-called leisure years (although Freud's seventieth birthday was celebrated by the International Association, represented by a good number of his pupils who presented him with a gift of money). Nor was his old age marked by his moving—or being moved—to what we call today a retirement home or a nursing home. For the most part old age was impressed upon him by his body—he *felt* it in his body. And in his old age, old age appeared in his writing and his words in various guises. One of those places is *An Autobiographical Study* (1925), which was published when he was sixty-nine.[29]

An Autobiographical Study is a rather formulaic chronological account of Freud's career. Only one anecdote of a private nature interrupts the uninflected flow of events. Freud, writing from the vantage point of his late sixties, pauses to insist on the vivid impression that William James had made on him when he met the philosopher some fifteen years earlier during his visit to the United States. Freud casts the difference between himself and James in terms of age: Freud was young and healthy, James old and sick. Freud was particularly struck, he tells us, by James's heroic bearing:

> Another event of this time which made a lasting impression on me was a meeting with William James the philosopher. I shall never forget one little scene that occurred as we were on a walk together. He stopped suddenly, handed me a bag he was carrying and asked me to walk on, saying that he would catch me up as soon as he had got through an attack of angina pectoris which was just coming on. He died of that disease a year later; and I have always wished that I might be as fearless as he was in the face of approaching death. . . . At that time I was only fifty-three. I felt young and healthy. . . . (SE 20: 52)[30]

With this passage I imagine Freud replacing the disturbing figure of the incontinent aging father of his early middle years and *The Interpretation of Dreams* with the figure of a suffering old man who continues nevertheless and with dignity to work. Or perhaps it would be better to say that the one is superimposed on the other like a Galton family portrait. This scene surfaced in Freud's writing when he had most need of it. Only a few years earlier he had been diagnosed as suffering from cancer. I imagine Freud carrying this memory of William James with him as a kind of talisman throughout his last fourteen years. I see the story for Freud as a kind of parable of ethical behavior, as another embodiment of the superego, as a cultivated form (as the Tai Chi Chuan is a form), as a way of submitting to another version of symbolic law.

Freud, we remember, had theorized that the young child acquires the necessary strength to resolve the Oedipus complex—that is, to renounce the object of his desire—by *borrowing* it from his father. As he explained in *The Ego and the Id*, which was published two years before *An Autobiographical Study*, "Clearly the repression of the Oedipus complex was no easy task. The child's parents, and especially his father, were perceived as the obstacle to a realization of his Oedipus wishes; so his infantile ego fortified itself for the carrying out of the repression by erecting this same obstacle within itself. It borrowed strength to do this, so to speak, from the father, and this loan was an extraordinarily momentous act" (SE 19: 34). The word "borrow" is critical here. It is in the nature of the social or symbolic contract that what we borrow we must return. This is in part what I understand by Lacan's jolting description of the unconscious as preeminently ethical: "Sublimate all you want, you still have to pay with something. This something is called pleasure [*jouissance*]. This mystical operation, I pay for it with a pound of flesh."[31]

Earlier Freud had borrowed strength from a father demanding of others. In later life we could say that he borrowed a certain strength—a form of stoicism—from another symbolic father, represented in the figure of William James. But at the end of our lives, unlike the beginning, we must complete the symbolic transaction. We pay for it literally with a pound of flesh.

In his letters to Lou Andreas-Salomé, Freud spoke of his own aging as a series of losses. His tone is not so much bitter as resigned and self-reproachful. He represented himself to her—she was only five years younger than he—as a bad example of an aging man, as a person more preoccupied with his body than with his work.[32] He felt isolated professionally, he said. He was no longer very good at walking and not much interested in reading. His body was failing him—his intestines, his heart, his speech. He could no longer smoke. He reported that his memory for recent events was declining. He could, at the end, no longer travel. Still we know that this is the period in which he wrote, among other things, *Inhibitions, Symptoms and Anxiety* (1926), *The Future of an Illusion* (1927), *Civilization and Its Discontents* (1930), "Female Sexuality" (1931), and *Moses and Monotheism* (1939).

Andreas-Salomé argued with him, presenting aging and old age eloquently if sentimentally in terms of compensation and even as a culmination of psychic and intellectual growth. In 1927 she wrote to chastise Freud for his pessimism with regard to his aging: "it always seems to me as if old age requites the losses, the lavas, with deeper movements."[33] Seven years later (three years before her own death at the age of seventy-five and five years before his), she wrote: "it delights me to note from year to year how long it takes for much that happens to one to become inner experience. It is only in old age that this process is completed, and for this reason it is right and proper to grow really old, despite the less pleasant reverse side in the shape of infirmity. It seems to me that this is true even in matters of the intellect, not only in emotional life. And since what we call living, from the cradle to the grave, is full of burdens and difficulties, it is often a consoling thought that by virtue of its length it paradoxically still has something to give us, in order that we shall not be tempted to abuse it overmuch."[34] Andreas-Salomé came close here to a Jungian vision of old age, which Freud quickly rejected as an illusion that offered no future for him, not even the comforts of consolation. He refused what he correctly called her "eulogy" of old age, her view of old age as completion.[35] He replied to her in the more familiar metaphor of western culture of aging as decline. When Andreas-Salomé spoke lyrically about the "sunny aspects" of old age, "about what still remains unravelled for me in the wondrous skein of life," Freud countered with metaphors of the moon and sterility; "with me," he wrote back to her, "crabbed age has arrived—a state of total disillusionment, whose sterility is comparable to a lunar landscape, an inner ice age."[36]

At least once Freud described his old age as a period not of simple decline but of regression. He was referring to his life in work. In a postscript added in 1935 to *An Autobiographical Study* he noted that he felt he had not contributed any original work in the last ten years. "This circumstance is connected with an alteration in myself," he wrote, "with what might be described as a phase of regressive development" (72). Yet he had been by any "objective" standard quite productive—and in fact he insists on his productivity over the last ten years in the same postscript. What he meant was that he had returned to the problems that had interested him in the early part of his career. Still it is difficult to know how to take his observation. It does seem to be of a somewhat confessional nature, although it is offered for the public reading eye in Freud's customary matter-of-fact way. Freud seems to be apologizing even as he offers us an explanation for his turn of mind toward the past. Did this in fact embarrass him? If it did, perhaps here Freud is rationalizing the backward turning of his mind by presenting it as analogous to the model of the return to conflicts of childhood in the space of psychoanalysis itself.

It has often been remarked—and it has been theorized as well—that when we are old we return in reminiscence to those points in our life which most express our subjectivity and which remain in some sense unfinished dramas.[37] As a literary form or as a mode of self-expression, reminiscence did not much interest Freud. It is for this very reason that Freud's "letter" to Romain Rolland holds such a fascination for me. Written expressly to be published on the occasion of Rolland's seventieth birthday in 1936, Freud's text is not so much a reminiscence as an analysis of one of his own experiences. This we might have expected. Freud returns to the scene of his visit to the Acropolis some thirty years before. He had gone there with his brother not long after the publication of *The Interpretation of Dreams*. But during the last few years, he tells his readers, this memory—or more precisely the *affect* associated with it—kept surfacing in his mind.

Freud opens and closes his analysis of this memory by underscoring the fact of his old age. In the first paragraph he notes his age in neutral and formulaic terms, referring rhetorically to his age as a way of politely apologizing for what he says are the diminished proportions of his "gift" (or is he by his very demur calling attention to his analytic strength?). "I am ten years older than you and my powers of production are at an end," Freud writes, adding, "All that I can find to offer you is the gift of an impoverished creature, who has 'seen better days'" (SE 22: 239). But at the end of the letter, in its last sentence which has the force of a prison sentence, we encounter an altogether different tone. I read in it an almost Poe-like cry, uttered as if in awful understanding of the truth of his analysis—his recognition that his present diminished place in life is a "tragic requital" for having taken the place of the father, which means having *overtaken* the father. "And now," he writes to us, "you will no longer wonder that the recollection of this incident on the Acropolis should have troubled me so often since I myself have grown old and stand in need of forbearance and can travel no more" (248).

In this text, so brilliantly titled "A Disturbance of Memory on the Acropolis"—as if the memory were an earthquake—Freud's lifelong preoccupation with the ambivalent relationship between father and son returns again.[38] What Freud seeks to understand are the puzzling feelings of doubt and uncertainty that clouded the quite successful trip he made with his brother to Athens. He tells us that he had longed to see the Acropolis, and that indeed he found it a glorious sight. Why then, he asks, did he resist the journey? Why did he doubt what he saw? Freud's analysis, thirty years later, reflects his typically pessimistic view of the course of life as something fated, with success and its corollary guilt inextricably entwined in the son's relation to the father. "It must be," he concluded, "that a sense of guilt was attached to the satisfaction of having gone such a long way: there was something about it that was wrong, that from earliest times had been forbidden. It was something to do with a child's criticism of his father, with the undervaluation which took the place of the overvaluation of earlier childhood. It seems as though the essence of success was to have got further than one's father, and as though to excel one's father was still something forbidden!" (456).

Why did this memory disturb Freud at this point in his life? Freud was almost eighty-one when he wrote "A Disturbance of Memory on the Acropolis." His father had died at the age of eighty-one and one-half. Thus Freud was soon, perhaps, to overtake his father again. But more important, I think, Freud's analysis of his memory gave him an "explanation" for his fate, which was a painfully difficult old age. The infirmities of old age were a kind of punishment—castration—for "having gone too far." Destiny came in the form of an inexorable old age. For Freud fate had long been associated with the superego, which is to say, with the father. As he wrote elsewhere in "A Disturbance of Memory," "the Fate which we expect to treat us so badly is a materialization of our conscience, of the severe super-ego within us, itself a residue of the punitive agency of our childhood" (451). As I have already mentioned, Freud had theorized that when we are young, the superego is formed by the introjection of the figure of the father (in this way the Oedipus complex is surmounted). What are the characteristics of the superego? Freud associated the superego with severity, punishment, power, and at times with harshness and cruelty. As he put it in his essay on "The Economic Problem of Masochism" (1924), ultimately the superego is figured by "the dark power of Destiny" (SE 19: 168). In this text Freud associates the death instinct with masochism, and masochism with a need for punishment. Thus from a Freudian perspective, what are the implications of the association of old age with suffering? In *The Ego and the Id* Freud discusses at some length the phenomenon of people who do not wish to relinquish their suffering. In explanation he again links suffering, as punishment, with guilt and thus moral or ethical behavior: "In the end we come to see that we are dealing with what may be called a 'moral' factor, a sense of guilt, which is finding its satisfaction in illness and refuses to give up the punishment of suffering" (SE 19: 49). Old age, associated with suffering, is a punishment which must be embraced.

And that is why Freud could not travel anymore.

In old age, then, which in Freudian terms is castration, one is both father and son, the person who punishes and the person who receives punishment. The effect is that of a double image, of a composite photograph which does not record visual imagery but *affect*. The incontinent father of Freud's middle age and the aged Freud who cannot travel, now so near his father's age when he died, coalesce under the pressure of the injunctions of filial piety and the disturbance of guilt. How to bear that guilt ethically? How to meet one's old age morally? One shoulders it stoically, as Freud imagined William James did.

Thus, from what I am calling a Freudian perspective, we should not rage against the dying of the light as Dylan Thomas exhorted us to do. (This has become a dreadful cliché. We should also remember that Dylan Thomas was only thirty-seven when he died; old age was not at stake.) One should bear one's old age as one's fate which in a sense has been chosen.

The model of stoic behavior as acceptance of one's fate has been thoroughly absorbed in accounts of Freud's life. Jones extols Freud's behavior, praising it as exemplary, particularly in the context of the doctor-patient relationship: "He was throughout a model patient, touchingly grateful for any relief and in all the years completely uncomplaining. There was never any sign of irritability or annoyance, whatever the distress. There was no grumbling at what he had to endure. A favorite expression was 'it is no use quarreling with fate.' His gracious politeness, considerateness and gratitude toward his doctor never wavered."[39] Peter Gay, entitling the last section of his biography of Freud "Death of a Stoic," portrays Freud's last years as a "wrestling match with death," a battle which Freud fought with "psychoanalytic poise," not rage, and a refusal "to surrender to pathos" (427). The last sentence of Gay's book is: "The old stoic had kept control of his life to the end" (657). Schur, Freud's personal physician during the last years of his life, notes that during Freud's last weeks, "Not once in all that time did I witness any impatient or angry reaction toward any person in his environment" (527). Paul Roazen also has written of Freud's "stoic" and "sagelike endurance of his cancer."[40] What is the effect of lauding stoic behavior in old age? of representing old age as the shouldering of suffering? Is it not itself a kind of repression of the discontents of old age?

The metaphor of old age as a period of decline is of course a familiar one in western culture and, generally speaking, in Freud's writing it is not particularly unusual. However, the way in which he refers to old age in a letter he wrote to Andreas-Salomé in 1925 is striking. In it he describes his experience of aging, phenomenologically and theoretically, in vocabulary reminiscent of *Beyond the Pleasure Principle*, which had been published five years before:

> I no longer want to [keep going] ardently enough. A crust of indifference is slowly creeping up around me, a fact I state without complaining. It is a natural development, a way of beginning to grow inorganic. The "detachment of old age," I think it is called. It must be connected with a decisive turn in the relationship of the two instincts postulated by me. The change taking place is perhaps not very noticeable; everything is as interesting as it was before, neither are the ingredients very different; but some kind of resonance is lacking. . . . The never-ceasing tangible pressure of a vast number of unpleasant sensations must have accelerated this otherwise perhaps premature condition, this tendency to experience everything *sub specie aeternitatis*.[41]

Freud was sixty-nine at the time. Yet he tells Andreas-Salomé that he considered old age a "condition" (like an illness, old age might be only a temporary "condition") which was "premature"—"perhaps." Would not the coming of old age always have been to him premature?

With this passage firmly in view, we may understand the puzzling notion of the death instincts in *Beyond the Pleasure Principle* in terms of aging. We can read the death instincts as expressing themselves silently in the aspect of aging. In his letter to Andreas-Salomé, Freud emphasizes the gradual nature of aging as a process which is not "noticeable," only felt. He describes old age here as an accretion, as if it took the form of a bodily excrescence which was slowly and imperceptibly accumulating around him, enveloping him in its crust.[42] What does he feel? Not *grauen* but indifference.

Freud's initial speculations on what he called the death instincts in *Beyond the Pleasure Principle* (1920), published when he was sixty-four, draw on the discourses of myth and biology. At the end of this long piece which proceeds by a kind of associational anarchy, Freud called on the Aristophanes of Plato's *Symposium* to provide him with a parable for the origin of the sexual instincts. Not for the origin of sexual *difference* (there were already three sexes—" 'man, woman, and the union of the two' ") but rather for the introduction of "fresh 'vital differences' " into the system of sexual reproduction—or as Freud generalized, into any animate system (SE 18: 57, 55).[43] Freud was seeking to explain his hypothesis that all animate systems (the word "system" is mine, not Freud's) display the behavior of working "*to restore an earlier state of things*" (36). I am more interested here, however, in the way in which he uses the discourse of biology to develop his notion of the death instincts. For in this strange and twisting text, Freud, in his early old age, was principally concerned with the problem of how or why an organic system maintains itself even as it proceeds toward an inorganic state, toward death. He describes the life instincts and death instincts in terms of "opposition," of the one checking the other on the "journey" (that familiar metaphor) of life: "It is as though the life of the organism moved with a vacillating rhythm," he proposes. "One group of instincts rushes forward so as to reach the final aim of life"—which is death—"as swiftly as possible; but when a particular stage in the advance has been reached, the other group jerks back to a certain point to make a fresh start and so prolong the journey" (41).

In *Beyond the Pleasure Principle*, Freud even casts into doubt the inevitability of aging as a biological process. Is this not a peculiar form of denial? He introduces his brief discussion with the surprising comment that "we may be astonished to find how little agreement there is among biologists on the subject of natural death and in fact that the whole concept of death melts away under their hands" (317). What does Freud offer as examples that contradict the universality of senescence and a "natural death" for all living things? He observes that some animals and certain forms of plant life live so long (they "reach a very advanced age") that scientists have not been able to compute their natural life span. Not even a weak argument, this is no argument at all. He calls on the work of a scientist who has made a distinction between the *soma*, which is mortal, and the germcells, which are "potentially immortal" (46). Freud is referring here to the immortality of lineage which sidesteps the *real* of the aging and death of an organism. Perhaps even more bizarrely, Freud cites biological experiments involving very small organisms which lead him, he says, to conclude that in some organisms aging is not inevitable and can be forestalled by certain procedures. What procedures? Senescence can be held at bay by introducing *fresh vital differences*. The process? "Conjugation" which is the forerunner of sexual activity. Superimposing experiments upon one another, Freud draws the following startling conclusion: "If two of the animalculae, at the same moment before they show signs of senescence, are able to coalesce with each other, that is to 'conjugate' (soon after which they once more separate), they are saved from growing old and become 'rejuvenated' " (48). Aging is something we must be *saved from*. And what will save us? The sexual instincts.

Here aging is clearly associated with the death instincts, or the death instincts are associated with aging. Furthermore aging is associated with a *lack* of sexual activity. Again Freud reflects the bias of dominant western views toward aging— old age and sexuality are antithetical.[44]

With this introductory discussion in view, I want to turn here to a consideration of two metaphors which explicitly or implicitly arise both in Freud's letter about aging to Andreas-Salomé and in *Beyond the Pleasure Principle*— the metaphor of the exterior "crust" of the organism and the metaphor of the inertia of the organism. These two metaphors correspond to Freud's view of the organism as being buffeted by stimuli from without and as being *animated* or destroyed by stimuli which arise from within in the form of the life instincts and the death instincts.

In *Beyond the Pleasure Principle* Freud, as we have already seen, asks us to imagine an elementary organism as the model against which to test hypotheses concerning the existence of the death instincts. In order to regulate the stimuli which it receives from the outside world, the organism develops, in Freud's words, a "shield" whose function is to resist those "most powerful energies." The passage in *Beyond the Pleasure Principle* is worth quoting at some length:

> This little fragment of living substance is suspended in the middle of an external world charged with the most powerful energies; and it would be killed by the stimulation emanating from these if it were not provided with a protective shield against stimuli. It acquires the shield this way: its outermost surface ceases to have the structure proper to living matter, becomes to some degree inorganic and thenceforward functions as a special envelope or membrane resistant to stimuli. . . . By its death, the outer layer has saved all the deeper ones from a similar fate—unless, that is to say, stimuli reach it which are so strong that they break through the protective shield. *Protection against* stimuli is an almost more important function for the living organism than *reception* of stimuli. (27)

In this passage we see clearly the emphasis in Freudian psychoanalysis on a kind of protectionism (as in the protectionism of a nation-state against the invasion of outside forces). And if we refer back to Freud's letter to Andreas-Salomé in which he described himself in analogous terms ("A crust of indifference is slowly creeping up around me; a fact I state without complaining. It is a natural development, a way of beginning to grow inorganic") we may conclude that, for Freud, as one ages the "crust" grows thicker, and stimuli from the outside world grow fewer and farther between. In aging, then, it would be as if one grew progressively *inorganic*. Or from a Lacanian perspective, that as one declined into advanced old age, one responded less and less to the call of the Other.

We must take care here to remember again that Freud's experience of old age was associated with illness. Illness conspired with Freud's theory of excitation and stimuli to produce a model of old age as "detachment" from the world. As he wrote candidly in 1924 in a letter to Andreas-Salomé, he had two preoccupations at the time—one was a professional matter concerning the psychoanalyst Otto Rank, and the other was his new prosthesis for his jaw. "You would be surprised," he told her, "if you knew how much more concerned I am about the prosthesis than about Rank. Perhaps you would see in this a proof of the increase of narcissism in old age."[45] In illness, as Freud had observed years earlier in his essay "On Narcissism" (and to which I will return in another chapter), we turn our attention away from the world and concern ourselves with our own bodies. For Freud in old age, the body was no longer a source of narcissistic pleasure. Libidinal energy—and that energy was diminishing—was required to attend to his pain. For Freud defined the life instincts and death instincts as psychical forces whose activity is calibrated in accordance with physiological changes in the body. One of the most striking of those instances is illness. One of the most imperceptible of those instances is aging. What Freud wished for was a cessation of sensation, which was pain. That is, I submit, he wished for the *quiescence* of the organism. What was required was *acquiescence*, an indifference, a detachment, a patient submissiveness, an acceptance—in short, stoicism. What was wanted, to borrow his words from *Civilization and Its Discontents*, was "an avoidance of unpleasure—a goal, as we might call it, of weary resignation" (SE 21: 82).

Here is the appropriate place to consider what aspect the death instincts assume—or better, under what *aspects* they appear. Freud was nowhere very clear on this point. He offered not one but several answers. Part of the problem, he insisted, drawing on the metaphors of sound and silence, is that while the life instincts express themselves *noisily*, the death instincts are *quiet*. In *The Ego and the Id* he put it this way: "the death instincts are by their nature mute and . . . the clamour of life proceeds for the most part from Eros" (SE 19: 46). In *Beyond the Pleasure Principle* he argued that we see the workings of the death instincts in the repetition compulsion and in sadism. Ten years later in *Civilization and Its Discontents* Freud almost wholly identified the death instincts with aggressivity, which expresses itself in destructiveness directed outwards from the self. In fact, in *Civilization and Its Discontents*, which gives us a kind of summary of his thought on the death instinct, Freud used the terms "death instinct" and "aggressive instinct" interchangeably.

Lacan has also linked the death instincts with aggressivity, although he has taken, aggressively, the opportunity to suggest that Freud had not sufficiently analyzed aggressivity. We find Lacan praising Freud even as he himself seeks to take his place: "The enigmatic signification that Freud expressed in the term *death instinct* . . . reveals the aporia that confronted this great mind in the most profound attempt so far made to formulate an experience of man in the register of biology." "This aporia," Lacan continued, "lies at the heart of the notion of aggressivity."[46]

But we have been led to suspect that the death instincts may assume different aspects at different times in our lives. In *The Ego and the Id* Freud explicitly argues that as we mature biologically, we deflect the death instincts away from ourselves and onto the external world by virtue of the very strength of our bodies—by the development of "the muscular apparatus" (SE 19: 41).[47] We are invited to wonder what can happen when the body slows down in old age and can no longer, as it were, deflect the death instincts away from itself. I will return to this question in the chapter on phantasms of the aging body. But for the moment I want to recall Freud's words in his letter to Andreas-Salomé. He no longer wanted, he said, *to keep going ardently enough.* The distinction is implicitly between *movement* and *rest.* In terms of aging, then, we could link the life instincts with movement, and the death instincts with rest.

The French psychoanalyst Françoise Dolto, breaking from Lacan, also links the death instincts in general with the desire to rest. In a brilliant book on the body, she concludes that "the death instincts prevail during deep sleep, absent-mindedness, comas."[48] We may add following our discussion here that the death instincts prevail during advanced old age. "It is not in the desire to sleep but in the desire to rest," Dolto continues, that the death instincts assert themselves. The death instincts "are *le fait* of the body which is insensible to desire" (34). In his old age Freud experienced, he said in his letter to Andreas-Salomé, "a decisive turn in the relationship of the two instincts postulated by me" (154). The death instincts were gaining ascendancy over the life instincts. This does not mean that death is actively desired—this aspect of the death instincts is misleadingly named—but rather that rest is longed for. Fatigue, and its psychic correlative *inertia*, were gaining ascendancy over energy, both somatic and psychic.

In the last paragraph of *The Ego and the Id* Freud uses the word "rest" to describe in general a wish for quiescence: the death instincts "desire to be at peace" and want to put Eros "to rest" (50). In aging, the predominance of the death instincts over the life instincts is characterized by a certain and inevitable *inertia*, a slowing down. The notion of inertia is key. As Freud wrote in *Beyond the Pleasure Principle*, "*It seems, then, that an instinct is an urge inherent in organic life to restore an earlier state of things* . . . the expression of the inertia inherent in organic life" (SE 18: 36).

If the death instincts are an expression of inertia, the fear of death is the expression of the fear of castration. Toward the end of his life, Freud understood the more specific fear of death as having developed out of the more general and all-pervasive fear of castration. Inertia and castration—they came together in old age. Although Freud emphasizes the aggressive aspect of the death instincts in *Civilization and Its Discontents*, he could also ask this rhetorical question: "what good to us is a long life if it is difficult and barren of joys, and if it is so full of misery that we can only welcome death as a deliverer?" (SE 21: 88). It is a good question. Although posed in the context of a discussion of technology and civilization, Freud's question invites us to think of his own experience in his old age. Elsewhere he wrote of his "apathy" and of his "increasing feeling of helplessness," which he felt was "the worst thing about old age."[49]

In the letters Freud wrote toward the end of his life, the rhetoric of the "struggle" between the life instincts and the death instincts, which has been so thoroughly absorbed into commentary on Freud,[50] shifts to the rhetoric of a difficult balance, a balance which must be endured, a balance which must somehow be chosen. Writing in 1933 to Ernest Jones, Freud ostensibly spoke about old people in general, but he was clearly writing about himself: "old people must be glad when the scales are nearly balanced between the inevitable need of final rest and the wish to enjoy a while longer the love and friendship of those near to one."[51] How to balance the equation? The mathematics were for Freud excruciating.

Some six months before his eighty-first birthday, Freud wrote to Marie Bonaparte, noting precisely and in a single sentence her age and his, *and* the ages at which his brother, his father, and his mother died: "When you at a youthful 54 cannot avoid often thinking of death you cannot be astonished that at the age of 80½ I fret whether I shall reach the age of my father and brother or further still into my mother's age, tormented on the one hand by the conflict between the wish for rest and the dread of fresh suffering that further life brings and on the other anticipation of the separation from which I am still attached."[52] The equation, as we see, is not so simple to parse out. Rest (in this context a kind of pseudonym for death) is to be wished for because it would mean the end of bodily pain, but rest is *not* to be wished for because it would bring the psychic pain of the loss of others. In a much earlier essay entitled "The Theme of the Three Caskets" (1913) Freud interprets the drama of *King Lear* this way: "Eternal wisdom, clothed in the primaeval myth, bids the old man renounce love, choose death and make friends with the necessity of dying" (SE 12: 301). Triumphing over death is realized only by embracing it.[53] It is as if at this late point in his life, behind every door stands either rest, which is *not* something to be feared (the death instincts have taken on another aspect), or pain, which is what remains of life.

But if Freud's pronouncement in "The Theme of the Three Caskets" may seem wise itself, from the vantage point of Freud's suffering in old age it also seems irritatingly pedagogical in its tone of implied superiority to the vanities of desire. But in the ever expanding field of inertia in Freud's last years, desire still flared up in his words and in the space of psychoanalysis. Old age, we could say, using Freud's own terminology from another context, was *breached* by desire. Lacan's correction to Freudian psychoanalysis here rings so very true: desire is the desire of what one understands is the desire of the other, which over our lives assumes forms peculiar to ourselves. The so-called crust of stoicism was penetrated from outside. What did Freud want? I cite two instances which I find particularly moving and which require, really, no elaboration other than to note that both testify to narcissistic wounds that could no longer be healed. The first is a kind of professional complaint, the second a cry of desire.

There is the thinly veiled lament and plainly articulated reproach voiced, however matter-of-factly, in a letter to Arnold Zweig which Freud wrote some four years before he died: "I have a lot of free time: i.e. very few hours of analysis. People seem to have learnt that I am fairly old"—he was more than "fairly old," he was eighty at the time!—"and they no longer flock to me; accordingly I am slowly declining but there ought to be a process of self-regulation between cause and effect."[54] Freud was feeling the loss of professional control and thus self-esteem in everyday life.

And then there is the remark that, some seven years before his death, Freud flung angrily at H. D., a beautiful and cultured woman who was in her forties. They were together in his consulting room. As she reports it, he took her by surprise, beating his hand on the sofa, bursting out, " 'The trouble is—I am an old man—*you do not think it worth your while to love me.*' "[55] The posture of stoicism in old age was at this moment unforgettably breached by the desire for the attention of a much younger woman. Freud was not able entirely to renounce love, choose death, and make friends with the necessity of dying. We see here again yet another version of aging and its discontents.

COUNTER-TEXT

It's odd, but even when I am in pain I have a sexual urge. Perhaps especially when I am in pain. Or I should say that I am more attracted, more fascinated by women who cause me pain?

Probably you could call it the masochistic tendency. I don't think I've always had it—it's something I've developed in my old age. . . .

I crouched over just as I had on the twenty-eighth of July, glued my lips to the same place on her calf, and slowly savored her flesh with my tongue. It tasted like a real kiss. My mouth kept slipping lower and lower, down toward her heel. To my surprise she didn't say a word. She let me do as I pleased. My tongue came to her instep, then to the tip of her big toe. Kneeling, I crammed her first three toes into my mouth. I pressed my lips to the wet sole of her foot, a foot that seemed as alluringly expressive as a face.

"That's enough."

Suddenly the shower came on; water streamed over my head, face, that lovely foot. . . .

—Seventy-seven-year-old Utsugi with his daughter-in-law Satsuko, *from* Jurichiro Tanizaki, *Diary of a Mad Old Man* 26, 66

3. The Mirror Stage of Old Age . . .
Marcel Proust's *The Past Recaptured*

AFTER SPENDING SOME YEARS in a sanatarium outside Paris, Marcel returns to the city to attend a reception at the home of the wealthy Guermantes. He is, we remember, a neurasthenic dandy recognized in elite circles for his literary gifts—although he has in fact published only a few sketches. The memorable psychological drama that takes place that afternoon in the closing pages of Proust's *The Past Recaptured* can be read as a frightening hyperparable of aging in the twentieth-century West. Like other more familiar psychological dramas of initiation (the witnessing of the primal scene, for example, or the celebrated Greek drama which gave Freud inspiration for his theory of the Oedipus complex), it is structured as a scene of recognition, followed by blindness—or repression. But unlike classical psychoanalytic dramas, this drama of aging and its discontents turns more importantly on the character's relation to future time than it does to past time.

Marcel's insight into his future is doubled over into two paradoxical and contradictory scenarios about what he can achieve in terms of work. On the one hand, the man who is tormented by doubts about his own talent and disillusioned about the institution of literature itself finds that his faith in both himself and literature is restored on the afternoon of what he calls the most beautiful day of his life. On the other hand, as he is confronted face to face with his advancing age, he is assailed by new doubts and despairs that he will ever finish the very work he has now resolved to complete. Long wishing to begin in earnest his literary career, Marcel finally feels ready to do so. But the fact of his age (he is around fifty and has always been sickly) depresses him, and he quite understandably worries that he may die before he finishes his work. Is it or is it not too late? Marcel's rendezvous with what he understands to be his destiny at the reception is a contradictory combination of hell and paradise, danger and pleasure. It is a *combination*, never perfect union, because Marcel himself is split in terms of his relation to time. The ecstatic psychic moments of what he calls perfect knowledge—of the past recaptured, of indeed *youth*—connect his past with his present, giving him a sense of a productive future. His new and grim knowledge of old age, however, threatens to separate him from that ideal union of past and present, projecting him into a future aborted by age.

As with the narrative of Oedipus, the moment of recognition of his own aging is preceded by a series of delays which can be understood as forms of unconscious denial. I will mention two only. I take the following incident as my first example of Marcel's unconscious denial of old age. Lingering on his way to the Guermantes' so as to postpone his arrival (this dallying is certainly not only for the sake of making a fashionable entrance), Marcel notices an old man "with staring eyes and bent shoulders [who] was sitting, or, rather, was placed and was making greater effort to sit up straight, like a child who has been told to behave properly."[1]

By comparing Marcel's reaction to this man with the way he responds soon after to the elderly guests at the Guermantes', we can gauge the degree to which he is as yet unable to see into the mirror of his own future. The narrative of this small scene condenses the narrative of the scene at the reception: lack of recognition is followed by shock of recognition. The old man whom Marcel at first takes to be just any old man suddenly assumes an identity in Marcel's eyes. He is revealed to be a longtime and once "important" acquaintance, the Baron Monsieur de Charlus. But this scene differs importantly from the one to be played later that afternoon. In a very real sense this scene involves only two characters—the nameless old man and Monsieur de Charlus. Marcel stands to the side. He does not implicate himself in this scene. Later that day he will be forced to participate when the drama assumes the proportions of a doubled double, a triangle in which Marcel oscillates between two positions depending upon whether he contrasts himself with the others or finds himself reflected in their eyes. This structural variance between the two scenes is clearly revealed in the difference between Marcel's rhetoric about old age here and his rhetoric later at the Guermantes'. Here he is too far removed from what he will later understand as the realities of his *own* old age to correctly interpret the painful nature of the old man's condition. Here Marcel remains clinically detached, fascinated to detail the physical characteristics of the frail Monsieur de Charlus (who has suffered a stroke) and almost eager to record the evidence of his loss of social status. Even more telling, Marcel sentimentalizes the old man's physical infirmities, musing, for example, that he preferred to see in his limited gestures "an almost physical gentleness, a sort of detachment from the realities of life" (183). Later Marcel will find himself repelled by old age—because he is dangerously close to it—and will resort to satire.

The space of the final pages of *The Past Recaptured* can be thought of as divided into two domains—the private and the public. They are related to each other complexly and correspond to Marcel's ambivalent relation to his new sense of the future. It is in solitude when he is isolated from others that his belief in literature is renewed and that he "recaptures" the past, experiencing precisely (or so he believes) what he had felt at certain precious moments long ago. For Marcel, this form of doubling is elating. It unites the past and the present by insisting on their sameness, their identity. During these brief moments which are occasioned by involuntary memory (they cannot be willed into being), time as change, as limit, and as death is banished. Marcel feels himself a "timeless person, consequently unconcerned with the vicissitudes of the future" (197). Or, we might say, at these moments he feels himself to be *ageless*.

Marcel associates the private with what is authentic and is located deep within his sense of himself. Thus theoretically at least, for him the most valuable literary work would represent that experience, and the most contemptible would be concerned with the *appearance* of things. Literature is furthest from "reality," he believes, when it merely gives "a miserable listing of lines and surfaces" (213). It is ironic of course that one of Marcel's greatest talents is for satire, for the parodic description of the appearance of things. He exercises his talent for the "listing of lines and surfaces" when he crosses the divide between the private and public, stepping from the solitude of the small library where he has been waiting for the concert to end and into the main drawing room. Marcel's entrance into the social world is preceded—or rather further *delayed* (this is my second example of unconscious denial)—by a long and eloquent meditation on art and literature. It is immediately followed by the most trenchant and sustained satirical description of the elderly in western literature. Proust's metaphor of the theater is perfect, for it is in the very nature of the theater to question what is real and what is appearance. Marcel is *dis*oriented.

Marcel's first impression on entering the drawing room (he calls it a *coup de théâtre*) is that he has unaccountably found himself in an oddly unsavory masquerade ball. He thinks the guests are bizarrely costumed and are all playing pathetic roles. He wonders if they have purposely made themselves up into old people. He peers into their faces, trying to see back into time in order to discover their identity by reconstructing in reverse their "successive facial stages." As with his solitary magical moments, the past has surfaced involuntarily. But these double exposures, these palimpsests of time, are deeply troubling to him.

Let us take the example of Monsieur d'Argencourt. Having succeeded in identifying a guest as indeed Monsieur d'Argencourt (once an enemy), Marcel at first concludes that he has put on a disguise, that he "had turned himself into an old beggar who no longer inspired the least respect and [that] he put so much realism into his character of a driveling old man that his limbs shook and the flaccid features of his unusually haughty face smiled continually with a stupidly beatific expression" (255). It is an unusually haughty and cruel description. By assuming that Monsieur d'Argencourt is only *acting* old, Marcel is able to deny the physical realities of old age. At the same time, however, by ascribing old age to Monsieur d'Argencourt—and to the other guests—Marcel is able to deprive them of power (old age and power are in his eyes antithetical) and to distinguish himself from them. It is significant that the man who had long been a personal enemy of Marcel is portrayed as a "beggar" who thus requires no special attention. By relegating d'Argencourt to old age, Marcel renders him impotent. And Marcel, in his vindictiveness, can distance himself from blame. Unlike Freud, he feels no sense of guilt and takes only pleasure in his revenge, which has been achieved, he can tell himself, through the mere and neutral passing of time. But as readers we clearly see his guilty writing hand in his representations of old age.

Simultaneously fascinated and repelled by this theater of old age, Marcel describes at great length the grotesque spectacle of the physical appearance of his old friends and acquaintances, using metaphors drawn from the animal and plant kingdoms and the mineral world as if to suggest that they are less than human. At times the theater takes on the quality of the exotic absurd. The Duchesse de Guermantes, for example, is described as "an ancient and sacred fish," her "salmon-pink body barely emerging from its fins to black lace" (260–61). At other times the scene resembles a menacing Gothic melodrama. The stiff body of the aged actress Berma, for instance, is described as a crypt that imprisons what remains of her life. "Her hardened arteries being already half-petrified," Marcel muses, "long, narrow, sculpturesque ribbons of mineral-like rigidity could be discerned traversing her cheeks. Her dying eyes lived relatively by contrast with the horrible ossified mask and shone faintly like a serpent asleep among the rocks" (343). The body of old age is represented as a tomb. *Rigor mortis* has already set in. Here we see again the insistent contrast between the body, which is represented in terms of its lifeless *surface*, and what is left of life *inside*, here gruesomely figured as less than human, a snake. More generally, Proust consistently uses the imagery of the disintegration of the body in old age, as if the body were made of crumbling stone.

Marcel dwells on the texture of the skin in old age, itemizing the irregularities he finds revolting, implying that the *normal* condition of the skin is to be smooth (that is, young) and that thus the flaccid, wrinkled skin of old age is *abnormal*.

But old age is not just a breach of social manners or merely aesthetically un-appealing in Marcel's eyes. He describes the Duchesse de Guermantes's cheeks, for example, "as composite as nougat" in which he could see "a trace of verdigris, a bit of pulverised pink shell, a swelling hard to describe, smaller than a mistletoe berry and less transparent than a glass bead" (274). And Mon-sieur de Cambremer, for instance, as having developed "huge red pouches on his cheeks, which hindered him from opening freely his mouth or his eyes with the result that I stood there stupefied, not daring to look at the carbuncles, so to speak, which it seemed to me proper he should mention first" (268). As Marcel stares surreptitiously at the carbuncles (painfully purulent inflammations of the skin which are symptoms of a severe and deep infection of the flesh), as he scrutinizes the skin of the other guests as if with a microscope, he is sickened to discover "a multitude of fatty splotches" under everyone's skin. Old age, in other words, is perceived by Marcel as a dangerous disease which may infect him as well.

How to avoid catching the disease? How to avoid not seeing the elderly? How to preserve the illusion that the world is populated by the young? The trick, Marcel concludes, is to keep a *correct distance*, that is to say, to keep one's distance from those who are old, to keep them at arm's length, as it were, to not come too close. Marcel puts it clinically, using a technological metaphor drawn from optometry: "with them [the guests] old age was dependent on the person looking at them; he had to assume the right position if he wished to see their faces remain young and had to cast on them only those distant glasses which make the object look smaller, without using the lens an optician selects for a far-sighted person; with them old age, as readily detected as infusoria in a drop of water, drew nearer, not with the progress of the years but in proportion as the vision of the observer moved along the scale of enlargement" (280). Note that old age is explicitly linked with "infusoria," minute organisms which my dictionary tells me are found especially in decomposing organic matter. And that keeping one's literal distance implies of course keeping one's emotional distance, of avoiding any form of intimacy. The avoidance of old age is made possible by a certain kind of spectatorship—of distance. I will return to the question of distance in the chapter on masquerade.

Interestingly enough, if a person has grown older but does not *look* older, that too Marcel finds disquieting and strange. The implication is that there is no way one can avoid the appearance of old age: it is signified by the *absence* of its telltale marks as well as by their *presence*. Marcel describes Madame de Forcheville, for example, as a brilliant oddity in whom the signs of old age—what today we refer to as age spots—at first seem to be assets, fantastic new growths, but at a second glance are confirmed to be liabilities, symbols of barrenness, as we see in this depiction of her appearance: it "was so miraculous that one could not even say she had grown younger but rather that, with all her carmines and russet spots, she had burst into new bloom. She would have been the chief curiosity and principal attraction in a horticultural exhibition of the present day. . . . Moreover, just because she had not changed, she scarcely seemed to be alive. She looked like a sterilized rose'' (289). The attempt to arrest the signs of the process of aging on the surface of the body results, paradoxically, in the impression of sterility and death, not youth. As with Madame de Forcheville, so with the Princesse de Nassau: to be ''well preserved'' is metaphorically equivalent to being ''embalmed'' (323). In Marcel's eyes these unchanging women are ''monsters.'' They ''did not seem to have changed any more than whales,'' he thinks to himself in a bizarre analogy (279). The effect here is similar to that of the artificial and uncanny body of youth produced by plastic surgery. I will come back to this also in the chapter on masquerade.

Madame de Forcheville, here so cruelly vilified by Marcel, is the mother of Gilberte, whom he once adored. It is of course the case that many daughters age in the image of their mothers. In the eyes of Marcel this uncanny doubling is the most shocking of all because for him it calls into question the passion of youthful love and the very notion of the continuity of an identity. But why does it? Because Marcel wants to preserve untouched by time his sense of Gilberte as young. As much as Marcel insists on the importance to him of affective memory, in fact he is obsessed by what people look like. And he is repelled by what he sees in old age. He has no capacity, no psychic resources, for imagining at all, never mind positively, the transformations the body of a woman will undergo as she ages to become the ages of her mother before her. Marcel later reflects, ''It does us no good to know that the years go by, that youth gives way to old age, that the most stable thrones and fortunes crumble, that fame is ephemeral, our way of forming a conception—and, so to speak, taking a photograph—of this moving universe, hurried along by Time, seems on the contrary to make it stand still. Consequently, we always see as young the people we knew when we were young'' (305). There is of course a truth in this. But it is complicated. On the one hand, continuing to see as young the people we have known for a long time could mean that we preserve a certain intimate relation to them. In Marcel's case, however, the opposite is true. He does not recognize Gilberte. It is Gilberte who must say to him: '' 'You took me for Mamma; it is true I am beginning to look very much like her' '' (285). And if he is shocked to discover these changes in her, at the same time he does not seem too much to care.

I suspect it is true that we persist in carrying into old age images of our first loves as they were when they—and we—were young. Those of us who have attended high school or college reunions may know something of this. But for Marcel it is not just a *surprise* to see his first love after many years (are we not often taken by surprise?). It is a *shock*. When he is greeted by a "stout lady" ("stout" of course carries negative connotations) he finds he must struggle to remember who she is. He recognizes this "stout lady" as Gilberte's mother. He then realizes that she is Gilberte. He is doubly blind to her. She has vanished into the past, or into the future—it is difficult for him to know which. As Proust so chillingly puts it, "A name is frequently all that is left to us of a human being" (308). Marcel has denied to Gilberte a future in maturity. All that is left of her in his mind is her "name," which he cannot imagine connecting to her middle-aged body.

While Marcel reflects on what he understands as the *distorting* power of time on others, on their masks and disguises which he has himself in great part constructed, it comes to him with a shock that he too has been subject to the punishing law of time. It is only by seeing himself in the eyes of others that this "truth" is made clear to him. For Marcel, the drawing room of the Guermantes is a dizzying hall of mirrors where each person possesses the dangerous potential of reflecting the aging Marcel: "Then it was that I, who from my early childhood had lived along from day to day with an unchanging conception of myself and others, for the first time, from the metamorphoses which had taken place in all these people, became conscious of the time that had gone by for them—*which greatly perturbed me through its revelation that that same time had gone by for me*. And though of no importance to me in itself, their old age made me desperately sad as an announcement of the *approach* of my own" (260, italics mine). Moments later the old people surrounding him force him to acknowledge that he too is old. They hold up the mirror to him. What was abstract is now palpably real. "I now understood," he reflects, "what old age was—old age which, of all the realities, is perhaps the one concerning which we retain for the longest time a purely abstract conception" (267). What he will never see, however, is that he is complicit in constructing a hideous vision of old age, that he is in part responsible for creating the double bind in which he feels he finds himself, that he has himself made the mirrors in which he sees himself reflected. Unable to identify himself sympathetically even in any small way with "this old man" or "that old woman," as Beauvoir urges us to do in *The Coming of Age*, he thus dooms himself to a similar future, perpetuating a cycle of ageism.

What I find particularly interesting, as well as problematic, is that for the remainder of *The Past Recaptured* Marcel vacillates between the rhetoric of unbridled enthusiasm for the future and his new work, and the rhetoric of anxiety and physical vulnerability. He oscillates between blindness to his age and insight into it. For a moment he lucidly understands and is worried by the lie that his experience of old age (which he understands as the embodiment of the destructive effects of time) gives to his *idea* of time. He puts it cogently: "a still graver reason explained my distress; I was discovering the destructive action of time at the very moment when I was about to undertake to make clear and to intellectualise in a literary work some realities that had no relation whatsoever to time'' (265). On a thematic level he sees the contradiction. But after the initial shock that he has in fact aged—and indeed he has—he ''forgets'' or represses that perception in his eagerness to get his work underway.

Like an adolescent, he intoxicates himself with the ambitiousness of his project and what it will require of him. He vows to himself that he will ''endure it like an exhausting task, accept it like a rule of conduct, build it like a church, follow it like a regimen, overcome it like an obstacle, win it like a friendship, feed it intensively like a child, create it like a world'' (38). There is something strangely *hyper*energetic and frenetic about his response. The rhetorical figures of strength, discipline, tenacity, perseverance, and power alternate with those of weakness, debilitation, impotence, and senility. Proust is as successful in expressing the latter as he is the former. Marcel fusses. He worries that he may have a stroke or a car accident on the way home, or that he may contract the same illness which befell his grandmother. He recalls with foreboding that only recently as he was going down a flight of stairs, he almost fell three times. He broods that lately he has been exhausted to the point of paralysis. He fears that his forgetfulness is a sign of old age. Tellingly, he compares his anxiety to the condition of an elderly man: ''Strictly speaking, I had no particular illness but I felt as though I had become incapable of anything, as frequently happens to an old man, who, active the day before, breaks his hip or has an attack of indigestion and may for some time to come lead a bedridden existence which is now only more or less long preparation for the now inevitable end'' (392). As with Freud, Marcel associates old age with physical infirmity and a lack of productivity. For Freud, however, his whole life, unlike Marcel's, had been characterized by finished and successful projects, and Freud continued his habits of a lifetime into old age.

The Past Recaptured comes to an end with these thoughts. As readers we cannot follow Marcel into his future. But perhaps it is just as well that Proust closes his book with the contradiction posed by Marcel's double discoveries that afternoon. The lack of conclusion or resolution raises the important question of whether we should indeed accept the definition given to us by others which in effect ''castrates'' us. Is it wise in personal terms to recognize oneself as old? Should, in fact, one incorporate one's mirror image of old age as reflected in the eyes of others, the social world? Or is it more productive to deny it? Should one acknowledge a lack of time when, like Marcel, one has the desire to achieve something important? Perhaps for Marcel or anyone else with ambition, blindness to one's own old age is the most profound insight. Perhaps the future should remain concealed. As Anthony Wilden has put it, explicating Lacan, ''Truth for the subject is not knowledge but recognition. . . . But a certain *méconnais-sance*—which we might call sublimation—is essential to health."² Or, perhaps, indeed, we have no choice. But if these are the questions posed by the text, they are not the questions we should ask in our actual world. The very definition of old age which is given to us by Marcel—and through him, Proust—should be called into question. The ideology associated with old age as decline must be brought to consciousness. This Marcel cannot do.

Yet the fictional world of *The Past Recaptured* prompts us also to ask if it is not precisely the relation between the two kinds of knowledge gained by Marcel that renders each insight possible. This would be paradoxical but not untenable. It does seem to me to make sense that on a conscious level one often struggles against limitations only when one is acutely aware of them. Certainly such a view of the relation between literature and life processes was held by Proust; as he insisted not too long before he died, creativity and illness are often linked, and often indissolubly so.³ In *The Past Recaptured* Marcel himself, earlier in the afternoon, had explicitly associated old age with suffering, and suffering with artistic achievement. Indeed he figured the body in and of old age as a *sign* of productivity. He is speaking of grief, and referred to the titans Rembrandt and Beethoven. "It is true that grief, which is not compatible with happiness or health, is sometimes prejudicial also to life," he muses. "At each fresh, overpowering shock we feel another vein stand out and develop its deadly swell-ings along our temples, beneath our eyes. Thus were produced little by little those terrible, grief-ravaged faces of the aged Rembrandt and the aged Bee-thoven, whom everyone used to scoff at" (237). And he concludes, romantically if not bombastically, "let us allow our body to disintegrate, since each fresh particle that breaks off, now luminous and decipherable, comes and adds itself to our work" (237).

But this is *before* he steps over the threshold, before he feels himself to be implicated in the *real* of old age. Later that afternoon Marcel concludes that productivity is often stanched by old age; "even the best writers often cease producing at the approach of old age" (351). Thus Marcel's ideas about aging, work, and time are contradictory and convoluted. Or as Walter Benjamin has put it, writing of Proust and reflecting on the notion that eternity for Proust was platonic or utopian, his "true interest is in the passage of time in its most real— that is, space-bound—form, and this passage nowhere holds sway more openly than in remembrance within and aging without. To observe the interaction of aging and remembering means to penetrate to the heart of Proust's world, to the universe of convolution."⁴

With these pages from Proust's *The Past Recaptured* in mind as a paradigm, we can imagine what I want to call a mirror stage of old age. Not only in Proust but elsewhere the image of the mirror dominates western literary representations of the aged body (I will come back to this in a moment). This is not surprising. Given the western obsession with the body of youth, we can understand the "horror" of the mirror image of the "decrepit" body as having been produced as the inverse of the pleasures of the mirror image of the body of Narcissus. In part this may help explain the psychological phenomenon that as we age, we increasingly separate what we take to be our real selves from our bodies. We say that our real selves—that is, our youthful selves—are hidden inside our bodies. Our *bodies* are old, *we* are not. Old age is thus understood as a state in which the body is in opposition to the self. We are alienated from our bodies. I take this as a common psychological truth. Ask people in their sixties, seventies, perhaps eighties if they think of themselves as old. Most will insist that they feel the same way they did when they were thirty or forty, that *they* haven't changed, although their mirror image has. Or they will say that their body— now a *foreign* body—has betrayed them (one is never so aware of one's body as when one suffers from it). Or more vociferously, they will assert that the body is the oppressor and that they are hostage to it, or as in the words of the Duke of York in Shakespeare's *Richard II*, that they are "prisoner to the palsy" (II.ii.104).[5] As Marcel observes in an earlier volume of *Remembrance of Things Past*, "It is in the moments of illness that we are compelled to recognise that we live not alone but chained to a creature of a different kingdom, whole worlds apart, who has no knowledge of us and by whom it is impossible to make ourselves understood: our body."[6] Or as Marcel bluntly puts it in *The Past Recaptured*, "Having a body constitutes the principal danger that threatens the mind" (387).

We may think of ourselves as young, but others will perceive us as old, perhaps even ancient. As we have seen, this is marvelously dramatized in *The Past Recaptured*. "We did not see ourselves or our own ages in their true light," reflects Marcel, "but each of us saw the others as accurately as though he had been a mirror held up before them" (265). In *The Coming of Age*, Beauvoir explains this phenomenon by arguing, following Sartre, that old age belongs to the category of the "unrealizables." *We* are not old; it is the Other, the stranger within us, who is old. We cannot simply say that if we feel young, then we are young. Age is socially as well as biologically determined. As Beauvoir concludes, the recognition of our own old age comes to us from the Other, that is, from society. We study our own reflection in the body of others, and as we reflect upon that reflection, we ultimately are compelled to acknowledge the point of view of the Other which has, as it were, installed itself in our body. In *The Coming of Age* Beauvoir explains the complex "truth" of old age this way: "for the outsider it is a dialectic relationship between my being as he defines it objectively and the awareness of myself that I acquire by means of him. Within me it is the Other—that is to say the person I am for the outsider—who is old: and that Other is myself'' (420). As we saw in *The Past Recaptured*, we may be complicit in producing the meanings associated with what is now or will be our own condition.

I have insisted on the fact that in *The Past Recaptured* the affect of *shock* (terror, horror, disgust, fear) is associated with Marcel's recognition that he has grown definitively old. A scene from the history of psychoanalysis can help us understand the psychological etiology of this reaction and at the same time show us how embedded both Freudian analysis and modern literature, here exemplified by Proust, are in the western idolatry of youth and fear of aging. With Freud's essay on ''The Uncanny'' (1919) in mind, I want to suggest that to see, like Marcel, one's own aged body with a shock of recognition is to experience the *uncanny*. Freud describes the uncanny as ''related to what is frightening—to what arouses dread and horror,'' ''feelings of repulsion and distress'' (SE 17: 219). He theorizes that the origins of the uncanny lie in the infantile stage of the psychological development of the individual and in the primitive phase of the development of the human species when mankind believed the world to be populated by the spirits of dead. In terms of the uncanny, then, ontogeny recapitulates phylogeny. Freud further analyzes the uncanny as something ''familiar that has been repressed,'' and concludes that ''an uncanny experience occurs either when infantile complexes which have been repressed are once more revived by some impression, or when primitive beliefs which have been surmounted seem once more to be confirmed'' (SE 17: 249). He associates the uncanny with castration anxiety and a feeling of ''frightening things'' (SE 17: 241) as well as with the image of the double. Finally, following Otto Rank, Freud observes that whereas in the early stages of human history the double was an assurance of immortality and a powerful weapon against death, it later became a harbinger of death which it has remained to this day. This theory of the double is particularly interesting in terms of the subject of aging, and I will return to it in a moment.

But first I want to pursue Freud as he inscribes himself in his essay on the uncanny. Freud presents his essay as a tentative exploration of the phenomenon of the uncanny rather than a definitive study. He protests in the opening pages that he has had little personal experience of the uncanny and thus must turn to literature for evidence. In his customary self-deprecating manner, he asserts, ''the writer of the present contribution, indeed, must himself plead guilty to a special obtuseness in the matter where extreme delicacy of perception would be more in place.'' He insists, ''It is long since he has experienced or heard anything which has given him an uncanny impression, and he must start by translating himself into that state of feeling'' (SE 17: 220).

These demurs are curious in two respects. First, this is the only passage in

"The Uncanny" where Freud refers to himself in the third person. Elsewhere he writes with ease in the first person, both singular and plural. Here, appearing uncomfortable, he finds it necessary to create, as it were, another character, referring to himself as "he." Secondly, later in the essay Freud does in fact recount an experience of the uncanny drawn from his own life. It had occurred some time earlier while he was traveling in Italy. In a small town he found himself in the red light district, and trying to escape, kept returning involuntarily to the very same piazza, not once, but twice.

Far more significant for our purposes, however, is another of his personal experiences of the uncanny—no doubt a much more recent one—which finds its way into a footnote near the end of the essay. In it Freud describes the shock of recognition of meeting his double who is "elderly" (Freud was sixty-three when the essay on the uncanny was published). It is as if Freud could not incorporate this experience into the body of the text and into the main line of his speculations on the uncanny. But like the uncanny itself, what one desires to remain concealed does indeed surface. Freud found it necessary to relegate it to the margins, repressing his own experience. The passage deserves to be quoted in full:

> Since the uncanny effect of a "double" also belongs to this same group it is interesting to observe what the effect is of meeting one's own image unbidden and unexpected. Ernst Mach has related two such observations in his *Analyse der Empfindungen* (1900, 3). On the first occasion he was not a little startled when he realized that the face before him was his own. The second time he formed a very unfavourable opinion about the supposed stranger who entered the omnibus, and thought "What a shabby-looking school-master that man is who is getting in!"—I can report a similar adventure. I was sitting alone in my *wagon-lit* compartment when a more than usually violent jolt of the train swung back the door of the adjoining washing-cabinet, and an elderly gentleman in a dressing-gown and a travelling cap came in. I assumed that in leaving the washing-cabinet, which lay between the two compartments, he had taken the wrong direction and come into my compartment by mistake. Jumping up with the intention of putting him right, I at once realized to my dismay that *the intruder was nothing but my own reflection in the looking-glass of the open door*. I can still recollect that I thoroughly disliked his appearance. Instead, therefore, of being frightened by our "doubles," both Mach and I simply failed to recognize them as such. Is it not possible, though, that our dislike of them was a vestigial trace of the archaic reaction which feels the "double" to be something uncanny? (SE 17: 248n, italics mine)

Freud's mirror image of himself as elderly is that of the trespasser, of the interloper in the private domain of narcissism. In this little drama we see the material of the unconscious rising through the open door into the conscious. Or, we could say, paraphrasing Freud, who believed that in the unconscious everyone is persuaded of his own immortality, *in the unconscious everyone is*

persuaded of his own youth. It is not so much our own death which is uni-
maginable, as Freud has it, as our own old age. Freud says he was not "terrified"
by his double. He is specific about the affect associated with his recognition of
his own mirror image, which is more subtle than blunt terror. He was "dis-
mayed" by it, he "thoroughly disliked his appearance." For that appearance
represents the future absence of Freud himself, *nothing* (it "was nothing"), his
own death. Aging is explicitly linked with death through the affect of the uncanny.[7] What Freud sees is the image of the Other, to use Beauvoir's terminology, an image Freud would prefer not to recognize. The mirror image is
uncanny because, as I argued in the previous chapter, it is something familiar
that has been repressed—old age.

Clinical research has confirmed that Freud's experience was not uncommon.
Robert Butler's seminal essay on what he has theorized as the late-life phenomenon of the life review contains a fascinating report of clinical cases of
pathological disturbances in elderly people involving mirrors. Although Butler
refers to the "apparently common phenomenon" of "mirror-gazing" only in
passing, his remarks are provocative and suggest the fruitfulness of further
research along these lines, as the following clinical summary reveals:

> Another patient, eighty-six years old and periodically confused, often stood before
> the mirror in his hospital room and rhythmically chanted either happily or angrily.
> He was especially given to angry flareups and crying spells over food, money,
> and clothes. When angry he would screech obscenities at his mirror image, so
> savagely beating his fist upon a nearby table that the staff tried to protect him
> by covering the mirror. . . . [He] denied that the image was himself, and when
> an observer came up beside him and said, "See, this is me in the mirror and
> there you are in the mirror," he smiled and said, "That's you in the mirror all
> right, but that's not me." (68)

We can understand this patient's radical rejection of his mirror image as the
pathological equivalent of Freud's failure in the train to recognize his own
mirrored double.

In *The Coming of Age* Beauvoir chronicles countless instances from the
historical record of this obsession of the elderly with their mirror images. The
weight of their testimony is impressive. I repeat here some of their words, all
of which record their despair at their mirrored images. The aging Michelangelo:
"I am betrayed: my mirror image is my traitor, and my fleeting days" (763).
Gide at eighty: "Oh, come now, I really must not meet myself in a mirror—
these eyes with bags under them, these hollow cheeks, this lifeless look. I am
hideous and it depresses me terribly" (443). Wagner, on seeing his reflection
in a store window: "I do not recognize myself in that grey head: can I possibly
be sixty-eight?" (443). Madame de Sévigné at sixty-one: "If at the age of twenty
we were given the position of the eldest member of the family and if we were

taken to a mirror and shown the face that we should have or do have at sixty, comparing it with that at twenty, we should be utterly taken aback and it would frighten us'' (424). And Madame de Sévigné at sixty-three: ''It appears to me that in spite of myself I have been dragged to this inevitable point where old age must be undergone: I see it there before me; I have reached it; and I should at least like so to arrange matters that I do not move on, that I do not travel farther along this path of the infirmities, pains, losses of memory and the disfigurement'' (427). For ''inevitable'' (''I have been dragged to this inevitable point where old age must be undergone'') we might read instead ''invisible.'' But paradoxically this invisible point is also the point of *hypervisibility*. What was invisible, what she did not recognize—her own old age—is now made painfully visible. This denial of one's image is also dramatized in Louis Aragon's novel *La Mise à mort* in which the hero, incapable of conceiving of himself as old, literally does not see his own reflection in the mirror. (We should not forget that late in life Aragon himself refused to appear in public without a smooth mask that covered his wrinkled face.)

Although Beauvoir maintains that we respond to our mirror image in accordance with whether our attitude toward old age is basically positive or negative, her analysis points toward the latter. We inevitably despair, she insists, insofar as old age ''is summed up by the words decrepitude, ugliness and ill-health'' (60). She believes that to so respond is *natural*, that ''we must always have some cause for uneasiness before we stand and study the reflection offered us by the looking-glass'' (425). Note, however, that Beauvoir is defining old age here only in terms of the *body*—what it looks like, what its state of health is. In this respect her analysis of old age unwittingly in part reinforces our culture's negative assessment of old age.

Is the obsession with mirrors a symptom of this ''stage'' in life—old age— or is this stage triggered by one's mirrored image, by the reflections of others, that is, by the values held up to us by our society? Although knowledge of old age certainly can come to us from our infirmities (our own bodies can speak to us of old age), I want to insist again that old age is in great part constructed by any given society as a social category, as is, for example, adolescence. The mirror our culture holds up to the elderly contains the feared image of death. This is why Freud did not at first recognize himself in that image of an elderly gentleman. This is why that image aroused the ''dread and creeping horror'' he associates with the uncanny, for the Other was indeed oneself. It uncannily prefigured the coming years of suffering which Freud was destined to live out.

Psychoanalysis insists of course on the alienating effects of identification with an image. This insistence is perhaps strongest in the work of Lacan. By now in fact it will have become clear to many readers that we can hypothesize the mirror stage of old age as the inverse of the mirror stage of infancy proposed by Lacan.[8] Observing that an infant from six to eighteen months is fascinated by his mirror image, Lacan theorizes that the infant *perceives* the image of his body as a harmonious whole and ideal unity while simultaneously *experiencing* his own body as uncoordinated. It is this discrepancy between the visual image of unity and the lived experience of fragmentation that gives rise to the ego and to the subject forever split, to pleasurable anticipation of wholeness in the future as well as to alienation. The mirror stage ushers the subject into the domain of the imaginary, a domain prior to language and largely dominated by images.

In "The Line and the Light" (1964), Lacan stresses that in the "matter of the visible, everything is a trap" (*FF* 93). In old age we might say, following this analysis, that in western culture all mirrors are potentially threatening. As in the mirror stage of infancy, in the mirror stage of old age the subject is confronted with an image. If he identifies with it, he is transformed. In the mirror stage of infancy, the infant enters the imaginary. In the mirror stage of old age, the subject enters the social realm reserved for "senior citizens" in the western world. But the point is that the subject *denies* this identification rather than embraces it. The mirror stage of old age is the inverse of the mirror stage of infancy. What is whole is felt to reside *within*, not *without*, the subject. The image in the mirror is understood as uncannily prefiguring the disintegration and nursling dependence of advanced age.

In theorizing the mirror stage of infancy, Lacan writes of the structural relation between paranoia and mastery. From the beginning one is structured as a rival with oneself. Human knowledge is paranoiac. According to Lacan, the infant holds his mirror image in an amorous gaze. But the elderly person wishes to reject it—and thereby to reject old age for himself. What Lacan writes of the mirror stage of infancy in "The Freudian Thing" (1955) can be applied to the mirror stage of old age: "It is thus that the functions of mastery, which we incorrectly call the synthesizing functions of the ego, establish on the basis of a libidinal alienation the development that follows from it, namely, what I once called the paranoiac principle of human knowledge" (*Ecrits* 138). In the mirror stage of old age, one is libidinally alienated from one's mirror image. If the psychic plot of the mirror stage of infancy is the anticipated trajectory from insufficiency to bodily wholeness, the bodily plot of the mirror stage of old age is the feared trajectory from wholeness to physical disintegration. The affect associated with it is one of despair, not joy. And the hostility toward others which is associated with the mirror stage of infancy is now reflected back upon oneself as well as projected onto others. Aggressivity, about which I will have more to say in the next chapter, is intensified and now directed back upon oneself: this aging body is not my self.[9]

If the mirror image of infancy is a lure in the Lacanian sense, we might say that in the old age our culture has constructed we desire our mirror image to function as does *trompe l'oeil*, to reveal itself precisely *not* as what it so shockingly presents to us as ourselves. As Freud emphasizes in developing his theory of the intricate entwining of the body and the psyche, "the ego is first and foremost a bodily ego . . . the projection of a surface" (SE 19: 26). The I or ego which is developed in the mirror stage of infancy is structured precisely to resist the anxiety of bodily fragmentation. In old age, with one's position reversed before the mirror, the ego finds it more difficult to maintain its defenses. The Lacanian ambivalence that has been felt all one's life before mirrors—the constant checking and comparing—is exacerbated to an almost intolerable point. Like one of Robert Butler's elderly patients, one may want to turn the face of the mirror to the wall. Or like Marcel at the reception at the Guermantes', one may avoid identification with one's age counterparts.

This too would be a reversal of the trajectory of development in infancy. After the infant identifies with its mirror image (its ideal ego), Lacan theorizes that there is a "deflection of the specular *I* into the social *I*" (*Ecrits* 5). The child identifies—literally at first—with the images of others. Lacan brilliantly explicates desire as the desire to be recognized by the other. He puts it succinctly this way: "man's desire finds its meaning in the desire of the other, not so much because the other holds the key to the object desired, as because *the first object* of desire is to be recognized by the other" (*Ecrits* 58, italics mine). At stake in the mirror stage of old age is the relation between the imaginary other and the symbolic Other, which Lacan himself associates with death.[10] Thus, *the last object* of desire may be *to not be recognized by the other*, which in the case of old age is the Other, represented by the very old themselves. At this point perceptual unpleasure, as elucidated by Freud, escalates to almost ontological proportions. In *Beyond the Pleasure Principle* Freud writes, "Most of the unpleasure that we experience is *perceptual* unpleasure. It may be . . . external perception which is either distressing in itself or which excites unpleasurable expectations in the mental apparatus—that is, which is recognized by it as a 'danger' " (SE 17: 11). In the hallucinatory drawing room of mirrors crowded with grotesque images of old age in *The Past Recaptured*, the danger prompts the psyche to repress, or deny, it. The theater of old age provokes Marcel's gaze in the Lacanian sense. As Lacan says in "The Split between the Eye and the Gaze" (1964), when the world begins to provoke our gaze, "the feeling of strangeness begins too" (*FF* 75).

Strangeness, the uncanny, old age, decrepitude, death, fear, danger—all are linked together in this momentary drama of the mirror stage of old age. In the mirror stage of old age, the narcissistic impulse directs itself *against* the mirror image as it is embodied literally and figuratively in the faces and bodies—the images—of old people. If, then, the mirror stage of infancy initiates the imaginary, the mirror stage of old age may precipitate the loss of the imaginary. Where then would we be located? Outside the mirror? Caught between the double and the absent?[11]

As Lacan conceives it, the mirror stage of infancy is primarily a biological and psychological phenomenon (interestingly enough, he refers to experimentation with other species—the pigeon, the migratory locust—which suggests that development is contingent upon the presence of an image of one's own species). Basically the mirror stage is prior to socialization and prior to language, although the role of the mother is crucial and although we can understand the phenomenon of the mirror stage only retrospectively and through language. As Lacan puts it in his essay on "The Mirror Stage," the mirror stage enacts the formation (he uses the vivid term "precipitation") of the I before "it is objectified in the dialectic of identification with the other, and before language restores to it . . . its function as subject" (*Ecrits* 2). In contrast, the mirror stage of old age is more obviously rooted in the social and economic theater of a given historical moment. Thus we might further speculate that if the mirror stage of infancy is distinguished by the perception of binary opposition, the mirror stage of old age is more problematic. It is inherently triangular, involving the gaze of others as well as two images of oneself. In addition, one understands—consciously or unconsciously—that there is a relationship between the two terms (the two images of the self) such that one is incorporated within the other. It is not so much a matter of either-or as it is a matter of both-and. But within the terms of the mirror stage of old age as I have been describing it, one blocks knowledge of one of the two terms.

If (temporarily) blinding ourselves to our own aging may give us a kind of psychic reprieve, we must also be aware of the social consequences of perceiving the elderly as alien to ourselves. If our vision is fundamentally narcissistic, the way we look at others functions to protect ourselves. Those like Marcel who see themselves as on the threshold of old age deny full humanity to an aged person so as to preserve their own illusion of immortality. I will develop this at some length in the next chapter. Christopher Lasch points out in *The Culture of Narcissism* that our dread of old age has its origins not in a cult of youth but in a cult of the self.[12] But the two come to the same thing. It is important to stress here the relationship between narcissism and aggression. When one's narcissism is wounded, the result is aggression. The observations of the psychoanalyst Gregory Rochlin, who has written on aggression as well as the psychology of loss in old age, are particularly useful in this context. Rochlin asserts, "No experience brings out the effect in self-esteem more immediately than when it is associated with the body. The integrity of one's shape and bodily function holds the deepest and perhaps longest-standing investment in respect to self-esteem.''[13] As we have seen, hostility borne toward others is also feared from them through projection, and aggression can complete its return in the form of self-destruction.

Perhaps most significant, such narcissistic hostility allows the elderly to be rejected as a class more easily—as an alien species or, as in *The Past Recaptured*, as unreal, a mere illusion, a grotesque and transitory spectacle, a hyperscene of total theater that hopefully will soon be over, covered by the fall of the curtain. As we see with Marcel, for him to preserve psychological "health" (*méconnaissance*) on a personal level requires him to regard the elderly as an inferior class. Such a psychic habit of mind reinforces and perpetuates oppression of the elderly on the level of society. (I am here conflating old age and decrepitude which, although they are by no means identical, are for the most part equated in our cultural imagination.) For like sexism and racism, ageism is prejudice rooted in physical difference as well as in discrepancies in social power. As we know, throughout western history the elderly have been rejected as a class which consumes more than it produces. Recently the aged have been forgotten and hidden from sight in nursing homes and hospitals by the narcissistic younger social body, by those in power.

In *The Denial of Death* Ernest Becker argues that a culture is built primarily not on the repression of sexuality, as Freud believes, but on the repression of death, whose symbol is the human body, the "curse of fate."[14] Old age in our culture is characterized by a double bind, by personal and social conflict as intense as the Oedipal conflict that arises in childhood. This helps us understand Beauvoir's disillusioning statement in *The Coming of Age*: "whatever the context may be, the biological facts remain. For every individual age brings with it a dreaded decline. It is in complete conflict with the manly or womanly ideal cherished by the young and fully-grown. The immediate, natural attitude is to reject it, in so far as it is summed up by the words decrepitude, ugliness and ill-health. Old age in others also causes an instant repulsion. This primitive reaction remains alive even when custom represses it; and in this we see the origin of a conflict that we shall find exemplified again and again" (60). Old age is constructed as a social category, but it has a biological dimension which she believes the young cannot help but reject. Her words echo these of Nietzsche: "every table of values, every 'thou shalt' known to history, requires first a physiological investigation and interpretation."[15] In old age, then, as we saw in the last chapter, we may encounter yet again another form of the battle between civilization and its discontents.

Can we invent in our culture new meanings of old age so that we need not fight this battle with ourselves and others? Can we imagine mirrors which reflect other images of old age back to us? Can we associate not shock but other kinds of affect with growing old? Erikson has repeatedly argued that we oscillate between despair and acceptance—what he calls integrity—of our lives and our approaching death in advanced old age. He embraces an ego psychology with an assurance as strong as the contempt with which Lacan rejects it. As Erikson said in an interview when he was eighty-six, "You've got to learn to accept the law of life, and face the fact that we disintegrate slowly."[16] Erikson is not, on balance, in shock turning the mirror to the wall. In part I think it is because he has been looking into a different theoretical mirror throughout his life in psychoanalysis. He has consistently looked into a mirror populated by several generations. He is not *shocked* by aging because he has been anticipating it and expecting it, not repressing it. His mirror resembles Winnicott's mirror, not Lacan's. For Winnicott, "*The precursor of the mirror is the mother's face.*"[17] What the baby sees is already a reflection of his mother's response to him. The interplay is endlessly interrelated and animated (hopefully) by love, not motivated by a solipsistic narcissism. A mirror is then something to be looked *into*, not looked *at*. As Barthes writes in *Camera Lucida*, "it is not indifference which erases the weight of the image . . . but love, extreme love."[18] We can extend this reflection further across time, beyond infancy. In the same essay Winnicott observes that "when a family is intact and is a going concern over a period of time each child derives benefit from being able to see himself or herself in the attitude of the individual members or in attitudes of the family as a whole" (188). Although he is referring to a young child, we can expand this notion throughout the years. We may wish to reject our body in old age, but we may find the strength to accept it through a kind of familiarity with its images reflected to us in the bodies of generations older. This would be to emphasize genealogical continuities rather than discontinuities.

At the same time there may be a limit beyond which we cannot go. At this limit, which is not located in a middle age of physical health, being repelled by (or even disinterested in) one's own body may be part of the process of accommodating death in the aging body. This would be a process through which we acknowledge the reality we would like to reject but cannot, a process by which we define a form of separateness through rejection, a form of adaptive repulsion in advanced old age analogous to the function of depression, guilt, and other negative states of childhood. This would be a process which is a sign of achieved psychic organization, not failure.[19] I think here of one of Beauvoir's observations about her mother in *A Very Easy Death*. Her mother, in her seventies, desperately ill and near her death, had passed beyond the mirror stage of old age: "She had not asked for a mirror again: her dying face did not exist for her."[20]

COUNTER-TEXT

[Silence. The Young Woman approaches Madeleine, and shows her the dress.]

The Young Woman: Look . . . you know, this is the dress you wore in the film *Le Voyage au Siam*.

Madeleine: Oh yes . . . yes . . . it suits you perfectly . . . perfectly . . .

[The Young Woman draws Madeleine into the spotlight where an imaginary mirror is located. They both look together at Madeleine's reflection.]

The Young Woman: Look at yourself . . .

[Silence.]

Madeleine (transparently): I think I look beautiful.

[Silence.]

Madeleine: Red looks very good on me . . . it always has . . . and it's also this particular dress . . .

> —Madeleine, an actress of advanced
> age, eighty perhaps, *from* Marguerite
> Duras, *Savannah Bay* 105–106

4. The Look and the Gaze: Narcissism, Aggression, and Aging . . .
Virginia Woolf's *The Years*

AS WE SAW IN THE PREVIOUS CHAPTER, Lacan's stress on the strict structural relationship between narcissism and aggressivity is useful in understanding our culture's dominant representations of aging. In "Aggressivity in Psychoanalysis" (1948), we read: "This narcissistic moment in the subject is to be found in all the genetic phases of the individual. . . . This conception allows us to understand the aggressivity involved . . . with each of the great phases that the libidinal transformations determine in human life, the crucial function of which has been demonstrated by analysis: weaning, the Oedipal stages, puberty, maturity, or motherhood, even the climacteric."[1] In the last chapter I drew on Lacan's theory of the mirror stage of infancy, which is structurally the primary (and preparatory) moment of narcissistic identification and alienation. What interests me here is that Lacan invokes a dramatic conception of the life course with its "great phases" and libidinal transformations (not "stages") which we might more readily associate with his psychoanalytic opposite, Erikson. Lacan's emphasis on *libidinal* transformations is significant. As he puts it elsewhere in the same essay, referring to the Oedipus complex, "the energy for that identification is provided by the first biological upsurge of genital libido" (*Ecrits* 22). The biological is not, in other words, completely absent from Lacan. We are invited to wonder what would be associated with the climacteric in terms of biological libido. We have already pursued this question in relation to Freud, and I will return to it in this chapter.

What characterizes Lacanian psychoanalysis, however, is the emphasis on repetition of the narcissistic moment across our lives in time and in particular during the "great phases." It is a moment characterized by aggressivity. *"Aggressivity,* " he asserts, *"is the correlative tendency of a mode of identification that we call narcissistic, and which determines the final structure of man's ego and of the register of entities characteristic of his world"* (*Ecrits* 16). Narcissism, in short, entails aggressivity. Does aggressivity also entail narcissism?

Just as aggressivity is involved in each of the "great phases" of life, in the Lacanian model the fear of castration is also repeated at all stages of development following the resolution of the Oedipus conflict. If we extrapolate from these two "moments"—the mirror stage, which is associated predominantly with aggressivity (Lacan does not dwell on the affect of joy), and the Oedipus conflict, associated with aggressivity *and* castration anxiety—we can imagine an intriguing cumulative Lacanian model of the life course: each stage of libidinal transformation will be accompanied by the specific affects associated with all the previous stages. But his published work contains no extended commentary on the "transformations" of puberty, maturity, motherhood, menopause, or old age. Moreover, Lacan explicitly rejects a developmental model of the life course, emphasizing instead its backward turnings and returnings. For Lacan the narrative of a life is figured in terms of a regressive spiral. The narrative of a life is "a retroversion effect by which the subject becomes at each stage what he was before and announces himself—he will have been—only in the future perfect tense" (*Ecrits* 306).

Lacan also dismisses out of hand, indeed tauntingly, the possibility of any fruitful relationship between psychoanalysis and developmental psychology. For him a developmental psychoanalytic theory would be a contradiction in terms. "The very originality of psycho-analysis," he insisted in 1964, "lies in the fact that it does not centre psychological ontogenesis on supposed *stages*—which have literally no discoverable foundation in development observable in biological terms" (*FF* 63). Yet as we have seen, Lacan himself had earlier acknowledged that libidinal changes (which we may associate with social as well as biological changes) "determine" the "great phases" of life. We may understand his rejection of a psychogenetic or developmental psychoanalysis in part as a rhetorical stance assumed on the political battlefields of psychoanalysis. Lacan was concerned to counter the notion of the *autonomous ego,* as he called it, and he took every opportunity to ridicule his so-called opponents.

One of the main opponents in the schism between Lacanian psychoanalysis and American ego psychology is Heinz Kohut (although he goes unnamed in

Lacan's works just as Lacan does in his). I single out the Vienna-born Kohut, who practiced in Chicago for much of his life, because his work on narcissism is widely acknowledged in the United States as having shifted the theorization of narcissism from negative to positive terms. Furthermore, unlike Lacan, Kohut provides us with a developmental model of narcissism. As is all too well known, dialogue between these two schools of psychoanalysis has been virtually impossible. I want in this chapter to work in the space opened up by the vast difference between the two positions as I explore further the relation between narcissism—that is, *forms* of narcissism—and old age. I will turn to Virginia Woolf's *The Years*, a novel which offers us differentiated and moving views of the coming of old age. Along the way I will refer to the work of Freud, Pontalis, and René Girard.

In *The Years* Woolf follows a generation of the Pargiter family (there are seven brothers and sisters) from childhood to old age, from a childhood in a British family of wealth and status to an old age of genteel poverty on the eve of the Second World War. I am drawn in particular to the novel's final chapter. Like *The Past Recaptured*, the final scene of *The Years* is cast in terms of a party. But the tone of the two gatherings could not differ more. If the reception at the Guermantes' in Paris is a gathering of the elite of cultured society, the dinner party in London is a sprawling family affair. Four generations of this large family gather together in a celebration of the family's years. The party lasts until dawn. It is a bustling reunion marked by ambivalence and admiration, by laughter and haphazard collisions between relatives of all generations. Significantly, if in *The Past Recaptured* we see others only from Marcel's late middle-aged point of view, in *The Years* we are given multiple perspectives from people of varying ages. The most complex perspectives on age in this spectacle of the family sphere are provided by the *crossing* of sight lines between generations: we the readers watch the old as they gaze on the middle-aged and the young, and the middle-aged as they survey the old.[2]

These lines of sight converge on the figure of Eleanor. She is the character who interests me the most and who, I confess, has been a shadowy figure in my own mind since I first read *The Years* some ten years ago. Eleanor never marries. She lives at home into her fifties, taking care of her father until he dies. She (and Woolf) then surprises me by making a new and interesting life for herself (I expected her, I guess, to devolve into a dreary spinsterhood). When we find her again in the final chapter, she is vigorous and now in her seventies. Thus I turn to *The Years* not only as a way to write about narcissism and aging but also in order to retrace my reading steps, to review and elaborate my own hazy memories of the luminous party at the novel's end, to think again (I myself have grown older by ten years) about a character I remember I admired. In the following pages I approach the question of narcissism and old age by focusing on several paradigmatic moments in the final scenes of *The Years*. In all of them Eleanor figures prominently.

THE LOOK

In the midst of the wandering talk at the party and somewhat late in the evening, Eleanor—surrounded by her nephew and niece, her brother and sister—drops off to sleep. What interests me in this little scene is the glaring disparity between Eleanor's experience and her nephew's view of her. North, a bachelor in his late thirties, has just returned to London after many years abroad in Africa. He has not seen his aunt in years. Earlier in the evening he paused to admire Eleanor as magnificently energetic and independent. But as she falls asleep, in North's eyes she goes out of focus. She becomes less distinct, less *distinctive*. She is assimilated to the family. She takes on the look of her sister Milly whose bloated body repels him, whose arms are "so fat that they reminded North of asparagus; pale asparagus tapering to a point" (373).

This disturbing comparison of Milly's body to something that may be eaten reveals North's palpable fear of being incorporated into the family body, his dread of being absorbed into the look of the family. He imagines Milly's flesh as extending beyond its seemly boundaries, as threatening to engulf him: "He noticed how the rings were sunk in her fingers, as if the flesh had grown over them. . . . She cast a net over them; she made them all feel one family" (373–74). To his eyes the aged Milly and her husband Hugh are "obese, shapeless, they looked to him like a parody, a travesty, an excrescence that had overgrown the form within, the fire within" (379). To him they are omnivorous, less than human, "amorphous" sea creatures with long and floating "white tentacles" who want to trap him in endlessly boring conversation. He fears that he represents "food" to them, that they want to "suck" him in (377).

As in *The Past Recaptured*, in this remarkable scene we are presented clearly with the relation between (a certain form of) narcissism and aggression. The figure of the mirror is apt here also. Faced with the frightening mirror of the family, the middle-aged North wants to shatter the looking glass of old age. For him the cycle of generations represents the potential loss of a part of himself to others, the submergence of his individuality into marriage and into the tedium of family routine. The mirroring of the infant by the mother provides the foundation on which the structures of a healthy narcissism are built, as Kohut, Béla Grunberger, and others have theorized. In contrast this mirror deals a severe blow to North's narcissism. His thoughts turn murderous. In self-defense he wants to transform the old in his own image. He wants sharply defined boundaries, not blurred and sentimental edges. He desires rationality, which to his eyes does not characterize the behavior of the elderly. He imagines enlisting the medical establishment on his side to fix the elderly, as if they were sick. "You doctors, he thought, you scientists, why don't you drop a little crystal into a tumbler, something starred and sharp, and make them swallow it? Common sense; reason; starred and sharp. But would they swallow it?" (375).

Terrified of being consumed, North would make *them* swallow *him*. In *A Room of One's Own*, published some years before *The Years*, Woolf had used the figure of the mirror to describe a relation of power between men and women. As she wrote in what has become a celebrated and touchstone passage, "women have served all these centuries as looking-glasses possessing the magic and delicious power of reflecting the figure of man at twice its natural size."[3] In *The Years* the middle-aged hold up a mirror to the elderly which has a malicious and distorting power.

In his essay "On Narcissism," Freud theorizes that the "charm of a child lies to a great extent in his narcissism, his self-contentment and inaccessibility. . . . It is as if we envied them for maintaining a blissful state of mind— an unassailable libidinal position which we ourselves have since abandoned" (SE 14: 89). For Freud, "proper" or normal development entails a movement from narcissism to love for others; as we grow up we must surrender our narcissism. But this little scene in *The Years* together with Lacan's analysis of aggressivity suggests that we do not so easily proceed from narcissism to love for others (or "object" love). However, the "we" here is qualified by age. Here "we" refers to the middle-aged who in relation to the elderly remain locked in a narcissism which is linked with aggression. The middle-aged, represented by North, deny to the elderly the "self-contentment" and "inaccessibility" associated with a child's narcissism. What is often considered charming in a child—in this example, falling asleep at a party—is generally regarded as a regrettable lapse of control in the elderly if not outright bad manners. Children may very well be envied in their narcissism, as Freud suggests, but it is not envy that prompts the middle-aged North to represent the sleeping Eleanor to himself as obscene: "Eleanor snored. She was nodding off, shamelessly, helplessly. There was an obscenity in unconsciousness, he thought. Her mouth was open; her head was on one side" (378). Not envy but instead a complex fear of death and abandonment.

With the aged dead (sleep in the elderly is figured as death, not bliss), the middle-aged stand alone before death, no longer middle-aged, constituted in the look of the family which at this point is the look of death. If a sleeping child calls forth a tender gaze, *The Years* asks us to consider that the sight of an old person in sleep elicits dread. The fear of one's own mortality in turn calls forth aggression, as we see in North's description of Eleanor's body as she sinks into sleep. Earlier in the evening he had found her resplendent in her red-and-gold cloak. Now he imagines her as lacking color, as disintegrating. She is, in his eyes, "colourless save for a brown stain on her forehead; and her hair colourless save for a stain like the yolk of an egg on it. All over he suspected she must be soft and discoloured like a pear that has gone sleepy" (376). To echo Herbert Blau, we all know what follows ripeness. In sleep Eleanor takes on the look of the family, and North punishes her for it.

We see here corroboration of Lacan's theory that narcissistic identification entails aggressivity or, as he puts it in "What Is a Picture" (1964), that "there is no trace anywhere of a good eye, of an eye that blesses," that the eye "cannot be beneficent—it is maleficent" (*FF* 115). North resists identification with Eleanor at the cost of disfiguring his aunt in his mind's eye. In North's will to power to separate himself from his heritage, from what he imagines to be his future, his eye enacts a willful power play of difference. Thus age relations are power relations. In this little scene the middle-aged man does not wish really to *see* his elderly aunts and uncle. As he arrogates a position of superiority to himself, they are disregarded and distorted—in effect, discarded. At work is the powerful mechanism by which one term is what it is by excluding another term: the middle-aged remain potent by excluding the aged.

THE DREAM AS AN OBJECT: FORMS AND TRANSFORMATIONS
OF NARCISSISM

But what appears "obscene" to North is to Eleanor a precious object. Waking from her doze, she reflects that "there had been a gap—a gap filled with the golden light of lolling candles, and some sensation which she could not name"; "she felt extraordinarily happy. Most sleep left some dream in one's mind—some scene or figure remained when one woke up. But this sleep, this momentary trance, in which the candles had lolled and lengthened themselves, had left her with nothing but a feeling; a feeling, not a dream" (31). Freud, we recall, stresses that the primary language of dreams is visual. In this context Eleanor's insistence that her dream did not produce complexly articulated scenes or figures is telling. Her dream is not primarily characterized by dream-work, a message in disguise, the concealed representation of a wish. Rather it belongs to the incommunicable register of feeling-tones. Importantly, Eleanor does *not* want to tell her dream to anyone but instead wishes to keep it to herself lest in the telling it vanish. She insists on the pleasure principle of her dream. Woolf: "She wished, thought Eleanor, to protect the extraordinary feeling of happiness that still remained with her. Covered up from observation it might survive, she felt"

(381). Her immediate response is to evade the willful and separating look, to resist observing eyes, to protect her dream from interpretation. How are we to understand her act of not wanting to give up her dream?

In Pontalis's fine essay "Dream as an Object" we find theoretical reflections of this fictional scene.[4] Arguing that in privileging the hermeneutics of the dream Freud neglected the *experience* of the dream, Pontalis distinguishes two aspects of the dream—the dream as message and the dream as an object or place to which we would attach ourselves. In the first part of his essay, I find him particularly persuasive. Pontalis insists on the pleasure principle of the dream as if he would recuperate this pleasure, shifting the long-honored emphasis from the interpretation of the dream to the preservation of the incommunicable subjective experience of the dream. "In a way," Pontalis declares, "psychoanalysis is strangling the eloquence of oneiric life" (130). We also find this welcome insistence on the value of dreaming as experience in the work of the British analyst Masud Khan. Like Pontalis, Khan was also influenced by Winnicott. But unlike Pontalis, Khan writes of the dream as a *space*, not an object, a space akin to Winnicott's transitional space which is a space of creativity. "The dreaming subject is the entire subject," he writes. "The dreaming experience is an entirety that actualizes the self in an unknowable way."[5] Or as Milan Kundera puts it in *The Unbearable Lightness of Being*, observing that Freud overlooked the aspect of the aesthetic in his theory of dreams, "Dreaming is not merely an act of communication (or coded communication, if you like); it is also an aesthetic activity, a game of the imagination, a game that is a value in itself."[6]

Ultimately, however, Pontalis identifies the dream-space *negatively* as representing the narcissistic space of primary narcissism, as an undifferentiated idyllic primary state from which we must rouse ourselves. Finally he follows Freud, concluding that we must separate ourselves from the dream (and the negative narcissistic space, or place, it has established) and come to interpretation.[7] As he writes, in an almost moralistic tone, "we owe it to the dream to *come to the surface*" (133). For Pontalis, who is of course writing as an analyst and in terms of the space of analysis, the very *act* of dreaming the dream which one refuses to give up is a manifestation of secondary narcissism and represents a resistance to the other (the analyst) which is not fruitful and must be overcome. Reading the dreaming Eleanor in the theoretical light of Pontalis, we may be tempted to understand her silence as an obstinate or regressive *refusal* to give up the feeling-traces of her dream which, like all dreams in Pontalis's view, refers "to the maternal body" and represents an effort "to preserve an undivided totality" (128).[8]

But might we not imagine a dreamer holding on to her dream for other than negative reasons? Treasuring her dream and not just clinging to it as might an anxious child? Wishing not to relinquish her dream, not so much to refuse to give something up which someone else wants, as to keep something—an experience—for herself? The figure of the dreaming Eleanor (along with Khan and Kundera) invites us to ask these questions of Pontalis. For given Eleanor's pliant character and the dynamics of the social group in *The Years* which is divided by age (I will come back to this later), *refusal* or *resistance* seems much too strong. I would rather put it positively, shifting the emphasis from *resistance* to *preference*: Eleanor *prefers* to keep her feelings of extraordinary happiness to herself. In the character of Eleanor we find a figure of maturity who stands in marked contrast to Pontalis's final view of the dreamer who attaches herself in a childishly regressive way to the dream as an object. Eleanor's wish to keep her dream to herself is not regressive. Rather her "transitional dream" (I here borrow Pontalis's suggestive term but lend it positive connotations) resembles what the British analyst Winnicott has theorized as the cultivation of that part of us which always remains uncommunicated.[9] It is an intentional noncommunication which preserves individuality. Thus Eleanor's preference to keep her dream to herself should not be confused with regression to primary or secondary narcissism. We might say that her dream is an example of a *transformed* narcissism. It *expresses* a part of herself, it is a place of experience. It does not *represent* herself to herself.

Here Kohut's work on narcissism can be helpful. Where Lacan stresses the structural relationship between narcissism and *aggressivity*, Kohut emphasizes the intimate relationship between narcissism and *idealization*. Where Lacan insists that the libidinal transformations associated with the major stages in life entail aggressivity, Kohut offers instead a theory of social cohesion based on our developing and properly narcissistic concern for the continuity of values which have been important to us over a lifetime.

Kohut's departure from Freud's account of primary narcissism is the most radical aspect of his work.[10] With Freud he agrees that normal development requires that we relinquish our primary narcissism and turn toward others. Ultimately Freud theorizes narcissism in negative terms. But Kohut differs from Freud in positing another line of development, one leading from primary narcissism to mature narcissism. For Kohut, then, primary narcissism has two distinct aspects or forms: the idealized parental imago, which will come to be associated with love for others (object love), and the narcissistic self, which will come to be associated with mature narcissism. For Kohut mature narcissism is characterized by such qualities as creativity, humor, and empathy. Thus he views mature narcissism not as "a regression effect" but as "an integral, self-contained set of psychic functions" which is culturally as well as personally valuable.[11]

Kohut also theorizes that in the line of psychic development leading from primary narcissism to mature narcissism there is the possibility of a further development, or *transformation*, of narcissism into what he calls "cosmic" narcissism. Narcissistic energies are transferred to other, intangible domains, "from the self to a concept of participation in a supraindividual and timeless existence" (*FTN* 266). How does such a transformation of narcissism come about? Kohut is nowhere clear on this point. But taking a cue from a few of his remarks, I would like to propose that it has to do with the aging process itself, that is, with a biological diminishing of libido.

When he was fifty-nine, Kohut observed of his own aging: "The influence of aging (and with it the inescapable necessity of facing the reality of the final dissolution of individual existence) is producing a shift. . . . There is less enthusiasm in me now . . . and more concern for the continuity (i.e., for the survival of the values for which I have lived)."[12] This is commonplace enough, although what is *not* commonplace is to theorize aging. What I do find particularly arresting is Kohut's emphasis on the *gradual* nature of this change. He returns to this theme in "Forms and Transformations of Narcissism," arguing that the ability to accept our mortality is an achievement of the ego which entails giving up the narcissistic self. He adds that this release of the self takes place *slowly* over a long stretch of time. Kohut's final remark—it is almost an aside—I find quite suggestive. Using the time-honored analogy of the ego as the rider and the narcissistic self as the horse, he notes that our mastery over the narcissistic self "may after all have been decisively assisted by the fact that the horse too has grown old" (*FTN* 269).[13] What does growing old mean here? That the normal process of aging itself, which takes place over a long period of time and which entails a gradual rearrangement of narcissistic energy, facilitates our accepting the approach of our own death. That the biological diminishing of libido may have certain positive psychological effects.

This emphasis on gradual change invites me to insist again that for most of us old age is not characterized—or figured—by a dramatic crisis as are, for example, other major stages in life such as the Oedipal stage or adolescence. As I mentioned earlier in the chapter on Freud, certainly we can speak of someone aging overnight. But this is in fact rare, and often such an abrupt perception of aging in others occurs in the eyes of the perceivers for two reasons—either these elderly people have suffered a severely debilitating (or what we commonly refer to as a *ravaging*) illness, or we have not seen them for a long period of time. We have not aged with them. For most of us old age is distributed—perhaps almost imperceptibly—over many years.[14] Aging is a process, not an event. And is it not possible that in that long period of old age the narcissistic self is slowly left behind, much as is the transitional object in infancy?[15] Similarly, in the long period of old age is it not possible that the aggressivity associated with the narcissism of Lacan's mirror stage of infancy (and other stages) might simply be left behind as energy decreases? This would be a psychic process similar to *mourning*, which I will take up in the next chapter. I am led to the conclusion that the process of growing old may facilitate a *benevolent*, not aggressive, narcissism which may coexist with mature relations with others. From this perspective the relationship between narcissism and relations with others (object relations) would be dialectical, not mutually exclusive.[16] On the contrary, a benevolent narcissism would be a condition for benevolent relations with others.

Let us return to the dreaming Eleanor. If we were tempted at first to read the blissfulness of her sleep as a regressive desire to revert to the space of primary narcissism, in the light of the above discussion we may understand Eleanor's narcissism as an expanded and transformed narcissism, a mature narcissism, a benevolent narcissism. For what is most remarkable about Woolf's presentation of the sleeping Eleanor is that Eleanor both *preserves* her magical dream in a narcissistic space, *preferring* not to give it up,[17] and also offers to others a utopian vision of old age.[18] Thus her dream does not represent fundamentally the dream as nostalgia, as Pontalis would have it. It is not regressive or retrogressive but *progressive*. It yields a utopian impulse, part of which Eleanor *chooses* not to communicate and part of which she does. There is, in a sense, then, an active politics to Eleanor's stance. If she *prefers* to keep part of her experience to herself, she does not completely withdraw from the social contract of generations. She also *speaks* her experience which is her experience of aging. She offers to share her experience, which is, in Winnicott's phrase, the "experience of mutuality."[19] She transforms the feeling-tones of her sleep into social vision. Woolf: "Her feeling of happiness returned to her, her unreasonable exaltation. It seemed to her that they were all young, with the future before them. Nothing was fixed; nothing was known; life was open and full before them" (382).

At first we may wish to interpret this vision of age transformed into youth—of unbounded possibilities in a world undivided by age—as mere wish fulfillment. It is true, after all, that Eleanor does imagine herself as young again. It is my suspicion, however, that such a reading reveals primarily the fears of the middle-aged: it is the middle-aged who, like North, are apprehensive about old age and thus assume that the elderly must, inevitably and unambivalently, wish themselves young again. I want to note too that Eleanor's inner voice, which she speaks, cautions us not to reduce her dream to the fulfillment of a wish.

For Eleanor, old age is precisely *not* a period in her life she longs to escape. "Isn't that why life's a perpetual—what shall I call it?—miracle?" she says to the others; "old age they say is like this; but it isn't. It's different; quite different. So when I was a child; so when I was a girl; it's been a perpetual discovery, my life, a miracle" (383). Woolf's figuring of Eleanor's experience proves wrong the cultural myth of old age as inevitable decline.

We age as we have lived. The character of Eleanor embodies this truth. It has been her nature to resist cultural stereotypes throughout her life even as she has seemed to live the most conventional of lives. She never consented to what "they" said childhood and girlhood and old age would be like. Instead she accepted the variousness of experience at different times in her life. Old age is for her "different; quite different." This is why, I think, Eleanor does not have a unified narrative of her life, or more accurately, perhaps, does not need or desire such an intelligible account of her life. At several points in the evening her nieces—the middle-aged—ask her about her life. To *have* a life means to possess its narrative. But Eleanor cannot tell the story; she has only moments. Nor does she wish to. As she muses to herself, "it was the second time that evening that somebody had talked about her life. And I haven't got one, she thought. Oughtn't a life to be something you could handle and produce? a life of seventy odd years. But I've only the present moment, she thought" (366).

Are we not often told that in old age we should see our lives whole as from a vast perspective? I suspect, though, that like Eleanor we do not see our lives as fluent narratives, only the lives of others, and then we must always question whether what we see is the stuff of projection. Still my conviction is that the understanding of the old for the young is deeper than the understanding the young and middle-aged have for the old. To this the pages of *The Years* speak eloquently. I want here to give one example of a flagrant if common misreading of the old on the part of the middle-aged. It arises precisely from the mistaken assumption that all lives assume the shape of an organic narrative, and more specifically that these shapes are different for men and women. I turn again to Eleanor and North.

At another moment during the party, North catches the uncanny and flickering sight of the youthful and womanly Eleanor in the demeanor of the old Eleanor. Eleanor smiles up at him, "just as she used to smile when she was a girl with her brother's friends." North is prompted to wonder about how she has lived her life. "Why hadn't she married one of them, he wondered. Why do we hide all the things that matter? he asked himself" (412). It is common enough to be stirred by the poignant sight of youth suddenly surfacing in a body long old. It may, however, be as misleading to those younger as it is somehow and sometimes mistakenly reassuring. For the sense of a person as simultaneously young and old may give rise to the mistaken notion of the very continuity of a life. Certainly it is not unusual for North to wonder why the now seventy-some-year-old Eleanor has never married. Indeed it is a mark of the amplitude of his spirit that he pauses to reconstruct the life of someone so much older than he. But we as readers know, given Eleanor's life, that her spinsterhood is not, as North puts it elsewhere, her "tragedy" (372). North projects a crude stereotype of spinsterhood onto her. Eleanor too peers into the windows of her past at the party. But she does *not* hide all the things that matter. Nor do the things that once mattered now matter so much, if, really, at all. Eleanor is not a victim and her life is not a tragedy. But this the middle-aged cannot understand.[20] The sour cynicism of North and his sister Peggy prevents them from realizing that, as Eleanor says earlier, "things have changed for the better. . . . What I mean is, we've changed in ourselves. . . . We're happier—we're freer . . . " (386). Nor do they comprehend what Eleanor means when she voices the feeling-traces of her dream, *expressing* and not concealing what matters: "old age they say is like this; but it isn't. It's different. So when I was a child; so when I was a girl; it's been a perpetual discovery, my life, a miracle." Eleanor's speech is a declaration of being, and a forceful if gentle assertion of the politics of age.

THE GAZE: BENEVOLENT NARCISSISM

Do we, regardless of class or racial or sexual difference, look at others differently at distinct points across the course of our lives? Might it not be possible that different forms of narcissism are associated with different ways of seeing? Might not the *look* of desire be associated with aggressivity and the *gaze* with idealization which is, paradoxically, realistic, tolerant, and benevolent? The figure of the aged Eleanor suggests a *benevolent* narcissism, a narcissism associated not with aggressivity but with idealization. It is a form of narcissism I have linked, following Kohut, with age, although it need not be associated with it.

Here I want to take a detour with Girard which will serve to remind us that we must keep the category of age firmly in sight when we theorize about narcissism. Girard in a fine essay reads Freud through Proust, concluding that self-centeredness (narcissism) and other-relatedness (object love) are not necessarily incompatible.[21] I agree, but I arrive at this conclusion differently. For Girard *Remembrance of Things Past*, whose subject is desire, provides a critique of the Freudian theory of narcissism. Proust's novel offers another model of narcissism, one which is fundamentally Lacanian. In a gesture recalling the mirror stage of Lacan, Girard insists that narcissism is a projection of desire.

Girard: "What Freud calls 'intact narcissism' is the main, even sole object of desire in the novel of Proust. Since 'intact narcissism' is defined as perfect self-sufficiency and since self-sufficiency is what the subject of desire does not have and would like to have, there is nothing 'incongruous' in the choice of 'intact narcissism' as an object of desire" (298). As an example Girard cites Marcel's fascination with a group of adolescent girls. Marcel is attracted to them because of their apparent self-sufficiency, which is precisely what Marcel does not possess. But as Girard correctly observes, their self-sufficiency is a mirage. "In Proust," he writes, "the 'blissful autonomy' and the 'self-sufficiency' of the desired object are not real. They are never experienced by anybody" (299).

I agree with Girard that a blissful autonomy and a perfect self-sufficiency are theoretical fictions defining narcissism which have obscured the fact that we always construct ourselves in relation to others. I also find Girard's example from Proust persuasive. The novel speaks to our seduction by others, whose images we have fashioned in the mirror of our own desire. It also speaks to our repulsion of others, as I discussed at length in the previous chapter. But I also find Girard's analysis misleading. It is age-bound, a description of only one of the many possible relations we may have to others.

Compare, for example, Eleanor's benevolent regard for the young with Marcel's self-absorbed fascination with this group of adolescent girls. In *Within a Budding Grove* we read:

> As I passed the dark one with the fat cheeks who was wheeling a bicycle, I caught her smiling, sidelong glance, aimed from the centre of that inhuman world which enclosed the life of this little tribe, an inaccessible, unknown world to which the idea of what I was could certainly never attain or find a place in it. Wholly occupied with what her companions were saying, this young girl in her polo-cap, pulled down very low over her brow, had she seen me at the moment in which the dark ray emanating from her eyes had fallen on me? . . . I knew that I should never possess this young cyclist if I did not possess also what there was in her eyes. And it was consequently her whole life that filled me with desire. . . . [22]

Marcel *yearns* for what he does not possess. That he so actively desires to *possess* or inhabit another world is critical. By contrast Eleanor is at this point in her life in her "own niche" (409). She is self-sufficient in a pliant, not excluding, way. Unlike the restless Marcel she is "tolerant, assured" (409). Imagine her, as Woolf did, sitting comfortably with her younger brother at the party and looking around, taking pleasure in the sight of a young couple who have eyes, we can guess, only for each other. Or recall Eleanor at the end of the night and the novel's end when as dawn breaks and she prepares to leave her sister Delia's party, she looks out the window and sees a young man and woman coming home together after the long night. Here is the final and moving passage of the novel:

> "It's been so good of you to come!" Delia exclaimed, turning toward them with her hand outstretched.
> "Thank you—thank you for coming!" she cried.
> "And look at Maggie's bunch!" she cried, taking a bunch of many-coloured flowers that Maggie held out to her.
> "How beautifully you've arranged them!" she said. "Look, Eleanor!" She turned to her sister.
> But Eleanor was standing with her back to them. She was watching a taxi that was gliding slowly round the square. It stopped in front of a house two doors down.
> "Aren't they lovely?" said Delia, holding out the flowers. Eleanor started.
> "The roses? Yes . . . " she said. But she was watching the cab. A young man had got out; he paid the driver. Then a girl in a tweed travelling suit followed him. He fitted his latch-key to the door. "There," Eleanor murmured, as he opened the door and they stood for a moment on the threshold. "There!" she repeated as the door shut with a little thud behind them.
> Then she turned round into the room. "And now?" she said, looking at Morris, who was drinking the last drops of a glass of wine. "And now?" she asked, holding out her hand to him.
> The sun had risen, and the sky above the houses wore an air of extraordinary beauty, simplicity and peace. (434–35)

Eleanor's gaze at the young is not motivated by the Lacanian lure of fascination or desire. We could not say of Eleanor that catching the sight of this young couple filled her with desire in the Proustian way. Nor is she seduced by the mirage of the self-sufficiency of these young couples. She understands it to be an illusion, one that may last for only a very short time—but nonetheless she finds it a lovely illusion, an illusion of youth, romance, and love. Assured, at ease in her own place in her life, she gazes at the young with pleasure, a pleasure almost aesthetic because paradoxically poignant and disinterested.[23] Eleanor, a woman who never had lovers or a husband, is not gazing into her own past. At the end of the novel and her life, she extends her hands to her brother Morris. Reciprocity is found in the company of her siblings. She realizes—and there is not the sting of envy in it or the demand of desire—that "there" is *then*, another time, time past, and that "now" is *here*. She does not desire to recapture the past, as does Marcel. She does not wish to possess others. Nor does she wish like Marcel to project herself into a future in which she will fashion her identity. The future is in a very real sense of no concern to the woman who now "so seldom thought about herself" (335).

Thus if Lacan posits the mirror stage in which the *look* is reflected and desire is defined in the mirror of the other, the benevolent *gaze* of old age is by contrast not returned. The seventy-some-year-old Eleanor is not seen by these two young people, nor has she really been seen by North. Nor is she heard. She insists that old age is "different; quite different." But no one understands what she has said.

In "On Narcissism" Freud wrote that "parental love, which is so moving and at bottom so childish, is nothing but the parents' narcissism born again, which transformed into object-love, unmistakably reveals its former nature" (SE 14: 91). For Freud the revival of secondary narcissism in parents, which is signaled by their overvaluation of their children, is regressive, "immature, childish." This is worthy of heated dispute, although I must leave that aside here. But with the figure of the elderly Eleanor in our mind's eye, we can suggest another model of the relationship between narcissism and other-relatedness which is characterized by an *appreciation* of others, or otherness. In the character of Eleanor we see represented an interdependence between her narcissism, her self-sufficiency, her capacity to be alone in Winnicott's sense, and her valuing of the young which is precisely not an *over*valuation. It is her security in her self that makes possible her benevolence. Interestingly enough, Kohut distinguishes between the look and the gaze this way: "in contrast to the idealized parent imago which is gazed at in awe, admired, looked up to . . . the narcissistic self wants to be looked at and admired" (*FTN* 250). At this point it should be abundantly clear just to what extent Kohut's own distinction between the look and the gaze also rests on an analysis of our development in the *early* years. From this perspective too, then, the figure of the elderly Eleanor invites us to speculate that at a certain point in our lives we may give up a large measure of our narcissistic self. Accordingly, we may relinquish our desire to be looked at in admiration. In turn we become those who gaze at others—and this too is a pleasure, one that works to strengthen social bonds. Here it cannot be emphasized enough that the object of Eleanor's benevolent gaze is highly abstract. If parents smile lovingly and at times blindly on their children, Eleanor by contrast gazes on *youth*.

I am reminded here of a remark which a woman who was in (I would guess) her seventies made during the discussion after a lecture I gave at Hunter College.[24] "I've never felt a maternal instinct," she said, "and now I'm surprised to find that while I'm riding the bus or walking, I'm drawn to babies and little children." And I'm reminded too of what Colette wrote in *The Blue Lantern* about her good friend, the actress Marguerite Moreno: "Shortly before her death she had invited a grand-niece to stay with her. She had been incapable of hiding her astonishment, her deep feelings, at the sight of a human flower full of health and intelligence. This I deduce from her last letters, in which I find an affectionate constraint, a feeling of watchful pride, even to the extent of discovering something quite new to her, the freedom to welcome by name the idea of the future, at the suggestion of a radiant, beautiful child."[25]

In her last essay written before her death, Melanie Klein speaks to this relation of the old to the young. The essay is entitled "On Feeling Alone" (1963). There is something unfinished about it, and in fact Klein never gave it out to be published. Still, in it the psychoanalyst who has been so definitively associated with theorizing the turbulent and violent emotional life of the infant, places her theory of the origins of love and gratitude in infancy in the context of later life and old age. "A child who, in spite of some envy and jealousy, can identify himself with the pleasures and gratifications of members of his family circle, will be able to do so in relation to other people in later age," she writes. "In old age he will then be able to reverse the early situation and identify himself with the satisfactions of youth."[26] This is precisely the capacity Eleanor represents for me—the capacity to identify with but not be envious of the satisfactions of youth.

Klein imagines psychic compensations in aging and old age through identification with the pleasures of the young. But for the most part aging and old age are regarded in terms of loss and decline, yielding a dark portrait of what is in fact a long span of years which are themselves characterized by difference. At the very least we must distinguish between a period of extreme frailty and failing health, which is likely to be relatively short, and a longer period of health (I will return to this in the chapter on Beckett). From the perspective of a healthy old age, it is possible to theorize the development of strengths in old age rather than the ravages of regression. The elderly can possess the strengths that come with survivorship.[27] Long years of experience, which inevitably confirm a phenomenology of loss, may prompt us to seek new sources of sustenance in, perhaps, what Kohut called "participation in a supraindividual and timeless existence." We need not interpret this in a religious or mystical vein. Turning again to Eleanor, we may theorize a late maturing capacity to invest energy in people and ideals that have no direct bearing on the self—in her case, in youth itself. But to what extent is this strength used by society? *The Years* is pessimistic on this point. Eleanor—and her brothers and sisters—celebrate the idea of the family and, more particularly, *youth*, without demanding an answer in return. But the middle-aged feel themselves to be outsiders at the family party. And if Eleanor gazes on the young with benevolent affection, her gaze is not answered. In the Pargiter family, in this time which is still in a sense our time, the shame of it is that only members of the same generation—whether they are young lovers or seventy-year-old brother and sister—return each other's gaze. Sight lines between generations have been broken.

THE READING EYE

To review. The middle-aged North in his fear and disgust disfigures the aging body: it is the travesty of the look. The elderly Eleanor turns both within and without: these are the pleasures of the gaze, solitary and benevolent. Both visions—North's alienating and aggressive representation of the elderly and Eleanor's dreamy idealization of the young—are fundamentally private, interior, uncommunicated. As a line describes a circle, so their lines of sight limn two separate worlds of age, realms incongruent and incommensurate. Herein lies the pathos of the years. For *The Years* contains two contradictory representations of old age—one which is aggressively negative (or paranoiac, to echo the previous chapter) and is projected onto the old by the middle-aged, and one which is fundamentally positive and is *embodied* in the figure of an old person.

But *The Years* is magical as well. We are not at a party but readers of a novel, and Woolf offers us a third perspective from which, if only for a moment, the worlds are brought close together as the generation of the middle-aged (represented by Nicholas, Sara, and Maggie) looks on the older generation, the seven brothers and sisters, as if they were in and of themselves a work of art. This is the privileged place of the reader's eye. Here is the long and lovely passage which comes near the end of the novel:

> "Wake your sister, Magdalena," [Nicholas] said, turning to Maggie. Maggie looked at her. Then she took a flower from the table and tossed it at her. She half-opened her eyes. "It's time," said Maggie, touching her on the shoulder. "Time, is it?" she sighed. She yawned and stretched herself. She fixed her eyes on Nicholas as if she were bringing him back to the field of vision. Then she laughed.
>
> "Nicholas!" she exclaimed.
>
> "Sara!" he replied. They smiled at each other. Then he helped her up and she balanced herself uncertainly against her sister, and rubbed her eyes.
>
> "How strange," she murmured, looking round her, " . . . how strange. . . ."
>
> There were the smeared plates, and the empty wine-glasses; the petals and the bread crumbs. In the mixture of lights they looked prosaic but unreal; cadaverous but brilliant. And there against the window, gathered in a group, were the old brothers and sisters.
>
> "Look, Maggie," she whispered, turning to her sister, "Look!"
>
> The group in the window, the men in their black-and-white evening dress, the women in their crimsons, golds and silvers, wore a statuesque look for a moment,

as if they were carved in stone. Their dresses fell in stiff sculptured folds. Then
they moved; they changed their attitudes; they began to talk. (432–33)

This portrait, this still life of the elderly, has something of the eerie about it.
Brilliant, it is also tinged with death, with the cadaverous. But for us in the
late twentieth century, this image of the elderly must inevitably possess a utopian
quality as well. For in our period of smaller and smaller families (many of us
are single children, as many of our own children and grandchildren may or will
be), this vision may be charged with a nostalgia not for what we have possessed
and will never regain, but for what we can never experience because of our
historical moment. This still life of seven brothers and sisters gathered together
in old age, in a perfect repose if only for a moment, suggests without exaggerated
sentimentality a rich private sphere defined by one's siblings, something our
future in our historical time may not hold, a familial solidarity in a healthy old
age.

COUNTER-TEXT

They were collected in the drawing room, all six of them; two wives and a husband bringing the number up to nine. A sufficiently formidable family gathering—old, black ravens, thought Edith, the youngest, who was always flustered and always trying to confine things into the shape of a phrase, like pouring water into an ewer, but great gouts of meaning and implication invariably ran over and slopped about and were lost. . . . It was not often that they all met together, none missing—curious, Edith thought, that Death should be the convener, as though all the living rushed instantly together for protection and mutual support. Dear me, how old we all are. Herbert must be sixty-eight, and I'm sixty; and Father was over ninety, and Mother is eighty-eight. . . .

They stood in the drawing room in a group, uncomfortably shifting from one foot to the other, but it never occurred to them to sit down. They would have thought it disrespectful. For all their good solid sense, death, even an expected death, disconcerted them just a little. Around them hung that uneasy, unsettled air which attends those about to set out on a journey or those whose lives have been seriously disturbed. Edith would have liked to sit down, but dared not. How large they all were, she thought; large and black and elderly, with grandchildren of their own. . . .

All these old people, thought Edith, disposing of a still older person! . . . Wrangle, wrangle, she thought—for she had had some previous taste of family discussions; they'll wrangle over Mother like dogs quarrelling over an old, a very old, bone.

> —The six children gathering after
> the death of their father, Lord
> Slane, at the age of ninety-four,
> *from* Vita Sackville-West, *All Pas-*
> *sion Spent* 9, 11, 15–16, 22, 26

5. Gender, Generational Identity, and Aging . . .
Eva Figes's *Waking*

THE PREVIOUS CHAPTER—and the last chapter in Woolf's *The Years*—concluded with a still life of seven elderly brothers and sisters standing close together. It is a portrait of a certain congenial and familial intimacy in an old age of physical health. This chapter will end on an altogether different and painful note—with the figure of a woman isolated and dying in old age. She is the main character in Figes's *Waking* who as an old woman takes no pleasure or comfort in everyday life in her grown children—that is, in the family sphere she has helped to create. But if this chapter ends with an analysis of a scene of an elderly woman on her deathbed, I want also to begin it by invoking a similar scene from a different novel, Anne Tyler's *Dinner at the Homesick Restaurant*. It serves to introduce the contents of a counter-scene to the Freudian drama of the middle-aged son's aggression and guilt played out over the body of the frail and dying father. In this chapter, then, I will be shifting the emphasis from the son's troubled and repressed identification with the elderly father to the daughter's poignant and accepting identification with the dying mother.

Let us imagine, then, a mother on her deathbed. What would a child hope from a mother as a legacy? Mothers, more than fathers, are judged by their children in terms of their love for them, love which from the point of view of the child seems never to be sufficient or adequate. Thus from the perspective of a child, such a deathbed wish should represent a supreme self-sacrifice. Tyler's fictional answer to my hypothetical question—what does a child want from her mother?—is superb, deep as drama and yet also the stuff of which fairy tales are made. It is a wish implacable in its simplicity, a wish that can never be fulfilled. With two of her middle-aged children gathered around her, the dying mother (a Faulknerian character named Pearl Tull) tries to tell them through the fog of her illness: "You should have got an extra mother."[1]

What child does not wish for another mother? We spend our lives as children evaluating and reevaluating our mother, measuring what we see as her faults in relation to our demands and desires, wishing she were more like this and less like that, taking up new positions in relation to her as we grow older and our lives change. Psychoanalysis revolves around our attachment to our parents (and in the past decades it has been concerned more with the mother than with the father), figures who are all the more powerful in our psyche because of their singular status, both biologically and phantasmatically. What mother would think of giving up this position of power? A Pearl Tull who, dying, would selflessly wish for another mother to take her place. A mother who would be the embodiment of the phantasmatic all-good symbiotic mother of whom the psychoanalyst Margaret Mahler has written.

Mahler has described the life course as characterized by a simultaneous and continual distancing from and searching for the all-good symbiotic mother who represents our desire for what we phantasize was an originary blissful state of oneness.[2] What Mahler put in terms of a child's romance with the mother, the psychoanalyst Alice Balint had expressed more matter-of-factly some years before. In her essay "Love for the Mother and Mother Love" (1939), Balint concludes that from the perspective of a child, *a mother should have no interests of her own*.[3] (We saw this represented in Freud's letter about his mother-in-law.) Balint arrives at her conclusion through an analysis of the first months in a child's life. She argues that during this period the young infant and mother coexist in a symbiotic relation based on a mutual identity of interests, that is, on a reciprocal interdependence of instinctual drives which do not characterize the infant's relation to the father (her argument is thus driven by biology). From this Balint concludes that throughout our lives, a child's love for (or attachment to) her mother is at base a love without a sense of reality. A child—and we never cease being children—will never relinquish the phantasm of the all-good symbiotic mother.[4] Whereas a child will understand that a father has interests of his own, a child will maintain a naive and narcissistic attitude toward her mother throughout her life, continuing to assume that her mother's interests should coincide with her own. "For all of us," Balint writes, "it remains self-evident that the interests of mother and child are identical, and it is the generally acknowledged measure of the goodness or badness of the mother how far she really feels this identity of interests'' (116). Today we would want to question Balint's argument about the original symbiotic relation between mother and child as stemming from a biological mutuality of interests. But culturally it remains the case in the West today, a child, whether male or female, continues to demand more in terms of selflessness and self-sacrifice from the mother than from the father.

Balint's conclusion about the strength of love for the mother and mother love will be important to the discussion of *Waking* in this chapter. In the second half of this chapter I will focus on two critical moments in a daughter's life in relation to the mother, moments which are psychically implicit one in the other, folded into each other in a kind of repetition which takes place in a sphere that is represented as both actual and phantasmatic, one moment in middle age and one in old age. What we will see at work is a process of doubling that can take the form of the psychic creation of the all-good mother.

Waking is a brilliant spare novel of growing up and growing old, a narrative of a woman's life constructed as an interior monologue in seven short scenes.[5] The novel recalls the lyricism of Woolf cut with the minimalism if not absurdist anguish of Beckett. But the melancholia is not ontological, as it is in Beckett. Instead it has specifically to do with gender. The drama of the story turns on the divergences over the life course between the psyche and the body of a particular if nameless woman. In *Waking* we meet a woman who has a premature sense of aging as doom and whose fulfillments come rarely, a woman whose interior life is rich with intense but often vague and private longings. In *Waking* we find no lineaments of a public sphere, as we do in Woolf's *The Years*. As with Beckett's Malone, all of this woman's thoughts dwell in an intimate domain. All of her reflections upon waking up into seven days of her life have to do with members of her family, her lover, her (private) self, and with the phenomenology of the body.

Throughout the seven scenes the mother is the single figure who persists, psychically framing the life of this daughter. In the first scene we encounter the musings of a girl who is only six or seven. She is listening to the voices of her parents filtering through the wall which separates their room from hers—''His deep voice speaking words in sequence, the other voice several shades higher breaking with laughter'' (9). To her these are the sounds of two distinctly gendered beings from whom she feels puzzlingly estranged, ''creatures'' whose bodies and interests do not seem to resemble her own. She thinks of her mother as ''the woman'' whose ''eyes are odd'' and who ''has too much hair'' (9), as a woman she does not know. In the last scene, we read the musings of an old woman dying in a room whose walls seem to have vanished and whose sounds are now indistinctly human. Figes: ''I hear whispers, is it leaves stirring overhead, throwing their shadows on the wall? But the walls seem to have gone, or perhaps they are shining so much I do not see them now'' (84).

The five scenes in between each represent other phases in her life. Puberty and adolescence, during which she struggles against her mother: "I have only to do something, lift, bend, reach for, and she will pull me up short. Not nice, unladylike, or words to suggest my body has become indecent, to be strapped in, hidden from prying eyes. I do not know what I have done wrong, only that I must be ashamed, and that my body has odours which will turn milk sour" (18). Marriage, pregnancy, and her own early years of motherhood, from which she feels herself largely alienated. She is exhausted and tense, and she strains against her new life: "am I the person I used to be before all this? I am an animal, bound by the cries of the flesh, tenderness, anxiety, each in turn, and beyond this a whole network of small domestic duties which compromise and are bound to such feeling. But I have not changed" (37). Pleasures in the sexual body, during which after her divorce she takes a lover at the midpoint of her life, telling herself "I am alive, at last I am fully alive" (48), looking in a mirror to find the body reflected back to her transformed by passion, her "wild eyes, black, burning," looking out "from skin not just glowing, but incandescent, a white shape surrounded by a wild bush of confused hair" (55–56). Late middle age and the death of her mother, during which her own body becomes "a dead weight," something with which she is "at odds" (61). And early old age, in which she finds herself a recluse, living listlessly alone with "nothing to wake up for" (80), alone with the landscape and her memories, away from her children who are "strangers" (81). *Waking* presents us with a woman locked in the subsequent places of her age, unable except at a few critical moments to psychically cross the barriers of generations even as she herself moves through them in time.

These seven scenes in this woman's life are represented as taking place in precisely the same space, the same house. The process of the daughter's growing up and growing old is played out as the minimalist theater of her shifting from one room to another in a small house, from one generational bed to another. The wall represents a barrier which is at the same time so porous and permeable that not only do sounds move through it but so does the daughter as well as she moves through time, which is age. As an adolescent, for example, she scorns her parents, and in particular her mother. She makes a pact with herself to *always* remember what she feels like at that precise time in her life so that she will never repeat what she takes to be her mother's mistakes, confiding to her diary, " 'I do not want to forget, ever, what it feels like to be me now,' " thinking that her mother is an "old" woman, whom she does "not want to turn into" (27–28). But later these strong feelings vanish as her attachment to her past adolescent self is broken through age. When she wakes up one morning in middle age to hear her teenage son and his girlfriend making love on the other side of the wall, she no longer remembers what she had felt like as an adolescent. Her response is not understanding but contempt. She reacts with an almost Beckettian disdain for their sexuality, thinking, "I would laugh if I did not pity them" (64).[6] What she once so urgently desired is for now meaningless to her. The daughter, now a mother, has interests of her own. Or, to take another example, as a child, the daughter finds the unfamiliar musty smell of her parents' lovemaking alien to her. But later as a woman in love, her body (this is an aspect of the tactile body) is suffused with the same odors of marsh and bog. It is as if as an adult the daughter not only has assumed the bed and position of the mother but has taken on her body as well, absorbing and releasing its very smell. As a child she finds the distance between her world and her mother's world psychically unbridgeable. Here that distance collapses to virtually nothing, although the daughter does not appear to be conscious of the fact that she has adopted the position once occupied by her mother.

The daughter's reactions at various ages represent one of the great limitations if not tragedies of growing up and growing old for many of us. As we move through our lives, we seem so often to have so little understanding for those who are younger and those who are older. And yet I think precisely this assumption of our age at each point in time gives us a certain self-confidence, permitting us to focus on what needs to be done and experienced at the moment rather than losing ourselves in others—or, alternatively, losing ourselves in our past selves and our future selves. We all have interests of our own at different points in time. Does this not help explain why so few people would really rather be their younger selves again? Here we have yet again another form of the double bind of age which I spoke of in the chapter on the mirror stage of old age. At times in *Waking* a certain blindness to others is represented as yielding the best insight for ourselves. But what of the others? On the one hand, self-confidence or comfortableness in our age may give rise to an attitude of benevolence, as we saw in Woolf's *The Years*, or to a tolerant good humor. But on the other hand, humor can devolve into *humoring* of the other in another age, and at its dangerous extreme it can assume the form of a dismissive arrogance, as we saw in Proust's *Remembrance of Things Past*.

The daughter thus repeats in a certain sense the life of her mother. If from birth on she is always a daughter to her mother, as she grows older she becomes a mother to her daughter. As she ages, she becomes a mother to her mother. Dying, she oscillates between the two identities, she is a mother, she is a child. *Waking* thus invites us to consider how polyvalent our generational place in the family is. As we grow up and grow old we become more and more differentiated.

But as we assume more and more generational positions both psychically and socially, we as daughters become more like our mothers. This is not a matter of becoming mothers by literally having children; as we age, we find ourselves in a maternal position as we relate to those a generation younger than we are. If life is a process of separation and individuation from the mother, it is also a process of deindividuation as one becomes a mother—in a sense and uncannily, one's mother, the *mother*. Initially we have only one place. Later our places multiply. Repetition in the generational cycles is more than mere doubling. It is also proliferation.

Thus if Freudian psychoanalysis has stressed repetition in an individual's life (the repetition and rehearsal of traumatic events both in everyday life and in the privileged space of transference), we may also think of repetition in the cycle of the family over generations. By this I do not mean repetition in the sense that the sins of the fathers are visited upon the sons. By generational repetition I mean, instead, that we move through various identities as we assume different positions over time, moving from one generation to another.

I want here to take an excursion through recent psychoanalytic theory to sketch the elements of a theory of female identity in terms of generational time, turning first to the work of Doris Bernstein. Bernstein argues that the tasks of differentiation and individuation are more difficult for a female child than for a male child. She insists (I do not disagree) that women are thus at a distinct disadvantage in contemporary society, which values traits defined as traditionally male (aggressiveness, competitiveness, and so forth). But I am more interested in one of the reasons she gives in concluding that the boundaries between the emergent self and the mother are more blurred for female infants than for male infants than in the conclusion itself. She argues that the mother sees herself in the body of the daughter. In her daughter, she sees an identity of two terms, she sees *sameness*, whereas in the body of her son she sees *difference*. "*All mothers,*" she writes, "*share one common experience: the mother sees herself in the body of her infant daughter. She relates to her daughter narcissistically.*"[7]

In recent years psychoanalysis has emphasized the role of the mother as the mirror of the child. But Bernstein has elaborated this proposition in a gender-specific way, focusing not only on the child's relation to the mother but also on the mother's relation to her daughter, reversing the roles of spectatorship. Thus we could say that (these are not Bernstein's terms) the female infant is a mirror for the mother just as the mother is a mirror for the little girl. With the mother and the infant girl facing each other, it is as if we have the fascinating phenomenon of two mirrors facing each other, reflecting each other's surfaces (and feelings?) in an infinity of endless reverberations and permutations of familiar and familial proportions. Conversely, the male infant is *not* a mirror for the mother. Although in traditional psychoanalytic terms he may represent the desire of the female for what she lacks (the phallus), he may also precipitate a sense of difference as well. And as we saw in the chapter on the mirror stage of old age, we all know how unsettling it is to look in the mirror and find someone else (someone other than who we take ourselves to be) reflected there. Yet the burden of that chapter is that mutuality of interests must be seen in the mirrors which reflect age as difference. How then could we understand *difference* as *similarity*? Are mirrors different for men and women? Or can they be? Can mirrors be theorized differently in terms of gender and in terms of age? Can we imagine a positive version of the myth of the mirror of Narcissus? One way to begin would be to rethink the mirroring relation in terms of age difference as well as gender difference. A mother could look in the face of her daughter as if it were a mirror and accept her own older age as difference with pleasure (this kind of relation of age to youth I elaborated in the previous chapter). Perhaps she would see the relation not in terms of *difference* but rather in terms of *similarity*. Or a daughter could look in the mirror of her older mother, and imagine her coming older age with a kind of acceptance, as I suggested in the chapter on the mirror stage of old age.

To Bernstein's conclusion that the boundaries between a female infant and a mother are more blurred than they are with a male infant, I want to add Ernest Abelin's provocative theory that gender identity for little girls and little boys takes two different paths.[8] Abelin situates the development of such identity (as we will see, the term ''gender identity'' is not entirely correct) not in the Freudian Oedipal triangle but in the pre-Oedipal triangle which forms at about eighteen months during the rapprochement subphase (Mahler's formulation of the first longing of the child to return to the mother after differentiation). What is crucial is that for little boys and little girls, the points of reference for this triangle are different. For little boys, the triangle is familiarly Freudian, and so is the story of gender identity based on the perception of difference with regard to the specular body of the mother (the mother lacks what he possesses): mother/father/self. For little girls, however, the triangle is surprising: mother/baby/self. The father is conspicuous by his absence. *At stake in this triangle is not gender identity, which is based on sexual difference, but generational identity based on similarity.* Abelin explains the difference between gender identity and generational identity in the following terms: ''Generational identity establishes the self 'between' two objects, along one linear dimension. 'I am smaller than mother, but bigger than baby,' or, rather, in terms of wishes: 'I wish to be taken care of by mother and I wish to take care of baby.' By contrast, gender identity classifies the self in relation to the dichotomy male/female (or perhaps at first only to the dichotomy male/nonmale)'' (158). The implication of his brilliant essay is that female identity is at base *generational* identity, which has to do with feeling oneself linked, unconsciously if not consciously, to the generations ahead and behind through the relation of caring.[9] To the closely knit triangle of mother/baby/self is only later added the term that intrudes sexual difference—the father.

Putting Abelin and Bernstein together, we can advance the following hypothesis. If, as Abelin argues, generational identity is established in little girls before gender identity as sexual difference, and if, as Bernstein argues, little girls experience sameness or similarity in the mirroring relation to the mother, then we can see how *generational continuity*—the identity of generations over time—stems from generational identity.[10] This is a gendered version of generational *mutuality* which I introduced, drawing on Winnicott and Erikson, at the end of the chapter on the mirror stage of old age. Women, as we observe every day, take on the responsibility of the family, and while we can give many reasons for this (social, economic, historical), we can offer a psychoanalytic explanation as well.

I do not want to be mistaken here as providing a theoretical justification based on biological difference for arguing that caretaking is women's work. Such a position would only work to perpetuate unfair social practices on the basis of gender. On the other hand, caring for others is not accorded the dignity and value it should be in our society. What is at stake for me in this line of argument is not whether it is true but rather that given a different starting point, we can read the structural relations of (gendered) bodies in the family sphere differently from Freud.[11] If we begin from an alternative point of reference, from relations characterized by similitude and caring rather than difference and repressed aggressivity, we can read the possibilities of our psychic and social lives differently.

Figes's *Waking* does not permit us, however, to adopt uncritically an untroubled vision of a generational family romance. As we have already seen, the daughter's relation to her mother was ambivalent. So too is her relation to her own motherhood. She had her children relatively early—the first when she was twenty-five, the second soon after. For her, motherhood was a period of imprisonment. During pregnancy she felt herself locked in a body no longer her own. Childbirth was excruciating, a scene of suffering, a site of bloody sacrifice in which her body was a mere agency for another being. As she describes the birth of her daughter, "Within five minutes of my coming into that room, cream walls, high bed, bloodstains on the floor from the previous victim, the whole structure had come tumbling down, just like a child's building bricks scattered on the floor. In the interim between screaming to deaf walls, unable to get down from the hard high bed placed like a sacrificial altar, I thought: So this is what it's all about, I am not a person but a pod, to be used and prised open, nothing but a tool for some huge blind force'' (30).

She experienced her years of raising the children as years of servitude to rote routine. Her future was reduced, she felt, to an endless ticking of a numbing clock. She despaired that taking care of the children measured her years out for her in advance, leaving her and her age chronologically tied to the ages of her children. She felt that she had become a hostage to her son and to her daughter who had forced her, somehow, against her very will, to become the mother— uncannily, her *mother*. If earlier the daughter had conceived of her age primarily in relation to her mother, now she gloomily measured her age in relation to the ages of her children. As she thinks while waiting for the birth of her second child, ''My life is clearly marked out now. When the child is fifteen I shall be forty. When she is a woman of twenty-five I will be fifty, the age of my mother'' (40). *Waking* is not a celebration of generational identity or a hymn in praise of motherhood. For this daughter, motherhood violently circumscribes her life— or so she feels during the early and adolescent years of motherhood.

But when the middle-aged daughter visits her mother in the hospital where she is dying (presumably of cancer), the generations which Freudian psycho-analysis keeps apart come together. The blurring of generations is at its most intense. The mother and daughter become intimate, peers, each other. Their interdependence is represented as truly reciprocal in the sense of which Balint has written. For Balint the *''almost perfect counterpart to the love for the mother''* is maternal love (121). Like love for the mother, maternal love is also remote from reality, yet actual. The daughter sits by her mother's side in the hospital: ''I hold her hand with the loose heavy rings, or perhaps she is holding mine, I do not know, and neither of us knows who is in most need of comfort, she who must go or I who must continue with nobody to comfort me, hold my hand or listen to my troubles, which will continue'' (67).

In this relentlessly melancholic and magical scene is represented the maternal love of both for the other. In this scene is represented one of the deep mysteries of the body—that in psychic space our bodies can lose their boundaries. This is represented by the figure of two hands intertwined, resting in each other, holding each other, a figure which is primarily tactile, not specular, a figure of physical intimacy. The scene is one of pain and consolation. At stake is generational identity, which is bound up with two wishes—to be taken care of by the mother and to care for the child. But if years before the differences were clear, now they are indistinct. Whose hand is holding the other hand? In age, who is the mother? And who is the daughter? At this particular moment, generational identity is experienced most intensely as generational simultaneity.

And in the mirrors of love and suffering which they hold up to each other, are not previous mothers and future daughters reflected there as well?[12] And is not the moment all the more painful because the mirror reflects the future absence of the mother?

In *Waking* it is in the process of losing her mother to death that the daughter finds the "good" mother as if for the first time. In *Waking* the process of reidentification with the mother is represented as taking place at the moment of her dying. But what *kind* of identity is reshaped? Is it predominantly gender identity or generational identity? Would it not be more likely to be the latter since for the daughter the project of motherhood would seem to be coming to an end? Yet this would be too literal, especially because generational identity is defined in terms of caring for others and thus entails mothering. Perhaps both generational and gender identity are so thoroughly intertwined at this point that they cannot be separated. Or, fundamentally, that female gender identity *is* generational identity. But what clearly is at stake at this critical and difficult moment is *not sexual difference* but the relation of *familial resemblance*, of caring. It is not a Freudian Oedipal triangle of sexual difference which resurfaces but the early female triangle of mother/self/child. In this scene the mother and the daughter become once again reflecting mirrors to one another. The death of her mother gives the daughter a new place in the lineage of the family.[13] She becomes the mother.

Figes represents the intensity of the identification of the daughter with her mother in yet another way. With her mother dying, it is as if the daughter takes on her mortal illness as a way of symbolically relieving, or living, her mother's suffering. She grows old and haggard. She looks in the mirror and sees her mother's sickly face: "I do not feel myself. I do not wish to get up and confront the hollow, even slightly horrific face which will look back at me from the glass. Self-hatred. She looks at me with loathing and disgust, the sick face which resembles my mother" (62). At the same time she experiences what she imagines her mother must be feeling—terror at the thought of death. The daughter feels "grey cobwebs of death" gathering around her own now "wintry flesh" (73). As she wakes up each morning, she feels she too must push death away from her: "I rise each morning with a layer of detritus, dead matter, old skin clinging to me, an invisible web of dust, cobwebs, falling hair and the skeletal outline of dried leaves which I cannot shake off" (61). When she was younger she had defiantly declared her separation from her mother, insisting, "I do not want to turn into somebody like her" (28). Now she understands herself not in opposition to her mother but in identification with her. Age itself has shortened the distance between them. She thinks to herself, "I am following behind, just a few years" (68).

At the same time that the daughter panics at being abandoned by her mother, it is as if, to echo Pearl Tull's wish, the daughter does in fact get another mother. The mother in illness and on her deathbed is represented as the all-good symbiotic mother in Mahler's sense, or the ideal mother craved for by the child in Balint's sense, the mother who has no interests of her own, the mother who cares only for her child.[14] As the mother grows thin in illness, her body diminishing in anticipation of its final disappearance, she becomes the mother who appears not to think of herself. Figes: "she is kind and very calm in the white cubicle, between spasms of pain. . . . Since she knows this is the end she has become quite calm, open, her face has a washed look, like the face of a child, it is soothed with relief which makes it easy for us" (67). The mother gives herself up to her child. In her wise way she reassures her middle-aged daughter about her trouble with her teenage daughter: "Yesterday she wanted to know about my daughter, had things improved? I shook my head. It takes time, she whispered" (67). The mother thus prophesies the repetition of the present in the future, offering a healing vision of repetition in generational time. But if this mother-in-death becomes for her daughter the all-good symbiotic mother, it is with an uncancelable difference. For Mahler, "the all-good symbiotic mother was at one time a part of the self in a *blissful state of well-being*" (my italics). In the daughter's middle age we find instead a tormented if poignant anguish in her identification with her mother. The affect is assuredly not one of a blissful state of well-being. In "Three Essays on the Theory of Sexuality" (1905), Freud wrote that the "finding of an object is in fact a refinding" (SE 7: 222). In this scene in this daughter's life, the finding of the all-good mother is in fact a refinding, but it is accompanied by altogether a different affect—by an eloquent pain.

In her thoughts and emotions occasioned by her mother's coming death, the daughter finds not only *her own mother*. The daughter thinks how happy they have been in past years in a commemorative act of reparation.[15] She discovers *herself as a mother* as well.[16] The death of the mother permits the daughter to embrace figuratively her own motherhood just as she literally does her mother. She reevaluates her past moments with her young children and reconstructs herself retrospectively with a moving and binding nostalgia as a mother to small children. The family portrait is one of three generations in harmony. The daughter's mind turns to what seems to her is the only recently developed close friendship with her mother. For the divorced daughter, the moments she and her widowed mother spent together with the children represent happiness. Is this not also what every daughter would wish? A perfect identity of interests between the daughter and the mother as if the difference in their ages has vanished? Together the mother and the daughter formed a couple spanning two generations and existing apart from gender difference even as they talked to-gether as if two women of the same generation (time has collapsed) about what is missing from their lives, the other third term (or should we say the fourth term)—men. As the daughter reflects, "Looking back, how good it was, only a few short years ago. We did not know how good life was. We took the children on outings to the park, we always wanted to lose them for a bit, closed the playroom door, longing for quiet and adult conversation, sat in a haze of smoke and discussed whether a good life was possible, by which we meant love, relationships with men" (71). The reunion is between daughter and mother, with the couple both wanting to be with the children and also to have a room of their own. But here it is a room for women only.

And yet—again in a painful irony—just as the daughter rediscovers her mother at the moment of losing her, her adolescent children reject her with a cold and murderous fury. The adolescent son turns with scorching hostility on the middle-aged daughter of the dying mother: "you are ugly, he tells me, you are hideous and old. . . . Why don't you go away, he asks, and drop into a hole in the ground? Cover yourself up, he says, walking through my door without knocking, your body is disgusting. . . . Why don't you jump out of the window, so I can have this place to myself?" (64–65). Represented here is the desire of the adolescent to murder his parents, a repetition of the daughter's earlier wish to destroy her own mother. But we are given to understand that just as her own mother survived these attacks, so will she survive, and that he too will come to recognize her later for what she is.

What is strong about Figes's representation of the daughter's mother on her deathbed is that she can be read both as a projection of the daughter (an ideal phantasy) and as something real (that is, a woman with whom her daughter shares a reality). These two readings correspond to Winnicott's distinction be-tween object-relating and object-use.[17] For Winnicott, object-relating, which may consist entirely of projective identifications, is prior to object-use. He theorizes that the important capacity for object-use is developed only after the infant has tried to destroy the mother and, finding that the mother has survived aggression, comes finally to understand that the mother exists in her own right. What is important here is that aggression is not a response to external reality but con-tributes instead to the *construction of externality*. Object-usage, Winnicott in-sists, "is a position that can be arrived at by the individual in early stages of emotional growth only through the actual survival of cathected objects that are at the time in process of becoming destroyed because real, becoming real because destroyed."[18] But as *Waking* suggests, this process of emotional growth with parental figures may span many years. For some forty years the daughter had tried to destroy her mother only to finally realize at the moment of her mother's death that her mother had all those years survived her attacks and existed in her own right. Only belatedly does the daughter recognize that the mother has interests of her own. Only in middle age does she learn to *use* her mother, which allows her to rewrite the narrative of her own life as a mother.

If before I have stressed the process of identification, I want here to turn to the process of introjection. I understand the scene in *Waking* of the middle-aged daughter with her dying mother as representing the doubling processes of identification and introjection. In "Group Psychology and Analysis of the Ego" (1921), Freud's first systematic discussion of identification, he distinguishes between identification and introjection this way: "First, identification is the original form of emotional tie with an object; second, in a regressive way it becomes a substitute for a libidinal object tie, as it were by means of introjection of the object into the ego" (SE 18: 107–108). Freud's emphasis on introjection as a compensatory process for the loss of a person we love is extended by Roy Schafer in his excellent book *Aspects of Internalization*. Schafer explains that the motive of identification is the *transformation of the self* in the image of the object; the motive of introjection, *the continuation of the relationship* with the object by putting the object inside. As he puts it, "in introjection, one imagines having what one lacks or may lose; in identification one becomes what one needs."[19]

Implicit in Freudian psychoanalysis is the reactivation of the male Oedipus complex. The middle-aged son identifies with and aggressively turns against the figure of the elderly father. In *Waking* the daughter identifies with her dying mother, whom she also produces as a figure of the all-good ideal mother, a figure she needs. She also introjects this figure of the mother so as to never lose her even as she is being irretrievably lost. Introjection is a way of providing oneself psychically with a sense of continuity and coherence, with the psychic reassurance that the idea of the mother and the ideal mother are indestructible. In introjection a relation with a person who exists in the external world is displaced into the inner world where the figure continues to exist, preserved there, independent of oneself. We may feel, as Schafer has astutely observed, that the introject has the "independent ability to influence us" (83). Both Freud and Schafer underline the regressive or conservative role of the process of introjection. But in the context of *Waking* and in the more general discussion of generational identity, here I would like rather to stress its preservative and progressive role. Introjection is a way of getting another mother.

In *The Hands of the Living God* the psychoanalyst Marion Milner enigmatically suggests that when we as children detach ourselves from the mother, our bodies *psychically* take on the role of the mother. "It is," she writes, "one's own inner body awareness that takes over the role of the external mother; not just in the sense that one learns to do for oneself the external acts of bodily care that one's mother once did, but in this sense of fashioning a kind of psychic sphere or a new womb out of one's own body image, as being the only secure place to inhabit, from which to put one's feelers to the world."[20] May we not say that in this last possible moment of identification we subtly fashion a new kind of potent psychic space, which is the opposite of the crypt in Nicholas Abraham's sense?[21] This would be one way of understanding the compelling claim Pontalis makes in his essay "Between the Dream as Object and the Dream-Text": "the *absent* mother makes our *inside*."[22]

With development, psychic processes are increasingly interiorized. Secondary-process thought gains ascendancy over primary-process thought. A corollary of this is that we speak less as we grow older.[23] "I have become unused to speech," the daughter, now an old woman, thinks (81). In early old age she chooses solitude. She lives alone in her house with her dreams. She attends to the small details of the everyday, creating the world through the acts of the imagination, giving color to what is now for her the gray world, flat as a "faded photograph." There is an impressive strength in the will of her mind. The days, she thinks to herself, "will not remain grey. I have learnt to colour them, like a child with a colouring book. That is the secret" (79).

But if a dimension of her psychic life is recuperated through the efforts of the imagination, what of the body? *Waking* represents this woman's life from middle age on as a continual and increasingly difficult effort to assemble the parts of the ever-fragmenting body. The problem is how the daughter can *inhabit her own body*. In late middle age (in *Waking* aging is presented as a disease), the daughter wakes up each morning to find that she must unite the parts of her body into a whole. The body is figured as inanimate, lifeless, in shreds. "Somewhere under the covers lie the remnants of a body, with a little or no life" (60). The process of aging as decline is portrayed as irreversible. In early old age the body is represented as so close to death that it must be daily "revived" (78). This body is incapable of sexual pleasure. Indeed the erotic is now regarded with complete contempt as if desire were itself an illness, "a virus, an idiotic condition" which she has thankfully survived (79). But in sleep the daughter does experience the palpable memory-feelings of her body when it was alive. Her unconscious, the domain of primary thought, speaks to her of pleasure. In the daily round of everyday life her reason rejects it.

It is significant that the daughter's *memory-dreams*, as I want to call them, refer us to a tactile, not specular, image of the body that has to do with motherhood and sexuality. Figes reminds us that our truly significant memories are not those of an event but those of emotions and feelings which suffuse us with subjectivity. For this daughter it is a tactile bodily subjectivity. It is the memory of the feeling of the body of her infant son in her arms. "How he wriggled to escape my clutches, as a child will do, slithering with his soft buttocks in my palms before I woke and remembered he is a man now" (78), she remembers through her dreams. It is also the feeling of her body in desire for a man.

What is the relationship between the tactile image of the body and the specular image of the body? In the narcissism of adolescence, the daughter is in love with the *sight* of her phantasized and mirrored body and in love with the *sense* of her body in movement. There is, in other words, a perfect congruence between body and psyche in adolescence which is, paradoxically, a potential already fulfilled, for it exists only in fantasy. But ever after throughout her life, she finds that her specular images reflect an unexpected and unfamiliar self back to her, whether it is a woman wild in passion, her hair all disheveled, or the sickly face in middle age which resembles that of her mother. *Waking* suggests that the two rarely if ever coincide throughout the long stretch of time between adulthood and death *except* in images of the fragmenting body.

All space is psychic space. In the end *Waking* presents us with a bleak vision of a woman aging, as solitary and self-confined to a small place as is Beckett's Malone. But the conclusion of the book, which comes to the daughter's death, is rich with a certain promise. It suggests that the daughter, having internalized (or introjected) the mother, has developed strong psychic resources of her own. The seventh and final scene of *Waking*, which begins with violent images of the body fragmenting in death, represents what I take to be that space between the dream and psychic pain to which Pontalis refers,[24] a space permeated with the qualities of primary-process thought which in this case are, as we will see, not regressive in the negative sense, but creative and adaptive.

The interior monologue of the closing scene suggests that the actual drama of the fragmenting body, which is relentlessly chronological and biological, is accompanied by the undertow of the psychic polyvalence of generational positions. The daughter returns to her former selves, first under the sign of abandonment and terror, finally under the aegis of rescue. First she is a young girl cruelly abandoned by her friends and mother, submerged in water, unable to will her body together, pleading, "Mother, won't you come and lift me up?" (83). Then she is a young and desperate mother whose children are lost on the beach while she remains helpless to rescue them. Figes: "My son, I cry out, but before I can utter two words he is swept away. . . . I see my daughter a small child filling her bucket in the dusk and I want to ask, why are you out so late, is it true there is nobody with you, but the black waves come . . . " (84). By the novel's end, the daughter herself has become a child again, as the psychic

narrative of her life has carried her forward and now back, like the waves upon
the shore figured in the chapter—to the mother. Here are the final two sentences
of this moving book:

> And though the night is cool and the tide is creeping silently along the dark damp
> sand and I am not afraid, no, though the wind is rising over the dark horizon,
> the small voice in my head is crying mamma, why do you not come, why have
> you left me alone on the seashore with night coming in all around? But now I
> see a small light bobbing in the dark, it quivers, trembles, is it a spirit, no, the
> light of a fishing boat putting out to sea on the far horizon, no, perhaps a single
> star, the north star, rising in the sky, but no, it is coming nearer, she has come
> for me, she has not forgotten, she holds a torch in her hand, mamma, she has
> come back to the seashore and I am safe, now that she has come to fetch me,
> pick me up and carry me home. (87–88)[25]

Having internalized the mother, having carried her safely inside her, the daughter
is able to deliver up the mother, to care for herself in a world which does not
care for her, to psychically create a maternal supplement to her body and being.[26]

Reciprocity, mutuality, continuity—all are implicit in the notion of generational identity. In an important essay on theories of the life span and women's
lives, the sociologist Alice Rossi argues, "The possibility cannot yet be ruled
out that seeing the self in the other in the same-sex relationship of mothers and
daughters lays the foundation for an important component in women's greater
affiliative tendencies. It may even be that the pivotal role women have played
in extended kinship ties and the special quality of a woman's culture that characterizes the informal networks of female kin or friends whom women so easily
transform into quasi-kin are extrapolations of the unique bond between the
mother and daughter."[27] But in terms of aging in the West, we have for the
most part not provided a social arena for the fulfilling or playing out of generational identity. With differing longevity rates for men and women (women
tend to outlive men by seven years), with the ever-increasing mobility of generations in a family, and with age segregation prevalent in many aspects of our
society, many women will find themselves alone at the end of their lives—or
may fear the possibility of a long solitude imposed on them in old age and, as
it were, *by* old age itself. *Waking* represents this fear in an unflinching way.
Waking takes place within the *psychic* sphere of the family, which in the last
two scenes has contracted to the daughter alone.

We never outgrow the need for a protective figure, and if as old women in
the western world we are alone with no one to help us—no children, no friends,
no men—then we must do what we can do to rescue ourselves. The introjected
object, here the mother, eases that burden. The cycle of identification and
introjection is completed by projection: the projection of the mother onto the

empty space of the world. If Lacanian psychoanalysis emphasizes the originary loss of the object, we see here on the contrary that the primordial mother can never be fully lost. In psychic space the object is immortal.

In the solipsistic amphitheater of the last scene of *Waking*, what we see played out by its absence is the poverty of the social theater. There is no social space for the playing out of identity, however it is constructed. The mid-twentieth-century nuclear family, never a secure source of care for the elderly, has contracted to one, and social institutions, again by implication in this novel, provide no meaning. The painful romance of the final scene is a moving phantasy that provides comfort and consolation to a solitary, suffering, dying old woman—and perhaps to us as well as readers.[28] But however meaningful, it is just that, a phantasy of the all-good mother that concludes a book whose theme is ambivalence about motherhood. Yet are we not always alone with our death? In a sense, but only in a psychic sense, the aged daughter got herself an extra mother.

COUNTER-TEXT

Nine of his original high school class of ninety died in the war. Afterward a Jesuit explained the percentage in this way: the boys had been Catholic, therefore idealistic; they had gone into the service in 1943, when the safe jobs were filled; they had been eighteen or nineteen, too young for special training, which would have delayed combat. When his father died his own doctor watched him closely, explaining that sons sometimes took the deaths of their fathers hard, developing irreversible high blood pressure. Nothing happened immediately, but a year later he became certain that he would die at any moment from a heart attack. He went to bed for two weeks, resenting that his daughters, who were seven and four at the time, would survive him. Later, when he told this to a psychiatrist, the psychiatrist pointed out that most people would have been upset at the thought of not being survived by their children. He took this for a rebuke, and the psychiatrist tried to recall the remark. When he learned on the subway, from a headline in a newspaper held by a weeping black woman, that Kennedy had been shot, for an instant he was glad, although he was an admirer of Kennedy: he had stayed up late many nights to see TV reruns of the press conferences, lifting his beer can or snapping his fingers at Kennedy's wit. . . .

—*from* Charles Simmons, *Wrinkles*
179–82

6. Between Mourning and Melancholia . . .
Roland Barthes's *Camera Lucida*

SCENES OF LOSS AND REUNION succeeded one another in the last chapter as the daughter in *Waking* grew up, grew old, and died. I want to return here to the scene of a mother's death which in that book occurred at the midpoint of a child's life, a return that will bring us ultimately and again to our own deaths when we are old and we are children still. I propose to go principally by way of Barthes's *Camera Lucida*, a book also haunted by a child's loss of his mother. But I will refer to other scenes of loss drawn from Freud (in particular the dream of the ''Burning Child'') and from psychoanalytic accounts of people in later life. In *Waking* we are witness to the palpable *anxiety* suffered by a middle-aged daughter as she watches her mother dying in the hospital and fears what her own life would be like without her. How could she endure that loss? In *Camera Lucida* our focus shifts to the *grief* which has taken hold of a son in his early sixties after his mother has died. After death, as we would say. But is there an *afterdeath*?

We speak of an afterbirth and it strikes me as an odd thing. The afterbirth is what protected and nourished the growing baby. It is what remains after a mother and a child are separated for the first time. The *remains* in fact of a body, or of parts of a body which are no longer necessary. But whose body? Upon reflection the afterbirth seems to have belonged to no body, neither to the body of the mother nor to the body of the child. It was used by them. An organic detritus to which our culture has ascribed no meaning, the afterbirth is cast aside without ceremony. It is thrown away, not buried. And what of an afterdeath? I do not say "afterlife" which is life after death. In the final separation of a child from his mother through death, is there something that remains in psychic terms, something not to be discarded but to be safeguarded in, perhaps, a psychic structure? In funeral rites we inter the dead body, preserving it in a place, investing it and what it represents (including our separation from our dead) with meaning. Wakes and funerals: these are preeminently social rituals, and I will not be concerned with them here. What I am primarily interested in are the emotions associated with loss (grief, longing, sorrow, relief, anxiety), and the psychic process of our separation from someone we have loved. In the last chapter we saw represented in *Waking* the introjection of the figure of the dying mother by the child as constituting a maternal supplement to the psyche. In this chapter I will be more explicitly concerned with the psychic process of separation theorized by Freud and others as mourning.[1]

Retrospectively we read our lives, as does the discourse of psychoanalysis itself, as having been shaped by a rhythm of attachments to and separations from people we have loved. When does separation constitute loss? When is anxiety replaced by grief? More important, perhaps, are these the proper questions to ask? Although we can speak of mourning the loss of an ideal, the loss of our youth, the loss of a possibility in our lives, or the loss of a part of our body, I want to reserve the term "mourning" here for the process of separation following the loss through death of someone we loved. We commonly refer to the deaths of those very "close" to us as "losses." I might say that I have lost my husband, or my grandfather, or my grandmother. Paradoxically this phrase is comforting because it allows us to foreground our role in the story we are telling, to assert a relation, to refer not so much to the event of the death as to what we have suffered by that death, to speak of *our* pain, our grief. And yet anxiety as well as grief is often experienced in mourning, especially perhaps in the loss of a husband or of a wife or of a parent who is not of extreme advanced age. For by asserting we have lost someone, do we not also mean that we *feel lost* ourselves, that in our grief we have lost our sense of direction? Or to insist once more on the emotional tie involved in the relation between two people, that we *have been lost*? That we have been abandoned? Our lives can be broken by such losses. They can also be impelled forward by them.

How do we come to terms (in that pregnant phrase) with the death of someone we love? This is the question Freud explored in "Mourning and Melancholia" (1917), to which we customarily refer as "seminal." By this we mean it is an original piece of work that has been central to the development of research since. And indeed "Mourning and Melancholia" is a founding text. But it has also been a puzzlingly constraining text. Although the bibliography of psychoanalytic investigations of mourning has grown rather lengthy, for the most part discussions of mourning have not developed in a particularly fertile way theoretically.[2] Lacan underscores this in his habitually high-handed manner in an essay on mourning and *Hamlet*. With apparent relish he indicts the psychoanalytic community for "the surcease of all speculation along the path that Freud nevertheless opened up in 'Mourning and Melancholia.' "[3] But in his own long essay, Lacan himself not once refers to any other theoreticians of mourning or to any other research on the subject. Nor in my judgment does he push speculation on mourning in any unusual way.

My disappointment with previous work on mourning, however, has not only or perhaps even primarily to do with the paucity of theoretical elaboration about it. I have wished for a discourse about mourning more expressive than that provided by psychoanalysis, a discourse that would combine the affective dimension of the experience of mourning with theoretical descriptions of mourning as a process. As Kathleen Kirby has written, "It seems that even in psychoanalysis, grief is that which is not or cannot be expressed."[4] In this chapter, then, I turn to first-person accounts and stories which express forms of grief. I also will return to Freud's "Mourning and Melancholia."

As the title of Freud's essay suggests, he took care to distinguish between mourning and melancholia. The distinction has persisted to this day in theoretical discussions and in our conversations in everyday life. In this chapter I want to read the "between" differently. I argue that the distinction between mourning and melancholia has been cut too sharply, that we may point to something *in between* mourning and melancholia, that we may refer to a grief which is interminable but not melancholic in the psychoanalytic sense. Thus I have found myself drawn in *Camera Lucida* to the tableau (it is scarcely even a parable) of Barthes's anguish over his mother's death. I understand it as a figure of *interminable grief*.

Three assumptions, all intertwined, constitute the context of my own discussion. None of them informed Freud's initial speculations on mourning, although some research since has proceeded in some of these directions. They all seek to differentiate a general model of mourning. First, the assumption that we respond differently to the deaths of people to whom we are intimately bound at various times in our lives. There is a good deal of research, for instance, on loss in childhood and adolescence, much of which turns on whether mourning is in fact even possible for a young child.[5] Secondly, the assumption that our responses to the deaths of figures who play different roles in our lives (our parents, our children, our husbands, our wives, our sisters and brothers) will depend in great part on whether those persons can in some measure and in due time be "replaced."[6] Thirdly, the assumption that the process of mourning grows both increasingly more difficult and yet paradoxically more familiar to us as we grow older, as losses inevitably accumulate around us, and as we find ourselves coming closer to death ourselves.[7] Who has not heard the seemingly desultory conversations of friends in their seventies who, reunited after several years, talk almost casually of the lives, which may well be the deaths, of their mutual acquaintances and friends? And what of . . . ? He died last year. Death has become a common occurrence.

Finally, I am prompted by these assumptions to suggest that we may theorize mourning itself differently at various times in our lives.[8] Freud's own confessed experience and commentary confirm that mourning *and* our thoughts about it are subtly differentiated over the life course. Freud wrote "Mourning and Melancholia" when he was fifty-nine. What if he had written it earlier, during the period of his father's debilitating illness and death? Instead he wrote *The Interpretation of Dreams* which he described as his "reaction" to his father's death. As I mentioned in the chapter on Freud, he concluded then that for a son, the death of his father "is the most important event, the most poignant loss, in a man's life" (SE 4: xxvi).[9] It is the word "poignant" which strikes me as inapt, as lacking the complexity and charge of ambivalence. For we know that soon after *The Interpretation of Dreams*, which testifies to Freud's hostility toward his father, Freud developed his theory of the Oedipus complex. It is a theory of desire and aggressivity rooted in particular moments in the life course for both the son and the father: the young son wants to take the place of the middle-aged father.

Or what if Freud had written "Mourning and Melancholia" not when he was in his late fifties but during his advanced old age? I think of the many losses he had to bear throughout his life. One he felt he could not. It was the loss of a four-and-a-half-year-old, his grandson Heinerle who died in 1923 when Freud was sixty-seven. With the death of this child, it was as if for Freud the generations collapsed together and he had lost his own son. Only a year earlier, in fact, his daughter Sophie, Heinerle's mother, had died at the age of twenty-six. But it was the loss of the child who was *still small* which devastated him. It has been said that this is the only time in Freud's life when he cried. Soon after Heinerle's death Freud wrote, "I don't think I have ever experienced such grief. . . . I work out of sheer necessity; fundamentally everything has lost its meaning for me."[10] Two years later he wrote to Marie Bonaparte that he no longer loved anyone.[11] Was it not the death of his small son (I wrote "son" by mistake but it seems exactly right) rather than the death of his father that was the most "poignant" event in his life? And his response in old age? Not aggressivity, or at least not that I can see. Rather an exhausted resignation, deadened affect contained by his attachment to the discipline of work.

What Freud's experience expresses is for our historical period the painful generational tragedy—so acute that it seems almost obscene—of the child dying before the parent. As Freud aged into his seventies, his mother Amalia aged before him, living far into an advanced old age. Ever fearful of his own death (which, as we saw earlier, Freud had felt would be imminent at so many different points in his life), he found the distance between their ages shrinking, as it does as people grow older. I imagine him as a "good" son worrying that he would die before his mother did. And when in fact she did die at ninety-five, at what we might call a ripe old age (a phrase I find offensively cheerful), Freud found her death brought him relief, not pain. He gauged his response. It was "peculiar," he judged. And yet he so astutely grasped the meaning of his response. As he wrote to Sandor Ferenczi about his reaction to his mother's death: it "has affected me in a peculiar way, this great event. No pain, no grief, which probably can be explained by the special circumstance—her great age, my pity for her helplessness toward the end; at the same time a feeling of liberation, of release, which I think I also understand. I was not free to die as long as she was alive, and now I am."[12]

Freud's analysis was wise. In our century with its abundance of resources, we feel that deaths in a family should succeed one another in generational order. If not we are outraged. Also critical was the advanced age of Freud's mother. She was certainly of an age to die. For expected deaths, we often prepare ourselves by anticipatory mourning. But for those who die at a very advanced age, there may be such a subtly incremental separation from them in expectation of their death that we cannot even call it anticipatory mourning. Perhaps in such cases mourning does not take place *either* before *or* after death. The work of mourning is primarily an unconscious process, and perhaps our separation from people of a very advanced age can be effected consciously. I do not mean to say here that Freud did or did not do the work of anticipatory mourning for his mother. But from his own account we may conclude that he consciously felt no grief.

As if in answer to Freud, who had seventy-five years earlier asserted that the death of the father is the most significant event in a man's life, Barthes in *Camera Lucida* mourns not the father but the mother whom he adored. We may take his text as a refusal of Freud's "Mourning and Melancholia" even as it bears it out in some significant ways. Certainly the differences between Freud and Barthes in terms of the deaths of their mothers were immense (but that is part of my point). First, their family structures and their positions within them could scarcely have been more dissimilar. Freud was the *paterfamilias*, the head of a vastly differentiated family of several generations, himself the father of six children. Barthes, in contrast, had never married and had fathered no children. *Camera Lucida* presents Barthes's family as never having grown beyond the originary unit of the mother and child. Secondly, Freud and Barthes occupied different places on that imaginary chronological plumb line that stretches from birth to the upper limit of old age. When his mother died, Barthes did not occupy old age himself in the way that Freud had. Freud was seventy-four when his mother died, and he would live another nine years. Moreover, Freud had suffered severe physical ailments and had himself grown quite frail. Barthes was sixty-five. And yet who was the older of the two?

Freud's purpose in "Mourning and Melancholia" was to investigate not mourning but melancholia. He wanted, he wrote, to use the process of mourning as a foil to understand melancholia: "Dreams having served us as the prototype in normal life of narcissistic disorders, we shall now try to throw some light on the nature of melancholia by comparing it with the normal affect of mourning" (SE 14: 243). The difference between mourning and melancholia is cast in clear-cut binary terms, and this false opposition has paralyzed discussions of mourning ever since. Mourning is defined as "normal." It is psychic work which has a precise purpose and goal: to "free" us from the emotional bonds which have tied us to the person we loved so that we may "invest" that energy elsewhere, to "detach" us so that we may be "uninhibited." Mourning is "necessary." It denotes a process which takes place over a long period of time. It is slow, infinitesimally so, as we simultaneously psychically cling to what has been lost and "test" reality only to discover that the person we loved is no longer there. By "reality" Freud means primarily that we compare our *memories* with what exists in actuality now. He portrays the process of mourning as a passionate or hyperremembering of all the memories bound up with the person we have lost. Mourning is a dizzying phantasmagoria of memory. *Every* memory must be tested. But not only the past is at stake. Also involved is what one had imagined the future might bring. And *each* of those phantasies of the future must be remembered as well. As Freud wrote: "Each single one of the memories and expectations in which the libido is bound to the object is brought up and hypercathected, and detachment of the libido is accomplished in respect of it" (SE 14: 245). While there is something compelling in this description, there is also something equally vague about it. And this is all that Freud could say about the mysterious process of mourning other than that it proceeds little by little as we withdraw our psychic investment from the person we loved. How does mourning "work"? Freud could not tell us. His explanation is that in the passage of time, mourning is "accomplished": "in mourning time is needed for the command of reality-testing to be carried out in detail" (252).

Inarguably for Freud, the most important aspect of this work of mourning is that it must come to an end. As he wrote, "We rely upon its being overcome after a certain lapse in time" (244). Or as he expressed it in the confident and contemporaneous little essay "On Transience" (1916), "Mourning as we know, however painful it may be, comes to a spontaneous end" (SE 14: 307). Thus Freud defined mourning as a way of divesting ourselves of pain, of getting it over and done with. If we speak of a person as being *in* mourning, what inevitably we have in mind in classical Freudian terms is that at some time in the future she, or he, will be *out* of mourning.

For Freud, melancholia by contrast is pathological. It is characterized primarily as a *state*, not a *process*. It is denial of the reality of loss. It is a "disorder," a "disease." Melancholia is ultimately failed, or unsuccessful, mourning. In this unequivocal distinction I find a peculiar kind of piety, an almost ethical injunction to kill the dead and to adjust ourselves to "reality." In "Mourning and Melancholia" Freud leaves us no theoretical room for another place, one between a crippling melancholia and the end of mourning. But some people come to terms with their grief by learning to live with their pain and in such a way that they are still *in* mourning but no longer *exclusively* devoted to mourning.

Although Freud distinguishes between mourning and melancholia, his essay also draws us to the conclusion that they are so intimately related as to be inseparable. If melancholia is failed mourning, then melancholia also may denote our emotional devastation after the death of a person we have loved. In enumerating the affects and behavior associated with melancholia, Freud identifies the characteristics of mourning as well with only one exception—self-reproach (this has been long ago revised by others). "The distinguishing mental features of melancholia," he writes, "are a profoundly painful dejection, cessation of interest in the outside world, loss of the capacity to love, inhibition of all activity, and a lowering of the self-regarding feelings to a degree that finds utterance in self-reproaches and self-revilings, and culminates in a delusional expectation of punishment" (SE 14: 244). These are also the aspects of grief. Or as the psychoanalyst Karl Abraham, Freud's contemporary, succinctly puts it, "melancholia is an archaic form of mourning."[13] If the specificity of Freud's essay inheres in its theorization of melancholia, Freud also accurately delineates aspects of mourning. Yet his discussion does not seem sufficiently informed by an experience of mourning or study of it.

I do not mean to indict Freud here. But when I turn to a piece he wrote a good many years later, I find him posing another question and introducing another dimension into the discussion of mourning. It is as if he had now come up against the facticity of pain suffered in losing someone. It was not until the end of his life that Freud recognized that the "key to an understanding of anxiety" is "missing someone who is loved and longed for" (SE 20: 137, 136). Freud distinguished between pain and anxiety this way: "Pain is thus the actual reaction to loss of object, while anxiety is the reaction to the danger which that loss entails and, by a further displacement, a reaction to the danger of the loss of object itself" (SE 20: 170). In an addendum to *Inhibitions, Symptoms and Anxiety* (1926) published when he was seventy, he asks: "when does separation from an object produce anxiety, when does it produce mourning and when does it produce, it may be, only pain?" (SE 20: 169).[14] Unfortunately Freud does not pursue the question. Instead he submits that he understands very little of the "economics" of pain, although he tellingly couches his discussion in terms of a young child's relation to his mother. These few pages are marked by Freud's ungainly and pseudo-scientific metaphor of pain as breaking and entering the body ("pain occurs . . . whenever a stimulus which impinges on the periphery breaks through the devices of the protective shield against stimuli and proceeds to act like a continuous instinctual stimulus" [170]). But as I read these pages I am reminded of his own psychic pain (not anxiety, not mourning) suffered over the death of his grandson only a few years before. In earlier defining mourning as synonymous with our giving up of the dead, Freud had not understood or foreseen the psychic pain that could be entailed in loss. André Green comes closer in his splendid essay "Le Temps mort." "What is truly terrible about mourning," he writes, "is that we know one day we will have forgotten everything."[15] But Green is still adhering to Freud's classical definition of mourning as relinquishing the dead, which implies finding a surrogate or substitute. Only then would we have forgotten everything.

The sentimental strength of *Camera Lucida,* ostensibly a book on photography, inheres in Barthes's figuration and meditation on his grief in the wake of his mother's death.[16] The text, defined as its contents and as a tangible object, represents the possibility of a response to loss that situates itself between mourning and melancholia. The book itself embodies a resistance to mourning which entails a kind of willed refusal to relinquish pain. Rejecting our conventional notion of mourning as it has come to us from Freud's essay on mourning and melancholia, Barthes makes a subtle distinction between pain and emotion: "It is said that mourning, by its gradual labor, slowly erases pain; I could not, I cannot believe this; because for me, Time eliminates the emotion of loss (I do not weep), that is all. For the rest everything has remained motionless" (75). Over time, he believes, what subsides are the emotions of grief, its wild flourishes (those associated with *Hamlet*'s Laertes, for example).[17] The emotions (what were they? despair? a sense of abandonment? Barthes does not tell us) have emptied themselves out, leaving him vacant and hollow and numbed. He has come to a dead stop. "For the rest everything has remained motionless." Does this not recall Freud's response to the death of his grandson?

Barthes insists on the particularity, the historicity, of his loss. He refuses to assimilate his loss to an abstraction, a generality, or even to the family structure. What he has lost, he writes, is "not a Figure (the Mother), but a being" (75). He will not even say here *his mother*. And he will qualify this further, so that even when he will have survived her death, his life nonetheless will remain impoverished. It is a kind of vow. What he has lost, he writes, is "not a being, but a *quality* (a soul): not the indispensable, but the irreplaceable. I could live without the Mother (as we all do, sooner or later); but what life remained would be absolutely and entirely *unqualifiable* (without quality)" (75).

In his meditation on photography, Barthes seeks to theorize subjectivity in relation to a photograph. It is as if he is theorizing the possibility of sustaining the in-between of mourning and melancholia. A photograph is motionless, he says, like his pain. Yet he wants to locate the *production* of affect in his relation to a photograph that holds emotional power for him. Affect, he writes, "was what I didn't want to reduce; being irreducible, it was thereby what I wanted, what I ought to reduce the Photograph *to*; but could I retain an affective intentionality, a view of the object which was immediately steeped in desire, revulsion, nostalgia, euphoria?" (21). He imagines a photograph will renew his numbing pain over his mother's death.

But which photograph? How can Barthes sustain "an affective intentionality" (this is a phrase which should somehow be awkward but is for me almost lovely)? The gesture of lingering over old photographs of a person after his death is a familiar one.[18] I have known children in mourning after their father's death to become frantic in their search for photographs of him. After the memorial service for my paternal grandmother, I remember feeling moved and honored when I was chosen to have the photographs of her; I also remember my doubled-over sense of loss and guilt when I left them for lost in a cab only a few hours later. In *Camera Lucida* we see Barthes in one of the few novelistic scenes alone at night in the room where his mother had died, sifting through photographs of her, looking for the one photograph which will express the quality he insists is unique to her: "the assertion of a gentleness" (69). We see him gradually moving back in time with her. The goal of this "gradual labor" is not to come to the end of mourning but to sustain it. The finding of the photograph—it is a photograph of his mother taken in a garden—and his writing of that scene do not serve to sublimate his pain but to seal it. This is what he wants (but we could not call it desire). He asks us to imagine him alone, gazing at the photograph of his mother: "The circle is closed, there is no escape. I suffer motionless. . . . I cannot *transform* my grief" (90). Nor does he wish to.

Mourning is a process that takes place unconsciously. As Freud and others have described it and as we saw earlier in my discussion of *Waking*, part of the process is the psychic taking into ourselves, the *internalization*, of the figure of the person we mourn. But in Barthes's gesture of *externalizing* the figure of his mother, he undertakes to block the work of mourning. We can read "I cannot transform my grief" as "I will not."[19] Thus my understanding of the representation of mourning in *Camera Lucida* with its emphasis on exteriorization goes counter to (but does not preclude for others) Nicholas Abraham and Maria Torok's explanation of the process at work in the inability to mourn. To the process of introjection in so-called normal mourning, they propose the process of *incorporation* in an impossible mourning. Their suggestive metaphor is that of the split-off crypt located psychically inside the body and containing what cannot be forgotten, or in Jacques Derrida's words in "Fors," "the very thing that provokes the worst suffering" (98). What is contained is a "secret" constituted out of "intolerable pain" (69). Of Abraham and Torok's theory of mourning refused, Derrida explains: "I pretend to keep the dead alive, intact, *safe (save) inside me*, but it is only in order to refuse, in a necessarily equivocal way, to love the dead as a living part of me, dead *save in me*, through the process of introjection, as happens in so-called 'normal' mourning. . . . Faced with the impotence of the process of introjection (gradual, slow, laborious, mediated, effective), incorporation is the only choice: fantasmatic, unmediated, instantaneous, magical, sometimes hallucinatory" (71). Cryptic incorporation is a secret process that "marks the effect of impossible or refused mourning" (78). It is hidden from oneself. But Barthes wishes to keep his pain no secret. In concretizing the production of his pain in relation to a photograph (not a fetish, not a transitional object), he seeks to remain in mourning, to retain his psychic pain. Pontalis has described psychic pain as referring to a state halfway between anxiety and attachment to others.[20] We may conclude here that it occupies a middle position *in between* mourning and melancholia.

In an essay on Paul de Man written after his death and after the disclosure of events in his life which have compelled us to alter our memory of him, Derrida asks, "What is an impossible mourning?" "What does it tell us, this impossible mourning, about an essence of memory?"[21] These are pregnant questions, and if Derrida did not answer them and if I cannot, still they open up space for meditation and speculation. One way of understanding an "impossible mourning" is as interminable grief. We could wonder then if the "essence" of a memory of someone would not have to be that which we could *not* remember, never having known it. I am thinking of the fact that Barthes came finally to rest, motionless, before a photograph of his mother taken years before he was born when she was only five years old, just a little older than Freud's grandson when he died.

I understand the attraction to these old photographs. We can experience a kind of wonder in front of them: these people who grew so old were once so young! Photographs like these require us to stretch our imagination over a long span of years. They enable us to possess what we did not know. Thus fittingly and creatively, Barthes chooses a photograph of his mother which *represents* his memory of her. It does not serve to restore to his memory a specific event or experience he had with his mother. In *Camera Lucida* grieving is not represented in terms of a Freudian hypercathexis of memories of the person lost to death. Barthes writes, "The Photograph does not call up the past (nothing Proustian in a photograph)" (82). "Not only is the photograph never, in essence, a memory . . . but it actually blocks memory, quickly becomes a counter-memory" (91). The "essence" of memory then? It is rooted not in the actual but in the imaginary. This particular photograph of his mother is a kind of imaginary *afterimage* which takes on value in its materialization after death.

This particular photograph is not a *souvenir*, one of whose purposes is, as Susan Stewart has written, to restore the past, most often to "evoke a voluntary memory of childhood."[22] Nor, although it is a concrete object, does it fulfill the function of a transitional object, about which I will say more in the chapter on Beckett's *Malone Dies*. This photograph is not a talisman. It does not provide comfort or serve to support the child in his separation from what he has lost, to transform his grief. Its purpose is to reinforce it.

As many have observed, Barthes does not publish the photograph in his book. To do so would have been to deny the "essence of memory" which the photograph represents and to reduce it to the status of a document, somehow converting his book itself into a souvenir. With the mass production of the book, with all of our reading eyes looking curiously at that photograph, it would come to be possessed by us, reduced to a cultural icon, a sign of sentimentality in an age of mass culture. The photograph remains a secret: it is a secret because Barthes both will not show it to us *and* has told us about it. The photograph he has kept to himself and for himself. In this gesture, as in Woolf's portrayal of the dreaming Eleanor, I see confirmed Winnicott's theory that "in the healthy person there is the need for something that corresponds to the state of the split person in whom one part of the split communicates silently with subjective objects."[23]

Pontalis opens his recent essay "Perdre de vue" with the following story which I take to be about Barthes in grief:

A man who since his youth had devoted his life to philosophical inquiry, a man of literature and ideas who had had, he confessed, the rare opportunity to make what he loved doing his life's work, lost his mother. For many years she had suffered physically. In the banality that surfaces at such times a close friend said, hoping to ease his pain: you loved her so much, remember that she is no longer suffering. He answered with an anger surprising in such a gentle man: "But you don't understand. I will never see her again!" The philosopher knew that imaginary conversations would pursue him, he even had the presentiment that from then on his thinking and writing would be suspended from her vanishing. But pain and only pain remained: *he would never see her again.* And never seeing her, he would never be seen by her.[24]

Pontalis's deft remark is deeply discerning. What is lost to Barthes is the gaze of his mother, a loss that can never be compensated by the internalization of the figure of the mother. What is irretrievable is a mutual mirroring. In the light of this story it seems no coincidence that Barthes would have chosen photography as mourning as his theme and a photograph of his mother looking at the camera eye as his sacred object.

Camera Lucida is haunted by a kind of death-work. Barthes makes it painfully clear that this photograph is a condensation of all deaths across the generations—of the child he never had, of his mother's death, of his own death. As Barthes nursed his mother into her death, she became his "feminized child," as did the daughter's mother in *Waking.* As he looks at the photograph he thinks, "the only 'thought' I can have is that at the end of this first death, my own death is inscribed" (92–93). If the mother is the mirror for the infant, this photograph of his mother, still a child herself, shows him his death, the death of the man who is not yet born. Not just in the ontological sense that death will come to all of us in due time but in a more literal way. Inscribed in the photograph of his mother is the genetic code of his family, "the truth of lineage," as he puts it (103). Gazing into the photograph of his mother as a young child, Barthes sees into the future which is old age. "The Photograph," he writes, "is like old age: even in its splendor, it disincarnates the face, manifests its genetic essence" (105). In old age we are increasingly dispossessed of our bodies. What remains is the idea of that body, an essence of genetic generational memory (this recalls the image which I invoked in the Introduction of Loren Eiseley gazing at his mother's old body and finding his future reflected in it).

The photograph represents the catastrophe of death, which is its repetition. In an almost Freudian way, Barthes forces himself to feel that our bodies carry death in them. "In front of the photograph of my mother as a child," he writes, "I tell myself: she is going to die: I shudder, like Winnicott's psychotic patient, *over a catastrophe which has already occurred*" (96). In the apartment that had belonged to his mother and in the space of his book, Barthes imagines for himself the repetition of the catastrophe, replaying it over and over in his mind, reliving the death which has already occurred, witnessing and producing his own loss.

So we have come unexpectedly to this: the image of the mother speaks not of security but of death. The loss of the mother entails the loss of ourselves. *Camera Lucida* is like a meditative theoretical dream whose purpose is the fulfillment of a wish. If Barthes will not abandon his mother, then in a sense he can't be lost. This recalls Lacan's haunting analysis of the first question a child asks of his parents. It is an inversion of the question implied in the *fort-da*, the young child's symbolization through play of the departure and return of the mother. In symbolically controlling the absence and presence of the mother, the child is asking the second question: can I lose my mother? But the first question is: can my mother or father lose me? Or we could put it this way: *what do my parents want*? Do they want me? In Lacanian psychoanalysis the anxiety of abandonment arises out of the dialectical structure of parental desire. In "The Subject and the Other: Alienation" (1964) Lacan insists that the first object that the child "proposes for this parental desire whose object is unknown is his own loss—Can he lose me? The phantasy of one's own death, of one's disappearance is the first object that the subject has to bring into play in this dialectic" (*FF* 214).

If there is a dialectic at work in the family structure of parent and child, so there is a dialectic in the emotions associated with it—anxiety and grief. In the nightmare of what has come to be called the "Burning Child" dream, first reported by Freud in *The Interpretation of Dreams*, we find a conflation (a conflagration?) of several scenarios: the *anxiety* of both child and parent linked to the threat of abandonment or to separation through death, and the *grief* linked to the death of one's child. Can my father lose me? Have I lost my child? I am lost because I have lost my child. Much of the power of the dream of the "Burning Child" inheres in this unbearable oscillation between anxiety and grief, grief and anxiety. The dream of the "Burning Child" is thus also a kind of inversion of the Barthesian tableau of a son grieving for his mother. Both testify to the pain associated with overwhelming grief—the dream of the "Burning Child" to a father's loss of his young son, *Camera Lucida* to an aging son's loss of his mother.

Freud recounts the dream of the "Burning Child" at the very beginning of chapter seven in *The Interpretation of Dreams*. It is a dream which one of his patients had heard in a lecture and repeated to Freud. Freud repeats the dream. Later Lacan and others repeat the dream. So here do I.[25] I quote Freud:

A father had been watching beside his child's sick-bed for days and nights on end. After the child had died, he went into the next room to lie down, but left the door open so that he could see from his bedroom into the room in which his child's body was laid out, with tall candles standing round it. An old man had been engaged to keep watch over it, and sat beside the body murmuring prayers. After a few hours' sleep, the father had a dream that *his child was standing beside his bed, caught him by the arm and whispered to him reproachfully: "Father, don't you see I'm burning?"* He woke up, noticed a bright glare of light from the next room, hurried into it and found that the old watchman had dropped off to sleep and that the wrappings and one of the arms of his beloved child's dead body had been burned by a lighted candle that had fallen on them. (SE 5: 509)

We repeat (that is, retell) this story for different reasons. I return to the nightmare because it rehearses grief in a way that Freud's essay "Mourning and Melancholia" could not. The scene is preeminently threatening, saturated with the emotions of fear, guilt, anger, and grief. I repeat it because it expresses an anxiety that I suspect is shared today by every parent of a young child: my child might die. But the powerful hold this nightmare has on us has to do with the fact that in this drama we identify (unconsciously perhaps) with every one of the characters. They represent age as it is distributed over the life course from youth to old age. Each of the three characters is represented in a deathlike sleep (the father, the watchman) or in a sleeplike death (the son wakes up from death in a kind of afterlife). At the center of the oscillation between anxiety and grief, between sleep and death, is the dead body, which is strangely missing. We have learned from Freud to repeat that death cannot be represented in the *mise-en-scène* of the unconscious. But the dead body represents death. It is a dead body that is an insupportable reality. We have a different word for it—a corpse. We comfort ourselves with the sentimental notion that the dead "repose" in peace. For if they are at peace, then perhaps we also can be at rest. This is one of the reasons why the return of the figure of the burning child may call to mind the return of the Ghost of the father in *Hamlet*. Remember me, intones the Ghost. You've forgotten me, reproaches the child. But nothing is further from the truth. Interminable grief has been set in motion.

Why did Freud feel compelled to tell the dream of the "Burning Child"? He says it is a dream which does not present any obvious problems of interpretation (that in itself is a problem for Freud, since *The Interpretation of Dreams* is devoted to the work of elucidating the way in which dreams express our repressed, unconscious wishes). Freud will argue that nonetheless the "Burning Child" dream does obey the law of dreams: it fulfills the wish that the child were alive, not dead. In his matter-of-fact conclusion, which is not so much analytically forced as it is lacking in affect, we see again how much Freudian psychoanalysis consciously accents desire at the expense of an analysis of anxiety or grief.

Following Freud, commentators on the dream of the "Burning Child" have surrounded the dream with discussions of issues that seem far from the emotional drama presented by the dream—its *mise-en-scène* of stabbing grief.[26] Lacan comes closest to the heart of the dream in "Tuché and Automaton" when he refers to the pain as unspeakable: "no one can say what the death of a child is, except the father *qua* father, that is to say, no conscious being" (*FF* 59). He writes, "perhaps these words perpetuate the remorse felt by the father" (*FF* 58). Yet Lacan also seems self-consciously flamboyant here.[27] I suspect this unintentional conspiracy of silence is a defense against the subject of grief and mourning, a defense which takes the form of intellectuality. We have avoided the pain of the manifest content of the dream. We do not know how to respond adequately to someone else's anguish in grief, or even to a representation of such personal devastation. Perhaps at times the best we can do is to remain silent and to allow the grief to be expressed or performed, which may mean in the context of critical discourse to *present* the text of grief. In "The Work of Art in the Age of Mechanical Reproduction" Walter Benjamin wrote, "In all mourning there is a tendency to silence, and this infinitely more than inability or reluctance to communicate. The mournful has the feeling that it is known comprehensively by the unknowable."[28] Even more silence characterizes the part of the person who listens, and who often does not hear.

If response to grief assumes two different discourses,[29] similarly *Camera Lucida* is a split text. Barthes surrounds the figuration of his grief with theoretical meditations on photography. He acknowledges his "uneasiness" (he puts it gently) with being "torn between two languages, one expressive, the other critical" (8). He invents awkward and precious terms—the punctum, the pensum, the studium—which distract us from what they are meant to refer to. What I remember of *Camera Lucida* is the tableau of grief. What I forget is Barthes's vocabulary of photography. But Barthes can also write movingly of mourning and photography together: "there [is] in every photograph: the return of the dead" (9). Anxiety and grief, endlessly repeated.

As Freud defines mourning, its aim is our adaptation to "reality." The metaphor is that of detaching binding ties, of undoing ties that bind and constrict. "The complex of melancholia," he wrote, "behaves like an open wound" (SE 14: 253). For Freud the work of mourning is the work of healing a wound. It is a rite of passage out of death and into reality. In *Camera Lucida* Barthes explored photography as a "wound," as a way of *refusing* to allow the wound of his mother's death to heal (21). In *Camera Lucida* Barthes etches his own death with the tones of fatality. "From now on I could do no more than await my total, undialectical Death,'' he wrote (72). As we know, in what was to be an uncanny and tragic coincidence, Barthes died in an automobile accident the very year that *Camera Lucida* was published.

Barthes's death is thus present for me in his words just as his mother's death was for him in the photograph of her as a little girl. Paul de Man's chilling reflection on reading Shelley's *The Triumph of Life* in the context of death is relevant here. ''The final test of reading, in *The Triumph of Life*,'' he wrote, ''depends on how one reads the textuality of this event, how one disposes of Shelley's body.''[30] To the event of Barthes's death I prefer to respond with the assertion of a gentleness, to sustain its poignancy, not to dispose of the body. In part that means pursuing the relation between aging, grief, and death.

We will never know if Barthes would have been able to sustain his grief. Nor would we have necessarily wanted to hold him to his vow. He died soon after his mother died, and he died at a relatively young age—sixty-five. For all that and perhaps because of it, I take the tableau of Barthes in mourning for his mother as *representing the limit in old age of coming to terms with our losses*. In loss and at the upper limit in old age (which will be different for every person), we may not want to ''free'' ourselves from the emotional bonds which have secured us to others we have loved so that we may ''invest'' our energy elsewhere. We do not detach ourselves from our losses. Instead we live with them. And then we die with them. If grief is painful, it is also absorbing.

The notion of attachment to life is commonly cast metaphorically in terms of bonds, ties, and threads. When we speak of detachment in old age, of the loosening of bonds to life, I think we may mistake the process at work. It may be not that we are detaching ourselves from others but that we have refused to untie the bonds which have attached us to those we have lost. We may begin to live with the dead. As the distinguished theologian Joseph Sittler observed, speaking feelingly through his own experience when he was eighty-two, ''Most of old age is a kind of ministerial to death. . . . Life is constituted by multiple webs of relationships. When a web breaks with the death of a family member or a friend, you receive a kind of tender, ministerial preparation for your own death.''[31] For Sittler, the loss of others helps to loosen the bonds to our own life. François Mauriac used the metaphor similarly: ''this preparation for death is indistinguishable from detachment. To prepare for death is to untie one by one all the bonds that hold us, it is to break as many moorings as possible, so that if the wind suddenly rises, it will bear us away without our putting up any resistance.''[32] But some attachments remain binding phantasmatically.

As *Camera Lucida* suggests, with some losses mourning may never come to an end. We may remain *in between* mourning and melancholy. I do not mean of course that this may be characteristic of grief in advanced old age only. I am thinking also of a parent losing a young child, or perhaps a child of any age. For the Freud of "Mourning and Melancholia," the end of mourning is concurrent with the understanding that our life must be reshaped through new attachments. But a life can be reshaped around the loss, around a sustaining pain. It often also cannot. Who has not heard of older people who have died not long after the deaths of their spouses?

Almost a decade before his essay on mourning and melancholia, Freud remarked presciently in "Creative Writers and Day-Dreaming" (1908), "we can never give anything up; we only exchange one thing for another. What appears to be a renunciation is really the formation of a substitute or surrogate" (SE 9: 145). However, he later cautioned that mourning was age-specific. In "On Transience" he wrote that when mourning "has renounced everything that has been lost, then it has consumed itself, and our libido is once more free (*in so far as we are still young and active*) to replace the lost objects by fresh ones equally or still more precious" (SE 14: 307, italics mine). Freud never pursued the implications of these important parenthetical thoughts where he associated the completion of the process of mourning with those who are young and active.

But we are led to conclude that in advanced old age the lifelong cycle of loss and restitution which has characterized our lives may come to an end.[33] Loss may yield only interminable grief. For when we are very old, we *might not wish to* "replace" what we have lost. And if we are very young or middle-aged, why should we insist of those older that out of some sort of moral necessity fashioned in the image of our own age they should relinquish their lives as they have lived them? Of his mother's death Barthes wrote in *Camera Lucida*, "at the end of this first death, my own death is inscribed" (93). Even before that book he had written of himself as old and tired. "I abandon the exhausting pursuit of myself, I do not try to *restore* myself (as we say of a monument)," he wrote in *Roland Barthes by Roland Barthes*.[34] He thought of himself—he represented himself—in Proustian terms. For him it was the odor of something which called up an involuntary memory linked to "desire, death, the impossible return" (135). "I recall odors with a certain mad intensity," he wrote, "because I am growing old" (136).

Barthes's wish was to forever seal the affect of grief, to render it immovable, unchangeable, unalterable, immutable. But his writing hand was moving across the page to achieve this effect of motionlessness. His grief was expressed creatively. In *Camera Lucida* Barthes turned to what was for him a new kind of writing. There is a surprising risk in his rhetoric of self-expression and a near self-indulgence in metaphor which earlier in his career he had denied. There is a stunning strength in his willful resistance to the teleology of mourning which takes the form of neither denial nor negation. With *Camera Lucida* as our text we may conclude that the refusal to allow mourning to run its so-called normal course can vivify and not impoverish a life. But loss may also be succeeded by impoverishment. And mourning may be intimately linked to self-aggression. And at its limit, grief (I now include the mourning of one's own coming death) may devolve into anxiety.

Barthes wrote in *Camera Lucida* that a "sort of umbilical cord links the body of the photographed thing to my gaze" (81). He was unembarrassed by this metaphor. As he had written earlier in *Roland Barthes by Roland Barthes*, "when he loved his mother . . . he was unfashionable" (125). For him, she was irreplaceable. For him the mother could never be fully mourned. As in the previous chapter, then, I find myself as I near the end of this chapter returning to the return of the mother. I do so reluctantly. Reluctantly because consciously if not self-consciously, I have considered the relatively recent and often romantic emphasis on the mother a largely sentimental and unsustainable utopian (if not fantastic) note in psychoanalysis. But Barthes's wish in *Camera Lucida* is to speak not on behalf of a theoretical discourse but of his personal pain. Earlier in *A Lover's Discourse* he wrote, "I love you has no 'elsewhere'—it is the word of the (maternal, amorous) dyad."[35] Coming from Barthes, we cannot take his "unfashionable" pronouncement as symptomatic of an uncritical romance with the theoretical pre-Oedipal mother. Later in *Camera Lucida* we find a *conscious* refusal to give up what the mother represents. But what does the unconscious speak? At the end of life, as we saw also in the last chapter, the unconscious often speaks of the maternal, amorous dyad, of the mother and child.

Charlotte Herfray, a French psychoanalyst who has worked with elderly people in nursing homes, has observed that the language of many old people on the edge of death is marked by the metaphors of arriving, of returning, of being called home, and of being found. She reads these metaphors as traces of *la langue maternelle* which stems from the originary word "mother." Such metaphors express the wish to return to one's phantasmatic beginnings in love. But the referent is real as well. The "mother" represents actual care which we all needed in infancy and childhood and which is urgently longed for and needed by many in old age as well. Herfray tells this poignant and striking story of an old woman near ninety whom she had seen regularly for several years:

> One day—it was Mother's Day—the very depth of her sorrow took me by surprise. She collapsed crying in my arms, telling me, "I'm so unhappy." Why, I asked. She began to recite this sentence as if it were a poem she had learned by heart. "If you still have a mother, *rejouis-toi*." The word *rejouir* is startling because it contains the signifier *jouir*. Mother's Day: a symbolic reminder of that happiness, *rejouissance*, which no longer existed. In tears, this woman wasn't

able to tell me anything else about what had overcome her on the last Mother's Day she was to live to see. Yet she had not forgotten that it was a holiday. "Mother's Day": for her this connoted the nadir of absence in her life. She died several weeks later—on the day of her mother's birthday.[36]

Michèle Grosclaude, a psychoanalyst who has treated elderly patients with senile dementia, has suggested that a person's deepest concerns continue to be expressed through even the most extreme deformations of memory imposed by this ravaging disease. Subjectivity continues to be voiced in the way in which one chooses objects, including words. She argues that the objects which are selected represent a return back through the arc of one's life to the first object of love. In a very real sense the central story of one's life—the psychic problematic one has been working out and working through during the course of one's life—can be condensed in that object or group of objects. Thus the return is not to be understood as a simple regression to infancy in a negative sense. Grief, desire, death, loss, *jouissance*, remembrance of things past—all figure in a brief case history reported by Grosclaude of a seventy-five-year-old woman who suffered from dementia. It is also a story about an elderly child and a mother. As different as her story is from the story I have told of Barthes, the two resonate in an almost uncanny way.

This woman (Mrs. M) was vigorous until her husband died. Within days of his death she was diagnosed as suffering from acute senile dementia. She did not recognize anyone close to her and returned to using her native tongue, which she had not spoken since she was five. She hallucinated various objects, among them photographs of herself as a five-year-old with her parents which she "saw" in the flowered wallpaper of the nursing home. For Grosclaude the telling detail is this: Mrs. M brings her a washbasin (*lavabo*), calling it a cradle (*berceau*).

This woman had never had children. The continuing psychic drama of her life, concludes Grosclaude, constellated itself around the uncertain location and identity of mother and child. Grosclaude interprets Mrs. M's act of bringing her the *lavabo* as the act of a child: she shows something to which she is attached to the "mother," asserting a return between a person who is present and a person who is absent. Grosclaude delicately reads in the word "cradle" the anguish, doubled over, for the lost child. Who is missing? The child who was never born? The child Mrs. M once was? And, I would add, the mother who never was?

This scene of loss takes shape around an object, a washbasin I imagine to be a porcelain-white curved basin, and a word, "cradle," which represents shelter for those who are in need of care. It calls up another scene. At a conference on geriatric psychiatry, Yannick Rimbert, a nurse who had been taking care of people in a hospice for two years, was asked to tell how she saw her patients to their deaths. She answered with this story:

> Yvonne died at eleven o'clock one night several weeks ago, no, several months ago. Her room was at the end of the corridor. Behind the door to her room there she was in a large armchair, a seventy-year-old woman, slight, fragile, frail, her body emptied out and aged by cancer of the bone. She suffered immensely. But her will to live would not allow me to help her. From the armchair to the bed, back and forth she slowly pulled her legs, which were all purplish and stiff.
>
> "Wait, I will get there."
>
> Tonight she is tired, and she collapses. I hurry to her. She can hardly talk. I carry her in my arms as if she were my child. Carefully I lay her down. Her entire body speaks of suffering. She rests. . . .
>
> "Yvonne, do you want me to call your family?"
>
> "Yes," she says, "but hurry. . . . "
>
> Nine o'clock. The family still isn't here.
>
> "I'm hungry, I'm cold. . . . "
>
> I take a damp cloth and press it to her lips. Her head is heavy. Her face grows emptier and emptier. Her large blue eyes are still there. They look at me. . . . She can no longer speak. . . .
>
> "Yvonne, does it hurt?"
>
> No answer. There is, it seems to me, a smile on her lips.
>
> Very carefully I lie down next to her. I gather her gently in my arms, as if to protect her, and little by little I realize that I am rocking her.
>
> There is in her blue eyes a deep sense of peace. Then her eyes close.
>
> She has trouble breathing. I cry for this woman who for these years knew how to express her love of life. In dying she left me her youth, her songs, her very past, for in my eyes her youth was always present. Then she died.[37]

Winnicott once astutely remarked that there is no such thing as a baby. What he meant is that wherever you find a baby you will also find a mother, the person who cares for the baby. The "cradle" of Mrs. M implies not just a baby but a mother to rock the cradle. Why should Yvonne not wish for the return of the mother, the person who will care for her, so vulnerable now in old age? If the mother and the father are among the figures in our lives who can never be replaced, still present in this scene is a surrogate figure, not a person to whom she is attached in the same way, but a person who cradles her in a tender ministerial to death, a woman in grief who mourns as if for her mother.

COUNTER-TEXT

Sitting next to me was a beautiful woman of about fifty who resembled a red apple that has been preserved and, although wrinkled, has kept its flavor.

"This is the photograph album of my father's and mother's generation, poor things. When their things were divided up among the children, I received the album. I keep it as a remembrance."

"Who's this woman?" I asked, pointing to the picture of a pretty young woman wearing a white veil, with a garland of flowers around her head and a Mass book in her hands.

"My mother, on the day of her First Communion." . . .

"Is she dead?"

"She's been dead for a long time, she died even before my father. Now she'd be more than eighty years old."

"What was her name?"

The woman hesitated a moment, almost as if she had to think back, then she hurriedly answered, "Fabiola. An unusual name. If it weren't my mother's, I wouldn't be able to remember it." . . .

One morning, while getting out of bed, Fabiola realized that time, which she had forgotten, had never forgotten her and now it was encircling her in so tight and slow a flight that she could count the revolutions. She was infinitely weary and only the earth's bosom could offer her weariness adequate rest.

Time flew about her name for an instant, then it went beyond, taking her memory from the heart of even her youngest daughter, whom she'd loved with all consuming love, and who now had to think back in her memory in order to remember that her mother's name was Fabiola.

—*from* Clarice Tartufari, "A Story,
Perhaps Lived"

7. The Transitional Object
of the Oldest Age . . .
Samuel Beckett's *Malone Dies*

THE LAST CHAPTER ENDED with a generational variation on the figure of the pietà: a younger woman cradling the body of an old woman through the transition from life into death, a woman whom the nurse mourns publicly in speech and in writing. The psychoanalyst Phyllis Greenacre has suggested that this maternal rocking eases our earliest transition in life. "It is probable," she writes, "that the rhythm of the maternal movements associated with body warmth offers the infant a partial reinstatement of prenatal conditions and helps bridge over the transition from intramural to extramural life."[1] What interests me here is the implicit analogy that we can draw—it is virtually inescapable—between infancy and what we may need in our oldest age. How the transition from life into death is represented in Beckett's *Malone Dies* will be one of the subjects of this chapter, as it was of the earlier chapter on Figes's *Waking*. Indeed the two novels have much in common. Both take place in the solipsistic *mise-en-scène* of the psyche. Both conclude on a hallucinatory note. But if the final emphasis in *Waking* is on a purely internal psychic process whose end is the conjuring up of the figure of the mother, in *Malone Dies* the focus shifts to a more creative and controlled process. The figure of the mother is not dominant. The role of actual objects—things, literally—is of more interest.

Like Barthes who in mourning for his mother wrote *Camera Lucida* (the book, a tangible object, is one of the shapes the shaping of his grief assumed), so the dying narrator of *Malone Dies* is represented as a writer who is surrounded by a spare world of concrete objects, including pencil (two, actually) and paper. As radically different as are infancy and what I have called our oldest age, the role of objects in *Malone Dies*, a novel about the transition from life to death, invites us to think about that process in terms of the transitional objects of infancy. At stake is the adaptive space of *illusion*, not the delusory dynamic of introjection and projection as represented in *Waking*—although the transitional object of infancy does testify to the need for contact with the body of the mother.

I choose in this chapter, then, to read *Malone Dies* as a portrait of a solitary old man who in his oldest age tells himself stories to help himself forget his increasing pain. Within the context of my book, such a reading will seem self-evident enough. But few literary critics of Beckett have in fact turned their attention to old age. What is blatantly manifest in Beckett's work over the length of his career—the representation of old age—seems to have been systematically misrecognized by his literary critics, just as Oedipus did not recognize his future in the figure of his father.[2] Again, I submit, we come up against the repression of aging and old age.

From the opening pages of the alternately grim and hilarious monologue that constitutes *Malone Dies* to the novel's conclusion (which I read as the death of Malone), the narrator is presented as perceiving this period of his life as radically different from the others. Positioned by Beckett in a small and somewhat barren room in a large house whose character is mysteriously indeterminate, Malone is confined to a bed near the room's only window. The setting itself is not an uncommon one. As Elaine Scarry has remarked in *The Body in Pain*, "This constantly diminishing world ground is almost a given in representations of old age."[3] But Beckett's version of it will be uncommonly different.

Malone refers to his age sarcastically. He is, he says, long past "sweet and seventy."[4] In this single phrase Beckett calls into question what most of his readers, depending upon their age and when they read the novel, will consider the chronological definition of old age (when *Malone Dies* was first published in 1956 in the United States, the number marking the onset of old age was sixty or sixty-five). Indeed Malone is so old that he cannot remember how old he actually is (apparently he is about one hundred). For many years now it has been customary to think of old age as a short span of life preceding death. But Beckett's story of Malone was prescient, foreshadowing the situation of many frail elderly today who live into their eighties, nineties, and beyond. Malone so aptly for our time—both literally and in terms of mirroring our fear—defines old age as a vast expanse of years followed by a relatively short period of strange "decomposition" (83), although at times this period of debilitation, of "second childishness," seems as if it will stretch on forever (59). That time, which corresponds to what Gutmann has called (rather infelicitously) the period of *termination*,[5] is the space of the present tense of the novel.

We can understand this period of "decomposition" as representing the last of the perilous zones of transition Beckett had earlier described in his monograph on Proust, as "dangerous, precarious, painful, mysterious, and fertile, when for a moment the boredom of living is replaced by the suffering of being."[6] In *Malone Dies* we do not find the figure of vegetative or medicated old age which is what so many of us fear. Instead we encounter an intense and restless subjectivity adroitly resisting the pressure of death. Malone insists, "I do not want to sleep. There is no time for that in my timetable . . . coma is for the living" (18). But I wonder what we would see if Beckett had given us another point of view as well, as Woolf did, for example, in *The Years*. From the vantage point of, say, a visitor touring the facilities where Malone lives, would we see only a silent, bedridden, decrepit old man who seems "dead to the world" and himself? To call on his words from *Proust*, Beckett's portrait of these oldest years of Malone is one of fertility as well as pain. To be sure the accent is on suffering, but it is not on boredom. Colette, unexpectedly connecting the specific bodily pain of old age with youth, commented almost rhapsodically in *The Blue Lantern* that "pain [is] ever young and active, instigator of astonishment, of anger, imposing its rhythm on me, provoking me to defy it; the pain that enjoys an occasional respite but does not want my life to end: happily I have pain" (9–10). By contrast Beckett's vision is sardonic, but pain is still an instigator in life.

Ruby Cohn has astutely remarked that Beckett's work is an "anatomy of suffering."[7] Malone's suffering is primarily bodily suffering. As the characters in the bizarre stories that Malone tells himself age from childhood into old age, so Malone, whose body is virtually impotent from the start, loses first his capacity to hear clearly, later his voice, and finally the ability to even move his head from side to side. These losses are accompanied by intensifying pain and by strange, unexpected changes in his sense of his body, changes which Beckett renders with great economy. Indeed the phenomenology of the lived body—or what we might better call here the old and dying body—is one of the great and little remarked achievements of *Malone Dies* (I will explore at greater length representations of the phenomenology of the aging body in my last chapter).

Beckett tells us that Malone feels he is near death, that something fundamental has changed, that "it is no longer I, I must have said so long ago, but another whose life is just beginning" (32). The pain precipitates a vivid sense of the splitting of the I from the body. "I shall never go back into this carcass," he declares at one point (17). Malone's body speaks to him, telling him that he has only a few weeks to live. Inexplicably his body feels heavier. Rather than shriveling as Malone thought it would, it seems to be dilating, swelling. Malone no longer has any sensation of his feet—they feel so far away—and imagines he would need a telescope to see them. At times he has the sensation that he "emits grey" (46–47). Although Malone determines not to speak of his suffering, staunchly maintaining that he is "far from the sounds of blood and breath, immured" (9), he soon abandons that resolution. Early in the novel he reports on pains that are unfamiliar to him, pains imaginatively presented by Beckett in terms of color and music. "They have a kind of rhythm, they even have a kind of little tune," as Beckett puts it. "They are bluish" (22). Later the pain is deftly described as mounting heat as if entries were being made in a psychiatrist's chart (in a way they are): "My head. On fire, full of boiling oil. . . . Incandescent migraine" (104). Malone's discourse on pain seems endlessly inventive. He is capable of deflating self-irony. If his pain is at times "almost unbearable," he can also refer to his style of suffering as "grandiose" (114).

What serves to combat the pain? In a sense it is precisely the association of this time in life with the early months of life, a connection that most of us find disturbing because it connotes regression. But *Malone Dies* calls this reading into question, if caustically. Generally, the analogy of the old age of decrepitude and senility with childhood demeans the person to whom it is applied. But the effect of Beckett's analogy is altogether different, in part because Beckett pursues it in such a sustained way and in part (it comes to the same thing) because Malone is by no means a pitiful character (not that there is anything necessarily wrong with pity, but I must leave this aside). Malone is presented as confronting his suffering with black-humored tenacity and a nutty, analytic intelligence that refuses to relinquish its own activity even, as we have already seen, in imaginatively taking an inventory of pain.

To characterize this time in life, Beckett uses the imagery of infancy and, surprisingly, of the *prenatal* period.[8] Malone is presented to us naked (he has been, however, discreetly covered by his author with bedclothes). He is toothless and from time to time sucks "happily" on his pillow, as infants and toddlers do. Acutely self-conscious of the resemblance between these two extremes of life, Malone wryly observes that the only other time he was not mobile was when he was an infant. He makes several rather gruesome references to himself as an old fetus. "Yes," he muses, "that's what I am now, hoar and impotent, mother is done for, I've rotted her, she'll drop me with the help of gangrene" (51). "What matters," he asserts bluntly, "is to eat and excrete" (7). And in charting his decaying physical condition, he sentimentally *and* ironically invokes his childhood: "My breath, when it comes back, fills the room with its din, though my chest moves no more than a sleeping child's. I open my eyes and gaze unblinkingly and long at the night sky. So a tiny tot I gaped, first at the novelties, then at the antiquities'' (22). ''Antiquities'' refers of course to people who seemed to him then incredibly ancient. But he now occupies that position, and the irony is not lost on him. Like a child he intends to fill his days with play. And like a child he will discover again—although he already knows this full well—that one cannot live only in the condition of play. Even in Beckett we find a limit to a postmodern poetics of the aging body.

I wish to pursue this analogy between infancy and old age unto death with Winnicott's suggestive theory of transitional objects. Like Erikson, Winnicott is concerned with the developmental psychoanalysis of health. He theorized that every healthy infant undergoes a maturational process between the ages of four to twelve months, selecting an object (a blanket, for example, or a pillow) that will help him make the transition away from the mother and into the objective world.[9] This object will exist for the child in the locus of objective and subjective states, in what Winnicott calls the ''intermediate'' area of experience. The teddy bear that is carried around by a toddler is typically referred to as the prime example of a transitional object. But in fact this proverbial bear often *represents* a relationship with a person whom the child already understands to be differentiated from himself (in psychoanalytic terms the teddy bear may signify a true object relation). For Winnicott, however, the choosing of the transitional object takes place prior to the child's being able to distinguish himself as separate from the world of things and other people. The transitional object exists, as if magically, in the fluid zone between the inside and the outside. The child construes it to be *both* a part of himself and *not* a part of himself at the same time (the object is both me and not-me). With the help of the transitional object, the infant passes from magical control (from the mother who is at first apparently inseparable from the infant and seems to respond perfectly to his demands) to illusionary control by manipulating an uncomplaining object: the infant takes possession of the object, thus making, as it were, the transition himself. While Winnicott understands the transitional object as serving as a defense against anxiety (it provides comfort), he does not emphasize that it is a substitute for what will be always lost and always desired. For him the importance of the transitional object is precisely its actuality, its corporeality, its materiality, *not* its symbolic value, not what it might represent. Indeed it exists in a state *prior* to representation proper.

The subtitle of Winnicott's essay is ''A Study of the First Not-Me Possession,'' which implies that there is a second not-me possession, a third, and so on. But Winnicott regards only the *first* as truly transitional, as existing for the infant in that psychically indeterminate and covalent space. What happens to the transitional object? Winnicott concludes that as the infant develops his capacity for distinguishing the me from the not-me, the transitional object simply loses its meaning. It is not so much lost—it would then need to be mourned—as it is left behind after it is no longer needed. The process is basically additive: the exchange of *the* transitional object for *many* objects. Important for our purposes, Winnicott theorizes that the transitional object of infancy is the ancestor of the cultural world of adulthood which is the sphere of illusion, of art, literature, and music.

Beckett's fictional scene of an old and dying man is staged as a reversal of this process. Instead of addition, the process is one of subtraction and contraction. Meaning is withdrawn from a number of objects and located finally in one only, the transitional object of the oldest age, the last possession. This is Malone's exercise-book, which we can imagine contains an intermittent chronicle of his suffering, his reminiscences, and the stories he tells, fictions that yield a measure of illusion and control. Or perhaps the exercise-book embodies the space of illusion but is virtually empty, not filled with writing. "It is a thick exercise-book," Malone thinks, "I hope it will see me out" (34).

As the novel opens, Malone, a kind of accountant of the past, decides to take an inventory of his possessions. It is a motley, curious Beckettian miscellany of "a good dozen objects" all jumbled together in the corner—a brimless hat, a button-boot, the bowl of a pipe, a needle stuck between two corks and garnished with a piece of black thread, a scrap of paper, some buttons and three socks, a photograph of a jackass, a stick, a stone, the cap of a bicycle bell, a half crutch, a club, a little packet tied up in yellowed newspaper. With Malone in bed are a stick, two pencils, and a child's exercise-book. We can read the project of Malone's taking inventory as a postmodern metaphor for taking stock of a life, for summing up a past, for reviewing it through the memories called forth by possessions. But Beckett will deflate this romantic notion, in part by the very character of the objects we find in Malone's company. They are eccentric and broken. They call up no rich past of emotion.

At first Malone bombastically regards the time remaining to him as an opportunity for coming to final conclusions, to "draw the line and make the tot" (4). But as he proceeds to number his objects, they recede from view. And as he lets go of his things, he acerbically dismisses the sentimental lure of wisdom. It is not possible to arrive at a totalizing view. At first his objects testify to his present existence (yes, he is still alive) and his periodic rummaging in them offers the consolation of the sense of continuity of the self (as we will see, this is also part of the problem). Malone even entertains the notion of gathering up all of his objects into bed with him, of swaddling and adorning himself with his "treasures," of literally internalizing some of his possessions so that they cannot escape him. It is a weird and brilliant phantasy of reassurance, familial security, and plenitude: "Perhaps I should call in all my possessions such as they are and take them into bed with me. . . . Then I shall have them all round me, on top of me, under me, in the corner there will be nothing left, all will be in the bed, with me. I shall hold my photograph in my hand, my stone, so that they can't get away. I shall put on my hat. Perhaps I shall have something in my mouth, my scrap of newspaper perhaps, or my buttons, and I shall be lying on other treasures still" (79).[10]

Beckett even subverts this bizarre narcissistic phantasy. The photograph is not one of him, but one of an "ass." And as Malone moves closer to death, these once-treasured objects simply lose their meaning (in psychoanalytic terms, they are decathected) rather than increase in meaning, as is often thought occurs in the psychic life of old people. In Malone's heap of broken objects we find no sweet keepsakes or even maudlin mementos of a fondly remembered past. On the contrary, Beckett is calling into question the entire notion of recapturing the past. The Malone who thought he knew his objects "by heart" is surprised to find that he does not even remember what is in his small pile of objects. Many of the objects he thought were in his possession are missing. And unfamiliar objects—things of which he has no memory whatsoever and which do not connect him in any way to his past—are unaccountably present. As Malone observes with measurable equanimity, "now I know that the image of these objects, with which I have lulled myself until now, though accurate in the main, was not completely so. . . . I see then that I had attributed to myself certain objects no longer in my possession. . . . I note on the other hand, in the heap, the presence of two or three objects I had quite forgotten and one of which at least, the bowl of a pipe, strikes no chord in my memory" (20–21).

It is a commonplace of our culture that the elderly invest themselves in souvenirs of their pasts which serve as emblems of their present selves. The phenomenon of collecting, of investing in concrete objects, is associated with old age (as it is with children of some eight to ten years old). The philosopher Harry R. Moody, for example, idealizes collecting in the elderly, distinguishing between souvenirs and collections: "Souvenirs are physical objects associated with unique personal experiences from a single point in time. But collections capture the past in a different way. By their mute presence, they invoke remembered time itself; collections create the sense of a bounded or comprehensible universe with an ordering principle."[11] More surprising, Benjamin, in his essay on book collecting, explicitly links collecting with old age. Without a trace of irony, he imagines that as the collector touches his books, as he turns them over and over in his hands, he sees into the past as if a seer. The metaphor is one of poetic inspiration. "One has only to watch a collector handle the objects in his glass case," Benjamin writes. "As he holds them in his hands, he seems to be seeing through them into their distant past as though inspired. So much for the magical side of the collector—his old-age image, I might call it."[12] The atmosphere is Proustian. Benjamin extols the figure of a collector, suggesting that his relation to his objects is one of privileged knowledge, that together the collector and his objects form an intimate sphere grounded in possession. It is the counterpart in the private domain of the museum in the public domain. As Benjamin puts it in the same essay, "for a collector . . . ownership is the most intimate relationship that we can have to objects" (67). Such a relation to objects is figured in romantic, almost hallowed terms. The relation is understood to endow both the object and the collector with an aura of meaning. Just as the museum can be understood as signifying a representational view of the world, so too a collection of such objects is understood as representing the collector to himself and others. Order and intentionality in the act of collecting are presumed to lend coherence and permanence to the collector.

The psychiatric geriatrician J. Wertheimer has written that the practice of *collectionnisme* in the elderly is a *defense* against aging.[13] He associates collecting with the rigidity of habits in everyday life that we may find in the elderly, the kind of habit against which Beckett railed in his book on Proust. Collecting has to do with the attempt to maintain a facade of permanence even as change is proceeding inexorably. Interestingly, Wertheimer draws attention to what I would call a double bind for the elderly in terms of their stance toward time. He refers to the practice of the elderly of seldom modifying their surroundings (not redecorating, for example, for perhaps some thirty years), as if not to disturb the past, which is to deny change. I suspect we are all familiar with this phenomenon. How many ·of us have not stepped across the threshold into the apartment or house of older people and felt ourselves to be in another era? Everything has its place. Nothing is to be rearranged. Wertheimer implicitly posits a spectator of a younger generation which perceives a kind of unbridgeable difference between its own domain of change and the *other* ordered world of changelessness. He concludes that the elderly who practice a form of *collectionnisme* may maintain a certain identity but at the cost of exile.

In this context, we see just how unusual Beckett's representation of the relation of the elderly Malone to his objects is. Malone cannot be said to be a collector. The pile of objects is not assembled by intention. It is a miscellany, a heap. Malone in his ever-analytic way undertakes to think through the very notion of possession. Are these his objects? What condition would render these objects his? "I see then," he concludes, "that I had attributed to myself certain objects no longer in my possession."

In western culture to attribute something to oneself is to understand it as belonging to oneself or as representing oneself. Malone's belongings are placed in doubt, and thus so is Malone himself. But for the most part Malone's rhetoric is not one of elegiac lament or resignation. His speech (his writing) is plain. He declares, "our business is not with what I have no longer, such things do not count at such a moment, whatever people may say" (80). If the assertion is firm, his unmooring from the world of objects has cast him somewhat adrift, as the deviation from the pronoun "our" to "I" represents. Instead of regretting his lost and fixing relation to the objects, the finical, intellectually scrupulous Malone devotes himself to what he sees now is properly his "business," his legitimate field of inquiry—the issue of the linguistic shifter of possession. Just which object can carry the possessive that will connect it to him?

"Only those things are mine," Malone answers, "the whereabouts of which I know well enough to be able to lay hold of them, if necessary, that is the definition I have adopted" (77). Being able to *see* his objects is not enough. He must be able to touch them, to handle them, to bring them near, to draw them to his body. Physical contact is crucial. This response may be of consequence for understanding the experience of the infirm and immobile elderly who inhabit a contracted physical space. What indeed is theirs? How do they represent themselves? Where do they locate the I? With what are they in contact? For Malone the necessary condition of possession is physical contiguity, which implies control and manipulability. As Malone's physical ability to come into contact with the world of things decreases, his objective world contracts finally to nothing. With the loss of mobility and maneuverability comes the dwindling of meaningful possessions, objects which speak to him about his past.

With the exception of the exercise-book, Malone's most important possession is his hooked stick. During the first three-quarters of the novel Malone maintains shaky communication with the "objective" world through its agency (the stick also used to serve an erotic purpose; Malone muses that he used to "rub" himself against it, saying, "It's a little woman" [75]). In *Malone Dies* is represented the importance of technology to the frail elderly body. Technology enhances the body. Some elderly bodies are prosthetic bodies.

The marked emphasis in *Malone Dies* on the grasping of objects as an important means of maintaining contact with the world recalls attachment theory of early infancy. Attachment theory insists on the significance of the tactile register in the constitution of the subject. Interestingly, the psychoanalyst Victoria Hamilton argues that it is the insertion of a concrete object (a rattle, for example) into the symbiotic relation between mother and infant that sets in motion the process of differentiation from the mother.[14] Attachment theory resonates with Winnicott's notion of transitional objects, especially in regard to the intermediate area in which they are perceived to exist. Winnicott calls this imaginary zone the *potential space* between mother and child, between the individual and the environment. For Winnicott *contiguity*, actual physical contact with objects, is crucial to the development of identity. As I suggested in the chapter on the mirror stage of old age, Winnicott advances a notion of mirroring that is different from Lacan's. Winnicott also stresses the importance of tactile body experiences in the intermediate area or potential space, supplementing the Freudian theory of the auto-organization of the body through its libidinal zones. As Winnicott explains, "It will be seen that if this area is to be thought of as part of the ego organization, here is a part of the ego that is not a body-ego [in the strictly Freudian sense], that is not founded on the pattern of body *functioning* but is founded on body *experiences*. These experiences belong to object-relating of a non-orgiastic kind, or to what can be called ego-relatedness, at the place where it can be said that *continuity* is giving way to *contiguity*."[15] From the perspective of Winnicott and attachment theory, then, we are led to wonder what the effect might be of our *detachment* from the world of things. Might it not be a form of *de-differentiation*? As Malone says, "I shall doubtless be obliged to forget myself in the bed, as when I was a baby" (83).

Malone cherishes his pencil (he sucks on it), which keeps slipping from his grasp. When he drops his hooked stick, it is one of the catastrophic moments in the novel. Yet Malone reconciles himself to his loss almost with alacrity. It is as if physical necessity is indeed the mother of invention.[16] What remains now to Malone? Nothing, he notes, "except my exercise-book, my lead and the French pencil" (83). This nothing has to be everything. Identity, control, and illusion are no longer bound up in any real way in an exchange with the world of objects and other people. Malone now inhabits a subjective world that is in great part shaped by his pain. As death comes to haunt the hallucinating Malone in the figure of a black-suited man with a tightly rolled umbrella, as Malone suffers yet another debilitating attack (it seems to be a stroke), he shifts his life as if it were a part of speech to his book, resolving never to say "I" again (although he does): "This exercise-book is my life, this big child's exercise-book, it has taken me a long time to resign myself to that" (105). The exercise-book is the place of both the me and the not-me. As Malone is increasingly alienated from his disintegrating body, the I comes to exist in the book itself. This is the illusion that sustains him. A more familiar way of putting it would be to say that Malone takes refuge in his stories. Without the power to shape language, "he" would not exist. We are in a world of paradox. Where is "Malone" located experientially? In two places at once?

An infant refuses substitutes for its transitional object. In the novel the old and dying Malone is represented as *accepting*—in fact welcoming—the substitution of different figures for himself (the bizarre stories Malone writes about

Sapo and Macmann are facets of his past selves). He also creates them, locating the I in the verbal world of both the mind and the book which, importantly, is an *actual* object. The process is a kind of magical extrusion of the I. What we see represented in the fictional world of *Malone Dies* is that the indeterminate state of being at the end of the character's life mirrors the intermediate area of infancy as theorized by Winnicott. But this dispersion of the I is achieved with only provisional success. The body reasserts its claims. Toward the end of his life, which is the end of the novel, Malone reflects, "things were going too well. I had forgotten myself" (97), rhetoric he immediately calls into question. "I exaggerate" (97).

I do not want to leave the impression that Malone is unambivalent about the effects of writing. The exercise-book, which represents the process of writing, is no perfectly safe harbor. On the one hand, even as he takes refuge in it, his writing threatens to refer himself back to himself. Malone acknowledges the ominous and irreducible autobiographical character of writing. Referring to Sapo's eyes as gull's eyes (as Beckett's eyes have been described), Malone rails: "I don't like those gull's eyes. . . . I know those little phrases that seem so innocuous and, once you let them in, pollute the whole of speech. . . . They rise up out of the pit and know no rest until they drag you down into its dark" (16). The danger is that his words will *represent* him to himself. In Lacanian psychoanalysis the overwhelming drive is to find an object with which we can identify, as in the imaginary scene of the mirrored self of infancy. In *Malone Dies* the wish is *not* to be reflected, to withdraw the I into an intermediate space that does not mirror the I, to lose the I in language.

On the other hand, Malone is troubled by the idea that language is itself an impersonal system. He arrives at this conclusion while meditating further on what it means to possess an object. Already having deduced that physical contiguity is a necessary condition for possession, he comes to the realization that it is not a sufficient condition. Why? In addition to the bed and the wardrobe, his room contains two pots for his waste. They serve as the starting point for further analytic inquiry: "The pots do not seem to be mine, I simply have the use of them. They answer to the definition of what is mine, but they are not mine. Perhaps it is the definition that is at fault. They have each two handles or ears, projecting above the rim and facing each other, into which I insert my stick. In this way I move my pots about. . . . They are not mine, but I say my pots, as I say my bed, my window, as I say me" (80).

The notion that one can possess something by virtue of *using* it does not bother Malone. But by this idea he is led to the disturbing realization that finally possession is a matter of the impersonal structure of language. At issue is the epistemological problem represented by the crafty linguistic shifter of possession. He charts an equivalency between objects and his self. It is a slippery slope. "I say my pots, as I say my bed, my window, as I say me." That his identity (his *self-possession*) is also structured by language distresses him (he may also realize that he can no longer *use* his own body in a way that signals possession). He makes a hasty retreat, abandoning his inquiry into the nature of possession. Here again we see his ambivalence about his relation to the language of his exercise-book, which is the language of the intermediate area. It is a poetic language whose function is, as Gabriele Schwab has argued, to mediate or reshape the relation between the primary process and secondary process of mental functioning.[17] Malone reverts to the secondary process, invoking a Newtonian view of the universe. Paranoically he attributes his disquiet to the objects themselves: "I shall stop. It is my possessions have weakened me, if I start talking about them again I shall weaken again, for the same causes give rise to the same effects" (80).

The objects in Malone's cell can all be thought of as transitional phenomena. But only the exercise-book is the transitional object of the dying Malone, his last and finally only possession, his last not-me possession, the container of transitional words, analogues (I quote Barthes) "to those pillow corners and pieces of sheet which the child stubbornly sucks."[18] "I cherish it, it's human," writes Malone (105). The exercise-book is a bridge between the comfortably familiar (the long span of old age) and the disturbingly unfamiliar (the period of strange decomposition and the specter of death). The exercise-book, both a tangible object and the container of that intangible system, language, preserves to the extent possible a kind of psychophysical equilibrium as disintegration, not individuation, progresses.[19]

If we were to describe Malone's environment in realistic terms (a single bare room, almost no apparent exchange with other human beings), it would seem scandalously cruel, a Kafkaesque vision of the debilitating sterility of many so-called nursing homes.[20] Indeed *Malone Dies* does suggest a surrealistic vision, filtered through a dying man's subjectivity, of nursing home life. Malone tells us that he is, if not cared for, at least "looked after! This is how it is done now. The door half opens, a hand puts a dish on a little table left there for the purpose, takes away the dish of the previous day, and the door closes again" (7). He alternately and paranoically fears that his life will be prolonged by every available means possible by his caretakers *or* that he will be starved to death. He imagines that his fate will be like that of other old men: "when they cannot swallow any more someone rams a tube down their gullet, or up their rectum, and fills them full of vitaminized pap, so as not to be accused of murder. I shall therefore die of old age pure and simple, glutted with days as in the days before the flood, on a full stomach" (81).

But such a reading would not account for Malone's resiliency. What fosters this psychic strength on the part of Malone, who is so *alone*? I turn again to Winnicott. In "The Capacity to Be Alone" (1958), he speculates that the ability to be alone "depends on the existence of a good object in the psychic reality of the individual . . . so that temporarily he or she is able to rest contented even in the absence of external objects and stimuli."[21] Observing that psychoanalysis has dwelt on the *fear* of being alone, Winnicott develops his idea of the capacity to be alone a few years later in an essay on the isolate to which I briefly alluded in my discussion of Woolf's dreaming Eleanor. Winnicott refers provocatively to his model of the isolate as representing a psychoanalysis of the *one-body relationship* (which we can contrast with the Freudian familial *triangle* of mother-father-child as dramatized in the primal scene and with the Lacanian *dyad* of self-other pictured in the mirror of the imaginary). Winnicott argues that *"each individual is an isolate, permanently non-communicating, permanently unknown, in fact unfound."*[22] Such noncommunication with others is by no means a symptom of neurosis. "At the core of the individual," he insists, "there is no communication with the not-me world" (189–90). Although Winnicott considers that his notion of the individual as isolate is particularly useful to the study of our early years (infancy, childhood, adolescence), with Beckett's Malone in mind, we may add the very old and dying as well.[23]

Toward the end Malone does not regard it as necessary or even desirable to communicate with the so-called outside world, the objective world of the not-I. He moves, alone, into the quasi-subjective world of his stories. Referentiality becomes intertextuality. The contents of his exercise-book are not intended for the eyes and ears of an audience. He is no longer motivated by the demand to be recognized by others. His exercise-book is a figure for the psychoanalysis of one-body relationships, for the ability to be alone, a figure of the individual alone with himself and his imaginary companions. For the solitary Malone the other is not desired, nor does the "self" seem to be constituted by what is absent. Indeed the "self" is not constituted at all. The I is dispersed into several fictional characters strung out over the life span. Yet paradoxically the I is also associated with the tangible object of the exercise-book and its protean language. In *Malone Dies* we do not so much find an "entrance" onto the stage of language as we find the site of language staging an "exit," the means by which the character's pure portion of agony may be endured.[24] The figure of the isolate endures the loss of all others and of all objects, except the transitional object of dying. And its fate too will be to be left behind.

I read *Malone Dies*, then, as the discourse not of desire but of the dying. "I want nothing," Malone asserts early on in the novel, reporting later that he has recently "had no wish to leave" his bed (83). In the tone of peasant wisdom he observes, "In the old days. . . . I was time, I devoured the world. Not now, any more. A man changes. As he gets on" (26). A lack of desire to invest oneself in the world does not necessarily imply, as we have seen, a lack of activity. In *Malone Dies* the work, a kind of life-work and death-work together, is the relocation of the I. As Malone heroically reflects with no trace of Freudian stoicism or resignation, "Death must take me for someone else" (104). As Lacan has defined the concept of aphanisis (a term first coined by Ernest Jones), what is represented is the *fading* of the subject in the context of old age.

I resolved in my introduction to this book to consider fictional texts apart from their authors, with the exception of Freud and Barthes. But as I come to the conclusion of this chapter, my mind keeps turning to Beckett. When *Malone Dies* was published in 1956, Beckett was fifty years old. The middle term of a literary trilogy, *Malone Dies* is quite different from *Molloy* and *The Unnamable*, having as it does more in common with the fictional techniques of modernism than with postmodernism. It is my guess that Beckett inserted *Malone Dies* in between the other two pieces in order to reduce the "danger" that the discourse of the dying Malone might be received as mawkishly sentimental. But for me today the poignancy of *Malone Dies* is not kept in check by its place in the trilogy. I find that I cannot help but conflate the fiction of *Malone Dies* with what I imagine of Beckett's life in Paris.

My husband introduced me to Beckett in 1985. We met in the bar of a large hotel. I was struck by Beckett's courtly behavior, his legendary keen blue eyes, his handsomeness. I noted that he was a bit shaky on his feet. I told him that I was writing a book on aging and was interested in his work.

In the summer of 1989 my husband visited Beckett again. He was eighty-three and living in a *maison de retraite* (a kind of nursing home) in Paris. His room was small and furnished laconically. He was virtually not writing. His wife, Suzanne, died a few months later.

In this chapter I have exaggerated Malone's capacity to be alone and adaptation to his pain to make my point about a certain discourse of dying and the transitional object of the oldest age. But we also occasionally hear in Malone the voice of someone who wants to remain attached to the world and who regrets leaving his life. Malone reminisces about the sounds of the trees of his childhood: every "tree had its own cry" (31). He confides to his exercise-book that all this is "mortal tedium" (43). He wonders if his final breaths will be a death rattle. And he drily considers suicide: if "I had use of my body I would throw it out of the window" (44). Although the transitional process of writing serves him as well as he can manage it, ultimately—never mind the splitting pain—the loss of life does not go easy. As we read toward the moving end of the novel,

"All is pretext, Sapo and the birds . . . my doubts which do not interest me, my situation, my possessions, pretext for not coming to the point, the abandoning, the raising of arms and going down, without further splash, even though it may annoy the bathers. Yes, there is no good pretending, it is hard to leave everything" (107).[25]

For me leaving this chapter was also difficult. I wondered if my continuing to circle around my own writing was not a pretext for not coming to the point, for not leaving the fictional Malone and Beckett, the old man I had met, alone in their rooms to die. I felt superstitious. Beckett died as this book was going to press.

COUNTER-TEXT

My shreds and remnants of years are scattered through it [the house] visibly in lamps and vases. . . . If I'm not somehow contained in them and in this house, something of all change caught and fixed here, eternal enough for my purposes, then I do not know where I am to be found at all.

—Hagar Shipley, ninety years old,
from Margaret Laurence, *The
Stone Angel* 36

8. Youthfulness as a Masquerade . . .
Denial, Resistance, and Desire

THE PREVIOUS CHAPTER DEALT with the subjective self-experience of a frail, aging body as represented in Beckett's *Malone Dies*. What is unusual about *Malone Dies* is that the fictional world represented is so relentlessly and exclusively an interior space in which other people play virtually no constituting parts, as they do, for example, in Figes's *Waking*. Malone's animating relation to the concrete world around him is figured almost entirely in terms of his connections to literal objects which diminish as the novel advances. As these links to the world are broken, Malone comes to inhabit a purely psychic space which is shaped in part by the body in pain. It is the kind of psychic space in which I imagine my mother's mother must have lived as she lay in her hospital bed, although assuredly what she was thinking and feeling would have been very different.

With no sense of eyes upon him, Malone does not think of his body in terms of how it looks to others and thus to himself. The visual register of his body holds no interest for him. In the last chapter of this book I will return to the phenomenology of the literary aging body. But here I want to explore further the social world and the specular body of old age which figured so prominently in the chapter on Proust and the mirror stage of old age. Marcel, we remember, mistook old age for masquerade at the reception at the Guermantes'. In this chapter, although the relation of spectatorship is always implied, I shift the perspective to consider masquerade primarily but not exclusively from the point of view of characters who put on a mask to solicit a certain gaze. I consider masquerade as a coverup through which old age nonetheless speaks.

In the ordinary sense of the word, "masquerade" has to do with concealing something and presenting the very conditions of that concealment. A mathematics of difference is posited between two terms—an inside and an outside, with the outside (the surface) understood as disguising what is within. In *Webster's Third International* we find this straightforward definition: masquerade is "an action, appearance, bearing or mode of life that is mere outward show concealing true character or situation: a pretense of being something that one is not." In this chapter I want to insist on the theatrical metaphor implicit in this formulation. As "pretense," masquerade is a form of self-representation. But I also want to call into question the unequivocal notion of the mask as "mere outward show" that hides a "truth." A mask may *express* rather than hide a truth. The mask *itself* may be one of multiple truths. Yet I do not want to romanticize masquerade and masking. At times the most radical gesture may be in fact to take off a mask and show what is underneath it. How, then, would we distinguish between different kinds of masks? The virtual undecidability of this question is echoed in the psychoanalyst Joan Riviere's theory of masquerade, which I will call upon in this chapter.

In a culture which so devalues age, masquerade with respect to the aging body is first and foremost a denial of age, an effort to erase or efface age and to put on youth. Masquerade entails several strategies, among them: the addition of desired body parts (teeth, hair); the removal or covering up of unwanted parts of the body (growths, gray hair, "age spots"); the "lifting" of the face and other body parts in an effort to deny the weight of gravity; the molding of the body's shape (exercise, clothing). In the following pages I discuss masquerade and the aging body from perspectives offered by twentieth-century western literary culture—Thomas Mann's *Death in Venice* and Patrick White's *The Eye of the Storm*—as well as mass culture in America, which seems recently to have "discovered" the aging body with a vengeance.

I have not been able to forget the striking scene that concludes *Death in Venice*. The elderly Aschenbach has collapsed in his beach chair facing the sea. He is dead. His makeup is running down his face. What I find so haunting is this slipping of the mask, the disintegration of the masquerade of youthfulness in a body that has come to be inhabited by death.

What was Aschenbach's desire? *Death in Venice* is a story so well known that it can be taken as a parable of the dominant discourse of aging in the West. We remember that Aschenbach is a failing writer (in this modernist narrative, aging and waning creativity are at the very least metaphors for each other, if not represented as mutually causal). He travels to Venice. The city is overcome by the plague (old age and the decay of a culture are both equated with disease). He falls in love with a beautiful boy who both presents and represents a fatal injury to his sense of himself, to his narcissism, as we might say. The equation is clear. Aschenbach longs for this young boy as he longs for youth itself. His attachment is strong and complex. He desires Tadzio and he also turns aggressively against him, which is to say against himself.

Aschenbach is filled, we learn, "with disgust of his own aging body."[1] How to mitigate his self-revulsion? How to attract youth? He turns to his appearance, adding the insignia of youthfulness. Mann: "Like any lover, he desired to please; suffered agonies at the thought of failure, and brightened his dress with smart ties and handkerchiefs and other youthful touches. He added jewelry and perfumes and spent hours each day over his toilette, appearing at dinner elaborately arrayed and tensely excited" (69). He allows himself to be taken in by a canny makeup artist who croons that what Aschenbach has lost he can regain, as if youth were a commodity to be purchased. He succumbs to the dangerous appeal that he is the sole judge of his youthfulness, that *subjective* experience is the only measure of age. The makeup man offers Aschenbach a seductive chestnut— "We are all as old as we feel, but no older, and grey hair can misrepresent a man worse than dyed" (69). Aschenbach, desperate in desire, takes it. To a certain degree the makeup man is right. To an extent we *are* as old as we feel, although this is something we cannot measure (most older people report that they "feel" younger than their chronological age).[2] But even more surely he is wrong. In addition to being a state of mind, aging is a biological phenomenon and a social construction. To subjective or personal age we must add social age, which is mediated by chronological age (how many years old we are) and biological age (the state of health of the body).

Predictably, the discourse of the makeup artist further pivots on the association of youth with what is natural. Youth is defined as private property, which in the West has been constructed as a natural *right*. Youth is thus understood as giving one the right to be seen and heard. The makeup artist: "You, for instance, signore, have a right to your natural colour. Surely you will permit me to restore what belongs to you?" (69). Restoration implies repossessing the original state of things, which is presumed to be the *authentic* state for all time. Aging is defined as a process of dispossession. Restoration is thus equated with rejuvenescence.[3] If youth is natural, in the sliding economy of age, old age is unnatural and perhaps by extension even unlawful.

There is a small scene early in *Death in Venice* that can be taken as a *mise-en-abyme* of the narrative. It serves as a warning signal, as a little morality play, as a cautionary tale. It poses the question of the extent to which we may be aware of the spectacle we may make of ourselves in masquerade in old age. It suggests that such masquerade is ultimately always visible to others, that the mask does not hide old age but that it makes it all the more visible, that it expresses the "truth," which is the desire for youth and the unimpeachability of death (old age in *Death in Venice* is equated with death). On his way to Venice, Aschenbach sees a man in a crowd of raucous young people. From a distance he seems to be one of them, that is, young. On closer inspection, however, Aschenbach discovers that the man is old. Mann: "Aschenbach's eye dwelt on him, and he was shocked to see that the apparent youth was no youth at all. He was an old man, beyond a doubt, with wrinkles and crows' feet round eyes and mouth; the dull carmine of the cheeks was rouge, the brown hair a wig. His neck was shrunken and sinewy, his turned-up moustaches and small imperial were dyed, and the unbroken row of double teeth he showed when he laughed was too obviously a cheapish false set" (17). Like Marcel in *The Past Recaptured,* Aschenbach is shocked by youthfulness as a masquerade for the aging body. He is unrelenting in his scorn. Pity is the most charitable response he manages. But unlike Marcel, Aschenbach's knowledge never extends even for a moment to self-knowledge. Later in the narrative Aschenbach looks at himself in the mirror and in a complete self-delusion sees "a young man who looked back at him from the glass" (70).

As *Death in Venice* dramatizes (and many conversations in everyday life confirm), the social codes of dress and behavior in relation to old age are strict and confining. Act your age, children are told. Many adults will survey the behavior of those older and, ever alert to infractions of the rules, note in conspiratorial, gossipy tones (which construct a comfortable, correct "we" and marginal "they") that *her* hair is too long for her age, *her* dress too short, *his* hair too dark, *her* makeup too gaudy. Like Aschenbach's arrogant response to the old man in the crowd, such judgments imperiously imply that *they* should know better—and that *we* do.[4] Makeup artists assert that an out-of-date style of makeup will announce a woman's age more insistently than will wrinkles, dating her by fashion decade. As Alison Lurie observes in *The Language of Clothes*, how we dress conveys age-related messages, and any deviation from the conventional norm is regarded by others as an offense that borders on the obscene. "Extreme disparity of age and costume," Lurie concludes, "is seen as disgusting or even frightening."[5] What interests me is the strength of affect associated with such a response. The spectator recoils from a spectacle he unconsciously regards as dangerous to himself. He thus establishes a distance (and metaphorically, therefore, difference) between himself and the other, not wanting to be drawn into the spectacle.

Above all it is old age that must be kept hidden. In this context we see again how Freudian analysis repressed the subject of old age, which was to remain concealed, a well-kept secret. This is represented succinctly in one of Freud's comments in *The Interpretation of Dreams* about the dream of ''Irma's Injection.'' To this specimen dream he adds an association which is not a detail from another dream but drawn from an actual examination of a female patient. The dream of ''Irma's Injection'' reminded him, he wrote, ''of an examination I had carried out some time before of a governess: at first glance she had seemed a picture of youthful beauty, but when it came to her opening her mouth, she had taken measures to conceal her plates. This led to recollections of other medical examinations and of little secrets in the course of them—to the satisfaction of neither party'' (SE 4: 109). Old age is figured as a dirty secret that had best remain undetected, latent, not manifest.

Death in Venice takes a dark if not tragic view of the aging body-in-masquerade. The implication in this modernist text is that youth and age—the two extremes of the body—cannot coexist simultaneously and in harmony without us making pathetic spectacles of ourselves. Reading *Death in Venice* in this vein, we might well ask what then would constitute a commensurate *heroics* of the aging body. As we saw in the chapter on Freud, *Beyond the Pleasure Principle*, another celebrated and contemporaneous text of modernism, suggests an answer. We remember that Freud came finally to the conclusion that the death instinct itself represents a choice that we make, giving us if not the reality, at least the illusion of mastery. We choose what is inevitable. What is inevitable is death. Analogously we may conclude that in the context of modernism, a heroics of the aging body would be to *choose* one's chronological age, that is, to accept it as if one were free to choose it rather than to deny it, as does Aschenbach. But is this not too easy an answer? As I indicated at the end of the chapter on Freud, we have evidence that in his old age, desire for what youth represents broke through the well-fitted mask of resignation. To suggest that we consciously can choose our age would mean that we have left behind the realm of the unconscious and desire for the realm of mastery. Is this ever possible?

In *Death in Venice* the aging body-in-masquerade is figured as a grotesque body. But it is not the grotesque body of the Bakhtinian space of carnival which is associated with a vitality and power completely lacking in the character of Aschenbach. When we turn to *The Eye of the Storm*, however, we do find in a stunning companion makeup scene a more Bakhtinian version of the aging body-in-masquerade. Comparing the two texts, we see just how far we have come from the turn of the century in terms of the social construction of old age. In his late fifties, Aschenbach is characterized as an ''elderly man.'' To call a person in his or her fifties ''elderly'' today would be both a mistake and a gross insult. The heroine of *The Eye of the Storm*, the wealthy widow Elizabeth Hunter, is over eighty. She represents the demographic category in the West called the old-old (those over seventy-five), or more precisely the frail elderly (those over eighty-five, although not everyone over eighty-five is frail). The old-old present for society the "problem" of providing health care for its elderly citizens. Elizabeth Hunter belongs to this group. Only some ten years before, her body was still beautiful. At near-seventy, as White describes it, her body was still "almost perfect," "long, cool, of that white which is found in tuberoses, with their same blush at the extremities" (150). But now decrepitude has definitively set in. Hunter has recently suffered several strokes. Bedridden and nearly blind, sustained in part by her considerable wealth, she continues to live at home where she is taken care of around the clock by three nurses (part of the drama of the narrative turns on the fact that her two children, both of them greedy and pathetic, want to put her in a nursing home, which she emphatically refuses, but this I must leave aside). Note that in *Death in Venice* the failing Aschenbach was carried off at a relatively youthful chronological age by an efficient disease, not by the slow deterioration of the body in advanced old age.

If Hunter's body is decrepit, her will, caustic wit, irony, and vanity are tenaciously intact. In a vivid scene she directs one of her nurses on how to get her up for a visit from her son. Unlike Aschenbach who places himself in the controlling hands of a makeup artist, Hunter is represented as remaining in charge. She possesses, if intermittently, the ironic distance of self-knowledge. If pathos characterizes the twin scene in *Death in Venice*, in *The Eye of the Storm* the scene of masquerade is by turns hilarious, gruesome, and moving. White insists that the drama of the decrepit body, its *facticity*, is indeed grim. But Hunter's gestures of sheer and bizarre extravagance lodge a refusal against old age and powerlessness. There is nothing coy or measured or demure about Hunter's masquerade. She takes pleasure in the decidedly artificial and the unnatural, which she ironically calls "natural." As we will see, masquerade works here both to conceal (to conceal the tawdriness and fragility of her aging body) and to reveal (to reveal Hunter's once-sheer loveliness if not her glamor and her well-hidden vulnerability with regard to her children).

White characterizes Hunter as having displayed throughout her life both a cynical view of the human condition and the capacity for the sublimity of romance. In keeping with her character, this scene combines spectacularly sardonic humor and poignant revelation. It runs for several pages in the novel and is told from shifting points of view—that of the young nurse (her voice predominates), Hunter herself, and the omniscient narrator. The scene begins in burlesque with the rhetoric of black gallows humor. The nurse reduces Elizabeth Hunter to a body, to an object, to a genderless "it." White: "The nurse gathered up the bundle of creaking bones and acerbated flesh and maneuvered it into a seating position.''[6] But Hunter, feeling herself ''transformed into a glimmering ghost of the past,'' takes charge, demanding rouge the shade of dusk rose, lipstick the color of deep carnation, and delphinium-silver for her eye shadow. The nurse traces ''on Elizabeth Hunter's eyelids the dreamiest of moonlit snail-tracks. Elizabeth Hunter, all but transmuted, lolled in a delphinium-silver bliss'' (109). She instructs her nurse to bring ''the expensively created, natural-yellow teeth'' (108). Hunter chooses the long lilac wig, which she decides to wear ''flowing free.'' ''I have decided to appear utterly natural,'' she says with a regal manner.

How are we to view Elizabeth Hunter? White uses the metaphor of finding the proper distance so as to regard her correctly. We should not be too far away or up too close (Aschenbach was both). The proper distance allows one to see the mask (it is grotesque, make no mistake about that) *and* what it reveals (not what it conceals in defense):

> [The nurse] backed up till she reached the best distance from which to contemplate what in one sense was nothing more than a barbaric idol. Frightening in its garishness of purple-crimson, lilac floss, and florescent white, in its robe of battered, rather than beaten, rose-gold, the claws, gloved in jewelled armour, stiffly held about the level of the navel, waiting apparently for some further motive which might bring them to rest on the brocaded lap. . . . [T]he younger woman might have been struck with horror if the faintly silvered lids hadn't flickered open on the milkier, blank blue of Elizabeth Hunter's stare. . . . Momentarily at least this fright of an idol became the goddess hidden inside: of life, which you had longed for, but hadn't dared embrace, of beauty such as you imagined, but had so far failed to embrace . . . and finally, of death, which hadn't concerned you, except as something to be tidied away, until now you are faced with the vision of it. (109–10)

Given the proper distance, the rhetoric of burlesque yields to the rhetoric of revelation. In this scene young and old do coexist in the body in their own idiosyncratic way. Gazing at Elizabeth Hunter from ''the best distance,'' the nurse sees so much more than did Aschenbach, who felt only scorn for the old man in the crowd, or for that matter Marcel at the Guermantes'. Furthermore, unlike Aschenbach, the nurse understands as a result that death casts a shadow on her life also. She realizes that the drama of Elizabeth Hunter's experience has something to tell her about her own experience to come.

Masquerade is the pathetic defense of denial in *Death in Venice*. In *The Eye of the Storm* it is an act of defiance. This distinction between the two scenes corresponds to two currently circulating notions of masquerade—as *submission* to dominant social codes and as *resistance* to them. Although this debate has taken place within the context of feminism and draws on the psychoanalyst Joan

Riviere's analysis in "Womanliness as a Masquerade" (1929) of the gestures of femininity itself as masquerade, it can be useful to us in a consideration of old age.[7] In brief, Riviere argues that "intellectual" women who have been successful in a typically masculine arena may find themselves putting on the signs of femininity (coyness, flirtatiousness) as a defense against their fear of retribution on the part of men. As Riviere concludes with regard to one such case, the display of femininity, which consisted of behavior designed to attract men, "was an unconscious attempt to ward off anxiety which would ensue on account of the reprisals she anticipated from the father-figures after her intellectual performance" (37). Femininity is worn as if it were a set of strategies which conceals a desire for masculinity.

Interestingly enough, Riviere refuses to conclude whether there is an elemental or essential femininity that is imitated in the act of masquerade or whether femininity consists precisely *in* the act of masquerade. She reflects, "The reader may now ask how I define womanliness or where I draw the line between genuine womanliness and the 'masquerade.' My suggestion is not, however, that there is any such difference; whether radical or superficial, they are the same thing" (38). Riviere accepts the paradox that masquerade both conceals and reveals *and* tells a certain truth of its own. Thus unconscious desire, which is mixed with castration anxiety, speaks through masquerade as a symptom. In terms of masquerade, then, the question of the unconscious is central. But for the moment I want to bracket the question of gender and transpose the discussion of masquerade onto the question of old age. My explicit concern here is to explore the extent to which the analysis of femininity as masquerade can be used to think through the question of youthfulness as masquerade.

For Irigaray womanliness as masquerade is a sign of submission to "the dominant economy of desire in an attempt to remain 'on the market' in spite of everything."[8] I find this formulation quite relevant to the analysis of masquerade in the context of aging and old age. In Aschenbach's gestures, for example, we read his submission to the dominant economy of desire. He wants to remain desirable to the young in spite of everything. Irigaray insists that this desire, constituted by patriarchy (that is, the dominant other), must be renounced if women are to find a desire specific to themselves. Analogously, would we ask of Aschenbach that he renounce his desire and seek his own voice in the specificity of his age? What would that mean? But Aschenbach's desire, which is the desire for a lost youth if not for desire itself, *is* specific to his age. Would it not be too simple to conclude that Aschenbach's desire has been constituted by a society dominated by youth and that it is therefore foreign to his specific desires? For when we are old, do we not carry youth within us? For Irigaray, female masquerade is associated with the symbolic register only and not with the imaginary.[9] *Death in Venice* suggests that youthfulness as a masquerade in old age intersects *both* the imaginary and the symbolic. Here Freud's conviction, amounting to a denial, that the unconscious cannot contain the idea of death takes on a new insistence. As I argued earlier in the chapter on Freud, his highly conscious theoretical preoccupation with death was a coverup, or masquerade, for anxiety about aging.

The psychoanalyst Martin Berezin has explored the territory Freud avoided and has concluded that certain of our drives and ego mechanisms are timeless, that is, they do not admit the category of age. Indeed Berezin opens an essay on narcissism and aging with a vignette of a fifty-five-year-old woman that recalls the aging body-in-masquerade of *Death in Venice*. "I was," he writes, "struck by her appearance and behavior. She was highly made-up with thick lipstick and eye shadow, her dress was flamboyant, her hat was a huge broad-brimmed affair. She talked affectedly and gestured as though she were still a flirting adolescent. Her behavior was obvious, and the reason for it became clear when later in the interview she told me she had won a contest at the age of 18. How pathetic, I thought, this woman's self-image is still that of an eighteen-year-old beauty-contest winner."[10] Berezin concludes that her mask spoke of the continuity of the "style" of an individual and of the "timelessness of the unconscious" (10).

In Irigaray's politics of *renouncing* something, we have come far from the discourse of psychoanalysis and the unconscious. For the unconscious is not something that can be renounced. We see this even more clearly in Mary Ann Doane's discussion of masquerade as a strategy of resistance in an essay on female spectatorship and film.[11] Doane refers to Marlene Dietrich's performance in *The Blue Angel*, which she reads as self-consciously calling into question the dominant iconography of woman. Doane concludes that by "destabilizing the image, the masquerade confounds the masculine structure of the look. It effects a defamiliarization of female iconography" (82). This could easily serve as a description of the scene of masquerade in *The Eye of the Storm*. White's representation of the aging body destabilizes conventional images of the aging body, confounding what I call the *youthful structure of the look*. (I want to note here also that Dietrich's performance itself reinforces the youthful structure of the look in its representation of the female body as beautiful, glamorous, and young. It is complicit in constructing an ageist culture.) White destigmatizes the conventional iconography of the aging female body with a flourish. In *The Eye of the Storm* the aging female body is not viciously or unconsciously debased. Neither is it romanticized.

Just as Doane endorses femininity as masquerade in terms of resistance, I have implicitly been privileging in terms of aging the masquerade of defiance over the masquerade of pathos. But this too must be called into question. For Doane the distance from which we view an image is crucial. I call it a *critical distance* because it depends on self-conscious knowledge, or what I referred to above in my discussion of Hunter as self-knowledge.[12] Doane places masquerade definitively in the register of consciousness. She writes, "The effectivity of masquerade lies precisely in its potential to manufacture a distance from the image, to generate a problematic within which the image is manipulable, producible, and readable by the woman" (87). How would we transpose this formulation into the symbolic economy of old age? Would we say, analogously, that the effectiveness of the aging body-in-masquerade would lie in its being manipulable and producible by the spectator (as well as by the person or character who is being looked at), by those who are old themselves? Yes, to the extent possible, but not exclusively because (among other reasons) old age, although it is constructed in a binary relation with youth, is a *position that most of us will inhabit*. At the same time, as I have already suggested, if we are old we carry youth with us; we identify in part with the young. Thus in terms of age, identification is not as clear-cut a phenomenon as it is (or at least as psychoanalysis has argued it is) in terms of gender. And thus at bottom our resistance to old age may be *unconscious*. Self-consciously and critically renouncing our culture's conventions of the iconography of the aging body may enlarge the arena within which we may act, but a difference between youth and age will still exist.

We all have a stake in representations of old age and the aging body. Age necessarily cuts across all our lives and our bodies in a way that other differences fundamentally do not. I am here pointing to the obvious, which is at the same time complex. If we are white, we will never be black. If we are Native American, we will never be Irish Catholic. Similarly the analysis of age must be different from the analysis of gender. We can resist and we can destabilize social constructions of old age. And we should. But death we cannot ultimately deny. Nor can we deny the imaginary, or the unconscious. And in dominant discourses of the West, death remains primary.

Jean-François Lyotard argues in *Just Gaming* for what I call a postmodern version of masquerade. "This is the ideal of games and masks," he writes, "the awareness that the relation between the proper name and the body is not an immutable one. This bars the way to the very notion of the subject identical to itself through the peripetia of its history. There is no subject because s/he changes bodies, and by changing bodies, s/he of course changes passions as well as functions."[13] What Lyotard observes is as profound as it should be commonplace: our bodies change as we grow older, and so do our interests, our desires, our responsibilities, our roles, our self-dramatizations. Lyotard phrases this insight in the language of poststructuralism: the subject is not identical to itself through time. I would put it this way: *We must add age to recent debates on difference*, which have been linked to desire and have resulted in some of the most important criticism in the last few decades in the areas of sexual difference, colonialism, ethnicity, race, and cultural difference. But I do not agree with Lyotard that our *awareness* that we change as we age is "the ideal of games and masks." It is true that I have insisted on the (relative) effectiveness of masquerade as resistance, and indeed masquerade can be effective at any age. Our body images are extremely changeable, unstable, flexible, labile. Whatever comes in contact with the surface of the body (clothing, medical and technological prostheses of all sorts, decorations and ornaments, even other people) is incorporated into our body, changing our body image. Like organic parts of the body, the trappings of masquerade can carry symbolic or imaginary meanings. But I also believe that in advanced old age there is a limit beyond which "games and masks" of masquerade cannot be an "ideal."

In the idealization of play is the avoidance of death. In this sense there can ultimately be no postmodern poetics of the aging body. In *Death in Venice* and in *The Eye of the Storm* the passages I have chosen of the aging body-in-masquerade express the limit toward which the body tends in old age—that is, death—and in this way the images are overdetermined. But as extreme cases they also allow us to speculate that in advanced old age masquerade serves primarily a narcissistic function in a theater which is predominantly private, not public. Unlike Dietrich's performance in *The Blue Angel* which derides masculinity,[14] masquerade in old age does not function as a derision of youth. Quite the contrary. It is concerned not so much with parody (although it can certainly contain elements of parody) as with forging links to one's past selves. *Masquerade itself* in fact can be regarded as an intermediate object in the psychoanalytic sense, serving as a bridge to lost objects, as a bridge which re-creates, momentarily, the past in the present.[15] What has been lost is youth—what one could have been (as in the case of Aschenbach) or what one was (in the case of Hunter).

In *Death in Venice* the implied reader (or implied spectator) occupies a position of relative superiority in part because of presumed youth. We are meant to pity Aschenbach and his pathetic behavior. Even with the admirable, fiercely resourceful Elizabeth Hunter who defies all conventions to appear "natural" but cannot resist the deterioration of the body, we still find ourselves as readers ultimately placed in such a position as well. Age is conflated with death, from which we are—at least for the moment—exempt. Thus even in *The Eye of the Storm* we find an ambivalence about aging that borders on the gerontophobic. To what extent is such gerontophobia endemic to literary representations of aging? I cannot answer this question, but I can point to another and quite different portrait of a woman both taking and giving great pleasure in masquerade in old age.

In their book *The Story of Louise: Old People in a Nursing Home,* Michèle Dacher, an anthropologist, and Micheline Weinstein, a psychoanalyst, present with acumen and sensitivity psychoanalytic portraits of eight people who live in a French nursing home. As I read through the absorbing case studies of (among others) the alcoholic sixty-two-year-old Georges and the seventy-two-year-old Emilienne, an orphan, I wondered who was the Louise from whom the book took its title. It was not until the last chapter that Louise was introduced by Michèle Dacher as the person who by personifying a voracious attachment to life had made it possible for her to continue her research. Across from the nursing home was a small, provincial bistro. After Dacher's first day of research in the nursing home, which she grew convinced was suffocating its inhabitants alive, Dacher tells us that, deeply discouraged, she stopped in the bistro. It was there she met Louise, who some years before had tended bar herself and now made this bar her home. Two other boarders were there with the owner. This is how Dacher remembers her first sight of Louise:

> In spite of her broken voice Louise was singing songs from the beginning of the century at the top of her lungs. The three others followed. Between songs they downed their liquor straight, laughed, and exchanged the most outrageous collection of obscenities. Louise was at the time seventy-seven years old, strong, compact enough so that you could see her body under the old coat which she always wore; her disheveled platinum blonde hair flew in all directions; her dark lipstick outlined a mouth well beyond its natural borders, just up to a mustache. Her face was covered with spots that at first I thought were traces of pigmentation but were in fact for the most part filth. Her nails were black, half painted with an old dark polish. Louise was astonishingly dirty and possessed a lack of all restraint (*incontinence*) that was incited by provocation: by herself she managed to animate the entire room of the bar. (214)

The point of course is that Louise's ferocious excess was a sign of her desire—quite literally her erotic desire for a man named Jean—and a measure of her more general powerful investment in life. Her remarkable appetite and energy, her flamboyance, which had nothing to do with parody, drew these two younger women to her. The way they looked at her ceased to be in any way judgmental. And as they came closer to her, their roles as uninvolved spectators diminished. As they became involved in the life of Louise, whom they followed finally to her death, their relation became one of reciprocity.[16] Louise was for Dacher a story of love and her death a kind of victory, because it was lived out in desire and was *chosen* by her, although not in the Freudian mode of resignation to fate. Louise provided these two women with a reference point from which to think their way through their research and through the nursing home, dialectically, and to conclude that in a nursing home there is no natural death. Whether an old person dies rapidly or lives for many years, it does not matter. Only nondesire remains, dissolving what little lives of life.

We both are and are not identical to ourselves throughout our lives. It is as important to stress continuity as it is difference. Masquerade can conceal or express different passions. A mask can be a coverup. It can be eccentric. It can point to change at the same time as it reveals the continuity of the subject. Was Louise's masquerade a mask? Yes, of sorts, but it did not hide anything. Was it herself? Yes. Is there represented in this portrait of an old woman the "ideal of games and masks," to refer once again to Lyotard? Definitely not. I read her masquerade in old age neither as a pathetic denial of age nor as a self-conscious, parodic act of resistance. Rather the story of Louise offers a third version. The theatricality of her unconventional and transgressive gestures did not conceal a pathetic denial of old age, nor did it assert a desire for youth. Hers was, still, a public stage, not a private forum. If for Riviere femininity as a masquerade is a disguise for a desire for masculinity, for Louise masquerade of the aging body did not express her wish for youth. Indeed the vitality of her behavior was so strong that it seems, I submit, to have effectively obliterated the centrality of the category of age. In Louise's version of the aging body-in-masquerade we do not find the self-conscious *critical* distance that we might encounter in certain readings of womanliness as a masquerade as conscious resistance.

Womanliness as a masquerade in Riviere's sense is not as symptomatic of our historical period as it was of hers. More specific to our time is youthfulness as a masquerade. Both men and women "put on" youth so as to not be classified as old. Those older may consciously or unconsciously fear retribution at the hands of those younger (this is an old story in western culture—power passes from the old to the young). The practice is, however, much more common among women whose marketability (to echo Irigaray) continues to depend in great part upon their attractiveness. In the mass media it is not surprising, therefore, that we encounter countless images of the aging body-in-masquerade as well as a discourse urging as utopia the virtual elimination of the aging body. Most of those images are of the female body. For the most part the discourse is addressed to women. As an older woman, one's success is defined in terms of how closely one approaches the model of the younger woman. The deep structure of the look of mass culture is youth versus age.

At the Academy Awards a few years ago, for example, there was a tribute to the actress Olivia de Haviland, best known for her role as the sweet and modest Melanie in *Gone with the Wind*. It took the ritualized form of a condensed retrospective of her screen roles with brief clips shown in chronological order. She was young, she was beautiful. The stated purpose was to honor the body of her work. The cinematic apparatus, of course, showcased her body. The point was to produce the uncomplicated flow of sentimentality for the millions of viewers (American and international) who were watching. And the sequence apparently did, easily. But the nostalgia was shattered when the curtains parted and Olivia de Haviland herself appeared to accept the award. The difference between her screen images and what the television cameras recorded in the present was indisputable. The distance was vast. The scrutinizing eye of the camera was ironic, calculating, cruel. She was old, she was overweight, she was disappointing. She was not so much making a spectacle of herself (although she did overact, painfully) as the image-making apparatus was making a spectacle of her.[17]

What are we to make of this mass-mediated form of the narrative of a life? Of the compression of the long process of growing up and growing old into a chronological collage of a few short segments, all of which were initially constructed for the silver screen of mass culture? Olivia de Haviland suffered disgrace at the very moment that she was being celebrated. Her scandal was that of the aging body, which was ruthlessly and relentlessly inspected by the panopticon of mass culture, the all-seeing television eye.[18]

With the American celebration of youth and with the growing number of older people in the United States, we are witnessing the proliferation of techniques for disciplining the aging body, ranging from age-calibrated exercises and new anti-aging creams to special diets and cosmetic surgery. We read about these products everywhere. A typical article in *The Ladies' Home Journal* (this one from November 1987) begins, ''The beauty buzzword these days is *anti-aging*. And it's oh-so-timely, since the segment of the population with the largest disposable income and the greatest interest in looking younger is growing older.''[19] Older people, primarily women, are urged to comply with changing fashions and increasing age. The paradox is that most women, if they maintain the continuity of their style, achieve the effect of masquerade which effectively ridicules them. A feature in *The New York Times Magazine* expresses it in this withering way: ''Some women do push the limits of consistency, wearing long hair well into their 60's, or styling their hair into a stiff bouffant, circa 1956. They might anchor their hair with two cute barrettes, or paint their lips a pale frosted pink.'' A psychology professor is quoted who makes the explicit and crude connection between anachronistic fashion, maladjustment, and old age. '' 'There are frozen dinosaurs who are locked into the way they looked when they were 16,' says Dr. Cash. 'It's almost as if their bodies don't belong to them.' ''[20]

These new techniques are spawned by the market economy. They are also used to evade (even while conforming to) the dominant ideology of youth—by joining it or infiltrating it. In years past and in the popular imagination, older Americans have been hidden in retirement communities and nursing homes. Now they are in hiding among the population. At precisely the historical moment that the elderly are appearing on the historical stage in record numbers, many are vanishing into the crowd, no longer visibly marked as old. This visual disappearing act is the analogue of the psychological repression of old age and of the social oppression of those visibly marked as old. What we see in some popular discourses on aging is not that traditional notions of aging are being accorded more currency (age as bringing wisdom, age as being synonymous with decline) or that aging is so much being redefined, but rather that the aging body is being remodeled so as to virtually eliminate it—to make it indistinguishable from a young or middle-aged body. Articles in national weekly tabloids (*The National Examiner, The Star, The National Enquirer*), whose staples and filler consist of stories on celebrities and on the body, have recently begun exploiting age as an issue, particularly and not surprisingly for women. As *The Examiner* puts it, "the theory of growing old gracefully is out-dated" (December 29, 1987). Beautiful older women, whose stock in trade is their mass-mediated images, are vaunted as models. The typically American self-help project for the aging woman is to erase the effects of time, or in the mathematics of age to subtract twenty years from chronological age. Chronological age is figured as shameful, as something one would rather not admit. *The Examiner* calls the roll—Angie Dickinson, Jane Fonda, Joan Collins, Sophia Loren, Elizabeth Taylor, and Diahann Carroll: "They have to admit they're past the half century, and they all manage to pass for twenty years younger with a few simple tricks that work for everybody." Here the mass-mediated aging body-in-masquerade is represented as a democratic body, potentially available to everyone.

Ironically then the panopticon is being evaded by the strategy of *trompe l'oeil*. I cite an extreme example, the case of Leona Helmsley, the "Queen," the hotel manager and magnate whose photograph has accompanied advertisements for the Helmsley "Palace" in such magazines as *The New York Times* and who was recently convicted on over thirty charges of tax evasion. With her coiffed dark hair and her smooth face, she might "pass for" fifty. But recently her mass-mediated image was unmasked by the media themselves who, covering the sensational story of irregular financial affairs, exposed her chronological age as sixty-nine. This was the real news! The panopticon, with its army of journalists (most of them young, no doubt), reasserted its power of surveillance.

In *The New York Times* Helmsley's age was printed in the neutral tone of facticity. In the national rags the journalistic glee in ferreting out contradictions in attitudes toward age is much more overt. Take, for example, the June 14, 1988, story in *The Star* about Jane Fonda. Her alleged behavior (surgery for breast implants) is presented as a contradiction to her words. Fonda: "I am really appalled by what I see going on in plastic surgery. We've got to make friends with those wrinkles and sags and gray hairs. We've got to understand that they represent our life experience. We see these women who have been nipped and tucked and injected and peeled to within an inch of their shiny taut lives." In effect this story, which was accompanied by the obligatory before and after photos, takes pleasure in punishing Fonda, detailing her difficulties with the operation and concluding that no matter how much she disciplines her body (aerobics, weights, running, biking), her body "still has to answer to Mother Nature." This is another version of democracy presented to and by age, yet again a reassertion of that symbolic economy whereby age represents the inevitable slide into death.

In terms of the aging body-in-masquerade, I want to single out one technique only—cosmetic surgery. Cosmetic surgery is, of course, available to people at any age, and it is used for any number of reasons. But more and more frequently it is being used to "correct" for youth.[21] This version of the aging body-in-masquerade is characterized by the aesthetics of smoothness, tact, and good taste. It is the opposite of Lacan's view of femininity as masquerade as the "piling up of crazy things, feathers, hats and strange baroque constructions which rise up like so many silent insignias."[22] What Michèle Montrelay has observed of masquerade in women—its silence—is relevant here: "The objective of masquerade is to say nothing. Absolutely *nothing*. And in order to produce this nothing the woman uses her own body as disguise."[23] With cosmetic surgery, the mask of the aging body is doubled over. The surface of the body is cut and stretched to disguise the surface of the body. Unlike the hysterical body whose surface is inscribed with symptoms, the objective of the surgically youthful body is to speak nothing.

How do we evaluate this version of masquerade? It corresponds to Doane's reading of masquerade as resistance when it produces "a certain lack in the form of a certain distance between oneself and one's image." But when is this form of masquerade collusion and complicity with an ageist culture? When does the image become part of oneself? When is the lack of relation between outer appearance and the interior disturbing? And when and if so, to whom? As a reader of mass-circulation magazines, I find an article about plastic surgery in a recent issue of *Paris Match*, France's most popular weekly magazine, to be emblematic of a distressingly violent rejection of the aging body. In 1987 *Paris Match* featured a twelve-page article, complete with double-spread color photographs, on cosmetic surgery to produce the illusion of "eternal youth." One of the most bizarrely compelling vignettes is of an older couple who underwent plastic surgery together. Faces swollen and bandaged, they are shown in a full-page photograph in their hospital room. Wearing their hospital nightgowns, they are holding hands and smiling *not* at each other but at the camera. The text comments, "If 'growing old together' is the promise upon which marriage is founded, today 'growing younger together' is a realistic basis for those who wish to prolong the happiness of being attractive to each other and of giving each other pleasure."[24] The body of youth is associated with giving the eye sexual pleasure; the aging body, conceived as its opposite, as impeding pleasure and offending the eye. Thus the aging body is to be extirpated. This is dubbed a "realistic" strategy, given technological improvements in cosmetic surgery. The aging body is to be literally effaced—at least on the surface.

The Lacanian psychoanalyst Eugénie Lemoine-Luccioni makes an important distinction between masking and cosmetic surgery. She argues that masking can sometimes both display symptoms *and* work as a cure. On the other hand, cosmetic surgery represents in the Lacanian sense the desire for the lost object (youth) which it can never restore. What is further lost in the process of surgery, doubling over the loss, are the traces of one's history. Thus cosmetic surgery serves to silence subjectivity.[25] It is a form of self-repression. At its worst, Lemoine-Luccioni argues, cosmetic surgery can result in depersonalization, in the uncanny sense that one's body is not one's own.

Mass culture, on the other hand, rests its case for cosmetic surgery on the appeal to the body as private property and ultimately on a person's narcissistic unassailability. Take, for example, an article in *USA Today* (April 27, 1988) which is calculated to appeal to a certain bizarre voyeurism—a *surgical* voyeurism. All the elements of a successful potboiler are here: beauty, wealth, celebrity, extravagance. Cher is reported as saying that "she didn't see the big deal about surgery." She is quoted as announcing, "I get to do what I want with my body. . . . When I need to get anything done I certainly mean to get it." We are informed that she has spent $40,000 on plastic surgery, "including procedures on her breasts, navel, buttocks, nose, chin, teeth, and removal of two ribs to make her look more boyish." This inventory of body parts is a "discursive surgery,"[26] aggression directed against the aging body as it is represented. But the aggression is not just discursive. The surgery took place in a literal operating theater.

Surgical voyeurism is also at stake in a recent sequence from the television soap opera *The Young and the Restless*. The television audience is shown scenes, including dizzying close-ups, from a real facelift being performed on the actress who plays Catherine Chancellor, a wealthy, vengeful, visibly old, "once beautiful'' woman. As Patricia Mellencamp has pointed out, the viewer inspects the results and concludes that they are woefully disappointing. Here again is another example of the scrutinizing panopticon dispersed into a society obsessed with youth and age.

What particularly interests me, though, is why this scene is so fascinating and so troubling to viewers. I think it has to do with the fact that we commonly associate surgery with medical matters, with illness or with severe disfigurement. Here pain is being willfully suffered for other purposes—the pressures of the ideology of youth, the resistance to death. Another scene in the history of bodily pain comes to mind—the scene of the torture of the regicide (his body was drawn and quartered) with which Michel Foucault opens *Discipline and Punish*.[27] To recall Foucault's argument: the public scene in which the King's justice was written on the body in pain and torture was replaced in the seventeenth century by a new kind of punishment, a discipline of the body represented in the institution of the prison modeled on the panopticon. But today we see *in public* another form of bodily pain. In the mass-mediated surgical scene from *The Young and the Restless*, the theater of bodily pain, which for centuries has been prohibited or concealed from view, is broadcast to millions of spectators. What was private is overtly public and accessible to voyeurism. Is this a scene of torture? Perhaps in part, for the purpose of torture is to produce the official speech of the State, which in this case is to silence age—to speak nothing. Indeed, this conflation of the public site of state torture with the private site of ''restorative'' surgery is figured in other contemporary cultural texts—in Terry Gilliam's film *Brazil* (1985), for instance, or in Thomas Pynchon's *V*. In these texts, the two sites of bodily pain are virtually interchangeable and indistinguishable, and sadism and masochism collapse into each other.

This prompts me to ask: what of the imaginary? There may be another, albeit similar, reason for the discomfort and interest aroused in the spectator by the scene from *The Young and the Restless*. It has to do with the blurring of the dichotomy between inside and outside. The surgeon Richard Selzer has remarked that there is a taboo against seeing the interior of our own bodies. Visual representations of the body are concerned predominantly with the exterior of the body (representations of the interior of the body are primarily cast in the form of standardized maps, like medical charts). Thus this may very well be a prohibition that concerns not only individuals but our culture as a whole. What is prohibited carries a fascination, of course. Autopsies (the results of which are routinely reported in the newspapers) deal with what we scarcely ever *see*. But history, and its time, is written not only on the body but *inside* the body. Opening up the body in age, then, may represent *seeing* the disturbing disjunction between the chronological age of the body (the organs of the body "speak" the age of the person) and its (soon to be) remodeled outside.[28]

I conclude then that the surgically youthful body is the postmodern version of Oscar Wilde's haunting tale of Dorian Gray, the man whose body never visibly aged. From this perspective the postmodern body is not, as Arthur Kroker and David Cook suggest, the body disfigured by what they call postmodern diseases (AIDS, anorexia, herpes).[29] It is rather the surgically youthful body, the uncanny aging body-in-masquerade.

COUNTER-TEXT

Tereza's mother blew her nose noisily, talked to people in public about her sex life, and enjoyed demonstrating her false teeth. She was remarkably skillful at loosening them with her tongue, and in the midst of a broad smile would cause the uppers to drop down over the lowers in such a way as to give her face a sinister expression.

Her behavior was but a single grand gesture, a casting off of youth and beauty. In the days when she had had nine suitors kneeling round her in a circle, she guarded her nakedness apprehensively, as though trying to express the value of her body in terms of the modesty she accorded it. Now she had not only lost that modesty, she had radically broken with it, ceremoniously using her new immodesty to draw a dividing line through her life and proclaim that youth and beauty were overrated and worthless.

—*from* Milan Kundera, *The Unbear-*
able Lightness of Being 46

9. **Phantasms of the Aging Body . . .**
The Companion/Empty/Fragmenting Body

SEVERAL YEARS AGO I TAUGHT an interdisciplinary honors course on literature and aging to college freshmen. I was surprised by several of their responses to the reading, although in retrospect I realize that I should have anticipated them. There was, for instance, a chasm between the way in which these eighteen- and nineteen-year-olds described their grandparents and great-grandparents (most of whom, if still living, lived nearby) and the way in which they described other old people, both literary and living. Their relatives were their familiars, and in general the students displayed a sympathetic understanding for them and for their lives. As for the others, the *other* is telling. The others were truly *other*. In language that was predominately stereotypical, they were defined simply and reductively as old. "Old" was understood to be only one of the many aspects of these students' relatives (and it was often not even a particularly important aspect at that). But for the others, "old" was the sole and subsuming feature. I know that this reductiveness may have been brought about in part—perhaps even in large part—by the focus of the course itself. But still I found it striking that there was no awareness on the part of the students of a lack of integration in their own readings and representations of aging. They "split" the old into two categories: those whom they knew well and did not see exclusively in terms of age, and those whom they did not know well and defined categorically as old. In the latter case, "old" took precedence over other culturally defined markers—over gender, race, and ethnicity.[1]

I am generalizing here to make my point. In fact the attitudes the students expressed were more complex. But I am not exaggerating when I report that not one of these twenty-some students could imagine in a concrete and however sketchy way what shape their own lives might take through the middle years and into old age. I had asked them to write a summary of their life stories from the perspective of old age (this exercise is not uncommon in classes in gerontology). What I found instead of narratives of lives sustained into old age was an abrupt series of deaths in their late twenties and thirties. As I mentioned earlier, I take it as commonplace that in western culture we now assume that, barring accident or an untreatable disease, we will live out our natural life span and thus into old age. But these students were simply not prepared—or refused— to imagine themselves beyond the decades so close to their own.

How could I help prepare my students to imagine old age? We were reading various works of twentieth-century American literature ranging from Saul Bellow's *Mr. Sammler's Planet*, Tillie Olsen's *Tell Me a Riddle,* and Arthur Miller's *Death of a Salesman* to May Sarton's *Journal of a Solitude* and Ernest Hemingway's *Old Man and the Sea*, my selection being dependent upon what was in print in paperback. But it occurred to me that the art and craft of acting, in its more literal guise, was preeminently suited to exercise the imagination in terms of the kind of identification Beauvoir had in mind when she urges us in *The Coming of Age* to "recognize ourselves in this old man or that old woman" (14). One of the professors of acting at the University of Wisconsin-Milwaukee agreed to lead my class through the exercises he used in preparing his young actors to play old characters. For upwards of an hour we worked under his direction in a dimly lit workshop studio. He impressed upon us the increasing weight of gravity over time, the dimming of our sight and hearing, and the accumulating sediment in our voices. What I remember most vividly after that hour was how heavy and tired my body felt.

No doubt there was some value in this exercise. Most important, it asked us to *feel* our bodies differently. But in retrospect I question its wisdom. The exercise addressed only the physical aspects of the passage of our bodies through the years. Its sole narrative was unmitigated physical decline, which was gradual and yet simultaneously precipitous. The exercise took the form of a litany of deficits chanted in a depressive monotone: the weakening of our eyesight, the clumsiness of our bodies in motion, the loss of our power of hearing. Instructors in geriatrics in medical schools have used similar techniques, asking students, for example, to take notes with their unaccustomed hand, or to tape their fingers together to simulate arthritis. In *The View from Eighty* Malcolm Cowley vo-

ciferously questions this approach. Cowley: " 'Put cotton in your ears and peb-
bles in your shoes,' said a gerontologist, a member of that new profession
dedicated to alleviating all maladies of people except the passage of years. 'Pull
on rubber gloves. Smear Vaseline over your glasses, and there you have it: instant
aging.' Not quite. His formula omits the messages from the social world, which
are louder, in most cases, than those from within" (5). In previous chapters I
have taken up the question of how the social body constrains the way we perceive
the physical body. Here I want to turn to a different body. The acting exercise
ignored the intertwining of the body and psyche, which in some cases seems
to bring compensation. Bracketed was the *psychic body*.

As we have seen in the previous pages, in western culture aging is represented
primarily in terms of the visual, in terms of the surface of the body. Hence the
emphasis in literature on the way the body looks, and hence the endemic cultural
practice of checking ourselves and others for physical signs of aging. Hence, as
I have shown, the emphasis on mirrors and masquerade in both literature and
life. This preoccupation with surfaces is a symptom of our culture of narcissism
and of our society of the spectacle and mass-mediated images. Unfortunately,
this view of the body as a *specular* body has achieved widespread currency at
the expense of other dimensions of the body. Yet we commonly talk about how
our bodies *feel*. I am hot, we will say. Or, I feel full of water. Or, I feel fat.
How might our bodies *feel* phantasmatically in old age? What about phantasms
and representations of the body-in-space, of the interior of the body, and of the
body-in-parts? In this chapter, then, I turn to literary representations of phantasms of the aging body.

But first I want to tell a personal story. It is my memory of a kind of
hallucination of an aging body. It is a waking dream of a psychic body, of my
own body in what I could imagine to be an aspect of my old age. As with so
many other stories about age, my starting point is chronological age. I begin
with a number.

I was twenty-four at the time and living in San Diego. I was going to graduate
school there at what was then called, if I remember correctly, San Diego State.
I took the bus to school. It was always very crowded. One afternoon after getting
off the bus, I turned around and looked back. I saw myself in the midst of all
the people getting off the bus again. I was my grandmother. I was in the body
of my grandmother. She was in her late sixties, near the age at which she had
been when she, like Barthes, was run over by a car.

My memory of this phantasm of an aging body has accompanied me for
some twenty years now. I do not remember any specific visual details, the color
of (I hesitate between pronouns) my dress, for example, or what I was carrying,
if anything. What I remember is the shape of my body. As long as I had known

my grandmother, her body had always been the same, or so it seemed to me. It was matronly, ample, gentle, energetic. For that moment it felt as if it were mine. My overwhelming impression was how comfortable I felt.

Although iconic, this phantasm of an aging body was predominantly and palpably corporeal, tactile not visual. The affect associated with it was a sense of equilibrium and assurance, not anxiety. The form it took was that of a tableau of stasis, not of a drama or a narrative structured by crises. The felt metaphor was that of being held by one's body. Being held by this body was a comforting feeling. Was this a reparative phantasy? Perhaps. It had something of the sense of *déjà vu* about it. There was the presence of the already-seen, of the uncanny, of the surfacing of the past in the present. I was bringing my grandmother back to life. But there was a prospective dimension to this phantasy as well. The future appeared in the present. Thus in the context of this book as well as of my life, I think of it as the kind of phantasy which helps make possible a certain disposition toward the future of our bodies as they age. With this image I counter, for example, Freud's dream of "My Uncle with the Yellow Beard," which I discussed in the chapter on aging as castration. And with it I counter the words of Madame de Sévigné which I quoted in the chapter on the mirror stage of old age: "If at the age of twenty we were given the position of the eldest member of the family and if we were taken to a mirror and shown the face that we should have or do have at sixty, comparing it with that at twenty, we would be utterly taken aback and it would frighten us."[2]

Freudian psychoanalysis, with its stress on the psychological and sexual development of infant and child, has given us narratives of the integration of the body parts into a whole and of the construction of identity. The metaphors are architectonic. It should not be surprising then that in old age with its accompanying physical decline, a psychoanalytic reading will revolve around, if not produce, the metaphors of disintegration. We may have the uncanny impression that processes have reversed themselves, are *undoing* themselves, are coming undone. The equation between childhood and old age has been made in countless time-honored representations of the so-called ages of man from Jacques's famous and sour speech on the seven ages of man in Shakespeare's *As You Like It* to Epinal's graphic portrayal in the visual arts of the twelfth and final stage as the age of imbecility or second childhood.[3] The equation between childhood and old age has passed into everyday speech (he is in his second childhood, we will say), and it makes people patently anxious (we will avoid it for ourselves but attribute it to others). Rather than deny the association of old age with childhood, however, we should confront it.

In the images of the psychic body which I discuss below—the immobile body, the empty body, the fragmenting body—the figure of *undoing* is central.

But the process of undoing is not presented as one of simple physical decline—the draining of color, the weakening of eyesight, the diminishing of strength, the fading of memory. That is without doubt a dominant aspect of aging, and one we cannot consciously deny, although powerful literary fictions, such as *The Portrait of Dorian Gray*, speak to our desire to do so.[4] Nor do these images counter decline with sugar-coated compensatory sentiment. Instead they show us that our cultural image-repertoire of aging bodies is more various and richer in meaning and subtlety than we might have thought.

THE IMMOBILE BODY/THE COMPANION BODY

I turn first to *The Afternoon of Monsieur Andesmas*, a short and mysterious novel by Marguerite Duras which deserves to be much better known than it is.[5] In it we find emphasized two aspects of the body other than the visual—touch and movement. But first we must take a brief detour.

Our sense of the unity of our bodies is three-dimensional. It is constituted by touch and movement, which together contribute to our idea of our body in terms of the *tactile*. Through the body image which we construct out of our sense of our bodies, we imagine the body in space and thus in a place. Schilder has insisted that our tactile image of the body is independent of our visual image of the body.[6] Perhaps it is even prior to our visual image of the body. The infant's developing sense of his body as a whole comes in great part from the touch of the mother. As she supports the infant's neck, as she washes the legs and arms, as she counts the toes, she assembles the body. As she cradles the baby, she encompasses the body in a single gesture. This corresponds to what Winnicott calls *holding*. By holding the infant, the mother helps the child to *feel* himself as an entity rather than as a jumble or hodgepodge of parts. Winnicott calls attention to the psychic catastrophe that can befall an infant if he has the experience of infinite falling, of being dropped and never being caught and never coming to rest. In such a case, he cautions, the psychic body may never resolve itself into a unity. I would add that in later years and over the life span, the loss of the affectionate touch of others can contribute to a sense of our derealization—and not just in the metaphoric sense.

And what part does movement play in the development of our sense of our bodies as whole? As a child grasps an object, she learns about how the parts of her own body are connected as well. Encountering the material world as she crawls, she develops a sense of her own boundaries. We have even given a name to this stage of learning how to move the body: the infant is a "toddler." In and of itself, then, movement is a means whereby we construct the tactile image of the body. In our early years holding and movement are linked together, and they continue to so be throughout our lives as we see in moments of fear and danger when we search for security. Psychoanalysis has called this "clinging"; its opposite, though linked, is "going in search."[7]

Freud theorizes that infants direct their energies narcissistically to different areas of the body in a certain sequence—a genetic sequence; I will come back to this in the next section. Lacan, as we saw in the chapter on the mirror stage of old age, insists that we cathect our own specular image. In addition we cathect movement itself when we are in the process of constructing a unified body image out of disparate parts. If Lacan observes that infants experience intense pleasure in recognizing their mirror image, similarly toddlers experience pleasure in sheer movement.[8] If, as Lacan theorizes, the specular image of the infant seems to it to be an "other," so movement itself takes the toddler in all directions seemingly independent of her volition or intention. Only later do intention and movement become integrated. What happens, then, when the body slows down in old age? What of the body's relation to touch in old age? *The Afternoon of Monsieur Andesmas* suggests several answers to these questions.

There is a torpor that stretches across the landscape, both psychic and natural, of Duras's novel. The atmosphere is hot and slow. We are in southern France, and before us is Mr. Andesmas. Or rather before us are his body and his mind, for the two are no longer quite connected. Mr. Andesmas is seventy-eight. All afternoon he has been waiting, sitting heavily in a wicker armchair. It is Beckettian, this waiting. In a sense nothing will come. But the body is not at all as I imagine the bodies of Beckett's old men, thin and frail. Rather this body has grown large and ponderous.

Mr. Andesmas is wealthy and has placed himself in a position of control. He is on a hill overlooking the Mediterranean and the village below. But he is represented as having lost mobility. He can no longer move toward what he wants, and what he wants will no longer come to him. Even his wealth cannot guarantee him that. Ultimately what he desires is youth, which is irrevocably lost to him, even in the form of others. But he does not resort to masquerade, as does Mann's Aschenbach.

At first the body of Mr. Andesmas seems to dominate the landscape. Its sinking weight, its sheer inertia, its low point of gravity, its massive bulk—all anchor it to its place. And yet the body is indistinct. It lacks a definite presence. It is as if this body had become a statue, an inanimate part of the landscape. It seems almost to disappear from view, to blend into the surroundings. For the imaginary spectator, this body (it is "ancient") has no clearly discernible boundaries or parts. Or rather, there is the head and then there is the rest of the body. The effect is not one of unattractiveness, however. The effect is, we could say, *arresting*. It is achieved in great part by the clothes of Mr. Andesmas, which serve several functions. First, the clothes separate the head from the rest of the body or, we might almost say, from the body itself. Duras: "Below the ancient, smiling and bare head, the body was richly covered with beautiful dark clothes, meticulously clean. You could see the immense shape only vaguely, it was very decently covered with those beautiful clothes" (19). Secondly, the clothes do not dress or adorn the body so much as they wrap it or enshroud it and its undefinable parts, which have grown huge. A scotoma is the sensation of having a body part where one no longer exists. Mr. Andesmas, on the contrary, has the distinct sensation that a part of him (his stomach) has grown gigantic. The proportions of his body have come undone. Parts are no longer unified but must be carried around or held by the rest of the body. Duras: "His belly, for example; resting on his knees, it was wrapped in a waistcoat of the same dark material" (37). In his old age it is as if Mr. Andesmas has accumulated extra or new body parts.

Thirdly, clothes serve to hide the body. In the masquerade of *The Afternoon of Monsieur Andesmas*, the adornment or display of the body, or the re-vision of the body in the guise of youth, is no longer at stake. "Clothing," in fact, seems the wrong term to describe what covers his body, for clothing suggests complexity and the articulation of parts. Rather, the body of Mr. Andesmas is, simply, covered with material. The body is draped as if it were a piece of large furniture. The draping is a strategy for not being seen, for being "forgotten" by those Mr. Andesmas instinctively understands may find his presence troubling, especially children. Mr. Andesmas is considerate of others. "At his age," as Duras describes him, "he knew how not to make his presence bothersome, ever, to anyone, particularly children" (21). ("Bothersome" is a gentle word; we may suspect that the feelings of children might be much stronger, as we will see in a moment in the writing of Colette.) Andesmas's strategy appears to be this: if his body disappears, then so in a sense does he, and then he will be secure or, as we might say of a boat or a house, *secured*. His body covered, he is undercover. Mr. Andesmas wears protective covering. Thus the clothes finally are not so much on him as he is somehow *inside* them. Clothes have openings; they are like doors which give access to the body. But Mr. Andesmas is covered in material which, like a nun's habit, is specifically designed to allow no entry. His body is not permeable to others. He is protected, but the cost is this: if he does not wish to make his presence palpably felt, then he will not be able to compel people to come to him.

Movement, touch, and desire are interrelated in this elemental story. The loss of movement in old age entails the loss of the touch of others, but the touch of others is precisely what Mr. Andesmas desires, although at the beginning of the story he does not altogether know that. We begin our lives being held and caressed. To echo Winnicott, our sense of being *real* in our bodies comes from being touched. The mother, as I have said, is a kind of body-mirror to the infant. But as we grow older, it would seem that we progressively lose the touch of others. There is no clinging, and there is no going in search. I suspect that one of the reasons many adults are drawn to children is that their bodies are potentially available to them. Is it not a great loss to be prohibited from touching and being touched?

In *The Blue Lantern* Colette tells us that she found herself in her mid-seventies "practicing" for the paralysis she imagined an even older age would bring her: "in anticipation of the time when I shall no longer move," she wrote, "I make no effort to move" (57). Here again movement and touch are linked. In a kind of Proustian way an involuntary memory of Colette's childhood returns to her. She remembers what it felt like when she was a little girl and old people touched her. Now an old lady, she remembers that when she was little she shrank from the touch of old people. She avoided, as she puts it, "the clutches of the small paralyzed hand, crumpled as a claw" (78). "I vividly recall my shudder or repugnance when I was very young . . . at the touch of old people," she writes, wincing as she wonders now if the young person who is visiting her is experiencing the same sensation (78–79).[9]

In *The Afternoon of Monsieur Andesmas* the most poignant and most dramatic moment occurs in the theater of the mind of Mr. Andesmas—his revelation that he has lost the touch of others. We associate the sense of sight with distance and perspective, the sense of touch with closeness. What Mr. Andesmas has lost is a certain intimacy and familiarity with others. A young woman is sent to tell him that the person he is waiting for will come later. Mr. Andesmas *feels* her presence—her hair brushes against his body—and at that moment he comprehends his utter solitude in old age. *No one touches him anymore.* Duras: "He felt upon him the smell of a summer dress and of a woman's loose hair. Nobody ever came so close to Mr. Andesmas anymore." His daughter Valerie is the single exception. But by the end of the novel she too will have disappeared from his life. He will be virtually and utterly alone.

I want to insist that "touch" here is not only metaphorical. Even more important, it is literal. When we say that we have been touched by someone, we may mean that we feel ourselves somehow close to that person. But for this old man, whose age seems to stretch out endlessly before him, what is lacking is the *actual* touch of others. It is the literal touch of others that entails metaphorical closeness and not the other way around. "Was the closeness" of this woman "more important than what she was saying?" he wonders. We can answer, yes.

I concluded the chapter on mourning and melancholia with an image of a dying old woman being cradled in the arms of a young woman. The importance of touch is that it *places* you. It is the medium of the articulation of a relationship. Touch yields two different senses—that of connection and that of separateness. It makes for a sense of oneness, as with the body of the mother or nurse, as well as for a sense of difference. One thing is sure: if we are not touched, we might begin to suspect that we are not here. As we have seen, Beckett represents Malone, who has no sensation of being touched, as dispersed. As Freud noted in *Inhibitions, Symptoms and Anxiety*, "one of the oldest and most fundamental commands of obsessional neuroses [is] the taboo on touching" (SE 20: 121). We have a lifelong need to be touched, a need which Ashley Montague has suggested may if anything increase with aging. In *Touching* he writes: "this is where we fail the aging quite miserably—as we do in so much else. Because we are unwilling to face the fact of aging, we behave as if it isn't there. It is this massive evasion that is the principal reason for our failure to understand the needs of the aging."[10]

The waiting in this novel is, as I said, Beckettian. Nothing happens—except that Mr. Andesmas is told to keep waiting, to wait longer. For many in advanced old age there is nothing to do but wait. I remember vividly in the nursing homes I have visited the old people sitting in the "day room." The position of the body is significant. Neither standing (which is active) nor lying down (completely passive),[11] they were simply sitting, waiting, perhaps in expectation. Waiting for what? I would like to replace that question here with another one: *with* what? We are brought back to the body and to *The Afternoon of Monsieur Andesmas*.

Mr. Andesmas experiences the weight and inertia of his body as a kind of paralysis which invades his mind, dulling his sense of life (we may think here of Freud's death instincts). In his vast solitude no one exists to call him out of his body. Yet paradoxically he also becomes dissociated from his body. Duras describes his sensations this way: "An insinuating heaviness slowly penetrated Mr. Andesmas, taking hold of his limbs, of his whole body, and slowly reaching his mind. His hands became like lead on the arms of his chair and his head grew remote even to himself, letting it be taken over by a discouragement, never experienced before, at the thought of going on" (26). These feelings are not specifically associated only with physical decline, as they were, for example, in the acting exercise I mentioned earlier. Nor are his sensations those of simple frustration. We seek out and create psychic compensation for what we have lost. If in old age we have lost the bodies of others, then we may turn for some sort of comfort to our own body, which may now have become to us an *other* body. The physical reality of the immobile body in solitude—its very persistence, its thereness—is inseparable from its psychic valence: one's body is one's only and constant companion. One dwells in it. It provides a kind of reassurance or stability. This investment in one's body would not be, then, a simple return to the Freudian stage of the infant narcissistically cathecting its body as an erotic object. Rather it would be a tenacious attachment to one's own body that is characterized by ambivalence, by a volatile and yet balancing affect. Duras, emphasizing the paradoxical distance that Mr. Andesmas places between himself and his body, puts it this way: "Mr. Andesmas looked at himself. And at the sight of himself he found some comfort. It was, that evening, the equivalent of the only certainty he had known in the course of his life" (37). Of all the bodies that have been lost over his long life, only his remains. In the physical heaviness of his body, in its massive corporeality, it is as if Mr. Andesmas has *accumulated* more and more body as a way of literally alleviating his solitude.[12]

Finally, then, in *The Afternoon of Monsieur Andesmas* we find represented the phantasm of the immobile body as a companion. In Vita Sackville-West's *All Passion Spent* (1931), the experience of the body in old age is represented in similar terms. *All Passion Spent* is a novel about an elderly woman who, after the death of her powerful and widely respected husband, shocks her children by firmly taking what remains of her life into her own hands. The novel is basically a sentimental romance of old age. The heroine *chooses* a solitude which turns out to be eminently fulfilling and which is relieved by the attentions of a man who had (of course) loved her from afar during all the long years of her marriage. But this passage about the body I find quite interesting:

> [her mind turned to] the growth of her bodily ailments, for which she was beginning to feel quite an affection. Her body had, in fact, become her companion, a constant resource and preoccupation; all the small squalors of the body, known only to oneself, insignificant in youth, easily dismissed, in old age became dominant and entered into the fulfillment of the tyranny they had always threatened. Yet it was, rather than otherwise, an agreeable and interesting tyranny. A hint of lumbago caused her to rise cautiously from her chair and reminded her of the day she had ricked her back at Nervl, since when her back had never been very reliable. The small intimacies of her teeth were known to her, so that she ate carefully, biting on one side rather than on the other. She instinctively crooked one finger—the third on the left hand—to save it from the pang of neuritis. . . . And all these parts of the body became intensely personal.[13]

A much more prosaic account of the body in old age than we find in *The Afternoon of Monsieur Andesmas*, this account of the body is primarily a list of infirmities of bodily parts. Thus I prefer to call it a description of the aging body rather than a phantasm, which speaks more mysteriously to our fears and desires. Yet it illustrates the way in which we may care for our body in old age as if it were a baby, *our* baby, paying attention to all its parts. In *All Passion*

Spent it is as if the body, and its parts, have become *real* objects. This woman treats her body as a mother would her baby. She is in a narcissistic relation to it. It absorbs, here, all her attention. For the moment, she needs nothing else. But more significant, *All Passion Spent*, like *The Afternoon of Monsieur Andesmas*, goes counter to the more familiar notion of being imprisoned in our bodies in old age which we saw dramatized in my students' acting exercise.

THE EMPTY BODY

We commonly will say of a person who is very thin and frail, he or she is "nothing" but skin and bones.[14] Generally our attitude is one of pity. As we see the body diminish, we wish it had more weight and more solidity. By this we seem to mean more life, for fragility is associated with vulnerability. At stake in this "nothing" is the dimension of mass. But the body is also figured in terms of an inside and an outside. Freud gave us the image of the skin as a sac containing what is inside. More recently Didier Anzieu has elaborated the skin as the base which furnishes the psyche with its representations of the self and its functions.[15] An exterior requires an interior. How do we imagine this interior—literally, phenomenologically, phantasmatically? And what precisely of the interior of the body in old age? In Sartre's words, the body in old age— *his* body in old age—was the *empty* body.

I take Sartre's words as they were given shape by Simone de Beauvoir in *Adieux: A Farewell to Sartre*. Beauvoir's response to Sartre's long decline in old age is both clinical and troubled. But here I will bracket her portrayal of Sartre and turn to Sartre's words as if we were reading an autobiographical account of the last ten years of his life.[16] Sartre's medical history of these ten years is marked by several strokes, diabetes, growing blindness, and, finally, uremia. What did it feel like? Sartre described his sensations and feelings in terms of emptiness. For Sartre this emptiness was associated with a lack of cognitive activity. When he felt "empty" he had ceased to exist as an intellectual. Empty for Sartre was the opposite of work. His emptiness took the form of silence. He was no longer full of life (that is, he no longer worked). He was dull. Sartre told Beauvoir: " 'I'm not stupid. But I'm empty' " (49). He told her that he "felt empty . . . at present he had no desire to work" (65). When they were having lunch with a friend and Sartre remained in silence, Beauvoir asked him, " 'What are you thinking about?' " He responded, " 'Nothing. I'm not here.' " Beauvoir persisted, " 'Where are you?' " Sartre answered, " 'Nowhere. I'm empty' " (65).

Beauvoir's question draws Sartre back into the world, but only momentarily. Her solicitation of him allows us to hear his voice, which without her demand would have remained silent. In his words I hear a dulled despair. " 'I'm not stupid,' " he insists. But he cannot locate himself in the social world. He has no place. He does not know if he is dead or alive. Unlike the body of Mr. Andesmas, his body does not serve him as a refuge or a shelter. He is not *in* his body. His body is empty. It is a shell, an envelope containing nothing. The implication is that of loss, that the body has not always been vacant but was once full. The mode is depressive.

Sartre's sense of emptiness is a confirmation of castration. In this scenario of castration, what has been lost is not visible, as it is in the Freudian narrative of emergent sexual identity. The "wound" is written not on the surface of the body but, somehow, inside it. And yet not really inside it either, for there is a dissociation between body and mind. As Sartre describes himself, the activity of his mind, *thinking*, has stopped.[17] But the psyche has continued to produce phantasms of emptiness. And emptiness is associated with unlocatability. In western culture we locate ourselves phantasmatically *in* the body. Winnicott has observed, for instance, that an infant generally locates himself in the belly or in the head, but that an adult invariably locates himself behind the eyes.[18] In Sartre's evocation of an empty, organless, mindless body, the self is *dis*located.

Emptiness and unlocatability are the effects of the progressive disorganization and disappearance of the libidinal body. In *Adieux* we find the Freudian narrative of libidinal development written in reverse. The functions of the openings (or erogenous zones) of the body atrophy one by one. The narrative of genetic development of the libidinal organization of the infant's body proceeds from the oral phase, to the anal, and then to the phallic phase. In *Adieux* we witness the unraveling of this narrative.

First, Sartre loses the desire to work, which had been his primary pleasure his whole life long as well as his claim to power. The phallic aspect of his life— undone. Secondly, he becomes incontinent. Strikingly he feels no shame. He understands his body no longer as the means of expressing himself but as an object. He is no longer interested in controlling what comes out of his body. He no longer feels compelled to organize aspects of his body into the realms of the sacred and the profane. He no longer experiences any necessity to take care of his body. He describes himself as a " 'living corpse' " (74). The anal aspect of his life—also undone. And thirdly, the oral phase. At times eating and drinking seemed the only pleasure left to him. Taking things into the body is a way of trying to fill up the primal cavity and to restore the sense of libidinal well-being that has been lost. Yet nonetheless Sartre felt himself to be empty. Nothing could satiate him.

The figure of the empty body is not specific to old age, of course. Borderline patients also describe themselves as "empty." More pertinent because more literal, we also can understand anorexia in terms of the figure of the empty body. The anorexic body is associated with a void, with the feeling of powerlessness, and with the inability to express desire. Like the empty body of old age, the anorexic body is also strangely indeterminant with respect to life and death. But there is a critical difference between the anorexic body and the empty body of old age. The anorexic is characterized by an indomitable discipline and a fierce marshaling of defenses. In the case of the aged person who feels his body to be empty, will and discipline have atrophied along with the libidinal organization of the body. The anorexic struggles against the sense of emptiness by hyperactivity. The empty body in old age, on the other hand, is linked with inactivity. It is as if the body itself no longer urges a defense against disintegration.

But in this inactivity there can be a kind of compensation, as if the body had returned to a primordial state of rest. Sartre often railed against his decline in old age. But it is significant that there were times when he did not. For Sartre the empty body in old age was at times associated with the *pleasures* of inactivity, with doing nothing. Indeed, the formulation "doing nothing" is inaccurate and inadequate. Everyday language requires that we describe Sartre's state in negative terms: he was *doing nothing*. But we could say instead that he was musing, resting, or daydreaming. Beauvoir tells us that Sartre liked to sit gazing at the world "doing nothing" for long periods of time. He was not anxious but content to do nothing, he said, content to merely exist. How incredibly different this description of a sense of being is from Melanie Klein's theoretical portrait of an infant's experience. In Klein's view of the infant, the body is phantasmatically crowded with part-objects and the psyche is teeming with violent emotions. I allude to Klein here not to endorse her portrait of the turbulent emotional life of the infant but to put in relief the quiescent aspect of the empty body of old age as we find it in *Adieux*. The quiescent empty body of old age, associated with the affect of contentment, is also different from the inert Freudian body of old age which is associated with a lack of affect, with a resigned stoicism, although *resting* is an important component of both images.

Others have also described such contentment in inactivity. The examples are numerous, and I pause to report only one here. I quote from the American analyst Martin Grotjohn who in a letter to the English medical journal *The Lancet* described how he felt after having a heart attack. Grotjohn was in his late seventies or his early eighties, I would guess. What we find is not a phantasm of the aging body—indeed the body has virtually disappeared from his discourse—but a phenomenological description of his sense of being in the world. His words are remarkable for their tone of equanimity. As we will see, Grotjohn is concerned primarily with time in all its modalities—the past, the present, the future—and with the emotions he associates with each aspect of time in his life. He associates the past with work, guilt, and inadequacy, and the present with the pleasures of tranquility, gentleness, and love. The present is figured as a kind of hiatus or *entre-temps* between the past and the future, which is death and which he imagines will be difficult:

> I feel like an old man. I don't work and what's more, I don't walk. It's strange but it doesn't bother me. Suddenly fifty years of work is enough. I no longer take care of patients, and I no longer accuse myself of not understanding them or knowing how to help them. I feel liberated from the guilt that accompanies our work and the feeling that I will never be as adequate as one would hope. It's for others to take up the banner. I'm through with my practice and with problems.
>
> I sit in the sun, watching the leaves fall in the pool. I think, I dream, I draw. I feel liberated from the world of reality. I still love, in a tranquil way, and I still feel loved by my family and friends.
>
> I have time. I don't know how much time remains to me, but I'm not in a hurry. I'm not in a hurry to arrive—even to the end. It can wait, and when it comes, I will try to accept it, without any illusions. It won't be easy. I live for and in the moment, and I want to stay here a little bit longer, in tranquility. I consider all age a success in itself. Now, I understand better.[19]

Winnicott has insisted that in the life of the infant what he calls *being* precedes *doing*. Perhaps in an advanced old age *doing* is succeeded by *being*, not necessarily for all time but for a time.[20] Grotjohn's sense of being in old age is not pierced by anguish or fear. But we must take care not to allow this image of old age—or any other one, for that matter—to represent old age in all of its complexity. With its emphasis on tranquility, Grotjohn's report of his experience in and of old age can work negatively to release those younger from a sense of responsibility, concern, or guilt regarding the elderly. And indeed the view of old age as a period of gentle peace corresponds to one of our dominant and reductive cultural images of aging. We may think of the endless variations on this—an old man sitting in a park, an old woman in a rocking chair on the front porch, old people drowsing in front of a fire. Yet it is equally important that we not err on the side of distrust, and disregard or irretrievably distort the testimony of a Grotjohn, a Sartre, or even a Freud, as we find him in some of his last letters.[21] In this image of the quiescent body in old age we are very far indeed from the medical body. The body is not so much defined in terms of sickness and health as it is figured in terms of activity and rest—or metaphorically, young and old. How can we understand the phantasm of the empty body as contributing to a sense of *well-being*?

On this point I find very suggestive the words of a seventy-six-year-old French woman named Amelie who lived out the last years of her life in a nursing home. At issue in her description of her body is what it means to be sick, which pivots for her on the distinction between the outside and the inside: "I'm not sick, my body is not sick . . . my legs hurt . . . my body . . . is in good shape, like always . . . never . . . intestinal trouble or stomach trouble."[22]

This woman distinguishes between *part-objects* of her body (her legs), which are not essential to her sense of health and to her sense of the wholeness of her body, and her *image* of her body as a whole, which is associated with the internal organs. We are invited to conclude that if one has the sensation of having no internal organs, then one can understand oneself as not being sick. When we are sick our attention is drawn to the ailing or painful part of the body. If our body is empty, we need not focus on a mortal illness or death.

A striking passage from a recent novel illustrates this point by its opposite. In Gabriel Garcia Marquez's *Love in the Time of Cholera,* the eighty-one-year-old Dr. Juvenal Urbino is described as being able to actually *feel* his internal organs, a phenomenon that is associated in his mind with the disease of old age which is signaled by the stink of mortality. "Until the age of fifty he had not been conscious of the size and weight and condition of his organs," Marquez writes of Urbino. But little by little as Urbino grew older, "he had begun to feel them, one by one, inside his body, feel the shape of his insomniac heart, his mysterious liver, his hermetic pancreas."[23] In *Love in the Time of Cholera* aging, figured as a fatal disease, and the body, filled with organs, are linked together in the spectacle of the autopsy. Marquez: "Dr. Juvenal Urbino knew that most fatal diseases had their own specific odor, but that none was as specific as old age. He detected it in the cadavers slit open from head to toe on the dissecting table" (40). It is as if the phantasmatic sense of individual organs (we cannot really—that is, literally—feel our internal organs) presaged the anarchy of these organs functioning independently of one another.

Or we may offer another interpretation which ultimately, however, only represents the other side of the death-coin. If old age is linked with illness, perhaps it is only a temporary condition, and the attention devoted to the various offending parts of the body might deflect our attention away from death itself. This would be hypochondria as a defense. As Lacan proposed in a translation of a passage from *Antigone* in *L'Ethique de la psychanalyse*, "Against death alone will there never be a talisman permitting us to escape it . . . but we have imagined something wonderful: flight into impossible illnesses. It is we who have constructed them, fabricated them" (321).

THE FRAGMENTING BODY

In *An American Childhood* Annie Dillard, writing from the vantage point of her early forties, tells the story of her early years primarily in terms of her growth into consciousness. For her the development of consciousness was linked with her perception of adult bodies as always old. In her child's eye there were none of the fine distinctions we learn to make later between people of twenty-five, forty-five, and so on. All adults were simply *old*. Their bodies were sagging and loose. They were coming apart. But the view from forty brings a different perspective—that of bemused affection for the perceptions of the child she had once been. She remembers that when she was a little girl she was astonished by the utter lack of concern her parents (they were in their twenties) displayed toward their disastrous condition. In a marvelous passage we read:

> Our parents and grandparents, and all their friends, seemed insensible to their own prominent defect, their limp, coarse skin.
> We children had, for instance, proper hands; our fluid, pliant fingers joined their skin. Adults had misshapen, knuckly hands loose in their skin like bones in a bag. . . .
> We were whole, we were pleasing to ourselves. . . . Our crystalline eyes shone from firm, smooth sockets; we spoke in pure piping voices through dark tidy lips. Adults were coming apart, but they neither noticed nor minded. My revulsion was rude, so I hid it. . . . (24)

I read this passage as a self-conscious revision of childhood perceptions of the fragmenting body. It does not point to an originary phantasm of the Lacanian fragmented body, although it is connected to it. Nor does it recall more generally the discourse of psychoanalysis from Freud to Mahler with its emphasis on how we acquire a sense of bodily unity. Rather it emphasizes the fragmenting body, the body in the process of going to pieces. In this section, I am concerned to make a distinction between the *fragmenting* body and the *fragmented* body.

The fragmented body has been the focus of much recent research, most prominently in feminist film theory and criticism which has turned its attention to the female body fragmented and fetishized by the male gaze. In contrast the fragmenting body is best understood not in terms of gender—at its base it is genderless—but in terms of old age. The phantasm of the fragmenting body is associated with old age and the death that decrepitude brings. In a somewhat enigmatic passage in "Subversion of the Subject," Lacan explains what he means by the phantasy of decrepitude. It derives from the constitution of the subject in the realm of the visual: "the specular image is the channel taken by the transfusion of the body's libido towards the object. But even though part of it [the libido] remains preserved from this immersion, concentrating within it the most intimate aspect of auto-eroticism, its position at the 'tip' of the form predisposes it to the phantasy of decrepitude in which is completed its exclusion from the specular image and from the prototype that it constitutes for the world of objects" (*Ecrits* 319).

Lacan's insight that we know unconsciously that we will never be identical or whole to what we perceive in others as the image of unity has been much elaborated. I myself took this up in my chapter on the mirror stage of old age. What interests me here, however, is that Lacan chooses the word "decrepitude" with its inevitable reference to aging and old age, specifically to the infirmities of old age associated with the weakening and wearing down of the body, the breaking down of the body, or more phantasmatically, the *decay* of the body. Lacan is arguing that we are predisposed structurally to the phantasy of decrepitude. Decrepitude is a process. The phantasy of decrepitude is a *prospective* phantasy, not a retrospective one, although it draws on our unconscious experience of the infantile fragmented body. As a prospective phantasy it may appear with more insistence at certain periods of our lives—at the midpoint of our lives or at the very end. The anthropologist Thomas Louis-Vincent reports, for example, that in France very old men and women (especially women) who live alone fear that their bodies will be found long after they have died. Louis-Vincent suggests that a beautiful death represents a challenge to our mortality; thus a corpse of a person of advanced age in a state of decay would represent a capitulation to death.[24] The fear of one's body being found in a state of decay points to the phantasm of the fragmenting body. As we will see, the phantasm of the fragmenting body may be invoked to evoke, from a phenomenological point of view, the aging body unto death.

How do we deal with the phantasm of the fragmenting body or the decrepit body? What defenses do we erect? We can understand our culture's obsession with dismemberment in horror films as the repression or denial of the fragmenting body of old age, for the body is threatened and dismembered violently by outside forces. It does not fall apart in and of itself through age. We may project our fears of the fragmenting body in old age onto others, thus distancing ourselves from the specter of the fragmenting body by externalizing our anxieties and fears. Elsewhere in this book I have suggested that one of the aspects of the process of aging that renders it somehow acceptable to us is its gradual nature. For the most part aging proceeds almost invisibly. Thus Colette, remarking on her failing senses in *The Blue Lantern*, can still say with a measure of equanimity at seventy-five: "We should not be unreasonably perturbed when our precious senses become dulled with age. . . . My chief concern is lest I should mistake the true nature of a condition which has come upon me gradually." Indeed interestingly enough, Colette here takes up the gradual nature of aging as a challenge: "it keeps me in a state of vigilance, of uncertainty, ready to accept whatever may fall to my lot" (5). If aging is acceptable to us when it proceeds imperceptibly, it is a shock when it does not. We will report a shock in seeing someone who, as we commonly say, has aged overnight, as if aging were biological work that needed to be done in stealth and under the cover of darkness. Similarly we may find ourselves morbidly fascinated by the cases of progeria (the disease of premature aging) that are reported every so often in the newspapers and with more frequency in the national tabloid press.

But in this section I am more concerned with reports and representations of the fragmenting body as experienced or prospectively phantasized than with phantasms of the fragmenting body as projected onto others. By way of a preface I turn to a strange and wonderful passage in *Roland Barthes by Roland Barthes*. In it we find Barthes reflecting on the loss of a part of his body, a rib which had been removed. The interest for me in this passage lies in its tracing of the change in the status of this excised body part over time. The rib is first regarded as a sacred relic to be treasured, if somewhat oddly. In time the rib's aura breaks down. It decays, as we would say of radioactive material. Finally the rib is nothing but refuse to be discarded. In the stylistic hands of Barthes, the rib is dispensed with in a flash of ceremony:

> For a long time I kept this fragment of myself in a drawer, a kind of body penis analogous to the end of a rib chop, not knowing quite what to do with it, not daring to get rid of it lest I do some harm to my person, though it was utterly useless to me shut up in a desk among such "precious" objects as old keys, a schoolboy report card, my Grandmother B.'s mother-of-pearl dance program and pink taffeta card case. And then, one day, realizing that the function of any drawer is to ease, to acclimate the death of objects by causing them to pass through a sort of pious site, a dusty chapel where, in the guise of keeping them alive, we allow them a decent interval of dim agony, but not going so far as to dare cast this bit of myself into the common refuse bin of my building, I flung the rib chop and its gauze from my balcony. . . . (61)

I take this little story as a parable of the transitional or reparative phantasy of the fragmenting body. A body part is lost but the loss is accepted. How does this happen? The body part is granted the status of a transitional object.[25] As we saw in the chapter on transitional objects and *Malone Dies*, a transitional object is understood to be both a part of the self and not a part of the self at the same time. At first the rib is highly charged with symbolic meaning, although Barthes is half-joking. And as with a transitional object, the rib is not mourned. Rather its value simply diminishes over time.

More generally, phantasies of the fragmenting body are transitional phantasies in that they stage the passage from life to death. The psychoanalyst Elliott Jacques argues that such phantasies occur with more frequency in the transitional years of middle age than in earlier years. Indeed he insists that at the midpoint of our middle years, our fears of decline and death reach crisis proportions.[26] He suggests that we carry in us a sense of our life being divided into two parts— that of growing up and that of growing old, which are figured in terms of ascent and decline. At the midpoint, then, we would inevitably face decline. Jacques argues that our awareness of our personal death is expressed in unconscious and conscious ways, thus contradicting Freud's celebrated postulate that the unconscious cannot contain the idea of our own death. As Freud wrote in "Thoughts for the Times on War and Death" (1915), "at bottom no one believes in his own death . . . in the unconscious everyone is convinced of his own immortality" (SE 14: 289). But the question to ask is if the unconscious does not have a particular sense of time. It may be precisely that the western unconscious cannot contain the idea of one's personal death when one is in the first half of one's life, but that in the second half of life the unconscious does admit (in the sense of opening a door) the notion of one's death. This would mean that in our culture, a life is divided into two halves in terms of time and that we have a curious arithmetical relation to time. In this sense, the unconscious could be said to be able to count only up to two.[27]

Jacques illustrates his argument with material from his patients. What I find most striking is a dream of a forty-seven-year-old woman of the fragmenting body. The dream expresses this woman's anxieties and fears of death. Her apprehensiveness is figured in terms of immobility and helplessness, both of which are explicitly associated with the second half of life. Growing old is the work of this half of life. In her dream she is lying in a coffin: "She had been sliced into small chunks, and was dead. But there was a spider's-web-thin thread of nerve running through every chunk and connected to her brain. As a result she could experience everything. She knew she was dead. She could not move or make any sound. She could only lie in the claustrophobic dark and silence of the coffin" (507).

I suggested that the story of Barthes's rib contains a reparative element. He accepts the loss of his body part. Jacques (and George Pollock after him) argues that reparation in terms of our anticipated loss of our own lives is possible if we accept consciously what the unconscious is telling us. The process of reparation is accomplished, paradoxically, by mourning. As Jacques writes of midlife, "Mourning for the dead self can begin, alongside with the mourning and reestablishment of the lost objects and the lost childhood and youth" (512–13). Unlike a transitional object which is not mourned, what one has lost must be both given up and reestablished.

We should note that Jacques, like Erikson and others before him, reproduces a narrative of crisis which characterizes Freudian psychoanalysis and its descendants. We should also ask how we might historicize Jacques's essay. His essay was written in the early fifties. At the time it made an important contribution to theorizing aging, and it still does. But one of the problems it raises is in its criterion for the definition of the midpoint of a life. Jacques asserts that the midpoint of our lives coincides with physiological changes in our bodies. While there is some truth to this, we are today living longer and living healthier lives. Furthermore Jacques argues that the midpoint also generally coincides with social changes in our lives which contribute to a sense of our approaching decline. Of such social changes, he writes: "The sense of the agedness of parents, coupled with the maturing of children into adults, contributes strongly to the sense of ageing—the sense that it is one's own turn next to grow old and die. This feeling about the age of one's parents is very strong—even in patients whose parents died years before there is awareness at the mid-life period that their parents would then have been reaching old age" (510). But these social changes have themselves been changing rapidly. Many women are having children later in life. And many men in later life are having children in second and third marriages. From the point of view of the middle generation, parents are dying later. But from the point of view of the children born of older parents, parents may be dying earlier. Today, just where the midpoint of a life is located is difficult to ascertain from a social point of view. Intergenerational cycles, to use Erikson's term, are much more complex.

At the same time, a new discourse on aging is emerging which is characterized by a new mathematics of the life span. Life is being divided into four parts rather than two. In France advanced old age is now designated by the term "the fourth age." In the United States, Alan Pifer has proposed a similar way of thinking about the life course.[28] If our culture internalized this mathematics of the life span, one of the effects might be to leave middle age untouched by old age. If so, would anticipatory phantasms of the fragmenting body appear later in life at the three-quarters mark?

Finally, what of the phantasms of the fragmenting body that express the experiences of the body in old age and near death? Our literature does not lack for examples. A very old woman, who is described as having let herself slide bit by bit into indifference, says, " 'My legs are falling just to the end of the world.' "[29] Another woman, in her seventies and dying of intestinal cancer, touches her own face as if to verify that all of its parts are in order. She says, " 'I had the feeling that my eyes were in the middle of my cheeks and that my nose was right down at the bottom of my face, all bent.' "[30] The body is felt as bizarrely distorted, as losing its shape, its parts becoming anarchic. In *Adieux* Beauvoir quotes Sartre as saying in a moment of weary resignation, " 'When you're old it no longer has any importance. . . . You know it won't last long. . . . It's natural to come to pieces, little by little. When you're young it's different' " (19).

It is a reflex of cultural criticism today to call into question the process by which something is labeled *natural*. To speak of something as "natural" all too often conceals a cultural practice that carries its own biases and prejudices. How would we evaluate, then, Sartre's use of the word "natural"? Sartre divides the world into young and old. This, we could argue, is not inevitable. There could be more distinctions and gradations, and in fact, as I have already mentioned, our culture is in the process of trying to do just that (however, even in the now-prevalent terminology of "young-old" and "old-old," the same two terms are deployed). And we could further argue that our culture could have invented a different discourse in which Sartre could have described what was for him the physical and psychic ordeal of the frailty and failings of old age, thereby transmuting the experience, for example, by sublimating it in religious terms. Here we can think of the discourses of martyrdom, asceticism, and self-sacrifice. Or, we might work to invent a discourse which recuperated these failings of frailty.[31] Instead we find the dominant discourse is one of deterioration, marked by degradation and dependence, both highly negative terms in western culture, particularly in the United States.

Still, if we live long enough it is inevitable that we will experience some form of bodily fragmentation—the loss of a degree of mobility, perhaps the loss (as we say) of our minds, the loss of . . . functions. This is in the order of things. It is *natural*, if understood as tragic in our culture. But if the process of coming apart is biologically natural, the way we describe it is not. Lacan gave us the term "the fragmented body," and it is appropriate to cite his description of it here. Lacan theorizes that the phantasms of the fragmented body arise in psychic structures that have their base in infancy. They may reappear, as he put it in "Aggressivity in Psychoanalysis," with "each of the great phases that the libidinal transformations determine in human life" (*Ecrits* 24). They surface, he insists in "The Mirror Stage," in the "aggressive disintegration in the individual" (*Ecrits* 4). Lacan's description of the fragmented body reverberates with Kleinian overtones. The images of the fragmented body include those of "castration, mutilation, dismemberment, dislocation, evisceration, devouring, bursting open of the body" (*Ecrits* 11). The very violence of these phantasms leads Lacan to conclude that a severe injury to our bodies is more terrifying to us than is death itself. For the body is in phantasy (or in Lacan's imaginary) the principle of unity.

We must add that the body also represents the principle of disunity. We can imagine the dismemberment of our bodies, but not our deaths. Thus the horror of the dream of the fragmented body of the forty-seven-year-old woman. She was in pieces and she was still alive, trapped in the pieces of her body. For some this is a literal condition in old age. Lacan rightly emphasizes that the fear of death, which is dominant in our culture, is in fact secondary to our fears of mutilation or injury. As he insists in "Aggressivity in Psychoanalysis," "we have not sufficiently recognized the extent to which the fear of death, the 'Absolute Master,' presupposed in consciousness by a whole philosophical tradition from Hegel onwards, is psychologically subordinate to the narcissistic fear of damage to one's own body'' (28).

Does not aging inevitably imply the narcissistic fear of damage to our own bodies *and* death at the same time? Is it any wonder that aging, then, and the phantasm of decrepitude, should inspire such anxiety? Yet we must not dismiss the phantasm of decrepitude as a ''mere'' phantasm, for decrepitude is in fact a *literal* condition. Lacan speaks of imagos of the fragmented body as revealing themselves not just in phantasms—in painting, in literature, in dreams—but also at the organic level. The fragmented body, he writes, ''is even tangibly revealed at the organic level, in the lines of 'fragilization' that define the anatomy of phantasy, as exhibited in the schizoid and spasmodic symptoms of hysteria'' (*Ecrits* 5). Here the phantasm is converted into a symptom that is written on the body. But how much more terrifying when it is not a symptom but a literal condition. In the context of Lacanian psychoanalysis, ''fragilization'' seems too delicate a word. And yet in the context of old age it calls up the delicate ''frailty'' of the elderly.

As I come to the end of this book, I want to return to the last chapter of Figes's *Waking* and take up in a bit more detail its representation of the phantasm of the fragmenting body in old age. The experience of the daughter as she ages and dies is represented in terms of how she feels in her body, or in terms of how her body feels to her. There is a kind of teleology to her experience which is expressed through a proliferation of phantasms, or metaphors, of the fragmenting body over the last years of her life. The term ''fragilization'' may be used to describe the first set of metaphors, which are feminine and domestic. The body is likened to ''an old broken doll, its members dislocated,'' which must be ''painfully reassembled'' every morning (60), and to an old glove which has long ago taken on the shape of the psychic body but grows stiff after being slipped out of at night. In the morning it is hard, even painful, for her to find her way back into the body-glove, the body-as-envelope. Figes: ''I am reminded of a fumbling hand trying to inhabit an old leather glove. The glove is familiar, well worn, so much so that it never loses the singular contours of this hand, but overnight, each night, it has been dropped and forgotten on the midnight lawns of sleep which are white with hoar frost. By dawn it is stiff and hard from exposure, and I cannot enter it. It hurts to try'' (78). In old age, as the images of the body as a broken doll and the body as a stiff glove imply, the psyche and the body are inevitably incongruent. The psyche longs for youth, and the body is an insult and an impediment.

In *Waking* aging is associated vaguely with illness, as we have seen it so often is in the West. What particular illness is left unspecified. Thus aging is represented ambiguously and in negative terms. As I suggested earlier, if the body is suffering from a disease, then we may think that perhaps the disease can be cured and by implication the body can return to normal. What is not "normal," then, is aging. But if aging is identical to illness, then it is necessarily understood as an ordeal, as the opposite of health. What does the daughter's body feel like now? Figes uses the metaphors of the walls of the body cracking, of dead parts of the body sticking to her. Old age feels repulsive:

> I rise each morning with a layer of detritus, dead matter, old skin clinging to me, an invisible web of dust, cobwebs, falling hair and the skeletal outline of dried leaves that I cannot shake off. Something terrible has begun, that is why I feel so bad first thing in the morning. Inside something must have given way, walls have begun to leak or crumble, so I do not function as I should. I think about the organs which lie under the skin, according to the diagrams in the textbooks, which I have not had to think about before now. Perhaps it is my liver which aches. (61–62)

Finally, in the death scene the body of this old woman is figured as bursting violently apart. She feels as if she is in danger of being dashed against rocks and as if she is being invaded by black waters. "She" and "her body" are at this point identical, and yet at the same time she is dissociated from her body, which she describes as "helpless" without her:

> I can feel a slight wind, cool on my face, it comes with the dark, with the sea pounding against rocks, I can hear it rushing in my head. Now I am tossed, thrown this way, and that, I am in terror of being thrown onto rough rocks, of being torn apart, but already the hollow in my head is filling with water . . . black liquid, gushing, moving dark shadows come, waver . . . now my head is full of it swirling, gurgling, it will not come out, though I open my mouth nothing is heard. . . . I gasp for air, my head bobs up for a moment, out of dark water, but the night is black also, I am submerged, I must find my body which is helpless without me. . . . (84)

This representation of the fragmenting body—violent mutilation which stops just short of death by drowning—is central to a dominant tradition in the West: old age finds an end in the fragmentation of the body, in the return to the body in parts.

But as with the phantasms of the immobile body and the empty body, we find psychic compensations here as well. Once the imago of the body as a unity is accepted as imaginary, a certain relief is possible. One of Lacan's most brilliant contributions to psychoanalysis is his insistence on the illusion of the wholeness of our bodies. In *Waking*, we find an unusual description of what it might feel like in old age to have *experienced* that disunity at the level of the psychic body: "no more pain, now my body has been swept away I am light as a bird, no more trying to find bits of myself, the ache of effort with each breath, holding myself together like my poor old dislocated doll, how many years now, finding an arm, now a numb foot, pulling on aching muscles and still hot joints on first waking. Admit it, the hollow head, the mechanism for making eyes open and shut could no longer be connected to the rest of it. The illusion was shattered" (87). At this point, the illusion of the whole body shattered, the complete dissociation of the psyche from the body is felt as relief. The self is felt to be located no longer inside the body (in the head, for example) but outside the body. We saw a similar process represented in *Malone Dies*.[32]

The notion of being liberated from our bodies has a long tradition in the West, of course, in Christianity in particular. But the phenomenon can be understood in psychoanalytic terms as well. Freud long ago theorized in "The Libido Theory and Narcissism" (1917) what common sense has not failed to tell us: when we are sick we turn our attention to the part of the body which is presenting pain. There is, in Freud's words, "an increased cathexis of the diseased part of the body" (SE 16: 419). But we also set apart that painful part of the body. As Schilder has put it, we have "a tendency to push it out of the body-image. When the whole body is filled with pain, we try to get rid of the whole body. We take a stand outside our body and watch ourselves" (104). Schilder's words themselves suggest the strength of our unconscious will to defend ourselves. We *take a stand* against our bodies. Or, we might say, we discard the fragments of our body. Or, that in old age unto death the body is itself understood psychically as a fragment.

COUNTER-TEXT

Slowly Avey Johnson stood up. She unhurriedly picked up her chair and, holding it easily with one hand against her side, began walking over to where the musicians were playing, away from the voice in her ear.

Once there, she set the chair down close to the bottle-and-spoon boys standing beside the drummers.

And then she did an odd thing. Instead of sitting down she turned and slowly retraced her steps to her old place beside the tree, and stood there. Her face was expressionless, her body still and composed, but her bottom lip had unfolded to bare the menacing sliver of pink.

The dancers in their loose, ever-widening ring were no more than a dozen feet away now. She could feel the reverberation of their powerful tread in the ground under her, and the heat from their bodies reached her in a strong yeasty wave. Soon only a mere four or five feet remained between them, yet she continued to stand there. Finally, just as the moving wall of bodies was almost upon her, she too moved—a single declarative step forward. At the same moment, what seemed an arm made up of many arms reached out from the circle to draw her in, and she found herself walking amid the elderly folk on the periphery, in their counterclockwise direction. . . .

She began to dance then. Just as her feet of their own accord had discovered the old steps, her hips under the linen shirtdress slowly began to weave from side to side on their own, stiffly at first and then in a smooth wide arc as her body responded more deeply to the music. And the movement in her hips flowed upward, so that her entire torso was soon swaying. Arms bent, she began working her shoulders in the way the Shouters long ago used to do, thrusting them forward and then back in a strong casting-off motion. Her weaving head was arched high. All of her moving suddenly with a vigor and passion she hadn't felt in years, and with something of the stylishness and sass she had once been known for. *"Girl, you can out-jangle Bojangles."*

> —Sixty-some-year-old Avey Johnson
> doing the Carriacou Tramp, *from*
> Paule Marshall, *Praise Song for*
> *the Widow* 247, 249

Epilogue

I HAVE ARGUED IN THIS BOOK that Freudian psychoanalysis is complicit with our culture's repression of aging. In the founding text of psychoanalysis, *The Interpretation of Dreams,* Freud casually assesses a woman's "old" age in the following negative terms (he is referring to a figure in one of his dreams): "She was an imposing figure with discontented features, of an age not far from the time of the decay of feminine beauty" (SE 5: 457). She is, in his eyes, "elderly" (458). What might the age of "decay" have been for Freud?

Thirty-three years after *The Interpretation of Dreams* Freud gives an answer to this question in his lecture on "Femininity." He was seventy-seven at the time and, I think, should have known better. Toward the end of this text Freud contrasts men and women in terms of age and their "possibilities for development." If men at the age of thirty are still "youthful," women, it is implied, are old, which is to say incapable of change and rigid. Freud: "A man of about thirty strikes us as a youthful, somewhat unformed individual, whom we expect to make powerful use of the possibilities for development opened up to him by analysis. A woman of the same age, however, often frightens us by her psychical rigidity and unchangeability. Her libido has taken up final positions and seems incapable of exchanging them for others. There are no paths open to further development; it is as though the whole process had already run its course and remains thenceforward insusceptible to influence—as though, indeed, the difficult developments to femininity had exhausted the possibilities of the person concerned'' (SE 22:134–35). Fatigue—to Freud's mind a symptom of a kind of ''normal'' yet premature aging by the age of *thirty*—is associated with the exhausting work of femininity. Also associated with a woman of that age is *fear*. Analytically, Freud is afraid of old women. Theoretically, he relegates the ''problem'' of female sexuality to the gray continent of old age, demeaning both women and the elderly in the process. As he puts it in ''Female Sexuality,'' published in 1931, ''Everything in the sphere of this first attachment to the mother seemed to me so difficult in analysis—so grey with age and shadowy and almost impossible to revivify'' (SE 21: 226).

The ideal Freudian (analytical) woman is young, under thirty. By extrapolation we should, according to Freud, always wish ourselves to be young. But other psychoanalytic traditions and practices question the dominant discourse of Freudian psychoanalysis. I pause only to note a remark of Melanie Klein which I take as embryonic of a counter-position. In January of 1941 Klein— she was fifty-nine—told Winnicott, ''We are nearly snowed in here. Everything is covered with snow and the country is beautiful to look at. I wish I could do some winter sports which implies the wish to be 30 years younger. (But I am not so sure whether I'd really like that. It has given me enough trouble to get where I am—meaning to get as old as I am.)''[1] Drawing on her experience, Klein calls into doubt the unquestioned Freudian valuation of youth over aging and old age. Like Eleanor in Woolf's *The Years*, she does not unequivocally desire to be younger.

One of the unresolved questions in *Aging and Its Discontents* is the extent to which we can alter or inflect our experience of aging and advanced old age by changing our representations of it. Certainly our old age—our various experiences of old age—are inseparable from our culture's representations of aging. Certainly the profound gerontophobia in our culture should be extirpated, and one of the ways to begin that process is to examine critically our representations of aging and to work to produce new ones. As I have insisted throughout this book, in the West the dominant trope for aging has been the decay and decline of the body. Time or age, we will say, writes itself on the body. For the most part we fear what will be written there. As I have shown, we adopt many defenses to deal with our anxiety. We repress the subject of aging. We relegate aging to others. We do not recognize it in ourselves. And as I have insisted, it is only with great effort and perhaps even courage that our culture will rewrite its discourses about aging.

But even if we do succeed in measure in rescuing aging from the scandalous contempt in which it is held, at critical points we will inevitably encounter the tension between the social construction of the body and the lived experience of the body, the facticity of the *materiality* of the body, the phenomenology of the body in advanced old age. My guess is that as we move toward the limits of old age—and that limit is death—we move toward the limits of representation. It will be easier to change meanings associated with aging in the middle years as they extend into vigorous and healthy years of late life than the meanings associated with the years of very advanced or frail old age. As we approach the extremity of old age, we approach in the West the limit of the pure cultural construction of aging.

The stakes are high—for all of us. Repression of aging in psychological terms contributes to the very real oppression of the elderly in our society. In the preceding pages I have used the terms "gerontophobia" and "ageism" interchangeably; both refer to prejudice against aging and the elderly. It might be helpful, however, to think through possible distinctions between them. We might, for example, borrow the distinction made by Gloria I. Joseph and adopted by Adrienne Rich between "homophobia" and "heterosexism," and apply it to "gerontophobia" and "ageism." "Homophobia" is understood as an individual response of panic, "heterosexism" as "a deeply ingrained prejudice, comparable to racism, sexism, and classism—a political indoctrination which must be recognized as such and which can be re-educated."[2] Similarly, gerontophobia would be an individual's response of fear and anxiety, ageism a political prejudice. Yet as I have argued in this book, the fear of death is so strong in western culture where it is linked with aging and old age that it might be impossible to separate individual responses, that is, phobic responses, from social constructions and practices of aging, from ageism. How are we to understand, for example, the grisly crime reported on the front page of *The New York Times* on April 18, 1989, of the murder of some fifty frail and hospitalized elderly by a group of four nurse's aides in Vienna? One of the aides is reported as saying, "The ones who got on my nerves were dispatched directly to a free bed with the good Lord." Or more generally, what are we to make of the fact that many of the elderly who live alone in the United States receive virtually no medical care? The historian Peter Laslett has concluded that "everyone living in an advanced industrial society seems to have a guilty feeling about the elderly and the aged."[3] I emphatically disagree.

What can be done to undermine what I refer to in the chapter on masquerade as the *youthful structure of the look*? Our historical moment is propitious. At the same time as the material conditions of aging are undergoing change, so too our culture is producing new representations of aging. The aging body in the United States, for example, is changing—literally. It is older, it is healthier. The present generation of Americans aged sixty to seventy-five (and many who are older too) is in effect refusing to be labeled "old," as the cover illustration of the February 22, 1988, issue of *Time* magazine so energetically demonstrates.

Carrying the caption "And now for THE FUN YEARS! Americans are living longer and enjoying it more—but who will foot the bill?" the cover shows a vigorous silver-haired couple dressed in jogging outfits. The man is holding a tennis racket in his lowered arms and is smiling broadly and benignly at us, the readers. The woman, made up with very red lipstick, her clenched fists upraised in victory, is laughing in triumph—at, perhaps, an imaginary opponent? (The spectator of old age in America is placed in two positions which contradict each other: the viewer is invited to join old age as unproblematically "fun"; she is also threatened with being beaten at the game of generations.) In the cover story the aging body is presented primarily in terms of statistics ("fully half of all people now 75 to 84 are free of health problems that require special care or that curb their activities") and of photographs (people ranging from 69 to 105 are shown smiling, working, exercising). A heading reads, "Aging no longer has to mean sickness, senility, and sexlessness." It is significant, I think, that the body is not presented within the confining matrix of beauty and its opposite. It is, rather, health that is at stake. On the one hand, this is all to the good: a story such as this one can help reshape the dominant cultural attitudes toward aging as an inevitable decline to be feared. On the other hand, at issue in the story is the cost of health care for the elderly; if "aging no longer has to mean sickness," then why should the nation "foot the bill," as the cover caption so crudely puts it?

Or, consider a remarkable photo essay which appeared in *The New York Times Magazine* on August 27, 1989. Entitled "Victories of the Spirit," this piece by Mary Ellen Mark features photographs of people who participated in the second national senior olympics held in St. Louis in the summer of 1989. These photographs linger in my mind's eye as counter-texts to the photographs by Gundula Schultz with which I opened *Aging and Its Discontents*. Instead of a penurious and listless old man sitting alone in his dingy room, a man who goes nameless, and whose age is undefined, we see George M. Richards, age eighty-two, wearing running shorts and crouched at the starting line for the 100-yard dash. His body is wiry, his pose exceptionally relaxed. In another full-page photograph (not just the fact of these photographs but also their *size* is unusual), we see Catherine Cress, seventy-nine, stretching out her body in preparation for a swimming meet. She is wearing a black tank suit. The photograph is not what we would call "flattering." Our attention is drawn to the lumpy flesh on her thighs. But, importantly, the overall effect is not one of embarrassment, either on her part or on the part of the spectator. Her body seems just right, it is what it is, it is fit. The presence of it in public constructs a different, accepting space for the body—in all its differences—in old age.

Socially, politically, physically—the meanings of old age are changing. On the whole our literary tradition has lagged behind, continuing to produce predominately dark portraits of aging. But the youthful structure of the look is being challenged by more subtle and variegated and eccentric contemporary explorations of aging and old age in all kinds of mediums. I have mentioned some of them in the course of this book. I am thinking, too, of several of the pieces of the performance artists Rachel Rosenthal and Suzanne Lacey, of Robert Coles's *The Old Ones of New Mexico*, of Barbara Myerhoff's *Number Our Days*, of Cecelia Condit's videotape *Not a Jealous Bone*, of Anne Noggle's photographs of aging women from across the United States in her *Silver Lining*. Or of Herbert Blau's portrait of his mother, an old woman who was unsurprised by aging and not the least bit interested in denying it, who unswervingly adorned herself with "a bright penumbra of crimson on her lips and a lurid swath of rouge on her cheeks," wearing her garish lipstick until the day she died, unembarrassed by her excess.[4] I am thinking too of Margaret Simons's thumbnail portrait of Simone de Beauvoir. Of her first meeting with Beauvoir, Simons reports: "I was shocked when she opened the door. In spite of looking old and wrinkled, she had the audacity to wear red lipstick and bright red nail polish!"[5] There is pleasure in this shock.

In all of these texts *an* image of an aging body does not represent *the* aging body. In this work and embodied in these people, bodies in age are not figured in terms of youthfulness as a masquerade, as something disagreeable and unpalatable to be concealed, hidden, denied, as a material object with which we associate a gruesome feeling (*grauen*) in Freudian terms. Either the masks of youth have been taken off, or they were never put on in the first place, or the pleasures in the body remain in force. These bodies are presented and present themselves in the light of changing times.

NOTES

1. INTRODUCTION

1. Virginia Woolf, *The Years* (New York: Harcourt, 1937) 383.

2. Ernest Jones, *The Life and Work of Sigmund Freud* (New York: Basic, 1953) 1: 3.

3. Lydia Flem, *La Vie quotidienne de Freud et de ses patients* (Paris: Hachette, 1986) 170. My translation.

4. Simone de Beauvoir, *Adieux: A Farewell to Sartre*, trans. Patrick O'Brian (1981; Harmondsworth, England: Penguin, 1984) 48.

5. Jacques Lacan, "The Function and Field of Speech and Language in Psychoanalysis" (1953), *Ecrits: A Selection*, trans. Alan Sheridan (New York: Norton, 1977) 87. In subsequent references to texts in Lacan's *Ecrits*, I will identify the first reference to a particular essay either in the body of my text or in a note, after which references will be abbreviated to the short title of the book (*Ecrits*) and the page number.

6. Patricia Mellencamp, "Aging Fashionably on TV," presented at a conference on "Women and Aging" at the Center for Twentieth Century Studies, U of Wisconsin-Milwaukee, November 1987.

7. Philippe Ariès, *Centuries of Childhood: A Social History of Family Life*, trans. Robert Baldick (New York: Knopf, 1962). See Tamara K. Hareven, "The Last Stage: Historical Adulthood and Old Age," *Aging, Death, and the Completion of Being*, ed. David D. Van Tassel (Philadelphia: U of Pennsylvania P, 1979) 165–89. See also David Hackett Fischer, *Growing Old in America* (New York: Oxford UP, 1977), W. Andrew Achenbaum, *Old Age in the New Land* (Baltimore: Johns Hopkins UP, 1978), and Carole Haber, *Beyond Sixty-Five: The Dilemma of Old Age in America's Past* (New York: Cambridge UP, 1983), which contains an excellent essay on research done by historians.

8. Robert Magnan, in "Sex and Senescence in Medieval Literature," reaches the same conclusion: "Although a long line of works present various schemes for the division of life into stages, the tendency in literature is to polarize, to reduce these divisions to the most basic, the dichotomy of *juventus* and *senectus*" (29). In *Aging in Literature*, ed. Laurel Porter and Laurence M. Porter (Troy: International, 1984) 13–30. The essays in *Aging in Literature*, which includes a selective bibliography on aging, literature, and the humanities, for the most part approach aging from the point of view of developmental psychology.

9. Toni Morrison, *The Bluest Eye* (1970; New York: Washington Square, 1972) 20.

10. Letter from Sigmund Freud to Ernest Jones, May 3, 1928, qtd. Max Schur, *Freud: Living and Dying* (New York: International UP, 1972) 406.

11. William Shakespeare, *The Passionate Pilgrim*, poem 12, *Shakespeare: The Complete Works*, ed. G. B. Harrison (New York: Harcourt, 1948) 1586. The first line of the poem echoes Freud's point: "Crabbèd age and youth cannot live together. . . ."

12. Thomas Mann, *The Black Swan*, trans. Willard R. Trask (New York: Knopf, 1954) 5. For a discussion of literary representations of gerontophobia in the English tradition, see Richard Freedman's excellent "Sufficiently Decayed: Gerontophobia in English Lit-

erature," *Aging and the Elderly: Humanistic Perspectives in Gerontology,* ed. Stuart F. Spicker, Kathleen M. Woodward, and David D. Van Tassel (Atlantic Highlands: Humanities, 1978) 49–61.

13. John Hawkes, *The Passion Artist* (New York: Harper, 1978) 89.

14. See, for example, Barbara F. Lefcowitz and Allan B. Lefcowitz, "Old Age and the Modern Literary Imagination: An Overview," *Soundings* 59.4 (Winter 1976): 447–66.

15. I consider the question of late literary style in *At Last, the Real Distinguished Thing: The Late Poems of Eliot, Pound, Stevens, and Williams* (Columbus: Ohio State UP, 1980). For discussions of how representations of age change over the lifetimes of individual authors, see my "Simone de Beauvoir: Aging and Its Discontents," *The Private Self: Theory and Practice in Women's Autobiographical Writings,* ed. Shari Benstock (Chapel Hill: U of North Carolina P, 1988) 90–113, and "May Sarton and Fictions of Old Age," *Gender and Literary Voice,* ed. Janet Todd, *Women and Literature* NS1 (New York: Holmes, 1980) 108–27. See also the essays of Anne M. Wyatt-Brown: "Late Style in the Novels of Barbara Pym and Penelope Mortimer," *The Gerontologist* 28.6 (1988): 835–39; "The Narrative Imperative: Fiction and the Aging Writer," *Journal of Aging Studies* 3.1 (1989): 55–65; and "Creativity in Midlife: The Novels of Anita Brookner," *Journal of Aging Studies* 3.2 (1989): 175–81.

16. Barbara Pym, *Quartet in Autumn* (London: Macmillan, 1977) 218.

17. See Meridel Le Sueur's remarks in *Women and Aging: An Anthology by Women,* ed. Jo Alexander, Debi Berrow, Lisa Domitrovich, Margarita Donnelly, and Cheryl McLean (Corvallis: Calyx, 1986), which preface her reading of her poem "Rites of Ancient Ripening," whose opening line is "I am luminous with age" (10). Le Sueur says, "Since I was 60 I've written more and had better energy and more energy than I ever had in my life" (9). Florida Scott-Maxwell, *The Measure of My Days* (1968; New York: Penguin, 1979) 13. Scott-Maxwell opens her journal with this meditation: "*We who are old* know that age is more than a disability. It is an intense and varied experience, almost beyond our capacity at times, but something to be carried high. If it is a long defeat it is also a victory, meaningful for the initiates of time, if not for those who have come less far" (5). Scott-Maxwell writes about advanced old age as a time in life which must be understood as both physical and psychological, or spiritual, challenges.

18. For an excellent critical discussion of the origins of ageism in the United States, see Thomas R. Cole, "The 'Enlightened' View of Aging: Victorian Morality in a New Key," *What Does It Mean to Grow Old?: Reflections from the Humanities,* ed. Thomas R. Cole and Sally Gadow (Durham: Duke UP, 1986) 115–30.

19. Sigmund Freud, *The Ego and the Id* (1923), *The Standard Edition of the Complete Psychological Works of Sigmund Freud,* trans. and ed. James Strachey, 24 vols. (London: Hogarth and Inst. of Psycho-Analysis, 1953–74) 19: 33. Hereafter abbreviated as SE and cited parenthetically by volume and page.

20. Charlotte Herfray, *La Vieillesse: une interprétation psychanalytique* (Paris: Desclée de Brouwer; Épi, 1988).

21. Several important subjects go undiscussed in this book, including sexuality and aging, and the folding over of the narrative of a life in remembrance in old age.

22. Jacques Lacan, "Of the Network of Signifiers" (1964), *The Four Fundamental Concepts of Psycho-Analysis,* ed. Jacques-Alain Miller, trans. Alan Sheridan (New York: Norton, 1978) 45. Subsequent references will be cited as *FF* in the body of my text.

23. Kierkegaard, qtd. Richard Wollheim, *The Thread of Life* (Cambridge: Harvard UP, 1984) 283.

24. I am referring of course to the famous *fort-da* which Freud discusses in *Beyond the Pleasure Principle* (1920), SE 28: 14–17.

25. Loren Eiseley, *All the Strange Hours* (New York: Scribner's, 1975) 222.

26. Simone de Beauvoir, *The Coming of Age* (1970), trans. Patrick O'Brian (New York: Warner, 1978) 14.

27. One of the fascinating areas of research that remains largely unexplored is the question of reading and age. How do our readings of various texts change as we grow older? Would we find in our subsequent readings the expression of an identity theme, as Norman Holland suggests, or would the change in readings be more remarkable than their similarities? See Norman Holland, "Not So Little Hans: Identity and Aging," *Memory and Desire: Aging—Literature—Psychoanalysis*, ed. Kathleen Woodward and Murray M. Schwartz (Bloomington: Indiana UP, 1986) 51–75.

28. Hans Robert Jauss, "Literary History as a Challenge to Literary Theory," *Toward an Aesthetic of Reception*, trans. Timothy Bahti (Minneapolis: U of Minnesota P, 1982) 39.

29. See, for example, David L. Gutmann, "Psychoanalysis and Aging: A Developmental View," *Adulthood and the Aging Process*, ed. Stanley I. Greenspan and George H. Pollock (Washington: NIMH, 1980) 489–517; Bertram J. Cohler, "Adult Developmental Psychology and Reconstruction in Psychoanalysis," *Adulthood and the Aging Process* 149–99; George H. Pollock, "Aging or Aged: Development or Pathology," *Adulthood and the Aging Process* 459–85. These three essays are deep and wide-ranging. Cohler in particular calls our attention to the problems which can arise when one theorizes the life cycle in general from the conflicts and processes of infancy and is not critically self-conscious of doing so. Containing twenty-four contributions, *Adulthood and the Aging Process* is a ground-breaking and ambitious collection of essays. See also Herfray's *La Vieillesse*, Michèle Dacher and Micheline Weinstein, *Histoire de Louise: des vieillards en hospice* (Paris: Seuil, 1979); Michèle Grosclaude, "Mémoire, Souvenir, Savoir, Démence," *Temps, vieillessement, société* (Paris: SOPEDIM, 1982) 117–36. Interestingly enough, the work by these women in France is more openly moving and relies more on personal experiences with elderly patients who have touched them than is the work by the American men listed above.

30. See Patrice Petro, *Joyless Streets: Women and Melodramatic Representation in Weimar Germany* (Princeton: Princeton UP, 1989), for a succinct rehearsal of many of these debates and a significant contribution to them.

31. Susan Sontag, "The Double Standard of Aging" (1972), *No Longer Young: The Older Woman in America*, Occasional Papers in Gerontology 11 (Ann Arbor: Inst. of Gerontology, U of Michigan; Wayne State U, 1975) 31–32. On women and aging, see Audrey Borenstein, *Chimes of Change and Hours: Views of Older Women in Twentieth Century America* (Rutherford, N.J.: Fairleigh Dickinson UP, 1983) and *Older Women in Twentieth Century America: A Selected Annotated Bibliography* (New York: Garland, 1982). See also *Women and Aging: An Anthology by Women*; Mary Sohngen, "The Writer as an Old Woman," *The Gerontologist* 15.6 (Dec. 1976): 492–98; and the special issue on "Women and Aging" of *Women's Studies Quarterly* 17.1–2 (Spring-Summer 1989).

32. I am alluding to Naomi Schor's use of the phrase "anxiety of difference" in "For a Restricted Thematics: Writing, Speech, and Difference in *Madame Bovary*," trans. Harriet Stone, *The Future of Difference*, ed. Hester Eisenstein and Alice Jardine (New Brunswick: Rutgers UP, 1985) 187.

33. Malcolm Cowley, *The View from Eighty* (New York: Viking, 1980). Cowley places the definitive onset of old age at eighty. He writes, "Seventy-year olds, or septuas, have the illusion of being middle-aged, even if they have been pushed back on a shelf. The 80-year-old, the octo, looks at the double-dumpling figure and admits that he is old" (2).

34. May Sarton, *After the Stroke: A Journal* (New York: Norton, 1988) 35, 188.

35. Bernice L. Neugarten, "Personality and Aging," *Handbook of the Psychology of Aging*, ed. J. E. Birren and K. W. Schaie (New York: Van Nostrand Reinhold, 1977) 633.

36. See Teresa de Lauretis's persuasive book *Alice Doesn't: Feminism, Semiotics, Cinema* (Bloomington: Indiana UP, 1984).

37. Bernard Berenson, *Sunset and Twilight: From the Diaries of 1947–1958*, ed. Nicky Mariano (New York: Harcourt, 1963) 18.

38. Muriel Spark, *A Far Cry from Kensington* (1988; London: Penguin, 1989) 6.

39. Spark's epigrammatic reading of old age as a medium through which we move rather than as a period of special psychological work is amplified in Sharon R. Kaufman's *The Ageless Self* (Madison: U of Wisconsin P, 1986). An anthropologist, Kaufman concludes on the basis of interviews with sixty Californians that being old "is not a central feature of the self" (7); "people crystallize certain experiences into *themes*. Thus themes, as reformulated experience, can be considered building blocks of identity. Identity in old age—the ageless self—is founded on the present significance of past experience, the current rendering of meaningful symbols and events of a life" (26).

40. For an excellent study of female adolescence from the twin perspectives of literature and psychoanalysis, see Katherine Dalsimer, *Female Adolescence: Psychoanalytic Reflections on Works of Literature* (New Haven: Yale UP, 1986).

41. David L. Gutmann, *Reclaimed Powers: Toward a New Psychology of Men and Women in Later Life* (New York: Basic, 1987).

42. For a discussion of the concept of the life course from the point of view of critical social science, see Mike Featherstone and Mike Hepworth, "Aging and Old Age: Reflections on the Postmodern Life Course," *Being and Becoming Old*, ed. T. Keil Byetheway, P. Allatt, and A. Bryman (Newbury Park, Calif.: Sage, 1989) 143–57.

43. For bibliographies of literature on aging, see Walter G. Moss, ed., *Humanistic Perspectives on Aging: An Annotated Bibliography and Essay* (Ann Arbor: Inst. of Gerontology, U of Michigan; Wayne State U, 1976), and Joanne Trautmann and Carol Pollard, *Literature and Medicine: Topics, Titles and Notes* (Philadelphia: Soc. for Health and Human Values, 1976). For a recent anthology of short stories about aging, see Constance Rooke, ed., *Night Light: Stories of Aging* (Toronto: Oxford UP, 1986). For an excellent critical survey of scholarship in the area of literature and aging, see Anne M. Wyatt-Brown, "The Coming of Age of Literary Gerontology: A Literature Review," *Handbook of Aging and the Humanities*, ed. Thomas Cole, David D. Van Tassel, and Robert Kastenbaum, forthcoming from Springer. See also Janice Sokoloff, *The Margin That Remains: A Study of Aging in Literature* (New York: Lang, 1987), for a discussion of *Moll Flanders, Persuasion, Jane Eyre, Middlemarch, The Ambassadors,* and *Mrs. Dalloway.*

44. Rebecca West, qtd. *The New York Times,* 16 March 1983.

45. Herbert Blau, "Introduction," *Ideology and Performance,* forthcoming from Routledge.

46. Robert N. Butler, *Why Survive?: Being Old in America* (New York: Harper, 1975).

2. READING FREUD

1. As is well known, analysis, as it has descended from Freud, has been presumed generally to be effective only with the young and with the middle-aged—and the early middle-aged at that. As Lou Andreas-Salomé remarked in a letter to Freud about two patients whom she was treating, "they are both on the wrong side of forty." She added, however, "it is on the other hand definitely a help to be dealing with *mature* people" (162). Letter from Andreas-Salomé to Freud, *Sigmund Freud and Lou Andreas-Salomé: Letters,* ed. Ernest Pfeiffer, trans. William and Elaine Robson-Scott (New York: Norton, 1972). Hereafter abbreviated as *The Freud/Andreas-Salomé Letters.*

2. Letter from Freud to Fliess, May 7, 1900, *The Complete Letters of Sigmund Freud to Wilhelm Fliess, 1887–1904,* ed. and trans. Jeffrey Moussaieff Masson (Cambridge: Harvard UP, 1985) 412. Hereafter abbreviated as *The Freud/Fliess Letters.* As an example of one of Freud's references to aging prior to 1900, here is a passage from a letter he wrote to Fliess on May 1, 1898: "I feel parched; some spring within me has gone dry and all sensibilities are withering. I do not want to give you too detailed a description lest it sound too much like complaining. You will tell me whether it is old age or just one of the many periodic fluctuations" (*The Freud/Fliess Letters* 312). Only a few weeks later, on March 23, Freud wrote again to Fliess, "You know that I have been going through a deep inner crisis; you would see how it has aged me" (*The Freud/Fliess Letters* 405).

3. Peter Gay, *Freud: A Life for Our Time* (New York: Norton, 1988) 134, 219. See Gay for other references in Freud's correspondence to his sense of being prematurely old.

4. Letter from Freud to Martha Bernays, August 17, 1884, *Letters* 123.

5. Letter from Freud to Minna Bernays, February 21, 1883, *Letters* 38.

6. For example, in a manuscript on paranoia sent to Fliess, and dated January 24, 1895, Freud referred to a woman of about thirty as an "aging spinster" (*The Freud/Fliess Letters* 108).

7. In another letter from the same period Freud condemned worldly desire in the elderly as unseemly. As he wrote of a certain professor, "He is not particularly talented, rather what is known as very shrewd, an old practitioner of most doubtful character, egotistic, completely unreliable, and in spite of being sixty-five or more, ready to indulge in any kind of pleasure" (Letter from Freud to Martha Bernays, June 8, 1885, *Letters* 150). We should not be too hasty to dismiss this prejudice on Freud's part as being merely a reflection of his relative youth; he accorded to other people of the same age the prospect of intellectual achievement. As he wrote in the context of praising the great French physician Charcot, "the great problems are for men between fifty and seventy" (Letter from Freud to Martha Bernays, November 24, 1885, *Letters* 185). Later, when he was seventy-three, he remarked that intellectually "the best and most eventful decade" is "from fifty to sixty" (Letter from Freud to Max Eitingon, December 1, 1929, *Letters* 392).

8. Peter Gay, commenting in *Freud* on Martha Freud's appearance as she grew older, provides us with a useful vignette of the bourgeois conventions of age in turn-of-the-century Vienna. "To judge from hints in Freud's letters and from her photographs, she soon traded her slender youthfulness for a neat, just slightly drab, middle age; she did little to resist the then accepted style of aging, which relentlessly turned the young wife into a stately matron" (60).

9. Later Freud interpreted a dream which Jung had had about Freud ("'I dreamt that I saw you walking beside me as a *very, very frail old man*'") as expressing his rivalry with Freud (Letter from Jung to Freud, November 2, 1907, *The Freud/Jung letters,* ed. William McGuire, trans. Ralph Manheim and R. F. C. Hull [Cambridge: Harvard UP, 1988] 96). In 1911 Freud reported in a letter to Jung a similar operation of revenge because of and through the medium of age. Here Freud is supremely aware of what he had done and why. Again we find him referring to a colleague upon whom he wished to revenge himself, this time precisely because the colleague (Putnam) had referred to Freud as old. In an essay in *The Journal of Abnormal Psychology* Putnam had written, "Freud is no longer a young man." Freud retorted that Putnam "'has left his youth far behind him,'" and confided to Jung with cold pleasure that this was "an act of vengeance" which he found "delicious" (Letter from Freud to Jung, April 27, 1911, *The Freud/Jung Letters* 419). Significantly, Freud added that he had an "old-age complex" which had an "erotic basis" (419). The economics of masochism, to which I will allude

shortly, may be involved here. In *The Psychopathology of Everyday Life* (1901) Freud had acknowledged his sensitivity to the question of old age. "I know I don't much like to think about growing old, and I have strange reactions when I'm reminded of it" (SE 6: 31). As an example he alluded to this incident with Putnam.

10. Freud to Fliess, February 13, 1896, *The Freud/Fliess Letters* 172.

11. To be more precise, H. Rider Haggard's *She* (1885) ultimately gores this utopian phantasy about aging (New York: Modern, 1957). It is an odd and fantastical tale of prolongevity and romance that is obsessed from its opening pages with the physical appearance of its characters. The point of the meandering plot of the story, which is very long, is to prolong the penultimate dramatic moment: the sudden aging of a mysterious and beautiful queen who has lived in isolation for over two thousand years. Interestingly enough Freud makes no reference at all to the denouement of *She*. At the end of the story, the aging of her two thousand years of youth is compressed into two minutes. The condensed weight of all those years inflicts deterioration at a horrific pace. The narrator of *She*—he is a witness to this nightmare of a scene—interprets the torture of the heroine's sudden aging as punishment for her sins.

The notion of aging as punishment is a theme I will be developing in this chapter. *She* is a version of the legend of the Sibyl of Cumae, who had begged Apollo to grant her as many years of life as there were grains of sand in her hand. But she neglected to specify that those years be years of youth, and as she aged she shriveled to a wizened, ugly shape. We have here a central image of aging in western culture: aging as torture. As Petronius tells the story in the *Satyricon,* the Sibyl of Cumae begged for death, for release from old age and the bottle in which she was imprisoned. Thus we see that when the tragic equation between old age and death is broken, we find that old age *without* death is even worse than when death accompanies it.

12. Letter from Freud to Fliess, July 15, 1896, *The Freud/Fliess Letters* 195.

13. Letter from Freud to Fliess, December 9, 1899, *The Freud/Fliess Letters* 390.

14. Letter from Freud to Fliess, November 2, 1896, *Letters* 232.

15. Letter from Freud to Fliess, December 11, 1893, *The Freud/Fliess Letters* 63.

16. In *Jacques Lacan: The Death of an Intellectual Hero* (Cambridge: Harvard UP, 1983), Stuart Schneiderman reports Lacan as having underscored the same point: "In a speech at a psychoanalytic congress in 1973 Lacan debunked the idea that people are apprehensive about dying. People are more apprehensive about living long, he said" (23).

17. When he was fifty-one Freud gloomily wrote in a letter to Jung, "I am celebrating my entrance into the climacteric age with a dyspepsia (following influenza) . . . " (Letter from Freud to Jung, September 2, 1907, *Letters* 257). The climacteric can be used to describe any critical period, but Freud clearly used the word with reference to aging as decline. The climacteric refers specifically in physiological terms to the period of decreasing reproductive capacity in men and women; since the climacteric occurs earlier in women than in men, old age has been associated as installing itself in the bodies of women earlier than in men. This is one area in which old age must clearly be decoupled from biological change. For as with gray hair, menopause occurs in middle age, not old age.

Freud's comment to Jung about entering old age was not an isolated remark. A few years later he confided, "My Indian summer of eroticism that we spoke of on our trip has withered lamentably under the pressure of work. I am resigned to being old and no longer even think continually of growing old" (Letter from Freud to Jung, February 2, 1910, *The Freud/Jung Letters* 292). Surely this is a denial. We should note that again Freud associates old age with a lack of sexual desire. A few months later he spoke to Jung of his old age, explicitly linking old age and anxiety. "One becomes so anxious and resigned in old age!" he wrote (Letter from Freud to Jung, May 2, 1910, *The Freud/*

Jung Letters 315). Resignation and anxiety: these are incompatible terms. But if anxiety was predominant, it at times abated. Freud's emotional state oscillated between these two poles—anxiety and resignation. Shortly afterwards Freud expressed himself in even more vociferous terms: ''I have little pleasure in working and constant *douleur d'enfantement*; in short, I feel rather gloomy and I am not quite well physically either. Old age is not an empty delusion. A morose senex deserves to be shot without remorse'' (Letter from Freud to Jung, November 2, 1911, *The Freud/Fliess Letters* 453). This is not the only place where Freud associated old age with labor pains.

18. Letter from Freud to Karl Abraham, July 3, 1915, qtd. Max Schur, *Freud: Living and Dying* 301. Later in his life Freud believed that he might die between the ages of sixty-one and sixty-two. Freud analyzed his conviction in this way: ''In 1899 when I wrote *The Interpretation of Dreams* I was 43 years old. . . . [T]he superstitious notion that I would die between the ages of 61 and 62 proves to coincide with the conviction that with *The Interpretation of Dreams* I had completed my life work, that there was nothing more for me to do and that I might just as well lie down and die'' (Letter from Freud to Jung, April 16, 1909, *The Freud/Jung Letters* 219).

19. Letter from Freud to Oskar Pfister, March 6, 1910, *Psychoanalysis and Faith: The Letters of Sigmund Freud and Oskar Pfister*, ed. Ernest L. Freud and Heinrich Meng, trans. Eric Mosbacher (New York: Basic, 1963) 35.

20. Jacques Lacan, ''Tuché and Automaton'' (1964), *The Four Fundamental Concepts of Psycho-Analysis* 64.

21. As I have been stressing, in the early texts of psychoanalysis old age is associated chronologically with a much ''younger'' age than it is today. Thus Jung, writing to Freud about the incest prohibition, could insist that an adult son could have no desire for his mother, for she would be old and physically unattractive. Characteristically, Jung put it crudely: ''In riper years, on the other hand, when the son might really be a danger to the father, and laws were therefore needed to restrain him, the son no longer had any real incestuous desires for the mother, with her sagging belly and varicose veins'' (Letter from Jung to Freud, May 8, 1912, *The Freud/Jung Letters* 503). Today the theme of the adolescent son and mother, represented as still sexually desirable, is being explored. The coupling of an older woman with a younger man has a history, which is currently being researched by Lois Banner for her book *Sunset Boulevard: Aging Women and Their Relationships with Younger Men in European Past and Present*, forthcoming from Knopf.

22. I am alluding to Margaret Gullette's *Safe at Last in the Middle Years* (Berkeley: U of California P, 1988). There has been considerable research on what has come to be known as midlife crises in the United States, which was launched by David J. Levinson's *The Seasons of a Man's Life* (New York: Knopf, 1978) and popularized by Gail Sheehy's *Passages*. I do not engage that research here, but confine myself instead to the discourse of psychoanalysis.

23. Still, if one is working with only two categories, as Freud did (young and old), and old is defined negatively, this presents a problem. If in one's middle age one's children have by and large grown up, then one would necessarily be defined as old. Freud winced at this, not only when it happened professionally but also in terms of his own family. ''Little by little the young people are becoming independent,'' he wrote in a letter to Jung, referring in particular to his sons, ''and all of a sudden I have become the old man'' (Letter from Freud to Jung, July 7, 1909, *The Freud/Jung Letters* 240).

24. Daughters can also take pleasure in their aging mothers' infirmities. Melanie Klein has theorized the child's desire to castrate the parent through age; she has also recorded this in one of her female patients. In ''Mourning and Its Relation to Manic-Depressive States,'' she writes: ''In my experience, the desire to reverse the child-parent relation, to get power over the parents and to triumph over them, is always to some extent associated with the impulse toward the attainment of success. A time will come, the child phan-

tasizes, when he will be strong, tall and grownup, powerful, rich and potent, and father and mother will have changed into helpless children, or again, in other phantasies, will be very old, weak, poor and rejected'' (*International Journal of Psycho-Analysis* 21 [1940]: 154). In "Infantile Anxiety Situations Reflected in a Work of Art and in the Creative Impulse'' (1929), she analyzes a woman who paints a portrait of an old woman which expresses her "wish to destroy her mother, to see her old, worn out, marred'' (*The Selected Melanie Klein,* ed. Juliet Mitchell [New York: The Free Press, 1986] 93).

Alice Adams's *Listening to Billie* (New York: Penguin, 1975) traces the life of a young woman on the eve of her marriage (she is pregnant) to her birthday in her forties. As we reach the end of the book and the main character nears another birthday, Eliza thinks of herself and her sometime lover as getting old. She finds that for the first time she is not interested in making love, and that fact scares her: "It was terrible, and frightening. Age? A somewhat early menopause?'' (200). She thinks that she has nothing else to write about: " 'I've said all the poems in my head' '' (201). When her mother (Josephine), a powerful woman in life and even more so in her daughter's imagination, has her second stroke (the mother is in her middle sixties), Eliza admits to herself as she confesses to her lover, " 'when Josephine had her first stroke, the first thing I thought was I'm safe from her now. You see? So she had to have another one.' '' Trying to reassure Eliza that her reaction was not untypical and that she is not guilty, Harry responds, " 'You're not exactly the first person who'd find a crippled parent easier to deal with than a powerful one' '' (202). Adams, who wrote the novel from the point of view of several of the characters, makes it clear that the mother does in fact feel punished by her daughters.

25. J.-B. Pontalis, *Frontiers in Psychoanalysis: Between the Dream and Psychic Pain,* trans. Catherine Cullen and Philip Cullen (1977; New York: International UP, 1981).

26. Jean Laplanche, *Life and Death in Psychoanalysis,* trans. Jeffrey Mehlman (Baltimore: Johns Hopkins UP, 1976).

27. Pontalis: "In my view the theme of death is as basic to Freudian psychoanalysis as is the theme of sexuality. I even believe that the latter was largely accorded a more prominent role in order to conceal the former'' (*Frontiers in Psychoanalysis* 184).

28. Freud's resources—I am not referring to his financial resources, which were slender—were great. He had vast reservoirs of professional admiration and power, and, perhaps most important, he was cared for attentively by his friends and family, and in particular by his grown daughter Anna, who stayed at home and nursed Freud until his death. This was the shape that the life of Virginia Woolf's Eleanor takes in *The Years,* which I discuss in a later chapter. Freud was aware of this aspect of his good fortune in old age. As he wrote, "I know too that were it not for the trouble of possibly not being able to work I should deem myself a man to be envied. To grow so old; to find so much warm love in family and friends; so much expectation of success in such a venturesome undertaking, if not the success itself [psychoanalysis]: who else has attained so much?'' Letter from Freud to Max Eitingon, March 19, 1926, qtd. Jones, *The Life and Work of Sigmund Freud* 3: 122.

29. As we have seen already, it is impossible to assign a specific date to the "beginning'' of Freud's old age. Indeed it seems at times as if he compacted his middle years into the time between the publication of *The Interpretation of Dreams* and his entry, as he had put it to Jung, into the climacteric, thus reducing his middle age to some six years. In his biography of Freud, Jones notes that after Freud's sixty-fifth birthday, his "constant complaints about getting old took a sudden turn'' (3: 79). In evidence he cites a passage from a letter Freud wrote to Ferenczi: "On March 13 of this year I quite suddenly took a step into real old age. Since then the thought of death has not left me, and sometimes I have the impression that several of my internal organs are fighting to have the honor of bringing my life to an end'' (Letter from Freud to Ferenczi, May 8, 1921, qtd. Jones, *The Life and Work of Sigmund Freud* 3: 79).

30. Interestingly enough, the other "event of this time which made a lasting impression" on Freud was meeting the Harvard neurologist James J. Putnam, who was apparently also older than Freud, a fact upon which Freud insisted, articulating the bias of psychoanalysis against those who are older. As Freud put it (un-self-consciously?), Putnam "in spite of his age was an enthusiastic supporter of psychoanalysis" (*An Autobiographical Study*, SE 20: 51). I take it that this is the same Putnam whom Freud delighted in slandering. See Note 10.

31. Jacques Lacan, *L'Ethique de la psychanalyse* (Paris: Seuil, 1986) 371. My translation.

32. "One learns to count up one's losses," Freud wrote in 1928 (Letter from Freud to Andreas-Salomé, May 9, 1928, *The Freud/Andreas-Salomé Letters* 175). In 1924 Freud contrasted himself with her husband: "Here is a person who, instead of working hard into old age (see the example beside you) and then dying without preliminaries, contracts a horrible disease in middle age, has to be treated and operated on, squanders his hard-earned bit of money, generates and enjoys discontent, and then crawls about for an indefinite time as an invalid. In *Erewhon* (I trust you know Samuel Butler's brilliant phantasy) such an individual would certainly be punished and locked up" (Letter from Freud to Andreas-Salomé, May 13, 1924, *Letters* 349). What I find particularly fascinating here is his seemingly jocular reference to *punishment* (I will take up the theme of aging as punishment later in this chapter). Only five years later Freud, seventy-three at the time (and he was to live another eleven years), referred to himself as a "rather frail old man" (Letter from Freud to Ludwig Binswanger, April 11, 1929, *Letters* 386).

33. Letter from Andreas-Salomé to Freud, May 20, 1927, *The Freud/Andreas-Salomé Letters* 165. Andreas-Salomé goes on to make an intriguing comment about her own experience of old age as a woman. "This does not seem to me to be solely the result of my own optimistic bias, but also of gradually acquired experience, e.g., in the sphere which touches women most nearly, the erotic," she writes. "For I had feared that old age might set in too late (because speaking physiologically it had only set in at sixty) and that in this way I might be cheated of what old age specifically has to offer. Fortunately, I was able to capture something of it. And certainly it did bring happiness—indeed, if I now had to choose between the two phases of life, I am truly not sure on which my choice would fall. For when one leaves erotic experience in the narrower sense, one is also at the same time leaving a cul-de-sac, however marvelous it may be, where there is only room for two abreast; and one now enters upon a vast expanse—the expanse of which childhood too was a part and which for only a while we were bound to forget" (166–67). Here old age is associated specifically with biological changes in the body. I take it that Andreas-Salomé is linking old age with both the cessation of menstruation (this is the setting in of old age in physiological terms) and the cessation of sexual activity. Or she may be simply linking old age with the cessation of physical desire. She suggests that the recuperation of what is lost is made possible by our increased consciousness of our accumulated experiences over the years—this is an altogether familiar construction about old age. But she adds something that is quite unexpected, drawing on the metaphors of domesticity and fertility: "One finds nests everywhere, lays eggs everywhere, takes things more easily and finally flies away" (166).

34. Letter from Andreas-Salomé to Freud, May 3, 1934, *The Freud/Andreas-Salomé Letters* 201–202.

35. Letter from Freud to Andreas-Salomé, May 16, 1934, *The Freud/Andreas-Salomé Letters* 202.

36. Letter from Andreas-Salomé to Freud, May 4, 1927, *The Freud/Andreas-Salomé Letters* 164; Letter from Freud to Andreas-Salomé, May 11, 1927, *The Freud/Andreas-Salomé Letters* 165.

37. See Robert N. Butler, "The Life Review: An Interpretation of Reminiscence in

the Aged,'' *Psychiatry* 26 (Feb. 1963): 65–76. See also my essay "Reminiscence and the Life Review: Prospects and Retrospects," *What Does It Mean to Grow Old?: Reflections from the Humanities* 137–61.

38. Gregory Jay discusses the figure of the daughter in "A Disturbance of Memory on the Acropolis." See his chapter on "Freud: The Death of Autobiography" in *America the Scrivener: Deconstruction and the Subject of Literary History,* forthcoming from Cornell.

39. Jones, *The Life and Work of Sigmund Freud* 3: 145. Toward the end of his account of Freud's life, Jones returns to this theme: "But with all the agony there was never the slightest sign of impatience or irritability. The philosophy of resignation and the acceptance of unalterable reality triumphed throughout" (245). Jones describes the scene of Freud asking his physician Max Schur to not allow him to suffer in pain any longer this way: "There was no emotionalism or self-pity, only reality—an impressive and unforgettable scene" (246). Jones was not present.

40. Paul Roazen, *Freud: Political and Social Thought* (New York: Knopf, 1968) 167.

41. Letter from Freud to Andreas-Salomé, May 10, 1925, *The Freud/Andreas-Salomé Letters* 154.

42. A theatrical analogue to this crust is found in Samuel Beckett's *Happy Days.* In the first act Winnie is buried in sand up to her waist; in the second act, up to her neck.

43. For an excellent discussion of how Freud departs from Plato's *Symposium,* see John Brenkman, "The Other and the One: Marxism, Psychoanalytic Criticism, and the Problem of the Subject," *Literature and Psychoanalysis: The Question of Reading: Otherwise,* ed. Shoshana Felman (1977; Baltimore: Johns Hopkins UP, 1982) 396–456.

44. One obvious index of this is the figure of the dirty old man, who as an object of ridicule and fear expresses the taboo of sexuality in old age. See Leslie Fiedler, "More Images of Eros and Old Age: The Damnation of Faust," *Memory and Desire* 37–50.

45. Letter from Freud to Andreas-Salomé, September 17, 1924, *The Freud/Andreas-Salomé Letters* 143.

46. Jacques Lacan, "Aggressivity in Psychoanalysis" (1948), *Ecrits* 8.

47. The context is this: "the death instinct of the single cell can successfully be neutralized and the destructive impulses be diverted on to the external world through the instrumentality of a special organ. This special organ would seem to be the muscular apparatus; and the death instinct would thus seem to express itself—though probably only in part—as an instinct of destruction directed against the external world and other organisms" (SE 19: 41).

48. Françoise Dolto, *L'Image inconscient du corps* (Paris: Seuil, 1984). Translation mine.

49. Letter from Sigmund Freud to Arnold Zweig, December 7, 1930, *The Letters of Sigmund Freud and Arnold Zweig,* ed. Ernst L. Freud, trans. Elaine and William Robson-Scott (New York: Harcourt, 1970) 25; Letter from Freud to Zweig, January 28, 1934, *The Freud/Arnold Zweig Letters* 60.

50. I cite only one of many examples. See, for instance, Peter Gay's *Freud for Historians* (New York: Oxford UP, 1985): "In the pioneering years, Freud had postulated two sets of instincts—sexual and egotistic—the one serving the perpetuation of the human race, the other that of the individual. Then, in the early 1920s, he confronted the mighty constructive energies of Eros with the equally mighty energies of destruction, the death instinct" (90).

51. Letter from Freud to Jones, March 7, 1933, qtd. Jones, *The Life and Work of Sigmund Freud* 3: 180. Freud goes on in this letter to repudiate the longing for rest as a primary aspect of the death instincts. "I believe I have discovered that the longing for ultimate rest is not something elementary and primary, but an expression to be rid of the feeling of inadequacy which affects age, especially in the smaller details of life" (180).

"Ultimate rest" is of course a euphemism for death, and I have been at some pains to distinguish between the two in this chapter. My guess is that the word "inadequacy" was delicately chosen and that beneath it we may read the word "castration"—and not only in the smaller details of life but in those matters of immense importance as well.

52. Letter from Freud to Marie Bonaparte, December 6, 1936, *Letters* 435. A year and a half earlier he had written to Andreas-Salomé in a tone of genial stoicism: "If one lives long enough (say about seventy-nine years), one may live to get a letter and even a photo from you—whatever the latter may look like. I refrain from sending you one of myself. What an amount of good nature and humor it takes to endure the gruesome business of growing old!" (Letter from Freud to Andreas-Salomé, May 16, 1935, *Letters* 425). Only a year later he adopted a completely different tone with Stefan Zweig: "For, although I have been exceptionally happy in my home, with my wife and children and in particular with one daughter who to a rare extent satisfies all the expectations of a father, I nevertheless cannot reconcile myself to the wretchedness and helplessness of old age, and look forward with a kind of longing to the transition into nonexistence" (Letter from Freud to Stefan Zweig, May 18, 1936, *Letters* 429). As these excerpts show, in his last years—for *sixteen* years he felt he was living under a death sentence, even when he was given a reprieve—we can read the traces of the oscillations of the life instincts with the death instincts in his letters.

53. For a reading of *King Lear* from the point of view of the intersection of male hysteria and aging, see Carolyn Asp, " 'The Clamor of Eros': Freud, Aging, and *King Lear*," *Memory and Desire* 192–204.

54. Letter from Freud to Arnold Zweig, June 13, 1935, *The Freud/Zweig Letters* 107.

55. H. D., *Tribute to Freud* (Boston: Godine, 1974) 16.

3. THE MIRROR STAGE OF OLD AGE

1. Marcel Proust, *The Past Recaptured,* trans. Frederick A. Blossom (New York: Modern, 1959) 198.

2. Anthony Wilden, trans., *The Language of the Self: The Function of Language in Psychoanalysis,* by Jacques Lacan (Baltimore: Johns Hopkins UP, 1968) 166.

3. Diana Festa-McCormick refers us to Proust's *Chroniques* (Paris: Gallimard, 1927) 216–17, in her "Proust's Asthma: A Malady Begets a Melody," *Medicine and Literature,* ed. Eric Rhodes Peschel (New York: Watson, 1980). Or as we read elsewhere in *The Past Recaptured,* "we wait for suffering before setting to work. The idea of suffering as an ineluctable prerequisite has become associated in our minds with the idea of work; we dread each new undertaking because of the suffering we know we must go through to formulate it in our imagination" (241).

4. Walter Benjamin, *Illuminations,* ed. Hannah Arendt, trans. Harry Zohn (New York: Harcourt, 1968) 213.

5. See Terrance Brophy Kearns, "Prisoner to the Palsy: A Study of Old Age in Shakespeare's History Plays," Diss. Indiana U 1978.

6. Marcel Proust, *The Guermantes Way,* trans. C. K. Scott Moncrieff (New York: Modern, 1952) 408.

7. Otto Rank reports that in early twentieth-century Germany, Austria, and Yugoslavia, the superstition persisted that one would die within a year if one saw one's double. Robert Rogers, commenting on the mirror image in *The Double in Literature* (Detroit: Wayne State UP, 1970), emphasizes that Rank regarded doubling as a narcissistic phenomenon and stressed the relationship between paranoia and doubling (much as Lacan did after him) insofar as both are characterized by projection.

8. See Lacan, "The Mirror Stage as Formative of the Function of the I" (1949), *Ecrits* 1–7.

9. In "The Subversion of the Subject and the Dialectic of Desire in the Freudian Unconscious" (1960), Lacan writes of the mirror stage of infancy: "what the subject finds in this altered image of his body is the paradigm of all the forms of resemblance that will bring over on to the world of objects a tinge of hostility, by projecting on them the manifestation of the narcissistic image, which, from the pleasure derived from meeting himself in the mirror, becomes when confronting his fellow man an outlet for his most intimate aggressivity" (*Ecrits* 307).

10. Lacan also associates the mirror stage of infancy with structurally producing the idea of death. He refers to what he calls "the mortifying gap of the mirror-stage" (*Ecrits* 211), a gap which widens—and whose affect intensifies—in what I will call the triangle of the mirror stage of old age. In "On a Question Preliminary to Any Possible Treatment of Psychosis" (1955–56), he writes, "it is by means of the gap opened up by this prematuration in the imaginary, and in which the effects of the mirror stage proliferate, that the human animal is *capable* of imagining himself as mortal, which does not mean that he would be able to do without his symbiosis with the symbolic, but rather that without this gap that alienates him from his own image, this symbiosis with the symbolic, in which he constitutes himself as subject to death, could not have occurred" (*Ecrits* 196).

11. I am alluding here to André Green's rich essay "The Double and the Absent" (1973), trans. Susan D. Cohen, *Psychoanalysis, Creativity, and Literature: A Franco-American Inquiry*, ed. Alan Roland (New York: Columbia UP, 1978), in which he refers to Proust's *Remembrance of Things Past* and James's *The Ambassadors*, among other texts. Green points to a structure present in literature and in literary production itself which he describes as being "caught between persecution and mourning, between the double and the absent," a "structure" which perfectly captures Marcel's dilemma in *The Past Recaptured* (289).

12. Christopher Lasch, *The Culture of Narcissism* (New York: Norton, 1978).

13. Gregory Rochlin, *Man's Aggression: The Defense of the Self* (Boston: Gambit, 1973).

14. Ernest Becker, *The Denial of Death* (New York: Free, 1975) 96.

15. Nietzsche, "On the Genealogy of Morals" (1887), *Basic Writings of Nietzsche*, trans. and ed. Walter Kaufmann (New York: Modern, 1968) 491.

16. Erik Erikson, qtd. Daniel Goleman, "Erikson, in His Own Old Age, Expands His View of Life," *The New York Times*, 14 June 1988, C1. Erikson explains his ideas about the interrelation of the generations in, among other places, *Insight and Responsibility* (New York: Norton, 1964) and most recently in *Vital Involvement in Old Age: The Experience of Old Age in Our Time*, by Erik H. Erikson, Joan M. Erikson, and Helen Q. Kivnick (1986; New York: Norton, 1989). The authors make the important point that "old age must be *planned*, which means that mature (and, one hopes, well-informed) middle-aged adults must become and remain aware of the long life stages that lie ahead. The future of these long-lived generations will depend on the vital involvement made possible throughout life" (14).

17. D. W. Winnicott, "Mirror-Role of Mother and Family in Child Development" (1967), *Playing and Reality* (London: Tavistock, 1971) 111.

18. Roland Barthes, *Camera Lucida: Reflections on Photography* (1980), trans. Richard Howard (New York: Hill, 1981) 12.

19. I am indebted especially to Murray S. Schwartz and to the members of the Center for the Psychological Study of the Arts at SUNY-Buffalo for helping me to formulate this point.

20. Simone de Beauvoir, *A Very Easy Death*, trans. Patrick O'Brian (1964; New York: Warner, 1973) 89.

4. THE LOOK AND THE GAZE

1. The entire quotation from Lacan's "Aggressivity in Psychoanalysis" is:

This narcissistic moment in the subject is to be found in all the genetic phases of the individual, in all degrees of human accomplishment in the person, in an earlier stage in which it must assume a libidinal frustration and a later stage in which it is transcended in a normative sublimation.
    This conception allows us to understand the aggressivity involved in the effects of all regression, all arrested development, all rejection of typical development in the subject, especially on the plane of sexual realization, and more specifically with each of the great phases that the libidinal transformations determine in human life, the crucial function of which has been demonstrated by analysis: weaning, the Oedipal stage, puberty, maturity, or motherhood, even the climacteric. (*Ecrits* 24–25)

If it seems that in the complete passage Lacan modulates his emphasis on aggressivity in phantasmatic life and social behavior by referring to the psychic mechanism of sublimation (and in particular, following Freud, to the resolutions of the Oedipus complex through identification), he insists earlier that "one cannot stress too strongly the irreducible character of the narcissistic structure" (24).
    2. What age, I wonder, did Woolf imagine her readers? Is there an implied reader in *The Years,* and if so, what is her age? During the past decade *The Years* has undergone a lively critical assessment. The contributors to the 1977 issue of the *Bulletin of the New York Public Library,* which was devoted to *The Years,* in general praise the novel, reading it as an allegory of the decline of British patriarchy, which includes the collapse of the family and the disintegration of the colonial empire. My reading of the novel does not preclude that one. But the effect of the insistence on the theme of the decline of patriarchy has led some critics to underemphasize the register of interior consciousness in the novel. At the same time *The Years* continues to be regarded by many as one of Woolf's weaker novels. Thus we find Eric Warner, for example, labeling *The Years* Woolf's "critical and creative nadir, a monument to that insecurity and lack of trust in her own insights and imagination" because in it she turns from "exploring interior riches to a pseudo-historical movement whose texture is flat, and unyielding, even repellent to any inner 'vision'" ("Re-Considering *The Years,*" *North Dakota Quarterly* 48.2 [1980]: 29, 19). In my judgment it is precisely in the interplay between interior "visions" and the perceptions of others that *The Years* succeeds so brilliantly. It does so by pointing to its historical specificity in a way not yet acknowledged by its critics, a point to which I will turn at the end of the essay. Thus I turn to Woolf's *The Years* and not to *The Waves,* an earlier Woolf novel that also tracks characters from their childhood to old age but which remains in what is to me the suffocating register of interior consciousness.
    3. Virginia Woolf, *A Room of One's Own* (New York: Harcourt, 1929) 60.
    4. J.-B. Pontalis, "Dream as an Object," trans. Carol Martin-Sperry and Masud Khan, *International Review of Psycho-Analysis* 1 (1974): 125–33.
    5. Masud Khan, *Hidden Selves: Between Theory and Practice in Psychoanalysis* (London: Hogarth, 1983) 46–47.
    6. Milan Kundera, *The Unbearable Lightness of Being* (New York: Harper, 1984) 59.
    7. Although Freud characterizes primary narcissism as blissful and insists that it is "normal" ("On Narcissism," SE 14: 74), he ultimately theorizes narcissism in negative terms. In "Formulations on the Two Principles of Mental Functioning," which was published three years before "On Narcissism," Freud writes that in sleep we "re-establish

the likeness of mental life as it was before the recognition of reality'' (SE 12: 219). In ''On Narcissism'' his odd comparison of both sleep and secondary narcissism to *illness* reveals his deep-seated ambivalence about narcissism. ''The condition of sleep, too,'' he writes, ''resembles illness in implying a narcissistic withdrawal of the positions of the libido on to the subject's own self'' (83).

8. What at first seems a salutary revision of the Freudian emphasis on interpretation in favor of an emphasis on the subjective and pleasurable experience of the dream itself is in the end a reassertion of the politics of analysis, which in Pontalis is also a politics of gender. For if the dream as an object in analysis refers to the maternal body, then interpretation, the drawing of the dream into the symbolic realm, is male. It is, in Pontalis's word, *penetration*.

9. D. W. Winnicott, ''Communicating and Not Communicating Leading to a Study of Certain Opposites'' (1963), *The Maturational Processes and the Facilitating Environment* (New York: International UP, 1965).

10. See especially Heinz Kohut's important essay ''Forms and Transformations of Narcissism,'' *Journal of the American Psychoanalytic Association* 14 (1966): 243–72. Hereafter referred to as *FTN*.

11. Heinz Kohut, ''Thoughts on Narcissism and Narcissistic Rage'' (1972), *The Search for the Self: Selected Writings of Heinz Kohut, 1950–1978*, 2 vols., ed. Paul H. Orstein (New York: International UP, 1978) 2: 618.

12. Heinz Kohut, ''On the Adolescent Process of the Transformation of the Self,'' *The Search for the Self* 2: 661.

13. Freud, of course, uses the analogy of the horse (the id) and the rider (the ego). See *The Ego and the Id* (SE 19: 12–66).

14. If I emphasize here the gradual nature of the process of aging, in Henry James's *The Ambassadors* (1902) we find an altogether different representation of the assumption of old age. I would have liked to have taken a passage from the novel as a counter-scene, but the very nature of the representation of aging in the novel prevents us from doing so. For the entire stretch of the long novel the main character, Strether, exists in what I would call, extrapolating from Winnicott, a transitional time. Strether's age is *undecidable*. He is both young and old at the same time. It is not that other people do not perceive his chronological age. In James's world, Strether is definitively categorized as old. Rather, the intriguing proposition of the novel is that one must *choose* one's age. The end of the novel surprises us with the abruptness of Strether's choice: he chooses old age. Moreover, unlike Marcel in the masquerade ball in *Remembrance of Things Past*, Strether's final assumption and not denial of old age is not so much imposed from without as it corresponds to his desire. At the same time, however, Strether is able to ''feel young'' because Chad, a character who is chronologically young, feels ''old.'' If Marcel decides for a future (which we as readers know to be truncated), Strether decides for the past: he accepts his life as he has lived it. The genius of the novel lies in its presenting Strether as evaluating his entire past life without involving a single event.

15. D. W. Winnicott, ''Transitional Objects and Transitional Phenomena: A Study of the First Not-Me Possession,'' *International Journal of Psycho-Analysis* 34.2 (1953): 89–97.

16. This is Béla Grunberger's position also. In his essays on narcissism, written between 1957 and 1971 and published in English in 1979 as *Narcissism: Psychoanalytic Essays*, Grunberger elaborates a dialectical theory of the relation between the drives and narcissism as a separate psychic agency, a relationship which in principle ends in a synthesis between the two components. Departing from Freud, he writes, ''The balancing between object libido and narcissistic libido must therefore be viewed in another light, not as a situation involving equilibrium between object cathexis and narcissism, but as a dialectic relation between instinctual and narcissistic components'' (*Narcissism*, trans.

Joyce S. Diamanti [New York: International UP, 1979] 6). Grunberger argues that narcissistic happiness, once it is accepted and is not accompanied by guilt, "forms the necessary and essential component of the fullest and most mature object relations" (201).

17. Woolf's description of Eleanor's experience corresponds to the description of narcissistic pleasures offered by Grunberger, who like Kohut has worked to rescue narcissism from contempt. Narcissistic pleasures, according to Grunberger, have "a tonality *sui generis*" that is characterized by "an inexpressible sense of well-being, a particularly gratifying bliss, which seems to derive primarily from an existential feeling of extending to infinity, giving the individual an impression of unrestricted autonomy and grandeur" (107).

18. C. Fred Alford argues that the revisionary theories of narcissism of Grunberger, Kohut, Chassequet-Smirgel, and Andreas-Salomé offer a theoretical foundation on which to build a model of reconciliation, which in Alford's framework is reconciliation with nature. See "Nature and Narcissism: The Frankfurt School," *New German Critique* 36 (Fall 1985): 174–92. See also Alford, *Narcissism: Socrates, the Frankfurt School, and Psychoanalytic Theory* (New Haven: Yale UP, 1988).

19. Winnicott (1970), qtd. Khan, *Hidden Selves* 106.

20. Nor, in my judgment, do many of her critics. Mitchell A. Leska, for example, reads Eleanor conventionally, not to say melodramatically. See his *The Novels of Virginia Woolf: From Beginning to End* (New York: Jay, City U of New York, 1977). For Leska, the Eleanor of the final pages is "the aged woman whose sunflower of youth has long been fissured," who has lived through "The Hell and Purgatory of the Years," who, left alone "with an indulgent and possessive father," has been—"like Antigone—buried alive" (223).

21. René Girard, "Narcissism: The Freudian Myth Demythified by Proust," *Psychoanalysis, Creativity, and Literature* 292–311.

22. Marcel Proust, *Within a Budding Grove*, trans. C. K. Moncrieff (New York: Modern, 1951) 2: 129–30.

23. My use of the word "aesthetic" raises complicated questions which I can only hint at here. As Pierre Bourdieu reminds us in *Distinction*, trans. Richard Nice (Cambridge: Harvard UP, 1984), post-Kantian aesthetics of disinterestedness are an expression of and depend on relative distance from economic necessity. But Eleanor is not in the position of power; as I have been arguing, her interests do not seem to be *self*-interests in the sense that we usually mean it. Paul Schilder, in *The Image and Appearance of the Human Body* (1935; New York: International UP, 1950), would give a psychoanalytic, not materialist, reading of aesthetic. He argues that "when we consider the beauty of the human figure, we see immediately that aesthetic interest is certainly closely connected with interest in sex and therefore with a very urgent and very actual need. . . . It is clear that the aesthetic influence disappears when the sexual desire becomes stronger . . . aesthetic enjoyment, although it offers rest and relaxation, does not bring a full satisfaction of desires, and remains, therefore, distant from the object" (265). Reading Schilder through Woolf, might we not conclude that Schilder overvalorizes a certain kind of desire, that his own reading is age-bound? For Eleanor's interest in people of other generations serves to strengthen social bonds, at least on her part.

24. I was asked to speak on "New Love in Old Age" for which I chose these texts: Herbert Gold's *Family* (1981), Isaac Bashevis Singer's *Old Love* (1979), and M. F. K. Fisher's *Sister Age* (1983).

25. Colette, *The Blue Lantern* (1949), trans. R. Senhouse (New York: Farrar, 1963) 131–32.

26. Melanie Klein, "On the Sense of Loneliness" (1963), *Envy and Gratitude and Other Works 1946–1963* (London: Hogarth and Inst. of Psycho-Analysis, 1975) 310–11.

27. See David Gutmann's wide-ranging and richly speculative essay "Psychoanalysis and Aging," to which I am much indebted. Gutmann concludes that in many elderly people we find "the late maturing capacity to cathect and make real those agencies which do not in any direct way bear on the security and priorities of the self" (492). Gutmann stresses that these strengths may be *affective* as well as cognitive. He argues that our experience of loss, honed over the years, prompts us to seek new sources of sustenance, "the ultimate trustworthy object": "the aged person is . . . set free to search for those objects that finally will be sustaining and security giving. The aged have learned that all things of seeming substance pass and fade: their parents and the leaders of their youth are gone, peers are dying, the social mores change, and their bodies fail them. Though social objects desert them, they still search for that which will be constant and trustworthy. Since substance has failed, they seek the sustaining object in the insubstantial abstractions that cannot be lost. Concomitantly, the diminution of instinct frees them to search for the trustworthy object in the realm of the impersonal—the realm of otherness" (492).

5. GENDER, GENERATIONAL IDENTITY, AND AGING

1. Anne Tyler, *Dinner at the Homesick Restaurant* (1982; New York: Berkeley, 1983) 1.

2. Margaret S. Mahler: "One could regard the entire life cycle as constituting a more or less successful process of distancing from and introjection of the lost symbiotic mother, an eternal longing for the actual or fantasied 'ideal state of self,' with the latter standing for a symbiotic fusion with the 'all good' symbiotic mother who was at one time a part of the self in a blissful state of well-being," "On the First Three Subphases of the Separation-Individuation Process," *International Journal of Psycho-Analysis* 53 (1972): 338.

3. Alice Balint, "Love for the Mother and Mother Love" (1939), *Primary Love and Psycho-Analytic Technique* by Michael Balint (London: Hogarth and Inst. of Psycho-Analysis, 1952) 109–27.

4. Balint thus concludes that the child can never really *hate* the mother. True hate entails ambivalence; it is more likely to develop in relation to the father than to the mother. True hate is "pure aggressiveness," whereas pseudo-hate is "originally a demand for unselfishness from the mother" (111).

5. Eva Figes, *Waking* (New York: Pantheon, 1981).

6. Who of us have not returned years later to our diary entries to find that we do not recognize the person who is inscribed in those pages which now hold so little meaning for us? Beckett's *Krapp's Last Tape* (New York: Grove, 1960) tells us this truth too. Krapp, who makes a rambling tape-recording of his thoughts each year on his birthday, possesses an archive of his past selves to which he finds, as he recedes into age, that he has virtually no relation. The words on the page in the diary, the sounds on the tape, are empty signs which do not precipitate remembrance in the Proustian sense.

7. Doris Bernstein, "Female Identity Synthesis," *Career and Motherhood*, ed. Alan Roland and Barbara Harris (New York: Human Sciences, 1979) 108. See also her essay "The Female Superego: A Different Perspective," *International Journal of Psycho-Analysis* 64 (1983): 187–201. Readers familiar with Nancy Chodorow's *The Reproduction of Mothering: Psychoanalysis and the Sociology of Gender* (Berkeley: U of California P, 1978) may wonder why I am not drawing on her book here. Certainly its influence has been enormous. To cite only one example: three-quarters of the essays in the anthology *The (M)Other Tongue: Essays in Feminist Psychoanalytic Interpretation*, ed. Shirley Nelson Garner, Claire Kahane, and Madelon Sprengnether (Ithaca: Cornell UP, 1985), reference Chodorow's book. And at first glance, Chodorow's arguments may appear to coincide with those of Bernstein. But this is misleading. Precisely what I find valuable

about Chodorow's book is the social and historical dimension she gives to mothering. Her answer to the question she poses—why do mothers mother—is primarily that of acculturation. This should come as no surprise. Chodorow is a sociologist by training, and psychoanalysis, while obviously a source of intellectual fascination to her in addition to constituting the bulk of the content of her book, does not constitute the heart of her argument.

In my judgment feminist literary and film criticism has relied too heavily on Chodorow's exposition of psychoanalysis when feminist psychoanalysts themselves offer work of greater subtlety and detail. Just as important (and even though this will sound like a truism, it needs to be said), feminist psychoanalysts, such as Bernstein, believe fundamentally in tenets of psychoanalysis. I prefer, then, to work within this tradition, one that includes the work of Irene Fast and Jessica Benjamin. See, for example, Irene Fast, "Developments in Gender Identity: Gender Differentiation in Girls," *International Journal of Psycho-Analysis* 60 (1979): 443–53; and Jessica Benjamin, "A Desire of One's Own: Psychoanalytic Feminism and Intersubjective Space," *Feminist Studies/Critical Studies,* ed. Teresa de Lauretis (Bloomington: Indiana UP, 1986) 78–101. Recently much critical work in feminist literary and cultural studies has focused on the figure of the mother and the relation between the mother and the daughter. See, for example, the splendid essays by Susan Rubin Suleiman, "Writing and Motherhood," *The (M)Other Tongue* 352–77, and Linda Williams, " 'Something Else besides a Mother': *Stella Dallas* and the Maternal Melodrama," *Cinema Journal* 24.1 (Fall 1984): 2–27. See also Judith Kegan Gardiner, "On Female Identity and Writing by Women," *Critical Inquiry* 8.2 (Winter 1981): 347–61. Drawing on Chodorow and other theorists, Gardiner concludes that "female identity is a process and primary identity for women is more flexible and relational than for men" (354).

8. Ernest L. Abelin, "Triangulation, the Role of the Father and the Origins of Core Gender Identity during the Rapprochement Subphase," *Rapprochement: The Critical Subphase of Separation-Individuation,* ed. Ruth F. Lax, Sheldon Bach, and J. Alexis Burland (New York: Aronson, 1980) 151–69.

9. According to Abelin, only little boys approach early triangulation having *dis*identified from the mother; only in little boys is there an early *sexual* triangulation. This means that the little boy who is some eighteen months, in his first identification with the father and now yearning for the mother from whom he has separated himself, wishes for a *different* kind of object—for an object that does not mirror his body. The little girl, on the other hand, longs for the mother who is her mirror. Abelin concludes, in contradistinction to Freud, that masculinity is something that is added to "an otherwise feminine core identity" (165), rather than something subtracted to yield the feminine. Drawing on research in other fields as well (including cognitive psychology), he further suggests that females tend to be more responsive than males to redundancy; that is, they tend to perceive relations in terms of *similarity,* which is measured in terms of size, time, and role. Boys, on the other hand, are more responsive to discrepancy; that is, they perceive relations in terms of *difference.*

10. The difference between female generational identity as I have been developing it and male gender identity based on the Freudian notion of sexual difference resonates with Carol Gilligan's distinction between female identity based on affiliation and male identity based on achievement. See Carol Gilligan, *In a Different Voice: Psychological Theory and Women's Development* (Cambridge: Harvard UP, 1982).

11. See also D. W. Winnicott, "Creativity and Its Origins," *Playing and Reality* 65–85. Although he confuses the issue by using the terms "male" and "female" to describe two different forms of relating to an other, Winnicott's speculations on this matter resonate with what I have been developing here. Drawing on this model of the interaction between the infant and the mother, Winnicott distinguishes between what he calls the "male

element,'' which has to do with *doing*, and the "female element,'' which has to do with *being*. Associating the male element in object-relating with the instinct drive as it has been traditionally conceived in psychoanalysis, Winnicott argues that the male element in object-relating presupposes the separateness of the object. He links the female element with primary identification, an identification that has nothing whatsoever to do with the instinct drives. "The pure female element,'' he writes, "relates to the breast (or to the mother) in the sense of *the baby becoming the breast (or mother), in the sense that the object is the subject*'' (79). It is not separateness that is at stake here but rather the continuity of being. Seen from this perspective the mother is a *subjective object*, "the object *not yet repudiated as a not-me phenomenon*'' (80). For Winnicott the female is associated with our first identification, with our taking hold psychically of the world as and in symbiosis. I want to insist that this capacity for creating subjective objects is the opposite of creating difference or of objectifying the object. In "Creativity and Its Origins'' Winnicott also emphasizes generational continuity. It is in the female form of object-relating that we find "a true continuity of generations, being which is passed on from one generation to another, via the female element of men and women and of male and female infants'' (80).

12. I am indebted to Susan Jeffords for this point.

13. In Saul Bellow's *The Dean's December* (New York: Harper, 1982), we see a different drama played out. The old mother of a middle-aged and childless woman named Minna dies. Minna's husband, the Dean, is psychologically astute enough to understand that the death of Minna's mother causes Minna to reevaluate *him*. Minna turns her measuring look on him in great part because he is all she has left. She never had children. Her father and now her mother are both dead. Minna has completely lost her place within the structure of the family. Her place in the lineage of her own family, as constituted by her parents, has disappeared. In a sense, her identity, her generational identity, has also vanished.

14. I want to add another voice as a cautionary note here. In an address to the National Women's Studies Association in 1985, Barbara MacDonald argued that the source of ageism of young and middle-aged women with respect to older women is the patriarchal family where children are raised to believe that "mother is there to serve you," or as Balint puts it, that a mother has no interests of her own. See "Outside the Sisterhood: Ageism in Women's Studies," *Women and Aging* 23. MacDonald's argument resonates with the point I made in the chapter on Freud regarding the valorization of the stoicism of the elderly *paterfamilias* as possibly contributing to neglect of the aged.

15. Luce Irigaray has written movingly about what I call here reparation, echoing Melanie Klein: "I don't know one woman who doesn't truly suffer from being in dissension with or having broken with her mother. The first step is to reconcile with the mother inside us, because we have internalized (introjected) her, our mother, so it is necessary to make peace with that mother." "Amant marine de Nietzsche" (1980), *Le Corps-à-corps avec la mère* (Montréal: Pleine lune, 1981) 62. In the same volume Irigaray insists that we as daughters (and I would add as mothers) must rethink and remake our relations with our mothers so as to destabilize generational gender relations. I translate freely: "It is necessary for us to somehow let go of the all-good mother (the last refuge) and to establish a relation of reciprocity with our mothers, of woman to woman, where they can also feel themselves to be our daughters. In short, to liberate ourselves with our mothers. It is an indispensable condition to our liberation from the authority of the fathers. The relation mother/daughter, daughter/mother constitutes a very explosive nucleus [*noyau*] in our society. To theorize it, to change it, will in turn [ignite] the patriarchal order" (86).

16. In *Reclaimed Powers* David Gutmann argues that parenthood is a pivotal developmental event in our lives. With regard to women in particular, he suggests that having

children allows us to mature in a certain way, making it easier for us to accept our own death and the death of our mothers. *Waking* also offers a paradigm for this tri-generational constellation of mother-self-child but it is the inverse of Gutmann's. In *Waking* it is the death of the mother which permits the daughter to accept her motherhood.

17. See D. W. Winnicott, "The Use of an Object and Relating through Identifications" (1969), *Playing and Reality* 86–94.

18. Winnicott, "The Use of an Object" 90.

19. Roy Schafer, *Aspects of Internalization* (New York: International UP, 1968).

20. Marion Milner, qtd. Pontalis, *Frontiers in Psychoanalysis: Between the Dream and Psychic Pain* 21.

21. See Jacques Derrida on the work of Nicholas Abraham and Maria Torok, "Fors," *The Georgia Review* 31.1 (Spring 1977): 64–116.

22. Pontalis, *Frontiers in Psychoanalysis* 46.

23. As Schafer has observed, "Interiorization of psychic processes increases with development: more and more, thought replaces diffuse affective and motor expressions, and later replaces much of action, including speech. In this development, the daydream, which once coexisted with play and also partly defined its course, becomes the heir of play to a large extent" (86).

24. Pontalis, "On Psychic Pain," *Frontiers in Psychoanalysis* 194–205.

25. We find in Annie Dillard's *An American Childhood* (New York: Harper, 1987) an echo of this passage as if it were an uncanny acoustical mirror. Dillard, in her forties, comes close to the end of her autobiographical book with this reflection:

> I write this at a wide desk in a pine shed as I always do these recent years, in this life I pray will last, while the summer sun closes the sky to Orion and to all the other winter stars over my roof. The young oaks growing just outside my windows wave in the light, so that concentrating, lost in the past, I see the pale leaves wag and think as my blood leaps: Is someone coming?
>
> Is it Mother coming for me, to carry me home? Could it be my own young, glorious Mother, coming across the grass for me, the morning light on her skin, to get me and bring me back? Back to where I last knew all I needed, the way to her two strong arms? (250)

26. I take the term "maternal supplement" from Phyllis Greenacre who has written about the psychic economy of a child with a defective body. The problem for the child is how to create the illusion of a maternal supplement to his body. See Greenacre, "The Transitional Object and the Fetish: With Special Reference to the Role of Illusion," *Emotional Growth: Psychoanalytic Studies of the Gifted and a Great Variety of Other Individuals*, Vol. 1 (New York: International UP, 1971) 335–52. What is represented in the last lines of *Waking* is the process of gratificatory hallucination. In the final process of aging unto death, what is being denied and cast off is the fragmenting body. Paradoxically it is as if another body—a young body—is created in its place. It is as if the dying daughter created another mother. Tor-Björn Hägglund and Heikka Piha argue that just as with the beginning of life when the infant has not yet differentiated himself from the body of the mother, so too at the end of life there is a lack of boundary between the psychic body of the dying person and the mother: "the boundary between the bodies of the infant and its mother is nonexistent . . . at the end of life when the deeply regressed dying person's conception of his or her own body merges with fantasies of life after death." Hägglund and Piha, "The Inner Space of the Body Image," *Psychoanalytic Quarterly* 49 (1980): 257.

27. Alice S. Rossi, "Life-Span Theories and Women's Lives," *Signs* 6.1 (1980): 4–32.

28. I have written this chapter from the point of view of a daughter. The novel itself places us as readers in the position of the daughter (more generally, the child) who seeks the all-good ideal mother. This is why we may find the conclusion of *Waking* so moving. Yet generational simultaneity is also at stake in the novel's ending. Because we may wish to take care of the daughter, we may position ourselves as the mother as well. In part this generational polyvalence on the part of the reader is encouraged by the fact that in the fictional world of *Waking* we are given none of the distancing anchors of realistic fiction. The village has no place, the characters have no names. The daughter speaks in the first person, as I, a pronoun which in the psychic *mise-en-scène* of reading can shift easily to the I of the reader.

6. BETWEEN MOURNING AND MELANCHOLIA

1. The confusion of mourning as *affect* with mourning as a *psychic process* is not at all unusual and may derive in part from Freud's own mixing of the two in the very first sentence of "Mourning and Melancholia": "We will try to throw some light on the nature of melancholia by comparing it with the normal affect of mourning" (SE 14: 243).

2. For an excellent critical review of psychoanalytic literature on mourning up to the mid-sixties, see Lorraine D. Siggens, "Mourning: A Critical Survey of the Literature," *International Journal of Psycho-Analysis* 47 (1966): 14–25. For recent readings of literature in terms of mourning, see Sharon Cameron, "Representing Grief: Emerson's 'Experience,'" *Representations* 15 (Summer 1986): 15–41 (an essay which strangely avoids psychoanalysis), and Neal L. Tolchin, *Mourning, Gender, and Creativity in the Art of Herman Melville* (New Haven: Yale UP, 1988), which contains a comprehensive bibliography of work (literary and otherwise) on mourning.

3. Jacques Lacan, "Desire and the Interpretation of Desire in *Hamlet*" (1959), trans. James Hulbert, *Yale French Studies* 55/56 (1977): 37. I comment on Lacan's reading in Note 17.

4. Kathleen Kirby (U of Wisconsin-Milwaukee), "Indifferent Boundaries: Studies in the Subject, Language and Power," ms. 1989.

5. Anna Freud and Dorothy Burlingame differentiate between *grief* in a child and *mourning* in an adult. For Melanie Klein, on the other hand, mourning is a critical phase in the development of the infant, with melancholia associated with the depressive position. See her "Mourning and Its Relation to Manic-Depressive States."

6. George H. Pollock has steadily made important contributions to research on mourning. He insists that we should study mourning in relation to the life course and in particular to aging:

> My studies of various object losses, notably childhood parent loss, childhood sibling loss, adult spouse loss, and adult loss of a child, convince me that it is necessary to describe the function, role and meaning of the important lost "object" at different periods of the life course. . . . When viewed on a chronological axis, the significance of that which is "lost" reveals different meanings and functions during the adult periods. For example, the meaning of a spouse is different when one is in the early twenties, thirties, forties, fifties, sixties, seventies, eighties. In a recent study I described the changing meanings siblings have for each other during the adult years and how these sibling relationships are related to adult friendships. . . . During the adult periods, parents and children change in their meanings for each other. The kinship relationships always remain, but the individuals may have different *significances* for each other at various periods of adult life. ("Aging or Aged" 552)

See also Pollock's "On Mourning, Immortality, and Utopia," *Journal of American Psychoanalytic Association* 73.2 (1975): 334–62.

7. Several empirical studies lend support to this view, of which I note only one. In "Grief Reactions in Later Life," Karl Stern, Gwendolyn M. Williams, and Miguel Prados conclude that in older people mourning is marked less by overt signs of grief and more by actual physical illness. *The American Journal of Psychiatry* 108 (Oct. 1951): 289–94. The authors also observe a tendency in older people toward the idealization and glorification of those whom they have lost. This is certainly the case in Barthes's portrayal of his mother in *Camera Lucida*.

8. Similarly, one may resist a certain theorization of mourning depending upon one's own experience of mourning. A fascinating instance of such resistance from the history of psychoanalysis itself comes to us from Karl Abraham. In "A Short Study of the Development of the Libido, Viewed in the Light of Mental Disorders" (1924), Abraham reports that when he first read "Mourning and Melancholia" he resisted the idea of the introjection of the figure who has been lost. Only later did he realize, he says, that his resistance was due to the fact that the previous year he had lost his father and had in fact displayed physical signs of the psychological process of introjection, which he did not wish to acknowledge. *Selected Papers of Karl Abraham,* trans. Douglas Bryan and Alix Strachey (London: Hogarth and Inst. of Psycho-Analysis, 1973).

9. Freud also wrote in *The Interpretation of Dreams* that "men . . . dream mostly of their father's death and women of their mother's" (SE 4: 256). To my knowledge this interesting observation, which could be explained on the basis of intergenerational gender identification, has not been explored since. It raises the issue of possible connections between mourning and gender. I do not know of any research that deals with mourning and gender other than studies of the different responses of men and women to the deaths of their spouses; the difference, however, is only noted, not accounted for theoretically. At the other end of the spectrum, Hélène Cixous has theorized mourning in terms of gender, speculating that women *do not* mourn (that is, do not come to an end of their suffering) but sustain themselves with pain. I make much the same argument here but not in terms of gender. See Hélène Cixous, "Castration or Decapitation," trans. Annette Kuhn, *Signs* 7.1 (Autumn 1981): 41–55.

10. Letter from Freud to Katá and Lajos Levy, June 11, 1923, *Letters* 344.

11. In *Tribute to Freud,* H. D. tells a story about Freud as a grandfather that I find harsh because of her apparent refusal to understand him. She remembers that when Freud was around seventy-seven, he expressed great concern about his grandchildren, asking the painful and paternalistic rhetorical question, " 'What will become of my grandchildren?' " (63). H. D. does not conceal her impatience ("I was worried about something else" [63]) and unfeelingly relegates his love for his young grandchildren to a tedious Jewish trait and to his ambitious desire for immortality.

12. Letter from Freud to Sandor Ferenczi, September 16, 1930, *Letters* 400. About a year earlier Freud had written: "The loss of a mother must be something very strange, unlike anything else, and must arouse emotions that are hard to grasp. I myself still have a mother, and she bars my way to the longed-for rest, to eternal nothingness: I somehow could not forgive myself if I were to die before her. But you are young, you actually have the best and most eventful decade, from fifty to sixty, still ahead of you. . . . " (Letter from Freud to Max Eitingon, December 1, 1929, *Letters* 392).

13. Karl Abraham, "A Short Study of the Development of the Libido" 437.

14. In *Inhibitions, Symptoms and Anxiety* (SE 20: 77–175), Freud associates *anxiety* with indefiniteness, *fear* with the danger of a known object, and *mourning* with the loss of an object. Bowlby has sharply and persuasively critiqued Freud's definitions of anxiety and mourning, and in particular Freud's association of anxiety with neurosis. John Bowlby is also one of the few analysts who argue that the process of mourning does not always

result in relinquishing the figure who has been lost. See *Separation: Anxiety and Loss* (1973; Middlesex, England: Pelican, 1975).

15. André Green, "Le Temps mort," *Nouvelle revue de psychanalyse* 11 (1975): 103–109. Translation mine. This calls to mind the words of the Japanese lover in Marguerite Duras's *Hiroshima, Mon Amour*, trans. Richard Seaver (New York: Grove, 1960): "In a few years, when I'll have forgotten you, and when other adventures, from sheer habit, will happen to me, I'll remember you as the symbol of love's forgetfulness. I'll think of this adventure as the horror of oblivion. I already know it" (68).

16. For a splendid reading of Barthes, sentimentality, and the mother, see Herbert Blau, "Barthes and Beckett: The Punctum, the Pensum, and the Dream of Love," *The Eye of Prey: Subversions of the Postmodern* (Bloomington: Indiana UP, 1987) 84–103.

17. What of Lacan's reading of Hamlet's celebrated "inability to mourn"? In "Desire and the Interpretation of Desire in *Hamlet*," Lacan is concerned with the trajectory of the tragedy toward Hamlet's "act," and thus with the fact that a crime has been committed. Like so many other commentators, he is fascinated with Hamlet's so-called procrastination: "Hamlet just doesn't know what he wants" (26). But if we think of grief (that is, the *state,* not its process of mourning) in terms of *not* giving something up, then we can understand Hamlet this way: he does not act because he *does not want to,* not because he *can't.* The object of Hamlet's desire is double: his own affect (his own pain), which he wishes to retain so as to maintain the conversation with the dead (the Ghost), the father. In his reading of *Hamlet* Lacan stresses mourning in its social appearances, observing that it is through discourse that we as social beings complete the work of mourning: "The work of mourning is accomplished at the level of the *logos*" (38). But from my perspective we can understand Hamlet as purposely not wanting to enter into symbolic rituals. Hamlet does not want to bury the dead, yet we could not describe his grief in terms of the crypt, in Abraham and Torok's sense.

Although Lacan observes in passing that Hamlet's desire is dependent upon the desire of his mother, Lacan does not pause to question just what in fact her desire is. Lacan takes her for granted, as is indicated by the fact that throughout his essay he mentions countless characters by name—Claudius, Fortinbras, Laertes, Ophelia, Polonius, Horatio—but the name Gertrude never once appears in his text. Gertrude herself recognizes that her marriage was "o'erhasty." And Lacan is on to something when he notes that for "this woman . . . there must be something very strong that attaches herself to her partner" (50). But this "something" Lacan does not explain. Can we not understand her "hasty" action—marrying the brother-in-law who murdered her husband—as a way of keeping her first husband alive, of not completing the process of mourning? In this sense Hamlet's desire would mirror hers: both of them desire *not* to complete the work of mourning.

18. In her essay "About Losing and Being Lost," Anna Freud stresses the importance of objects such as photographs in mourning: "The adult mourner consoles himself for his loss by holding on to mementos and heirlooms as external links to the lost object. Damage to these bridges to the past, or their real loss, is experienced as a personal injury and a desecration of the memory of the deceased." *The Psychoanalytic Study of the Child* 22 (1967): 9–19.

19. The point I am making in this essay pivots on the distinction between externalization and internalization (introjection, incorporation). Internalizing the lost object as a part of mourning has become something of a theoretical piety which may be born out of the superego. Pontalis has written that the "*work-of-mourning* [is] a complex process that operates no longer on representations but rather on an *object* incorporated into the shell, the container, of the ego; a process, therefore, that is intrapsychic in the strongest sense, and whose teleological purpose has been said to 'kill the dead.'" Pontalis, "On Death-Work in Freud, in the Self, in Culture" (1978), trans. Susan D. Cohen, *Psycho-*

analysis, Creativity, and Literature 85. Or as Hans W. Loewald has insisted: "Mourning involves not only the gradual, piecemeal relinquishment of the lost object, but also the internalization, the appropriation of aspects of this object—or rather, of aspects of the relationship between the ego and the lost object which are 'set up in the ego' and become a relationship within the ego system." Loewald, "Internalization, Separation, Mourning, and the Superego," *The Psychoanalytic Quarterly* 31 (1962): 493.

20. J.-B. Pontalis, "On Psychic Pain," *Frontiers in Psychoanalysis: Between the Dream and Psychic Pain* 194–205.

21. Jacques Derrida, *Memoirs for Paul de Man*, trans. Cecile Lindsay, Jonathan Culler, and Eduardo Cadava (New York: Columbia UP, 1986) 6.

22. Susan Stewart, *On Longing: Narratives of the Miniature, the Gigantic, the Souvenir, the Collection* (Baltimore: Johns Hopkins UP, 1984) 145.

23. Winnicott, "On Communication" (1963), *The Maturational Processes and the Facilitating Environment* 84.

24. J.-B. Pontalis, *Perdre de vue* (Paris: Gallimard, 1988) 275. Translation mine. In a remarkable letter to Freud written when she was sixty-six, Andreas-Salomé speaks passionately about the compensations which old age has brought her. One in particular, which she attributed specifically to her old age, was "new and unexpected"—an intensification of grief in which the figure of Rilke, who for thirty years had been so important to her, assumed firm and distinct form. Just as Barthes in the loss of his mother suffered from never being able to see her again, Andreas-Salomé suffered from not being able to talk to Rilke.

> From the moment Rainier was removed from the changing ebb and flow of his existence he acquired a firm outline in my mind. The totality of his essential character emerged from my inner preoccupation with him, from letters and memories, and from a new and unprecedented kind of communion. In the first place this took the form of an intensification of grief—a kind of lamentation that I could no longer *tell* him, no longer communicate to him, what would have been for him so important a piece of knowledge and experience. But he remained an utterly distinct figure.

Letter from Andreas-Salomé to Freud, May 20, 1927, *The Freud/Andreas-Salomé Letters* 166–67.

25. Psychoanalysis indicts repetition as blindness, as has recent psychoanalytic literary criticism. See the brilliant and influential issue of *Yale French Studies* 55/56 (1977) entitled "The Question of Reading: Otherwise," ed. Shoshana Felman. Her stunning reading of repetition in readings of *The Turn of the Screw* is one of the most forceful examples (See "Turning the Screw of Interpretation" 94–207). I want to insist, however, that repetition is not always testimony to entrapment. Instead it can be expressive of powerful dramas whose stories need to be continually retold *not* because we are blind ideologically to contradictory knots in them but because the *affect* associated with them, which may bind us together in our imagination out of concern for the suffering and pain of others, needs to be brought to life.

26. See, for example, Samuel Weber's discussion of the dream of the "Burning Child" in *The Legend of Freud* (Minneapolis: U of Minnesota P, 1982) 69–75, and Jane Gallop in her *Reading Lacan* (Ithaca: Cornell UP, 1985) 177–85.

27. Referring to the dream of the "Burning Child" in his seminar "Of the Subject of Certainty," Lacan does acknowledge the emotional power of the dream. If Freud somewhat perfunctorily labels it "moving," Lacan in his own hyperbolic way characterizes it as "a dream suspended around the most anguishing mystery, that which links a father to the corpse of his dead son close by, of his dead son" (FF 34). But no sooner

has he said this than Lacan submerges the dream in his gender-coded theory of the symbolic, placing the dream of the "Burning Child" in the tradition of *Oedipus* and *Hamlet*, narratives that deal with the economy of desire and the law. Lacan also discusses the dream of the "Burning Child" in "The Split between the Eye and the Gaze," *FF* 67–78.

28. Benjamin, *Illuminations* 224.

29. The work of Julia Kristeva is a remarkable exception to this rule. See *Soleil noir: depression et mélancholie* (Paris: Gallimard, 1987), whose discourse is both theoretical and expressive.

30. Paul de Man, *The Rhetoric of Romanticism* (New York: Columbia UP, 1984) 121.

31. Joseph Sittler, "Theological Perspectives on Aging," *How Does Our Society Today Value Aged Persons?*, ed. Elizabeth M. Lane (Madison: General Health Services; Yahara Center, 1986) 54.

32. François Mauriac, *The Inner Presence: Recollections of My Spiritual Life*, trans. Herma Briffault (Indianapolis: Bobbs, 1968) 56.

33. See Gregory Rochlin, *Griefs and Discontents: The Forces of Change* (Boston: Little, 1965). Rochlin argues that our lives are marked by an ongoing cycle of loss and restitution which itself changes over the life course. He distinguishes between the cycle of loss and restitution and the cycle of loss and impoverishment. According to Rochlin, the time of life which can properly be called old age is almost invariably characterized by impoverishment.

34. *Roland Barthes by Roland Barthes* (1975), trans. Richard Howard (New York: Hill, 1977) 125.

35. Roland Barthes, *A Lover's Discourse: Fragments*, trans. Richard Howard (New York: Hill, 1978) 148.

36. Herfray, *La Vieillesse* 198–99. Translation mine.

37. Yannick Rimbert, "L'Accompagnement des mourants," *Temps, vieillissement, société* 63–64. Translation mine.

7. THE TRANSITIONAL OBJECT OF THE OLDEST AGE

1. Phyllis Greenacre, "Considerations regarding the Parent-Infant Relationship" (1960), *Emotional Growth* 1: 215–16.

2. Waiting out life in old age for death is a persistent theme in Beckett's work. In the hands of most of his literary critics, however, death and old age are dissociated. Some distribute death evenly over the course of adult life, focusing on death as a metaphor for existential dread. Others concentrate on formal concerns, reading death as a metaphor for the absent author. We see the former in an essay by Laura Barge, "Life and Death in Beckett's Four Stories," *South Atlantic Quarterly* 76 (1977), in which she concludes that "physical death becomes for Beckett a metaphor for the existential anguish of sensing infinity in a finite world, of longing for selfhood in a universe of continual change that denies the possibility of being" (339). We find the latter in an essay by Charlotte Renner, "The Self-Multiplying Narrators of *Molloy, Malone Dies,* and *The Unnamable*," *The Journal of Narrative Technique* 11.1 (Winter 1981). Renner contends that at the halfway point of *Malone Dies*, a new and "temporarily anonymous narrator, being an amalgam of all earlier voices, is more authorial than any of its predecessors . . . this voice implicitly understands its birth and death to be metaphors for the self-mutation of the absent 'author' for whom it speaks" (22). Others read the process of bodily decay as a metaphor for something else. See, for example, J. D. O'Hara in his Introduction to *Twentieth Century Interpretations of* Molloy, Malone Dies, The Unnamable, ed. J. D. O'Hara (Englewood Cliffs: Prentice, 1970). He reads bodily decay in Beckett's trilogy as a metaphor for the

deadening effect of habit on our lives. An essay by F. D. Nuttal is an exception to this rule. See his "Samuel Beckett: *Malone Dies,*" *Jami'at San'a* 2 (1976): 81–94.

3. Elaine Scarry, *The Body in Pain: The Making and Unmaking of the World* (New York: Oxford UP, 1985) 33.

4. Samuel Beckett, *Malone Dies* (New York: Grove, 1956) 74.

5. In "Psychoanalysis and Aging," Gutmann writes: "The aging individual can maintain a relatively steady physical and emotional state over many years; it is the terminating patient who shows acute and rapid decrements in physical, mental, and emotional functioning. These quite distinct states are often compounded; and geropsychiatrists overgeneralize from the terminating patient to the aging individual. In effect, they make termination, the prelude to death, retroactive over the stages of later life; and they come to view most older individuals phobically, as creatures of profound loss" (490).

6. Samuel Beckett, *Proust* (New York: Grove, 1931) 8. A more ample excerpt regarding habit reads: "Life is a succession of habits, since the individual is a succession of individuals. . . . Habit then is the generic term for the countless treaties concluded between the countless subjects that constitute the individual and their countless correlative objects" (11).

7. Ruby Cohn, *Approaches to Teaching: Beckett's* Waiting for Godot, ed. Enoch Brater and June Schluter (New York: MLA, forthcoming).

8. Beckett also uses the literary metaphor of the epilogue to characterize the final "stage" of life. As he says of Macmann, a younger (but not so young) alter ego, "it must not be thought he will never move again . . . for he has still the whole of his old age before him, and then that kind of epilogue when it is not very clear what is happening and which does not seem to add very much to what has already been acquired or to shed any great light on its confusion" (58). In the history of western literature the epilogue has been linked primarily with the drama, with the final remarks which the actor addresses to the audience. Although last, the epilogue is clearly set off from the major body of the work—it is not the climax or denouement, for example, of a classic tragedy. And in the case of *Malone Dies,* it certainly does not "shed any great light on [the] confusion" of what went before.

9. For a rich collection of essays on the transitional object, see *Between Reality and Fantasy: Transitional Objects and Phenomena,* ed. Simon A. Grolnick and Leonard Barkin (New York: Aronson, 1978).

10. Grunberger has written provocatively of the treasure hoarding of children as a means of magically avoiding relations with others (Oedipus relations, in particular) and of maintaining the illusion of narcissistic autonomy. He writes, "Because the treasure is 'created' by the child, is his 'find' . . . he can project himself onto it in a magic narcissistic mode and thereby create a veritable universe, a separate realm where he is master" (285).

11. Harry R. Moody, "The Collector," *Human Values and Aging Newsletter* (Inst. on the Humanities, Arts, and Aging, Brookdale Center on Aging of Hunter College) 8.1 (Sept.-Oct. 1985): 2. To be fair, Moody also points to what he calls the "pathological version of this process," as it is expressed in the hoarding of old newspapers and other objects. Moody has made many important contributions to the study of aging. See, for example, his *Abundance of Life: Human Development Policies for an Aging Society* (New York: Columbia UP, 1988).

12. Walter Benjamin, "Unpacking My Library: Talk about Book Collecting," *Illuminations* 61. Benjamin also writes, "to a true collector the acquisition of an old book is its rebirth. This is the childlike element which the collector mingles with the element of old age" (61).

13. J. Wertheimer, "Les Mécanismes de permanence: le temps, support d'une hy-

pothèse psychodynamique du vieillissement psychologique,'' *Temps, vieillissement, société* 41–52.

14. See John Bowlby, *Attachment* (London: Hogarth, 1969), and Victoria Hamilton, *Narcissus and Oedipus: The Children of Psychoanalysis* (London: Routledge, 1982). Hamilton explains that "the achievement afforded by the successful grasp is . . . a differentiation *away* from the narcissistic type of relationship. The grasp frees the child from synchronous and mirroring interactions" (8).

15. D. W. Winnicott, "The Location of Cultural Experience," *Playing and Reality* 101.

16. As James Knowlson and John Pilling point out in *Frescoes of the Skull: The Later Prose and Drama of Samuel Beckett* (London: Calder, 1979), the enhancement of the activity of the mind through physical immobility is a persistent theme in Beckett's work. In Beckett's early and unfinished *Dream of Fair to Middling Women,* he "makes it clear . . . that the real satisfaction of thinking . . . can only be fully achieved when one is alone and when one has ceased to move" (5); "Belacqua regards being 'entombed and enwombed' in the mind with as much satisfaction as Murphy after him" (6). Although similar, the situation of Malone is radically different. Malone's immobility is not chosen but imposed by his body and is a sign of his approaching death.

17. Gabriele Schwab, "Genesis of the Subject, Imaginary Functions, and Poetic Language," *New Literary History* 15.3 (Spring 1984): 453–73. See also Schwab's essay "The Intermediate Area between Life and Death: On Samuel Beckett's *The Unnamable,*" *Memory and Desire* 205–17.

18. *Roland Barthes by Roland Barthes* 130.

19. I echo Phyllis Greenacre who has written of the transitional object in "The Transitional Object and the Fetish," "*I would see the transitional object—pliable, uncomplaining, and rich in its protean possibilities—as promoting a kind of psychophysical homeostasis as individuation progresses,*" *Emotional Growth* 1: 329.

20. In the last two decades several novels have appeared in the United States which portray the life of the elderly in nursing homes as debilitating, of which I mention four: May Sarton's *As We Are Now* (New York: Norton, 1973), Ellen Douglas's *Apostles of Light* (Boston: Houghton, 1973), John Updike's *The Poorhouse Fair* (New York: Knopf, 1969), and Hilda Wolitzer's *In the Palomar Arms* (New York: Farrar, 1983).

21. D. W. Winnicott, "The Capacity to Be Alone" (1958), *The Maturational Processes and the Facilitating Environment* 32. Winnicott argues that the basis of this capacity is "the early experience of being alone in the presence of someone" (32), which is to say with the mothering figure.

22. Winnicott, "Communicating and Not Communicating," *The Maturational Processes and the Facilitating Environment* 187.

23. In Beckett's fiction as a whole there is a movement from couples who are more or less objectively interrelated, to more indeterminate figures or shadows of couples, who are more like isolates. See Mary F. Catanzaro, "The Unmediated Voice in Beckett's Couples," *Critique,* forthcoming.

24. I am alluding here to a passage from Barthes's *A Lover's Discourse,* which is a discourse of desire. For Barthes the imagined or actual loss of a loved one produces intolerable anxiety. The only way to endure this "pure portion of anxiety" is by manipulating absence: one must "transform the distortion of time into oscillation, produce rhythm, make an entrance onto the stage of language" (16).

25. See H. Porter Abbott's fine essay "A Poetics of Radical Displacement: Samuel Beckett Coming up to Seventy," *Texas Studies in Language and Literature* 17.1 (Spring 1975), in which he ascribes a similar effect to Beckett's *Enough*: "the great beauty of *Enough* lies in the continual winning through of our perceptions to its essential human

content. The cumulative shock at the end is the discovery that the bizarre document we have been reading is a powerful and moving threnody of loss'' (232).

8. YOUTHFULNESS AS A MASQUERADE

1. Thomas Mann, *Death in Venice*, trans. H. T. Lowe-Porter (New York: Random, 1936) 69. I am foregrounding the category of age and bracketing other and profound differences which are involved in social constructions of the body, including race, class, ethnicity, and sexual orientation. Thus I do not consider here the explicit thematics of homosexuality and homoerotics in *Death in Venice*, nor a possible reading of the text as profoundly homophobic. In terms of gender and sexual orientation, it would be interesting to reflect on Adrienne Rich's contention that ''ageism'' is more ''pronounced'' in ''male homosexual standards of sexual attractiveness'' than it is in lesbian standards of sexual attractiveness. See Adrienne Rich, ''Compulsory Heterosexuality and Lesbian Existence'' (1980), *Blood, Bread, and Poetry: Selected Prose 1979–1985* (New York: Norton, 1986) 53.

2. See Robert Kastenbaum, Valerie Derbin, Paul Sabatini, and Steven Artt, '' 'The Ages of Me': Toward Personal and Interpersonal Definitions of Functional Aging,'' *Aging in the New Scene*, ed. Robert Kastenbaum (New York: Springer, 1981) 48–67.

3. See Eugene F. Gray, ''Balzac's Myth of Rejuvenation,'' *Aging in Literature* 73–83.

4. At a conference at which I gave a version of this paper, there was in the audience a woman in her late fifties (I would guess) who incarnated the version of the aging body-in-masquerade we see in *Death in Venice*. With her long and wavy blond Mary Hartline hair, with the poodle she cradled in her chaste lap, she looked as if she had made herself up for a modest, studiously pretty girl in her early twenties. I worried that she would be offended by my remarks. She appeared, however, not to recognize herself in the mirror I held up to *Death in Venice*, thereby uncannily confirming the narrative's emphasis on the blindness of our vanity—perhaps both of ours. I should add that a friend told me that in the after-hours and postmortems of the conference there was speculation about *my* age, which in turn led me to wonder about my appearance.

5. Alison Lurie, *The Language of Clothes* (New York: Random, 1981) 57.

6. Patrick White, *The Eye of the Storm* (New York: Avon, 1975). For a study of old age in the novels of White, see Mari-Ann Berg, *Aspects of Time, Ageing and Old Age in the Novels of Patrick White* (Göteborg: Acta universitatis Gothoburgensis, 1981).

7. Joan Riviere, ''Womanliness as a Masquerade,'' *International Journal of Psycho-Analysis* 10 (1929): 303–13. Reprinted in *Formations of Fantasy*, ed. Victor Burgin, James Donald, and Cora Kaplan (London: Methuen, 1986) 35–44, from which I quote.

8. Luce Irigaray, *This Sex Which Is Not One* (1977), trans. Catherine Porter with Carolyn Burke (Ithaca: Cornell UP, 1985) 133.

9. It is for Lacan as well: ''Masquerade . . . is precisely to play not at the imaginary, but at the symbolic level.'' ''From Love to the Libido'' (1964), *FF* 193.

10. Martin Berezin, ''Normal Psychology of the Aging Process, Revisited—II, *The Fate of Narcissism in Old Age: Clinical Case Reports*,'' *Journal of Geriatric Psychiatry* 10 (1977): 9.

11. Mary Ann Doane, ''Film and the Masquerade: Theorizing the Female Spectator,'' *Screen* 23.3–4 (1982): 74–87.

12. In an essay on fashion, Kaja Silverman also develops the notion of an ''ironic distance'' in theoretical correspondence with masquerade. She calls attention to the fact that exhibition (or masquerade) also plays an important part in the constitution of the male subject, as I have been implicitly suggesting in this essay. See her ''Fragments of

a Fashionable Discourse,'' *Studies in Entertainment: Critical Approaches to Mass Culture*, ed. Tania Modleski (Bloomington: Indiana UP, 1986) 139–52.

13. Jean-François Lyotard (with Jean-Loup Thébaud), *Just Gaming: Conversations* (1979; Minneapolis: U of Minnesota P, 1985) 40.

14. In ''Joan Riviere and the Masquerade,'' Stephen Heath, referring to Dietrich, notes that she ''gives the masquerade in excess and so *proffers* the masquerade . . . not [as] a defense against but a derision of masculinity'' (*Formations of Fantasy* 57).

15. I take the term ''intermediate object'' from Kestenberg, who has identified three different types of ''symbiotic bridges'' which are ''invented'' by the child (here Kestenberg follows Winnicott) in an effort to regain unity with the mother as well as to integrate the parts of the body into a whole. They are: *accessory* objects (for example, people other than the mother who take care of the infant), *transitional* objects, and *intermediate* objects (parts of the child's body). Kestenberg specifies different modalities of time for each of these symbiotic bridges: accessory objects serve to create continuity between past and future; transitional objects, to project the old, ''within the newness of the present,'' into the future; and intermediate objects, to re-create, momentarily, the past in the present (84). Although Kestenberg limits her analysis of symbiotic bridges to infancy and early childhood, we can see how it can be extended over the life course. See her ''From Organ-Object Imagery to Self and Object Representation,'' *Separation-Individuation: Essays in Honor of Margaret S. Mahler*, ed. John B. McDevitt and Calvin F. Settlage (New York: International UP, 1971): 75–99.

16. For an unsettling portrait of youthfulness as a masquerade, see Mary McCarthy's final chapter ''Ask Me No Questions'' in *Memories of a Catholic Girlhood* (1957; Harmondsworth, England: Penguin, 1963) which is devoted to her Catholic grandmother, whom she regards with chilling ambivalence and presents as an imposing eccentric. As opposed to Dacher's and Weinstein's generous portrait of Louise, McCarthy's representation of her grandmother seems motivated by some hideous revenge. The composite portrait of this aging body oscillates between scenes of elaborate masquerade (actually more a coverup for her failed cosmetic surgery in middle age than it is for the signs of old age) and scenes of the body (or parts of the body, specifically her thighs) naked. The former is the public body, constructed for the eyes of others, the latter is the private body, taboo to all eyes. In both cases the body is represented as being cultivated as a sacred relic and is regarded by the granddaughter with loathing, with awe, with admiration. McCarthy recalls her grandmother's afternoon ritual of making herself up to go shopping downtown, the final ''effect'' of which is one of ''indescribable daring'' (185). For a fine discussion of this chapter (although not in terms of masquerade), see Paul John Eakin, *Fictions in Autobiography: Studies in the Art of Self-Invention* (Princeton: Princeton UP, 1985) 42–55.

17. See Mary Russo, ''Female Grotesques: Carnival and Theory,'' *Feminist Studies/ Critical Studies* 213–29. Russo opens her essay by invoking a phrase which she says has resonated in her mind since childhood—that of a woman ''making a spectacle of herself''—and which has resonated in my mind, and now here, thanks to her.

18. I owe this formulation of television as the panopticon to Patricia Mellencamp, ''Video Politics: *Guerilla TV*, Ant Farm, *External Frame*,'' *Discourse* 10.2 (Spring-Summer 1988): 78–100.

19. Susan Sommers, ''Anti-Aging Beauty,'' *Ladies' Home Journal*, Nov. 1987, 68ff. For an excellent essay on video aerobics and aging, see Margaret Morse, ''Artemis Aging: Exercise and the Female Body on Video,'' *Discourse* 10.1 (Fall-Winter 1987–88) 20–53.

20. Linda Wells, ''What If . . . ?,'' *The New York Times Magazine* (September 17, 1989) 91.

21. That cosmetic surgery to ''correct'' aging is becoming more common is signaled

by an essay in *The New York Times Magazine* by Ann Louise Bardach on "The Dark Side of Cosmetic Surgery" (April 17, 1988) 24ff. The audience for *The New York Times* is monied and educated. The article serves not only to warn of the possible disfigurement that can accompany cosmetic surgery but also to inform its readers of the price ranges of the different procedures. Contrast this with the tabloids, whose audience is more solidly lower-class and which represent cosmetic surgery as a "splurge" (*The National Examiner,* Dec. 29, 1987). Interestingly, surgical "rejuvenation" of the face was advocated in the West as early as 1930. Jill Julius Matthews mentions this in passing in "Building the Body Beautiful: The Femininity of Modernity," *Australian Feminist Studies* (Summer 1987): 17-34.

22. Michèle Montrelay on Lacan, "Inquiry into Femininity," *M/F* (1978): 83-99.

23. Montrelay 83.

24. Jean-Claude Sauer and Roger Picherie, "L'Eternelle jeunesse: les derniers miracles de la chirugie esthéthique," *Paris Match,* 23 Jan. 1987, 82-93.

25. Eugénie Lemoine-Luccioni, *La Robe: essaie psychanalytique sur le vêtement* (Paris: Seuil, 1983).

26. I have borrowed the phrase "discursive surgery" from Francis Barker, *The Tremulous Private Body: Essays on Subjection* (London: Methuen, 1984) 90.

27. Michel Foucault, *Discipline and Punish: The Birth of the Prison,* trans. Alan Sheridan (New York: Random/Vintage, 1979).

28. In "Les Mécanismes de permanence," Wertheimer argues that the disjunction between the youthful appearance of the body (not necessarily only those who have had cosmetic surgery) and its interior produces what is only *apparently* a youthful vitality but is in reality a phantasmatic struggle against death. What we may approve as an energetic use of time in fact is the fighting of a losing battle: "Such apparent youth is only a facade behind which time in spite of everything does its work, even though the outer image of unfailing strength adjusts itself slowly in respect to the profound reality which continues to unfold within. Paradoxically, the vitality that is thus mobilized, that one believes to be an optimal usage of time, is in fact destined to struggle phantasmatically against the ineluctability of the real that leads the individual to his death. What appears to be vitality becomes an anachronism" (45, translation mine). On psychoanalytic grounds Wertheimer, then, makes a case for growing old "gracefully." What strikes me as particularly provocative is his notion of the anachronistic quality of a youthful energetic appearance in an aging body. In the extreme cases of cosmetic surgery to "correct" for age, we may say that people can become anachronistic to themselves.

29. Arthur Kroker and David Cook, *The Postmodern Scene: Excremental Culture and Hyper-Aesthetics* (New York: St. Martin's, 1986) 13.

9. PHANTASMS OF THE AGING BODY

1. How might we explain this phenomenon? As Beauvoir wrote in *The Coming of Age,* "We see those who are close to us *sub species aeternitatis*" (427). It is as though those close to us constitute a special group of people who do not grow beyond the age at which we first remember them. We continue to "see" (that is, to remember) this version of them. Close and repeated contact over the years helps preserve that timeless image (as it does with people who are our contemporaries). Such familiarity works to produce a certain blindness to changes which accompany the process of aging.

2. Qtd. Beauvoir, *The Coming of Age* 424.

3. Herfray opens *La Vieillesse* with a discussion of Epinal's chart which she reproduces (15-16).

4. See Ellie Ragland-Sullivan, "The Phenomenon of Aging in Oscar Wilde's *Picture of Dorian Gray*: A Lacanian View," *Memory and Desire* 97-113.

5. Marguerite Duras, *The Afternoon of Monsieur Andesmas* (1962).

6. In *The Image and Appearance of the Human Body* Schilder insists that "the touches of others, the interest others take in the different parts of our body will be of an enormous importance in the development of the postural body image" (126).

7. I. Hermann introduced the notion of a continuous and nonclimactic need for "clinging," which he believed was as primary a need as the need for food and which he also believed could serve as the basis for affectionate relationships. See "Sich-Anklammern-auf-suche-Gehen," *Int. Z. Psychoanalysis* 22 (1936): 349–70.

8. Margaret S. Mahler, "On the Significance of the Normal Separation-Individuation Phase," *Drives, Affects, and Behavior 2*, ed. M. Schur (New York: International UP, 1965) 161–69.

9. Roland Barthes has been associated with a celebration of the body in its various aspects, but he too recalls a memory of himself as a child shrinking from an old person, a memory which he underscores in his *Roland Barthes by Roland Barthes*, but does not examine critically in terms of aging: "*Straddling a chair at the corner of the Chemin des Arènes, Colonel Poymiro, purple-faced, the veins showing in his nose, mustachioed and myopic, at a loss for words, watched the crowd from the bullfight pass back and forth. What agony, what terror when the Colonel kissed him!*" (108).

10. Ashley Montague, *Touching: The Human Significance of the Skin*, 2nd ed. (New York: Harper, 1978) 321.

11. See Erwin Straus, *Phenomenological Psychology*, trans. Erling Eng (New York: Basic, 1966). Straus says of the upright posture that it is the "leitmotif in the formation of the human organization" and an "indispensable condition of man's self-preservation" (139).

12. The aspect of *stability* is critical. In its stability, this body in old age is roughly analogous to the dominant aspect of the infant's body in its second stage of mastering movement. What is at stake here is a *functional* body image, not a specular body image, although Lacan does refer to this phantasmatic form of body unity in the infant as "orthopaedic" (*Ecrits* 4). The functional body image is progressively constructed through movement of body parts and the body in space. In "From Organ-Object Imagery to Self and Object Representation," Judith Kestenberg proposes three stages in infantile development of this functional body image: the *prehensile*, which is associated with the grasping and seizing of objects to bring them to the mouth; the *stable*, which is associated with the newly achieved firmness of the infant's standing body and with a lower center of gravity in the body linked with crawling; and the *self-directional* (or *self-propelling*), which is associated with toddling and walking, that is, with a more accomplished level of bodily initiative in the world related to desire. Each phase, she argues, is characterized by a "united organ-object image" which is lost as the phases succeed one another. The term "united organ-object image" is misleading, for what is unusual in Kestenberg's approach is her emphasis not on the sequence of development of cathecting various places of the body (mouth, genitals) but on a psychoanalysis of a developing body image in the body's physical interaction with itself and the world.

13. Vita Sackville-West, *All Passion Spent* (Garden City: Doubleday, Doran, 1931) 189.

14. If in this chapter I were articulating a "somatic semiotics" of the aging body, to use Renate Lachmann's term, I would offer a counter-scene to the heavy and immobile body of old age in the frail body ("On Bakhtin," lecture at the Center for Twentieth Century Studies, U of Wisconsin-Milwaukee, March 1986). And indeed it does seem that bodies in advanced old age assume one of these two profiles. Both bodies are characterized by a lack of self-direction or self-propulsion. Think of the frail body as Colette describes it in *The Blue Lantern*, writing of an eighty-some-year-old friend of hers as "fragile and light as a vine-shoot" (149).

15. Didier Anzieu, *Le Moi-peau* (Paris: Dunod, 1985).

16. I have commented on Beauvoir's representation of Sartre in "Reminiscence, Identity, Sentimentality: Simone de Beauvoir and the Life Review," *Twenty-Five Years of the Life Review: Theoretical and Practical Considerations,* ed. Robert Disch (New York: Haworth, 1988) 25–46.

17. In his fascinating book *Le Moi-peau* (which I would translate as *The Self-Skin*), Didier Anzieu argues that one of the critical functions of the *moi-peau* is serving as a container of interior organs (101). What if the container contains nothing? Anzieu introduces the phantasm of the skin perforated by holes *(le moi-peau passoire)*. It is accompanied, he says, by the sense of anguish that the inside is empty. This phantasm is further associated with the sense that thoughts and memories are difficult to retain. Although Anzieu does not place his discussion in the context of aging, it would seem particularly apt to certain experiences, such as Sartre's, in old age.

18. If we locate ourselves behind the eyes, we also locate other people behind their eyes. I give an example from the literature of old age. In *The Old Man and the Sea,* Hemingway repeatedly insists that everything about the old fisherman was very old except his eyes, which remained youthful, which is to say, full of life.

19. Qtd. Peter Hildebrand, "Scène originaire—mort," *Temps, vieillissement, société* 20–21. Translation mine. Grotjohn describes himself as being given a reprieve, as it were, from the period of old age which is associated with death.

20. See Note 11 in the chapter "Gender, Generational Identity, and Aging."

21. As I suggested in the Introduction, Beauvoir's own attitude toward old age prevented her from accepting Sartre's description of the distinctive contentment he sometimes experienced in old age. What she writes speaks more insistently to *her* own anxiety about losing Sartre than to *his* experience. "I was glad," she writes reluctantly, "that he did not find weariness idlesome, but it rather wounded my heart that to find pleasure in it he should really be 'empty,' as he said to the doctor" *(Adieux* 52). On *Adieux*, see the excellent essay by Elaine Marks, "Transgressing the (In)cont(in)ent Boundaries: The Body in Decline," *Yale French Studies* 72 (1986): 181–200, and Alice Jardine, "Death Sentences: Writing Couples and Ideology," *The Female Body in Western Culture,* ed. Susan Rubin Suleiman (Cambridge: Harvard UP, 1986) 84–96.

22. Qtd. Michèle Dacher and Micheline Weinstein, *Histoire de Louise: des vieillards en hospice* 138.

23. Gabriel Garcia Marquez, *Love in the Time of Cholera,* trans. Edith Grossman (New York: Knopf, 1988) 40.

24. Thomas Louis-Vincent, *Rites de mort: pour la paix des vivants* (Paris: Fayard, 1985) 148–49.

25. Following Herfray, we could also read Barthes's story about his rib as a parable of defending himself against aging by giving up a part of his body—*sacrificing it*—in order to save himself. Herfray suggests that elderly people who exhibit marked hypochondria and submit themselves to multiple operations may be understood as performing just this magical gesture of sacrifice.

26. Elliott Jacques, "Death and the Mid-Life Crisis," *International Journal of Psycho-Analysis* 46.4 (1965): 502–12. Jacques is of course supremely aware that he has contradicted Freud on this important point, and this makes him uncomfortable. He questions Freud by invoking Melanie Klein, who earlier broke with Freud on just this issue. He ends unconvincingly by trying to reconcile Freud and Klein. He acknowledges that while the unconscious is not aware of death *per se,* nonetheless it *expresses* fears of death: "Does the unconscious, then, have a conception of death? The views of Melanie Klein and those of Freud may seem not to correspond. Klein assumes an unconscious awareness of death. Freud assumes that the unconscious rejects all such awareness. Neither of these views, taken at face value, is likely to prove correct. Nor would I expect that either of

their authors would hold to a literal interpretation of their views. The unconscious is not aware of death *per se*. But there are unconscious experiences akin to those which later appear in consciousness as notions of death'' (507).

27. See Ellie Ragland-Sullivan, ''Counting from 0 to 6: Lacan and the Imaginary Order,'' Center for Twentieth Century Studies *Working Paper* (Fall 1984).

28. See Alan Pifer, ''The Public Policy Response,'' *Our Aging Society: Paradox and Promise,* ed. Alan Pifer and Lydia Bronte (New York: Norton, 1986) 391–413.

29. Herfray 182. Translation mine.

30. Beauvoir, *A Very Easy Death* 69.

31. See Sally Gadow, ''Frailty and Strength: The Dialectic of Aging,'' *What Does It Mean to Grow Old?* 237–43.

32. Elizabeth Wright, in *Psychoanalytic Criticism: Theory in Practice* (New York: Methuen, 1984), reads Beckett's *Not I* in Lacanian terms as an illustration of the imago of the ''experience'' of the fragmented body. She writes, ''Mouth is reliving the trauma of the primordial moment when the body senses its split from the Real. This experience can neither be included in the Imaginary, the realm of illusory wholeness, nor can it be part of the Symbolic, the domain which grants a conditional identity. The traumatic moment can return in psychosis as the experience of the 'fragmented body' '' (113). By reading the phantasm of the *fragmenting* body as a repetition of the prior experience of the *fragmented* body, Wright overlooks the specificity of the experience in terms of aging and old age in *Not I*.

EPILOGUE

1. Qtd. in Phyllis Grosskurth, *Melanie Klein: Her World and Her Work* (New York: Knopf, 1986) 258.

2. Adrienne Rich, *Blood, Bread, and Poetry: Selected Prose 1979–1985* (New York: Norton, 1986) 200.

3. Peter Laslett, *Family Life and Illicit Love in Earlier Generations: Essays in Historical Sociology* (New York: Cambridge UP, 1977) 174.

4. Herbert Blau, ''The Makeup of Memory in the Winter of Our Discontent,'' *The Eye of Prey* 135.

5. Margaret A. Simons, ''In Memoriam,'' *Yale French Studies* 72 (1986): 204.

WORKS CITED

Abbott, H. Porter. "A Poetics of Radical Displacement: Samuel Beckett Coming up to Seventy." *Texas Studies in Language and Literature* 17.1 (Spring 1975): 219–38.

Abel, Emily, and Nancy Porter, eds. *Teaching about Women and Aging.* Special issue of *Women's Studies Quarterly* 17.1–2 (Spring-Summer 1989).

Abelin, Ernest L. "Triangulation, the Role of the Father and the Origins of Core Gender Identity during the Rapprochement Subphase." *Rapprochement: The Critical Subphase of Separation-Individuation.* Ed. Ruth F. Lax, Sheldon Bach, and J. Alexis Burland. New York: Aronson, 1980. 151–69.

Abraham, Karl. "A Short Study of the Development of the Libido, Viewed in the Light of Mental Disorders." 1924. *Selected Papers of Karl Abraham.* Trans. Douglas Bryan and Alix Strachey. London: Hogarth and Inst. of Psycho-Analysis, 1973. 418–501.

Achenbaum, W. Andrew. *Old Age in the New Land.* Baltimore: Johns Hopkins UP, 1978.

Adams, Alice. *Listening to Billie.* New York: Penguin, 1975.

Alexander, Jo, Debi Berrow, Lisa Domitrovich, Margarita Donnelly, and Cheryl McLean, eds. *Women and Aging: An Anthology by Women.* Corvallis: Calyx, 1986.

Alford, C. Fred. *Narcissism, Socrates, the Frankfurt School and Psychoanalytic Theory.* New Haven: Yale UP, 1988.

———. "Nature and Narcissism: The Frankfurt School." *New German Critique* 36 (Fall 1985): 174–92.

Anzieu, Didier. *Le Moi-peau.* Paris: Dunod, 1985.

Ariès, Philippe. *Centuries of Childhood: A Social History of Family Life.* Trans. Robert Baldick. New York: Knopf, 1962.

Asp, Carolyn. "'The Clamor of Eros': Freud, Aging, and *King Lear.*" *Memory and Desire: Aging—Literature—Psychoanalysis.* Ed. Kathleen Woodward and Murray M. Schwartz. Bloomington: Indiana UP, 1986. 192–204.

Balint, Alice. "Love for the Mother and Mother Love." 1939. *Primary Love and Psycho-Analytic Technique.* By Michael Balint. London: Hogarth and Inst. of Psycho-Analysis, 1952. 109–27.

Balzac, Honoré de. "The Girl with the Golden Eyes." *The Works of Honoré de Balzac: The Thirteen, Father Goriot and Other Stories.* Philadelphia: Anvil, 1901.

Banner, Lois. *Sunset Boulevard: Aging Women and Their Relationships with Younger Men in European Past and Present.* New York: Knopf, forthcoming.

Bardach, Ann Louise. "The Dark Side of Cosmetic Surgery." *The New York Times Magazine* 17 April 1988: 24ff.

Barge, Laura. "Life and Death in Beckett's Four Stories." *South Atlantic Quarterly* 76 (1977): 332–47.

Barker, Francis. *The Tremulous Private Body: Essays on Subjection.* London: Methuen, 1984.

Barkin, Leonard, and Simon A. Grolnick, eds. *Between Reality and Fantasy: Transitional Objects and Phenomena.* New York: Aronson, 1978.

Barthes, Roland. *Camera Lucida: Reflections on Photography*. 1980. Trans. Richard Howard. New York: Hill, 1981.

———. *A Lover's Discourse: Fragments*. Trans. Richard Howard. New York: Hill, 1978.

———. *Roland Barthes by Roland Barthes*. 1975. Trans. Richard Howard. New York: Hill, 1977.

Beauvoir, Simone de. *Adieux: A Farewell to Sartre*. Trans. Patrick O'Brian. 1981. Harmondsworth, England: Penguin, 1984.

———. *The Coming of Age*. 1970. Trans. Patrick O'Brian. New York: Warner, 1978.

———. *A Very Easy Death*. 1964. Trans. Patrick O'Brian. New York: Warner, 1973.

Becker, Ernest. *The Denial of Death*. New York: Free, 1975.

Beckett, Samuel. *Happy Days*. New York: Grove, 1961.

———. *Krapp's Last Tape*. New York: Grove, 1960.

———. *Malone Dies*. New York: Grove, 1956.

———. *Proust*. New York: Grove, 1931.

Bellow, Saul. *The Dean's December*. New York: Harper, 1982.

Benjamin, Jessica. "A Desire of One's Own: Psychoanalytic Feminism and Intersubjective Space." *Feminist Studies/Critical Studies*. Ed. Teresa de Lauretis. Bloomington: Indiana UP, 1986. 78–101.

Benjamin, Walter. *Illuminations*. Ed. Hannah Arendt. Trans. Harry Zohn. New York: Harcourt, 1968.

Berenson, Bernard. *Sunset and Twilight: From the Diaries of 1947–1958*. Ed. Nicky Mariano. New York: Harcourt, 1963.

Berezin, Martin. "Normal Psychology of the Aging Process, Revisited—II, *The Fate of Narcissism in Old Age: Clinical Case Reports*." *Journal of Geriatric Psychiatry* 10 (1977): 9–26.

Berg, Mari-Ann. *Aspects of Time, Ageing and Old Age in the Novels of Patrick White*. Göteburg: Acta universitatis Gothoburgensis, 1981.

Bernstein, Doris. "Female Identity Synthesis." *Career and Motherhood*. Ed. Alan Roland and Barbara Harris. New York: Human Sciences, 1979. 104–23.

———. "The Female Superego: A Different Perspective." *International Journal of Psycho-Analysis* 64 (1983): 187–201.

Blau, Herbert. "Barthes and Beckett: The Punctum, the Pensum, and the Dream of Love." *The Eye of Prey: Subversions of the Postmodern*. Bloomington: Indiana UP, 1987. 84–103.

———. *Ideology and Performance*. New York: Routledge, forthcoming.

———. "The Makeup of Memory in the Winter of Our Discontent." *The Eye of Prey*. 135–60.

Borenstein, Audrey. *Chimes of Change and Hours: Views of Older Women in Twentieth Century America*. Rutherford: Fairleigh Dickinson UP, 1983.

———. *Older Women in Twentieth Century America: A Selected Annotated Bibliography*. New York: Garland, 1982.

Bourdieu, Pierre. *Distinction*. Trans. Richard Nice. Cambridge: Harvard UP, 1984.

Bowlby, John. *Attachment*. London: Hogarth, 1969.

———. *Separation: Anxiety and Loss*. 1973. Middlesex, England: Pelican, 1975.

Brenkman, John. "The Other and the One: Marxism, Psychoanalytic Criticism, and the Problem of the Subject." *Literature and Psychoanalysis: The Question of Reading: Otherwise*. 1977. Ed. Shoshana Felman. Baltimore: Johns Hopkins UP, 1982. 396–456.

Butler, Robert N. "The Life Review: An Interpretation of Reminiscence in the Aged." *Psychiatry* 26 (Feb. 1963): 65–76.

———. *Why Survive?: Being Old in America*. New York: Harper, 1975.

Cameron, Sharon. "Representing Grief: Emerson's 'Experience.' " *Representations* 15 (Summer 1986): 15–41.

Catanzaro, Mary F. "The Unmediated Voice in Beckett's Couples." *Critique,* forthcoming.

Chodorow, Nancy. *The Reproduction of Mothering: Psychoanalysis and the Sociology of Gender.* Berkeley: U of California P, 1978.

Cixous, Hélène. "Castration or Decapitation." Trans. Annette Kuhn. *Signs* 7.1 (Autumn 1981): 41–55.

Cohler, Bertram J. "Adult Developmental Psychology and Reconstruction in Psychoanalysis." *Adulthood and the Aging Process.* Ed. Stanley I. Greenspan and George H. Pollock. Washington: NIMA, 1980. 149–99.

Cohn, Ruby. *Approaches to Teaching: Beckett's* Waiting for Godot. Ed. Enoch Brater and June Schluter. New York: MLA, forthcoming.

Cole, Thomas R. "The 'Enlightened' View of Aging: Victorian Morality in a New Key." *What Does It Mean to Grow Old?: Reflections from the Humanities.* Ed. Thomas R. Cole and Sally Gadow. Durham: Duke UP, 1986. 115–30.

Coles, Robert. *The Old Ones of New Mexico.* New York: Doubleday, 1973.

Colette. *The Blue Lantern.* 1949. Trans. R. Senhouse. New York: Farrar, 1963.

Cowley, Malcolm. *The View from Eighty.* New York: Viking, 1980.

Dacher, Michèle, and Micheline Weinstein. *Histoire de Louise: des vieillards en hospice.* Paris: Seuil, 1979.

Dalsimer, Katherine. *Female Adolescence: Psychoanalytic Reflections on Works of Literature.* New Haven: Yale UP, 1986.

de Lauretis, Teresa. *Alice Doesn't: Feminism, Semiotics, Cinema.* Bloomington: Indiana UP, 1984.

——, ed. *Feminist Studies/Critical Studies.* Bloomington: Indiana UP, 1986.

de Man, Paul. *The Rhetoric of Romanticism.* New York: Columbia UP, 1984.

Derrida, Jacques. "Fors." *The Georgia Review* 31.1 (Spring 1977): 64–116.

——. *Memoirs for Paul de Man.* Trans. Cecile Lindsay, Jonathan Culler, and Eduardo Cadava. New York: Columbia UP, 1986.

Dillard, Annie. *An American Childhood.* New York: Harper, 1987.

Doane, Mary Ann. "Film and the Masquerade: Theorizing the Female Spectator." *Screen* 23.3–4 (1982): 74–87.

Dolto, Françoise. *L'Image inconscient du corps.* Paris: Seuil, 1984.

Douglas, Ellen. *Apostles of Light.* Boston: Houghton, 1973.

Duras, Marguerite. *The Afternoon of Monsieur Andesmas.* Trans. Ann Borchardt. London: John Calder, 1964.

——. *Hiroshima, Mon Amour.* Trans. Richard Seaver. New York: Grove, 1960.

——. *Savannah Bay.* Paris: Minuit, 1983.

Eakin, Paul John. *Fictions in Autobiography: Studies in the Art of Self-Invention.* Princeton: Princeton UP, 1985.

Eiseley, Loren. *All the Strange Hours.* New York: Scribner's, 1975.

Erikson, Erik. *Insight and Responsibility.* New York: Norton, 1964.

Erikson, Erik, Joan M. Erikson, and Helen Q. Kivnick. *Vital Involvement in Old Age: The Experience of Old Age in Our Time.* 1986. New York: Norton, 1989.

Fast, Irene. "Developments in Gender Identity: Gender Differentiation in Girls." *International Journal of Psycho-Analysis* 60 (1979): 443–53.

Featherstone, Mike, and Mike Hepworth. "Aging and Old Age: Reflections on the Postmodern Life Course." *Being and Becoming Old.* Ed. T. Keil Byetheway, P. Allatt, and A. Bryman. Newbury Park, Calif: Sage, 1989. 143–57.

Felman, Shoshana. "Turning the Screw of Interpretation." *Yale French Studies* 55–56 (1977): 94–207.

Festa-McCormick, Diana. "Proust's Asthma: A Malady Begets a Melody." *Medicine and Literature.* Ed. Eric Rhodes Peschel. New York: Watson, 1980. 120–27.

Fiedler, Leslie. "More Images of Eros and Old Age: The Damnation of Faust." *Memory and Desire: Aging—Literature—Psychoanalysis.* Ed. Kathleen Woodward and Murray M. Schwartz. Bloomington: Indiana UP, 1986. 37–50.

Figes, Eva. *Waking.* New York: Pantheon, 1981.

Fischer, David Hackett. *Growing Old in America.* New York: Oxford UP, 1977.

Flem, Lydia. *La Vie quotidienne de Freud et de ses patients.* Paris: Hachette, 1986.

Foucault, Michel. *Discipline and Punish: The Birth of the Prison.* Trans. Alan Sheridan. New York: Random/Vintage, 1979.

Freedman, Richard. "Sufficiently Decayed: Gerontophobia in English Literature." *Aging and the Elderly: Humanistic Perspectives in Gerontology.* Ed. Stuart F. Spicker, Kathleen M. Woodward, and David D. Van Tassel. Atlantic Highlands: Humanities, 1978. 49–61.

Freud, Anna. "About Losing and Being Lost." *The Psychoanalytic Study of the Child* 22 (1967): 9–19.

Freud, Ernest L., ed. *The Letters of Sigmund Freud and Arnold Zweig.* Trans. Elaine and William Robson-Scott. New York: Harcourt, 1970.

Freud, Ernest L., and Heinrich Meng, eds. *Psychoanalysis and Faith: The Letters of Sigmund Freud and Oskar Pfister.* Trans. Eric Mosbacher. New York: Basic, 1963.

Freud, Sigmund. *The Standard Edition of the Complete Psychological Works of Sigmund Freud.* Trans. and ed. James Strachey. 24 vols. London: Hogarth and Inst. of Psycho-Analysis, 1953–74.

———. "An Autobiographical Study." 1925. SE 20: 7–74.

———. *Beyond the Pleasure Principle.* 1920. SE 18: 3–64.

———. *Civilization and Its Discontents.* 1930. SE 21: 59–145.

———. "Creative Writers and Day-Dreaming." 1908. SE 9: 143–53.

———. "A Disturbance of Memory on the Acropolis." 1936. SE 22: 238–48.

———. "The Economic Problem of Masochism." 1924. SE 19: 157–70.

———. *The Ego and the Id.* 1923. SE 19: 19–27.

———. "Female Sexuality." 1931. SE 21: 223–43.

———. "Femininity." 1933. SE 22: 112–35.

———. *The Future of an Illusion.* 1927. SE 21: 3–56.

———. "Group Psychology and the Analysis of the Ego." 1921. SE 18: 67–143.

———. *Inhibitions, Symptoms and Anxiety.* 1926. SE 20: 77–175.

———. *The Interpretation of Dreams.* 1900. SE 4–5: xi-338, 339–627.

———. "The Libido Theory and Narcissism." 1917. SE 16: 412–30.

———. *Moses and Monotheism.* 1939. SE 23: 3–137.

———. "Mourning and Melancholia." 1917. SE 14: 239–58.

———. "On Narcissism." 1914. SE 14: 69–102.

———. "On Transience." 1916 SE 14: 304 307.

———. *The Psychopathology of Everyday Life.* 1901. SE 6: ix-289.

———. "The Theme of the Three Caskets." 1913. SE 12: 290–301.

———. "Thoughts for the Times on War and Death." 1915. SE 14: 274–302.

———. "Three Essays on the Theory of Sexuality." 1905. SE 7: 125–243.

———. "The 'Uncanny.'" 1919. SE 17: 218–56.

Gadow, Sally. "Frailty and Strength: The Dialectic of Aging." *What Does It Mean to Grow Old?: Reflections from the Humanities.* Ed. Thomas R. Cole and Sally Gadow. Durham: Duke UP, 1986. 237–43.

Gallop, Jane. *Reading Lacan.* Ithaca: Cornell UP, 1985.

Gardiner, Judith Kegan. "On Female Identity and Writing by Women." *Critical Inquiry* 8.2 (Winter 1981): 347–61.

Garner, Shirley Nelson, Claire Kahane, and Madelon Sprengnether, eds. *The (M)other Tongue: Essays in Psychoanalytic Interpretation.* Ithaca: Cornell UP, 1985.

Gay, Peter. *Freud: A Life for Our Time*. New York: Norton, 1988.

————. *Freud for Historians*. New York: Oxford UP, 1985.

Gilligan, Carol. *In a Different Voice: Psychological Theory and Women's Development*. Cambridge: Harvard UP, 1982.

Girard, René. "Narcissism: The Freudian Myth Demythified by Proust." *Psychoanalysis, Creativity, and Literature: A Franco-American Inquiry*. Ed. Alan Roland. New York: Columbia UP, 1978. 292–311.

Goleman, Daniel. "Erikson, in His Own Old Age, Expands His View of Life." *The New York Times* 14 June 1988: C1.

Gray, Eugene F. "Balzac's Myth of Rejuvenation." *Aging in Literature*. Ed. Laurel Porter and Laurence M. Porter. Troy: International, 1984. 73–83.

Green, André. "The Double and the Absent." 1973. Trans. Susan D. Cohen. *Psychoanalysis, Creativity, and Literature: A Franco-American Inquiry*. Ed. Alan Roland. New York: Columbia UP, 1978. 271–92.

————. "Le Temps mort." *Nouvelle revue de psychanalyse* 11 (1975): 103–109.

Greenacre, Phyllis. *Emotional Growth: Psychoanalytic Studies of the Gifted and a Great Variety of Other Individuals*. Vol. 1. New York: International UP, 1971.

Grolnick, Simon A., and Leonard Barkin, eds. *Between Reality and Fantasy: Transitional Objects and Phenomena*. New York: Aronson, 1978.

Grosclaude, Michèle. "Mémoire, Souvenir, Savoir, Démence." *Temps, vieillessement, société*. Paris: SOPEDIM, 1982. 117–36.

Grosskurth, Phyllis. *Melanie Klein: Her World and Her Work*. New York: Knopf, 1986.

Grunberger, Béla. *Narcissism: Psychoanalytic Essays*. Trans. Joyce S. Diamanti. New York: International UP, 1979.

Gullette, Margaret. *Safe at Last in the Middle Years*. Berkeley: U of California P, 1988.

Gutmann, David L. "Psychoanalysis and Aging: A Developmental View." *Adulthood and the Aging Process*. Ed. Stanley I. Greenspan and George H. Pollock. Washington: NIMH, 1980. 489–517.

————. *Reclaimed Powers: Toward a New Psychology of Men and Women in Later Life*. New York: Basic, 1987.

H. D. [Hilda Doolittle]. *Tribute to Freud*. Boston: Godine, 1974.

Haber, Carole. *Beyond Sixty-Five: The Dilemma of Old Age in America's Past*. New York: Cambridge UP, 1983.

Haggard, H. Rider. *She*. 1885. New York: Modern, 1957.

Hägglund, Tor-Björn, and Heikka Piha. "The Inner Space of the Body Image." *Psychoanalytic Quarterly* 49 (1980): 256–83.

Hamilton, Victoria. *Narcissus and Oedipus: The Children of Psychoanalysis*. London: Routledge, 1982.

Hareven, Tamara K. "The Last Stage: Historical Adulthood and Old Age." *Aging, Death, and the Completion of Being*. Ed. David D. Van Tassel. Philadelphia: U of Pennsylvania P, 1979. 165–89.

Hawkes, John. *The Passion Artist*. New York: Harper, 1978.

Heath, Stephen. "Joan Riviere and the Masquerade." *Formations of Fantasy*. Ed. Victor Burgin, James Donald, and Cora Kaplan. London: Methuen, 1986. 45–61.

Herfray, Charlotte. *La Vieillesse: une interprétation psychanalytique*. Paris: Desclée de Brouwer; Épi, 1988.

Hermann, I. "Sich-Anklammern-auf-suche-Gehen." *Int. Z. Psychoanalysis* 22 (1936): 349–70.

Hildebrand, Peter. "Scène originaire—mort." *Temps, vieillessement, société*. Paris: SOPEDIM, 1982. 19–32.

Holland, Norman. "Not So Little Hans: Identity and Aging." *Memory and Desire:*

Aging—Literature—Psychoanalysis. Ed. Kathleen Woodward and Murray M. Schwartz. Bloomington: Indiana UP, 1986. 51–75.

Irigaray, Luce. "Amant marine de Nietzsche." 1980. *Le Corps-à-corps avec la mère.* Montréal: Pleine lune, 1982.

———. *This Sex Which Is Not One.* 1977. Trans. Catherine Porter with Carolyn Burke. Ithaca: Cornell UP, 1985.

Jacques, Elliott. "Death and the Mid-Life Crisis." *International Journal of Psycho-Analysis* 46.4 (1965): 502–12.

Jardine, Alice. "Death Sentences: Writing Couples and Ideology." *The Female Body in Western Culture.* Ed. Susan Rubin Suleiman. Cambridge: Harvard UP, 1986. 84–96.

Jauss, Hans Robert. "Literary History as a Challenge to Literary Theory." *Toward an Aesthetic of Reception.* Trans. Timothy Bahti. Minneapolis: U of Minnesota P, 1982.

Jay, Gregory. "Freud: The Death of Autobiography." *America the Scrivener: Deconstruction and the Subject of Literary History.* New York: Cornell UP, forthcoming.

Jones, Ernest. *The Life and Work of Sigmund Freud.* 3 vols. New York: Basic, 1953.

Kastenbaum, Robert, Valerie Derbin, Paul Sabatini, and Steven Artt. "'The Ages of Me': Toward Personal and Interpersonal Definitions of Functional Aging." *Aging in the New Scene.* Ed. Robert Kastenbaum. New York: Springer, 1981. 48–67.

Kaufman, Sharon R. *The Ageless Self.* Madison: U of Wisconsin P, 1986.

Kearns, Terrance Brophy. "Prisoner to the Palsy: A Study of Old Age in Shakespeare's History Plays." Diss. Indiana U, 1978.

Kestenberg, Judith. "From Organ-Object Imagery to Self and Object Representation." *Separation-Individuation: Essays in Honor of Margaret S. Mahler.* Ed. John B. McDevitt and Calvin F. Settlage. New York: International UP, 1971. 75–99.

Khan, Masud. *Hidden Selves: Between Theory and Practice in Psychoanalysis.* London: Hogarth, 1983.

Kirby, Kathleen. "Indifferent Boundaries: Studies in the Subject, Language and Power." Unpublished ms., 1989.

Klein, Melanie. "Infantile Anxiety Situations Reflected in a Work of Art and in the Creative Impulse" (1929). *The Selected Melanie Klein.* Ed. Juliet Mitchell. New York: Free P, 1986. 84–94.

———. "Mourning and Its Relation to Manic-Depressive States." *International Journal of Psycho-Analysis* 21 (1940): 125–53.

———. "On the Sense of Loneliness." 1963. *Envy and Gratitude and Other Works, 1946–1963.* London: Hogarth and Inst. of Psycho-Analysis, 1975. 300–13.

Knowlson, James, and John Pilling. *Frescoes of the Skull: The Later Prose and Drama of Samuel Beckett.* London: Calder, 1979.

Kohut, Heinz. "Forms and Transformations of Narcissism." *Journal of the American Psychoanalytic Association* 14 (1966): 243–72.

———. *The Search for the Self: Selected Writings of Heinz Kohut, 1950–1978.* Ed. Paul H. Orstein. Vol. 2. New York: International UP, 1978.

Kristeva, Julia. *Soleil noir: depression et mélancholie.* Paris: Gallimard, 1987.

Kroker, Arthur, and David Cook. *The Postmodern Scene: Excremental Culture and Hyper-Aesthetics.* New York: St. Martin's, 1986.

Kundera, Milan. *The Unbearable Lightness of Being.* New York: Harper, 1984.

Lacan, Jacques. "Desire and the Interpretation of Desire in *Hamlet*." 1959. Trans. James Hulbert. *Yale French Studies* 55/56 (1977): 11–52.

———. *Ecrits: A Selection.* Trans. Alan Sheridan. New York: Norton, 1977.

———. *L'Ethique de la psychanalyse.* Paris: Seuil, 1986.

————. *The Four Fundamental Concepts of Psycho-Analysis*. Ed. Jacques-Alain Miller. Trans. Alan Sheridan. New York: Norton, 1978.

Lachmann, Renate. Lecture on "On Bakhtin." Center for Twentieth Century Studies, U of Wisconsin-Milwaukee, March 1986.

Laplanche, Jean. *Life and Death in Psychoanalysis*. Trans. Jeffrey Mehlman. Baltimore: Johns Hopkins UP, 1976.

Lasch, Christopher. *The Culture of Narcissism*. New York: Norton, 1978.

Laslett, Peter. *Family Life and Illicit Love in Earlier Generations: Essays in Historical Sociology*. New York: Cambridge UP, 1977.

Laurence, Margaret. *The Stone Angel*. New York: Knopf, 1964.

Lefcowitz, Barbara F., and Allan B. Lefcowitz. "Old Age and the Modern Literary Imagination: An Overview." *Soundings* 59.4 (Winter 1976): 447–66.

Lemoine-Luccioni, Eugénie. *La Robe: essaie psychanalytique sur le vêtement*. Paris: Seuil, 1983.

Leska, Mitchell A. *The Novels of Virginia Woolf: From Beginning to End*. New York: Jay; City U of New York, 1977.

Le Sueur, Meridel. "Remarks from 1983 Poetry Reading." *Women and Aging: An Anthology by Women*. Ed. Jo Alexander, Debi Berrow, Lisa Domitrovich, Margarita Donnelly, and Cheryl McLean. Corvallis: Calyx, 1986. 9–19.

Levinson, David J. *The Seasons of a Man's Life*. New York: Knopf, 1978.

Loewald, Hans W. "Internalization, Separation, Mourning, and the Superego." *The Psychoanalytic Quarterly* 31 (1962): 483–504.

Louis-Vincent, Thomas. *Rites de mort: pour la paix des vivants*. Paris: Fayard, 1985.

Lurie, Alison. *The Language of Clothes*. New York: Random, 1981.

Lyotard, Jean-François, and Jean-Loup Thébaud. *Just Gaming: Conversations*. 1979. Minneapolis: U of Minnesota P, 1985.

MacDonald, Barbara. "Outside the Sisterhood: Ageism in Women's Studies." *Women and Aging: An Anthology by Women*. Ed. Jo Alexander, Debi Berrow, Lisa Domitrovich, Margarita Donnelly, and Cheryl McLean. Carvallis: Calyx, 1986.

Magnan, Robert. "Sex and Senescence in Medieval Literature." *Aging in Literature*. Ed. Laurel Porter and Laurence M. Porter. Troy: International, 1984. 13–30.

Mahler, Margaret S. "On the First Three Subphases of the Separation-Individuation Process." *International Journal of Psycho-Analysis* 53 (1972): 333–38.

————. "On the Significance of the Normal Separation-Individuation Phase." *Drives, Affects, and Behavior 2*. Ed. M. Schur. New York: International UP, 1965. 161–69.

Mann, Thomas. *The Black Swan*. Trans. Willard R. Trask. New York: Knopf, 1954.

————. *Death in Venice*. Trans. H. T. Lowe-Porter. New York: Random, 1936.

Marks, Elaine. "Transgressing the (In)cont(in)ent Boundaries: The Body in Decline." *Yale French Studies* 72 (1986): 181–200.

Marquez, Gabriel Garcia. *Love in the Time of Cholera*. Trans. Edith Grossman. New York: Knopf, 1988.

Marshall, Paule. *Praise Song for the Widow*. New York: Putnam's, 1983.

Masson, Jeffrey Moussaieff, ed. and trans. *The Complete Letters of Sigmund Freud to Wilhelm Fliess, 1887–1904*. Cambridge: Harvard UP, 1985.

Matthews, Jill Julius. "Building the Body Beautiful: The Femininity of Modernity." *Australian Feminist Studies* (Summer 1987): 17–34.

Mauriac, François. *The Inner Presence: Recollections of My Spiritual Life*. Trans. Herma Briffault. Indianapolis: Bobbs, 1968.

McCarthy, Mary. *Memories of a Catholic Girlhood*. 1957. Harmondsworth, England: Penguin, 1963.

McGuire, William, ed. *The Freud/Jung Letters*. Trans. Ralph Manheim and R. F. C. Hull. Cambridge: Harvard UP, 1988.

Mellencamp, Patricia. "Aging Fashionably on TV." Conference on "Women and Aging." Center for Twentieth Century Studies, U of Wisconsin-Milwaukee, November 1987.

———. "Video Politics: *Guerilla TV, Ant Farm, External Frame.*" *Discourse* 10.2 (Spring-Summer 1988): 78–100.

Modleski, Tania, ed. *Studies in Entertainment: Critical Approaches to Mass Culture.* Bloomington: Indiana UP, 1986.

Montague, Ashley. *Touching: The Human Significance of the Skin.* 2nd ed. New York: Harper, 1978.

Montrelay, Michèle. "Inquiry into Femininity." *M/F* (1978): 83–99.

Moody, Harry R. *Abundance of Life: Human Development Policies for an Aging Society.* New York: Columbia UP, 1988.

———. "The Collector." *Human Values and Aging Newsletter* (Inst. on the Humanities, Arts, and Aging, Brookdale Center on Aging of Hunter College) 8.1 (Sept.-Oct. 1985): 1–2.

Morrison, Toni. *The Bluest Eye.* 1970. New York: Washington Square, 1972.

Morse, Margaret. "Artemis Aging: Exercise and the Female Body on Video." *Discourse* 10.1 (Fall-Winter 1987–88): 20–53.

Moss, Walter G., ed. *Humanistic Perspectives on Aging: An Annotated Bibliography and Essay.* Ann Arbor: Inst. of Gerontology, U of Michigan; Wayne State U, 1976.

Myerhoff, Barbara. *Number Our Days.* New York: Simon and Schuster, 1978.

Neugarten, Bernice L. "Personality and Aging." *Handbook of the Psychology of Aging.* Ed. J. E. Birren and K. W. Schaie. New York: Van Nostrand Reinhold, 1977.

Nietzsche, Friedrich. "On the Genealogy of Morals." 1887. *Basic Writings of Nietzsche.* Trans. and ed. Walter Kaufmann. New York: Modern, 1968.

Noggle, Anne. *Silver Lining.* Albuquerque: U of New Mexico, 1983.

Nuttal, F. D. "Samuel Beckett: *Malone Dies.*" *Jami'at San'a* 2 (1976): 81–94.

O'Hara, J. D., ed. Introduction. *Twentieth Century Interpretations of* Molloy, Malone Dies, The Unnamable. Englewood Cliffs: Prentice, 1970. 1–25.

Petro, Patrice. *Joyless Streets: Women and Melodramatic Representation in Weimar Germany.* Princeton: Princeton UP, 1989.

Pfeiffer, Ernest, ed. *Sigmund Freud and Lou Andreas-Salomé: Letters.* Trans. William and Elaine Robson-Scott. New York: Norton, 1972.

Pifer, Alan. "The Public Policy Response." *Our Aging Society: Paradox and Promise.* Ed. Alan Pifer and Lydia Bronte. New York: Norton, 1986.

Pollock, George H. "Aging or Aged: Development or Pathology." *Adulthood and the Aging Process.* Ed. Stanley I. Greenspan and George H. Pollock. Washington: NIMH, 1980. 549–85.

———. "On Mourning, Immortality, and Utopia." *Journal of the American Psychoanalytic Association* 73.2 (1975): 334–62.

Pontalis, J.-B. "Dream as an Object." Trans. Carol Martin-Sperry and Masud Khan. *International Review of Psycho-Analysis* 1 (1974): 125–33.

———. *Frontiers in Psychoanalysis: Between the Dream and Psychic Pain.* Trans. Catherine Cullen and Philip Cullen. 1977. New York: International UP, 1981.

———. "On Death-Work in Freud, in the Self, in Culture." 1978. Trans. Susan D. Cohen. *Psychoanalysis, Creativity, and Literature: A Franco-American Inquiry.* Ed. Alan Roland. New York: Columbia UP, 1978. 85–95.

———. *Perdre de vue.* Paris: Gallimard, 1988.

Porter, Laurel, and Laurence M. Porter. *Aging in Literature.* Troy: International, 1984.

Proust, Marcel. *The Guermantes Way*. Trans. C. K. Scott Moncrieff. New York: Modern, 1952.
————. *The Past Recaptured*. Trans. Frederick A. Blossom. New York: Modern, 1959.
————. *Within a Budding Grove*. Trans. C. K. Moncrieff. New York: Modern, 1951.
Pym, Barbara. *Quartet in Autumn*. London: Macmillan, 1977.
Ragland-Sullivan, Ellie. "Counting from 0–6: Lacan and the Imaginary Order." Center for Twentieth Century Studies *Working Paper*. Fall 1984.
————. "The Phenomenon of Aging in Oscar Wilde's *Picture of Dorian Gray*: A Lacanian View." *Memory and Desire: Aging—Literature—Psychoanalysis*. Ed. Kathleen Woodward and Murray M. Schwartz. Bloomington: Indiana UP, 1986. 97–113.
Renner, Charlotte. "The Self-Multiplying Narrators of *Molloy, Malone Dies,* and *The Unnamable*." *The Journal of Narrative Technique* 11.1 (Winter 1981): 12–32.
Rich, Adrienne. *Blood, Bread, and Poetry: Selected Prose 1979–1985*. New York: Norton, 1986.
————. "Compulsory Heterosexuality and Lesbian Existence." 1980. *Blood, Bread, and Poetry: Selected Prose 1979–1985*. New York: Norton, 1986.
Rimbert, Yannick. "L'Accompagnement des mourants." *Temps, vieillessement, société*. Paris: SOPEDIM, 1982. 63–64.
Riviere, Joan. "Womanliness as a Masquerade." 1929. *Formations of Fantasy*. Ed. Victor Burgin, James Donald, and Cora Kaplan. London: Methuen, 1986. 35–44.
Roazen, Paul. *Freud: Political and Social Thought*. New York: Knopf, 1968.
Rochlin, Gregory. *Griefs and Discontents: The Forces of Change*. Boston: Little, 1965.
————. *Man's Aggression: The Defense of the Self*. Boston: Gambit, 1973.
Rogers, Robert. *The Double in Literature*. Detroit: Wayne State UP, 1970.
Rooke, Constance, ed. *Night Light: Stories of Aging*. Toronto: Oxford UP, 1986.
Rossi, Alice S. "Life-Span Theories and Women's Lives." *Signs* 6.1 (1980): 4–32.
Russo, Mary. "Female Grotesques: Carnival and Theory." *Feminist Studies/Critical Studies*. Ed. Teresa de Lauretis. Bloomington: Indiana UP, 1986. 213–29.
Sackville-West, Vita. *All Passion Spent*. Garden City: Doubleday; Doran, 1931.
Sarton, May. *After the Stroke: A Journal*. New York: Norton, 1988.
————. *As We Are Now*. New York: Norton, 1973.
Sauer, Jean-Claude, and Roger Picherie. "L'Eternelle jeunesse: les derniers miracles de la chirugie esthétique." *Paris Match* (23 Jan. 1987): 82–93.
Scarry, Elaine. *The Body in Pain: The Making and Unmaking of the World*. New York: Oxford UP, 1985.
Schafer, Roy. *Aspects of Internalization*. New York: International UP, 1968.
Schilder, Paul. *The Image and Appearance of the Human Body*. 1935. New York: International UP, 1950.
Schneiderman, Stuart. *Jacques Lacan: The Death of an Intellectual Hero*. Cambridge: Harvard UP, 1983.
Schor, Naomi. "For a Restricted Thematics: Writing, Speech, and Difference in *Madame Bovary*." Trans. Harriet Stone. *The Future of Difference*. Ed. Hester Eisenstein and Alice Jardine. New Brunswick: Rutgers UP, 1985. 167–92.
Schur, Max. *Freud: Living and Dying*. New York: International UP, 1972.
Schwab, Gabriele. "Genesis of the Subject, Imaginary Functions, and Poetic Language." *New Literary History* 15.3 (Spring 1984): 453–73.
————. "The Intermediate Area between Life and Death: On Samuel Beckett's *The Unnamable*." *Memory and Desire: Aging—Literature—Psychoanalysis*. Ed. Kathleen Woodward and Murray M. Schwartz. Bloomington: Indiana UP, 1986. 205–17.

Scott-Maxwell, Florida. *The Measure of My Days.* 1968. New York: Penguin, 1979.

Shakespeare, William. *The Passionate Pilgrim,* poem 12. *Shakespeare: The Complete Works.* Ed. G. B. Harrison. New York: Harcourt, 1948.

Siggens, Lorraine D. "Mourning: A Critical Survey of the Literature." *International Journal of Psycho-Analysis* 47 (1966): 14–25.

Silverman, Kaja. "Fragments of a Fashionable Discourse." *Studies in Entertainment: Critical Approaches to Mass Culture.* Ed. Tania Modleski. Bloomington: Indiana UP, 1986. 139–52.

Simmons, Charles. *Wrinkles.* New York: Farrar, 1978.

Simons, Margaret A. "In Memoriam." *Yale French Studies* 72 (1986): 204.

Sittler, Joseph. "Theological Perspectives on Aging." *How Does Our Society Today Value Aged Persons?* Ed. Elizabeth M. Lane. Madison: General Health Services; Yahara Center, 1986. 47–55.

Sohngen, Mary. "The Writer as an Old Woman." *The Gerontologist* 15.6 (Dec. 1976): 492–98.

Sokoloff, Janice. *The Margin That Remains: A Study of Aging in Literature.* New York: Peter Lang, 1987.

Sommers, Susan. "Anti-Aging Beauty." *Ladies' Home Journal* (Nov. 1987): 68ff.

Sontag, Susan. "The Double Standard of Aging." *No Longer Young: The Older Woman in America.* Occasional Papers in Gerontology II. Ann Arbor: Inst. of Gerontology, U of Michigan; Wayne State U, 1975. 31–39.

Spark, Muriel. *A Far Cry from Kensington.* London: Penguin, 1989.

Stern, Karl, Gwendolyn M. Williams, and Miguel Prados. "Grief Reactions in Later Life." *The American Journal of Psychiatry* 108 (Oct. 1951): 289–94.

Stewart, Susan. *On Longing: Narratives of the Miniature, the Gigantic, the Souvenir, the Collection.* Baltimore: Johns Hopkins UP, 1984.

Straus, Erwin. *Phenomenological Psychology.* Trans. Erling Eng. New York: Basic, 1966.

Suleiman, Susan Rubin. "Writing and Motherhood." *The (M)Other Tongue: Essays in Feminist Psychoanalytic Interpretation.* Ed. Shirley Nelson Garner, Claire Kahane, and Madelon Sprengnether. Ithaca: Cornell UP, 1985. 352–77.

Tanizaki, Jurichiro. *Diary of a Mad Old Man.* Trans. Howard Hibbett. New York: Perigee; Putnam's, 1981.

Tartufari, Clarice. "A Story, Perhaps Lived." *Unspeakable Women: Selected Short Stories by Italian Women Writers of the Twenties and Thirties.* Ed. and Trans. Robin Pickering-Iazzi. Unpublished ms., 1989.

Tolchin, Neal L. *Mourning, Gender, and Creativity in the Art of Herman Melville.* New Haven: Yale UP, 1988.

Trautmann, Joanne, and Carol Pollard. *Literature and Medicine: Topics, Titles and Notes.* Philadelphia: Soc. for Health and Human Values, 1976.

Tyler, Anne. *Dinner at the Homesick Restaurant.* 1982. New York: Berkeley, 1983.

Updike, John. *The Poorhouse Fair.* New York: Knopf, 1969.

Warner, Eric. "Re-Considering *The Years.*" *North Dakota Quarterly* 48.2 (1980): 16–30.

Weber, Samuel. *The Legend of Freud.* Minneapolis: U of Minnesota P, 1982.

Wells, Linda. "What If . . . ?" *The New York Times Magazine* 17 September 1989: 85–92.

Wertheimer, J. "Les Mécanismes de permanence: le temps, support d'une hypothèse psychodynamique du vieillessement psychologique." *Temps, vieillessement, société.* Paris: SOPEDIM, 1982. 41–52.

White, Patrick. *The Eye of the Storm.* New York: Avon, 1975.

Wilden, Anthony, trans. *The Language of the Self: The Function of Language in Psychoanalysis,* by Jacques Lacan. Baltimore: Johns Hopkins UP, 1968.

Williams, Linda. " 'Something Else besides a Mother': *Stella Dallas* and the Maternal Melodrama." *Cinema Journal* 24.1 (Fall 1984): 2–27.

Winnicott, D. W. *The Maturational Processes and the Facilitating Environment.* New York: International UP, 1965.

———. *Playing and Reality.* London: Tavistock, 1971.

———. "Transitional Objects and Transitional Phenomena: A Study of the First Not-Me Possession." *International Journal of Psycho-Analysis* 34.2 (1953): 89–97.

Wolitzer, Hilda. *In the Palomar Arms.* New York: Farrar, 1983.

Wollheim, Richard. *The Thread of Life.* Cambridge: Harvard UP, 1984.

Woodward, Kathleen. *At Last, the Real Distinguished Thing: The Late Poems of Eliot, Pound, Stevens, and Williams.* Columbus: Ohio State UP, 1980.

———. "May Sarton and Fictions of Old Age." *Gender and Literary Voice.* Ed. Janet Todd. *Women and Literature* NS1. New York: Holmes, 1980. 108–27.

———. "Reminiscence and the Life Review: Prospects and Retrospects." *What Does It Mean to Grow Old?: Reflections from the Humanities.* Ed. Thomas R. Cole and Sally A. Gadow. Durham: Duke UP, 1986. 137–61.

———. "Reminiscence, Identity, Sentimentality: Simone de Beauvoir and the Life Review." *Twenty-Five Years of the Life Review: Theoretical and Practical Considerations.* Ed. Robert Disch. New York: Haworth, 1988. 25–46.

———. "Simone de Beauvoir: Aging and Its Discontents." *The Private Self: Theory and Practice in Women's Autobiographical Writings.* Ed. Shari Benstock. Chapel Hill: U of North Carolina P, 1988. 90–113.

Woodward, Kathleen, and Murray M. Schwartz, eds. *Memory and Desire: Aging—Literature—Psychoanalysis.* Bloomington: Indiana UP, 1986.

Woolf, Virginia. *A Room of One's Own.* New York: Harcourt, 1929.

———. *The Years.* New York: Harcourt, 1937.

Wright, Elizabeth. *Psychoanalytic Criticism: Theory in Practice.* New York: Methuen, 1984.

Wyatt-Brown, Anne M. "The Coming of Age of Literary Gerontology: A Literature Review." *Handbook of Aging and the Humanities.* Ed. Thomas R. Cole, David D. Van Tassel, and Robert Kastenbaum. New York: Springer, forthcoming.

———. "Creativity in Midlife: The Novels of Anita Brookner." *Journal of Aging Studies* 3.2 (1989): 175–81.

———. "Late Style in the Novels of Barbara Pym and Penelope Mortimer." *The Gerontologist* 28.6 (1988): 835–39.

———. "The Narrative Imperative: Fiction and the Aging Writer." *Journal of Aging Studies* 3.1 (1989): 55–65.

Yahnke, Robert E., and Richard M. Eastman. *Aging in Literature: A Reader's Guide.* Chicago: ALA, forthcoming.

203 n.24; and aging, 29–37, 33; and anxiety, 63; and death, 50
castration anxiety, 154
childbirth, 99
childhood, 94; and aging, 135, 170; and narcissism, 93
Chodorow, Nancy, 212 n.7
cinematic apparatus, 160
Cixous, Hélène, 217 n.9
climacteric, 73, 202 n.17
Cohn, Ruby, 133
Cole, Thomas R., 198 n.18
Coles, Robert, 196
Colette, 87–88, 133, 174, 183
collectionnisme, 138
collectors and souvenirs, 137–38
Condit, Cecelia, 196
cosmetic surgery, 162–63, 165, 224–25 n.21; and Cher, 163; and voyeurism, 163; as self-repression, 163
Cowley, Malcolm, 19, 168–69, 199 n.33

Dacher, Michèle, 158, 180–81
Dalsimer, Katherine, 200 n.40
daughter, figure of, 94–97
death, 17–19, 35, 66, 68, 71, 77, 101, 124, 157; denial of, 70; fear of, 32; and Freud's father, 33; and its repetition, 121; and separation, 111, 112–13, 124; reactions to, 110, 121, 126
death instincts, 45–50, 151, 155, 185
death-work, 121
de Man, Paul, 125
denial, 20, 32, 38, 46, 54–55, 66, 116, 148
Derrida, Jacques, 119
desire, 28, 51, 68, 84–87, 154, 157–58, 173, 201
despair, 66–67, 71
developmental psychoanalysis, 20–21, 74
Dillard, Annie, 181, 215 n.25
Doane, Mary Ann, 155–56, 162
Dolto, Françoise, 49
double, 54–55, 59, 63–65, 69
dreams, theory of, 78–80, 82, 84, 87, 89; and gender, 217 n.9
Duras, Marguerite, *Afternoon of Monsieur Andesmas*, 171–77; *Hiroshima, Mon Amour*, 218 n.15; *Savannah Bay*, 72

ego psychology, 71
Eiseley, Loren, 13, 121
elderly, and invisibility, 161; representation of in *The Past Recaptured*, 54–61; representation of in *The Years*, 75–90
empty body, 177–81
Erikson, Erik, 20, 70–71, 73, 99, 208 n.16

essentialism and constructivism, 18
externalization, 119, 218 n.19

Fast, Irene, 213 n.7
father, figure of, 33–35, 44
Featherstone, Mike, 200 n.42; see also Hepworth, Mike
Festa-McCormick, Diana, 207 n.3
Figes, Eva, *Waking*, 37, 92–121, 131–32, 147, 189, 214–15 n.16, 216 n.28
Flem, Lydia, 3
Fliess, Wilhelm, 32, 34–35
Fonda, Jane, 162
fort-da, 12
Foucault, Michel, 164
fragilization, 188
fragmented body, 68, 105–106, 182–83, 187
fragmenting body, 106, 181–90, 228 n.32
Freedman, Richard, 197–98 n.12
Freud, Amalia, 3, 114
Freud, Anna, 218 n.18
Freud, Sigmund, 6, 68, 78, 80–81, 84, 99; and aging, 26–51, 202 n.17, 204 n.29; and his dreams, 29–32; and his father, 92; and femininity and his grandson's death, 113, 117, 120; and his mother, 3, 114, 217 n.12; and his mother-in-law, 93; *An Autobiographical Study*, 40, 42; *Beyond the Pleasure Principle*, 38, 45–49, 68, 151; "The Burning Child," 110, 122–24, 219–20 n.27; *Civilization and Its Discontents*, 48–50; "Creative Writers and Day-Dreaming," 126; "Count Thun," 33–34; "A Disturbance of Memory on the Acropolis," 43–44; "The Economic Problem of Masochism," 44; *The Ego and the Id*, 10, 40–41, 44, 48–50; "Female Sexuality," 193; "Femininity," 192; "Formulations on the Two Principles of Mental Functioning," 209–10 n.7; "Group Psychology and Analysis of the Ego," 104; "His Father on His Death-Bed Like Garibaldi," 34; *Inhibitions, Symptoms and Anxiety*, 117, 175, 217 n.14; *The Interpretation of Dreams*, 29–30, 33–34, 40, 113, 192, 217 n.9; "Irma's Injection," 151; "The Libido Theory and Narcissism," 296; "Mourning and Melancholia," 111–16, 123, 124, 126, 216 n.1; "My Uncle with the Yellow Beard," 30–32, 170; "On Narcissism," 48, 77, 87; "On Transience," 116, 126; "The Theme of Three Caskets," 50–51; "Thoughts for the Times on War and Death," 185; "Three Essays on the Theory of Sexuality," 102; "The Uncanny," 63–67
Freudian psychoanalysis, dramaturgical aspects of, 37–38

KATHLEEN WOODWARD is Director of the Center for Twentieth Century Studies and Professor of English at the University of Wisconsin-Milwaukee. She is the author of *At Last, The Real Distinguished Thing: The Late Poems of Eliot, Pound, Stevens, and Williams* and the editor of *The Myths of Information: Technology and Postindustrial Culture; The Technological Imagination: Theories and Fictions* (with Teresa de Lauretis and Andreas Huyssen); and *Memory and Desire: Aging—Literature—Psychoanalysis* (with Murray Schwartz).